TOKYO MEW MEW

MIA IKUMI & REIKO YOSHIDA

VOLUME SIX

TOKYOPOP®

HAMBURG // LONDON // LOS ANGELES // TOKYO

Tokyo Mew Mew Vol. 6
Created by Mia Ikumi and Reiko Yoshida

Translation - Ikoi Hiroe
English Adaptation - Stuart Hazleton
Contributing Editor - Jodi Bryson
Retouch and Lettering - Vicente Rivera, Jr.
Cover Design - Patrick Hook

Editor - Nora Wong
Digital Imaging Manager - Chris Buford
Pre-Press Manager - Antonio DePietro
Production Managers - Jennifer Miller and Mutsumi Miyazaki
Art Director - Matt Alford
Managing Editor - Jill Freshney
VP of Production - Ron Klamert
Editor-in-Chief - Mike Kiley
President and C.O.O. - John Parker
Publisher and C.E.O. - Stuart Levy

A  Manga

TOKYOPOP Inc.
5900 Wilshire Blvd. Suite 2000
Los Angeles, CA 90036

E-mail: info@TOKYOPOP.com
Come visit us online at www.TOKYOPOP.com

ISBN: 1-59182-549-0
First TOKYOPOP printing: March 2004
10 9 8 7 6 5
Printed in the USA

TOKYO MEW MEW

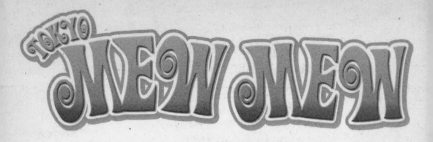

TABLE OF CONTENTS

About this story

Ichigo Momomiya was a normal junior high school student until a freak accident turned her into superhero Mew Mew! Ichigo and her partners are working hard to save the world!

東京ミュウミュウ
TOKYO MEW MEW

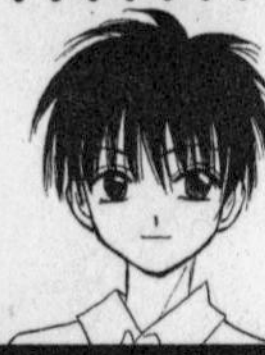

Masaya Aoyama
He's cute, smart and popular! Even better, he's on the kendo team.

CAFE MEW MEW

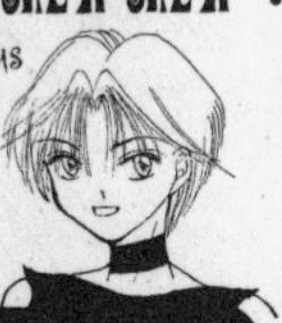

A mysterious wealthy high school student.
Ryou Shirogane

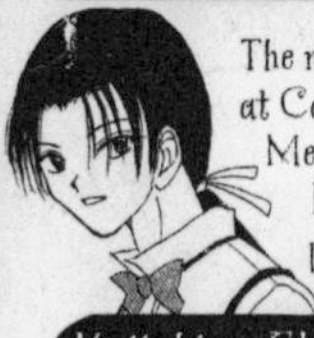

The manager at Café Mew Mew, and Ryou's partner.
Keiichiro Akasaka

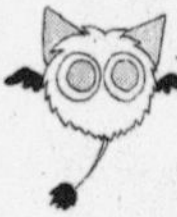

Masha
Ryou's pet robot.

Kish

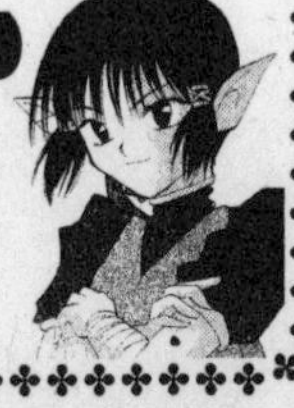

One of the aliens attacking Earth.

TOKYO MEW MEW

◀pre-transformation ▼post-transformation

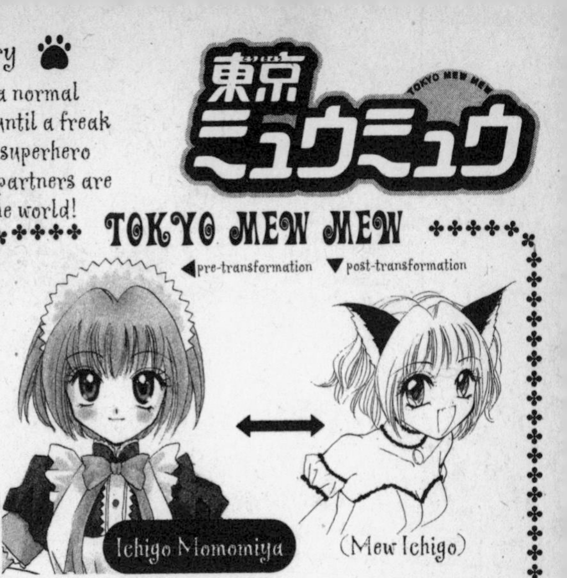

Ichigo Momomiya (Mew Ichigo)
I have a totally gigantic crush on Masaya, and I'm in seventh grade. I've been fused with the genes of an Iriomote Cat.

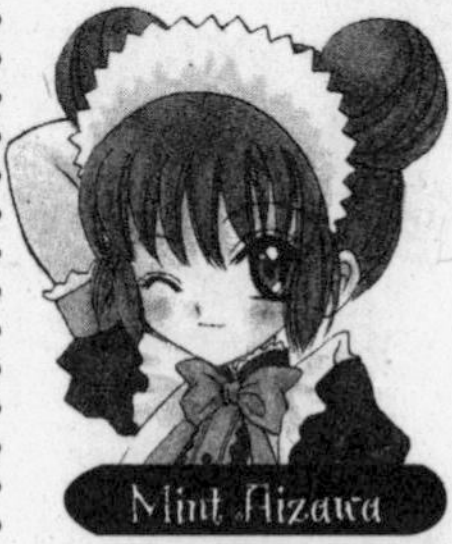

(Mew Mint)
Mint Aizawa
A wealthy chick with a totally sarcastic personality.

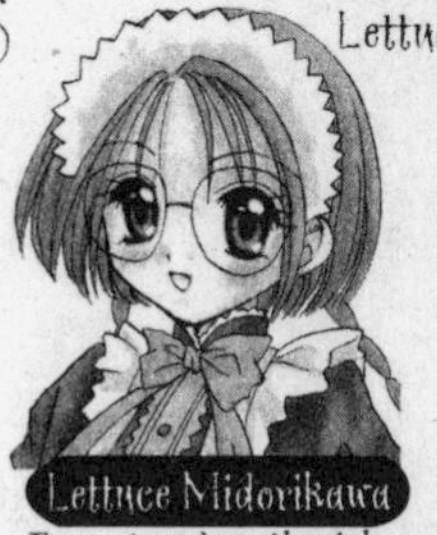

(Mew Lettuce)
Lettuce Midorikawa
A sweet and gentle girl, though she's a bit quiet.

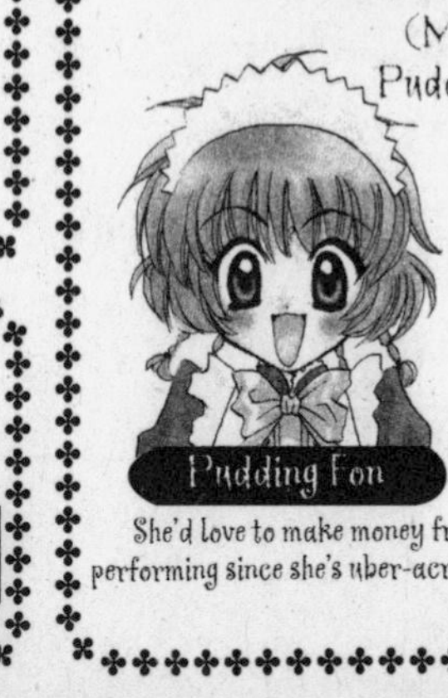

(Mew Pudding)
Pudding Fon
She'd love to make money from performing since she's uber-acrobatic.

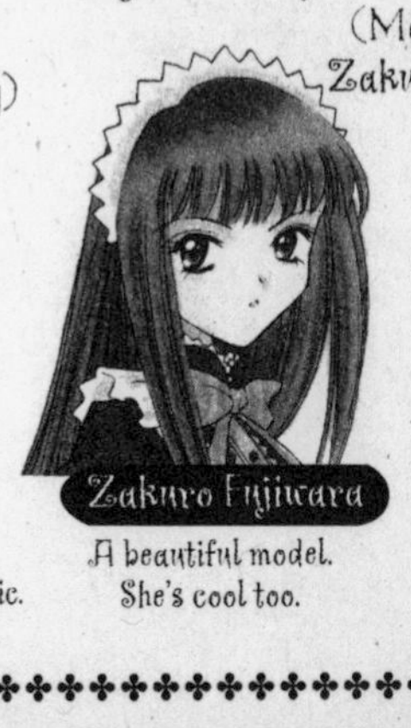

(Mew Zakuro)
Zakuro Fujiwara
A beautiful model. She's cool too.

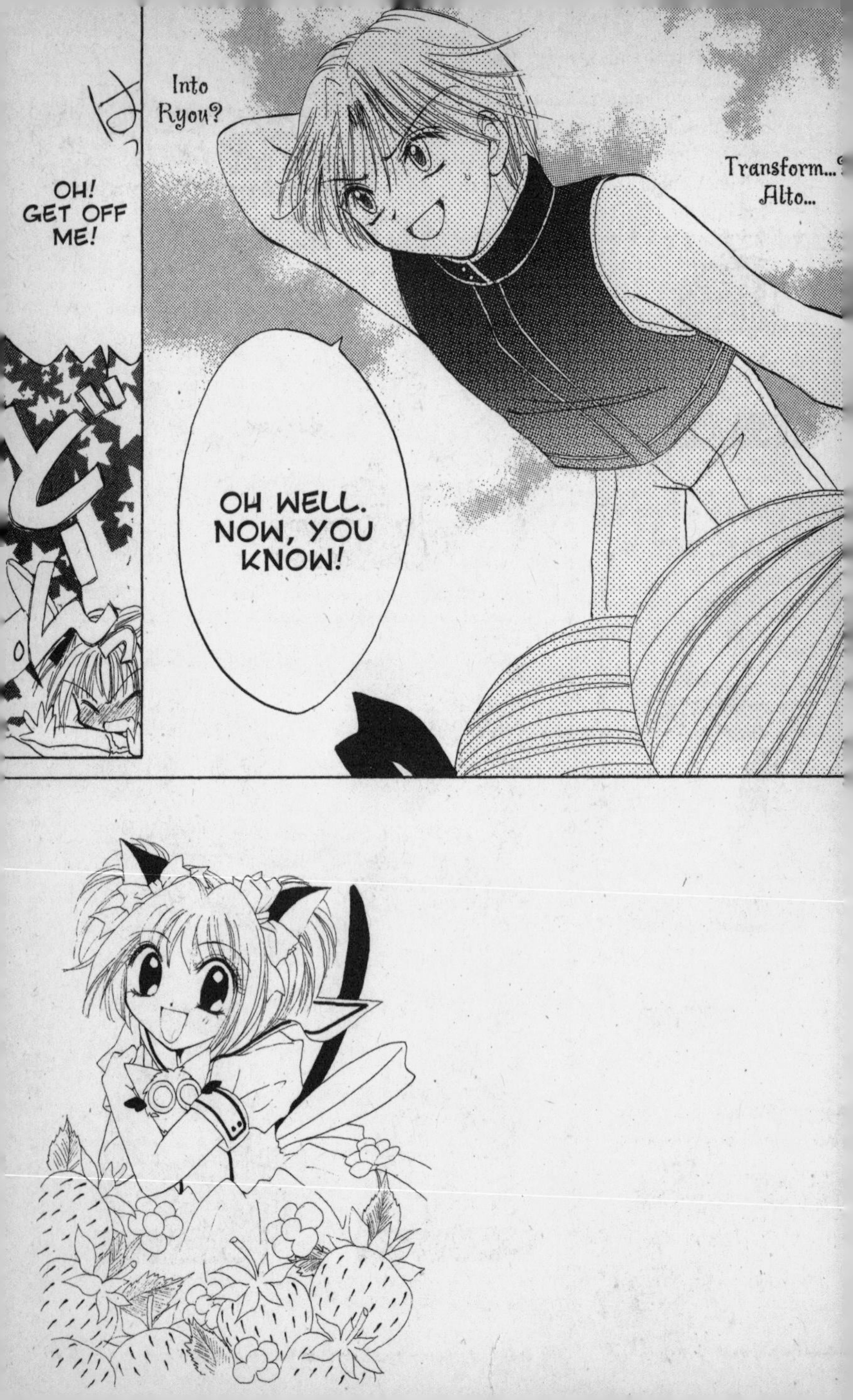
Transform...
Alto...
Into Ryou?
OH WELL. NOW, YOU KNOW!
OH! GET OFF ME!

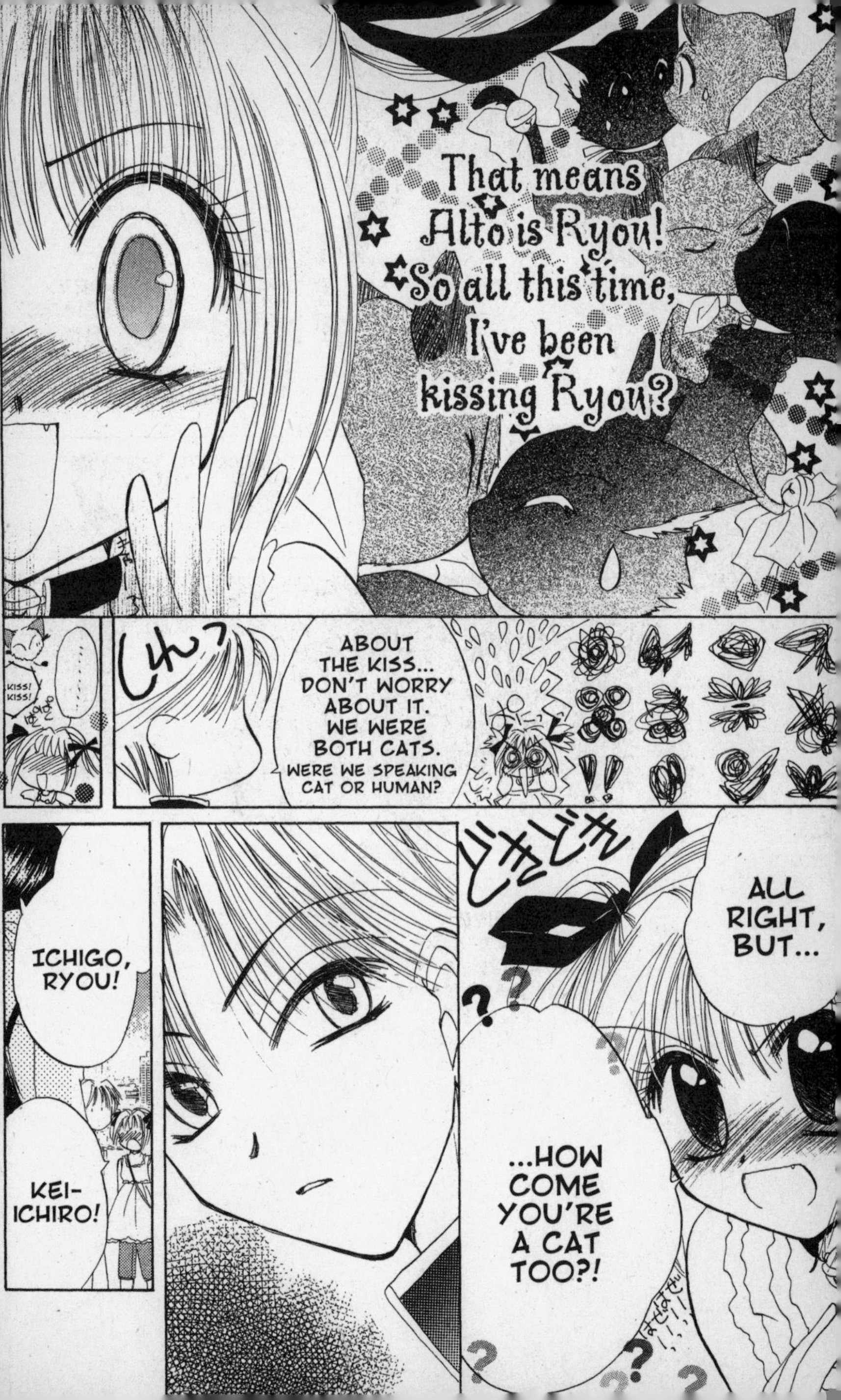

That means Alto is Ryou! So all this time, I've been kissing Ryou?
ABOUT THE KISS... DON'T WORRY ABOUT IT. WE WERE BOTH CATS.
WERE WE SPEAKING CAT OR HUMAN?
しれっ
KISS! KISS!
......
どきどき
ALL RIGHT, BUT...
...HOW COME YOU'RE A CAT TOO?!
ICHIGO, RYOU!
KEI-ICHIRO!

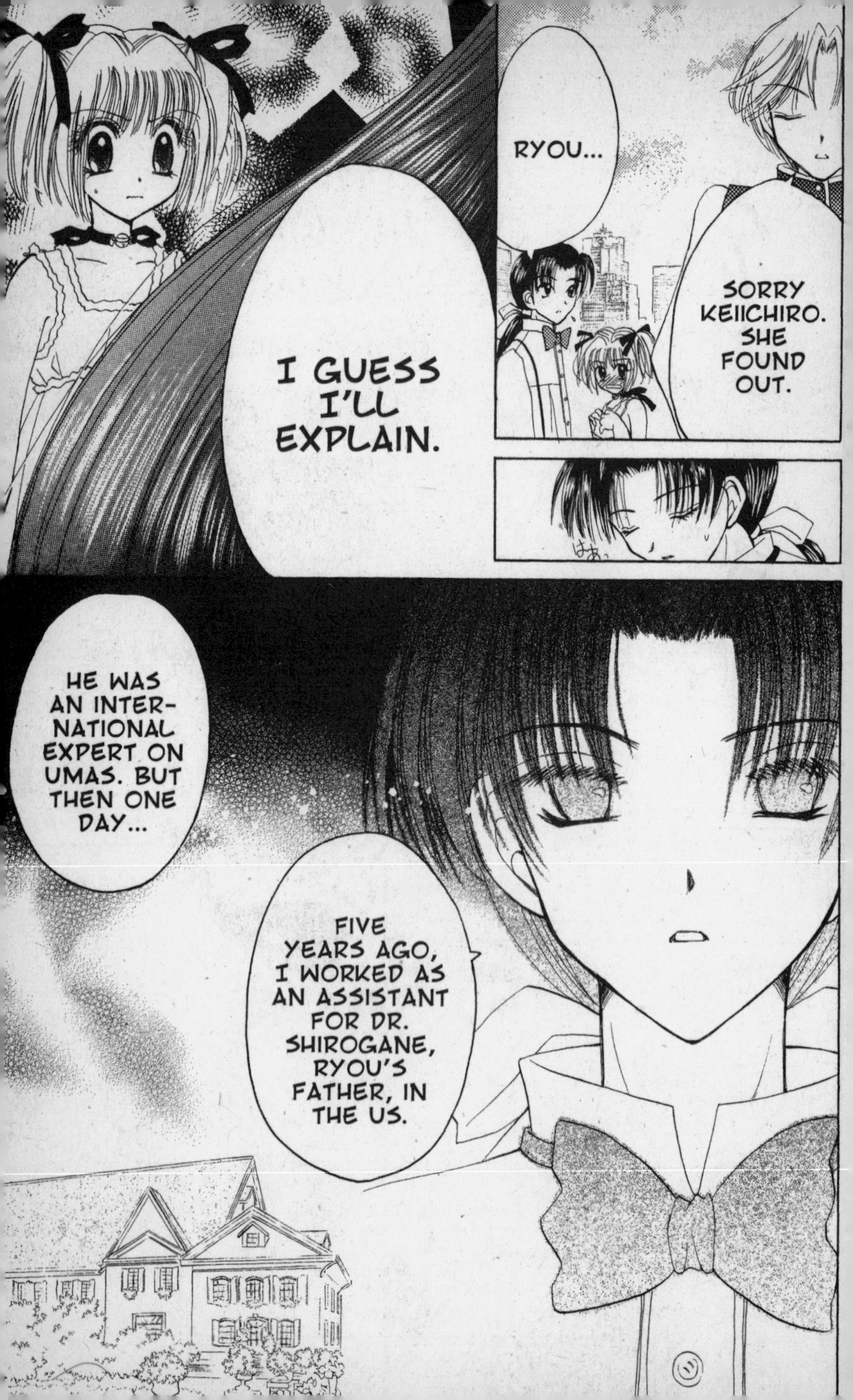
RYOU...
SORRY KEIICHIRO. SHE FOUND OUT.
はあ
I GUESS I'LL EXPLAIN.
FIVE YEARS AGO, I WORKED AS AN ASSISTANT FOR DR. SHIROGANE, RYOU'S FATHER, IN THE US.
HE WAS AN INTERNATIONAL EXPERT ON UMAS. BUT THEN ONE DAY...

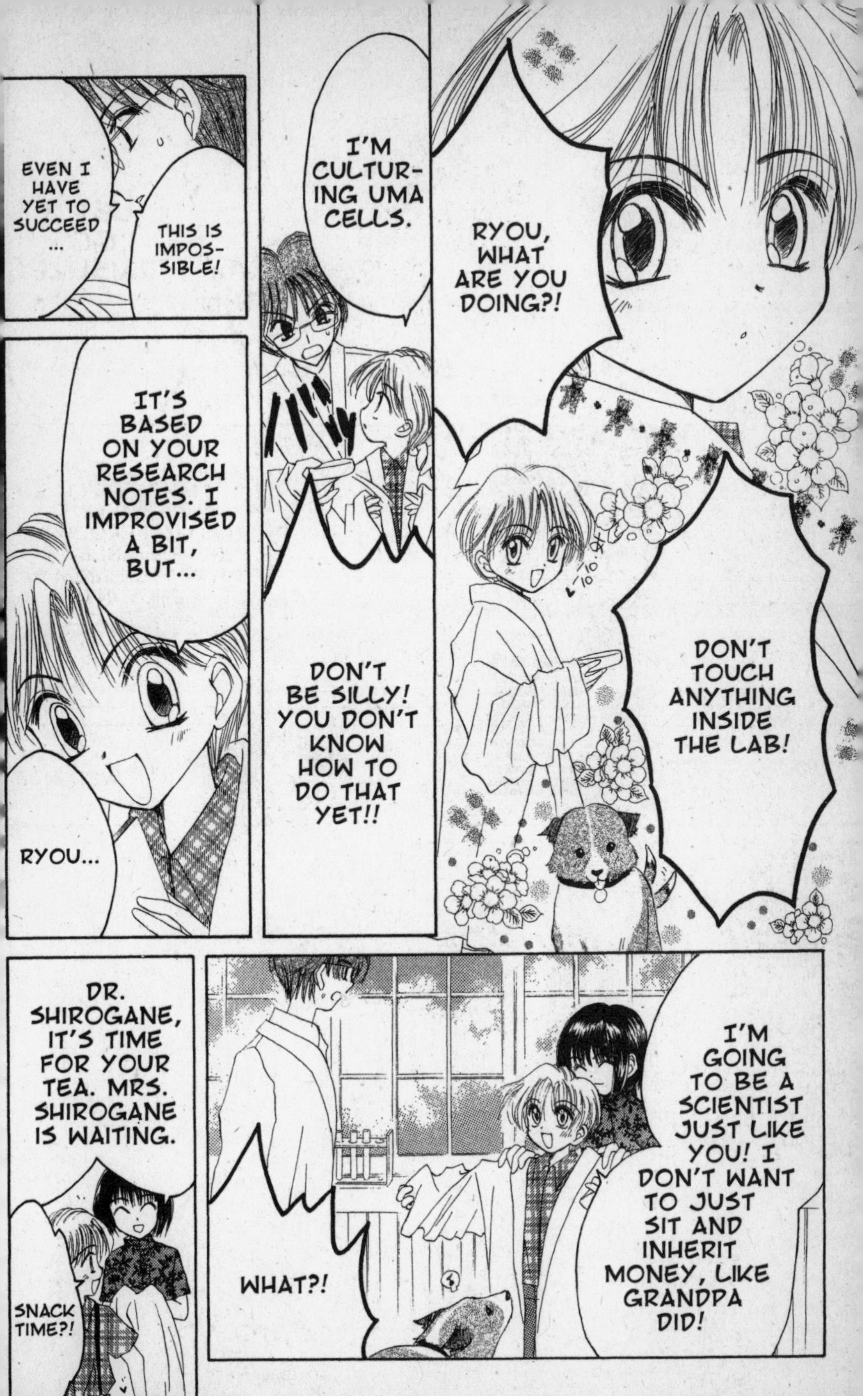
RYOU, WHAT ARE YOU DOING?!
DON'T TOUCH ANYTHING INSIDE THE LAB!
I'M CULTURING UMA CELLS.
DON'T BE SILLY! YOU DON'T KNOW HOW TO DO THAT YET!!
THIS IS IMPOSSIBLE!
EVEN I HAVE YET TO SUCCEED ...
IT'S BASED ON YOUR RESEARCH NOTES. I IMPROVISED A BIT, BUT...
RYOU...
I'M GOING TO BE A SCIENTIST JUST LIKE YOU! I DON'T WANT TO JUST SIT AND INHERIT MONEY, LIKE GRANDPA DID!
WHAT?!
DR. SHIROGANE, IT'S TIME FOR YOUR TEA. MRS. SHIROGANE IS WAITING.
SNACK TIME?!

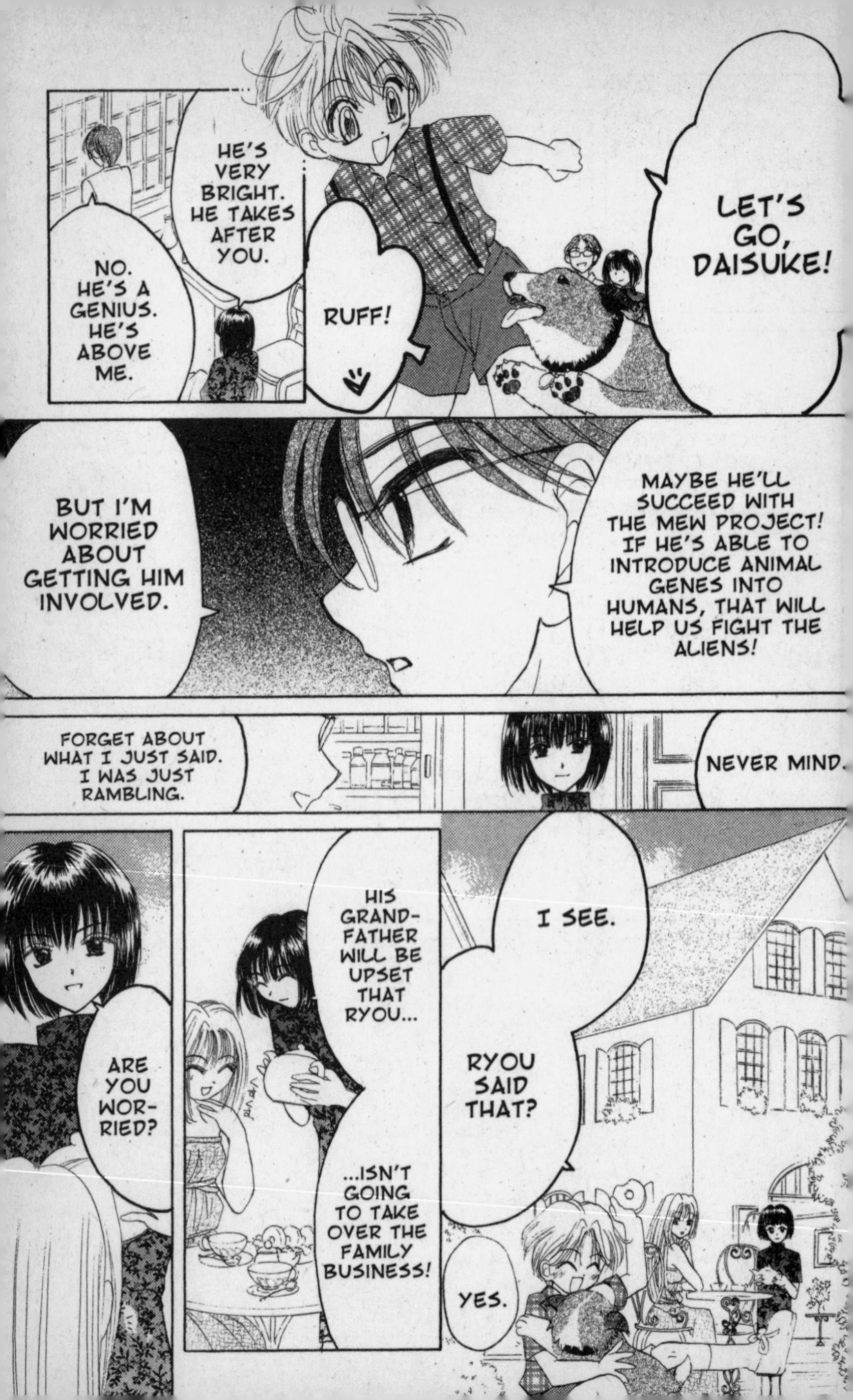

LET'S GO, DAISUKE!
RUFF!
HE'S VERY BRIGHT. HE TAKES AFTER YOU.
NO. HE'S A GENIUS. HE'S ABOVE ME.
MAYBE HE'LL SUCCEED WITH THE MEW PROJECT! IF HE'S ABLE TO INTRODUCE ANIMAL GENES INTO HUMANS, THAT WILL HELP US FIGHT THE ALIENS!
BUT I'M WORRIED ABOUT GETTING HIM INVOLVED.
NEVER MIND.
FORGET ABOUT WHAT I JUST SAID. I WAS JUST RAMBLING.
I SEE.
RYOU SAID THAT?
YES.
HIS GRAND-FATHER WILL BE UPSET THAT RYOU...
...ISN'T GOING TO TAKE OVER THE FAMILY BUSINESS!
ARE YOU WOR-RIED?

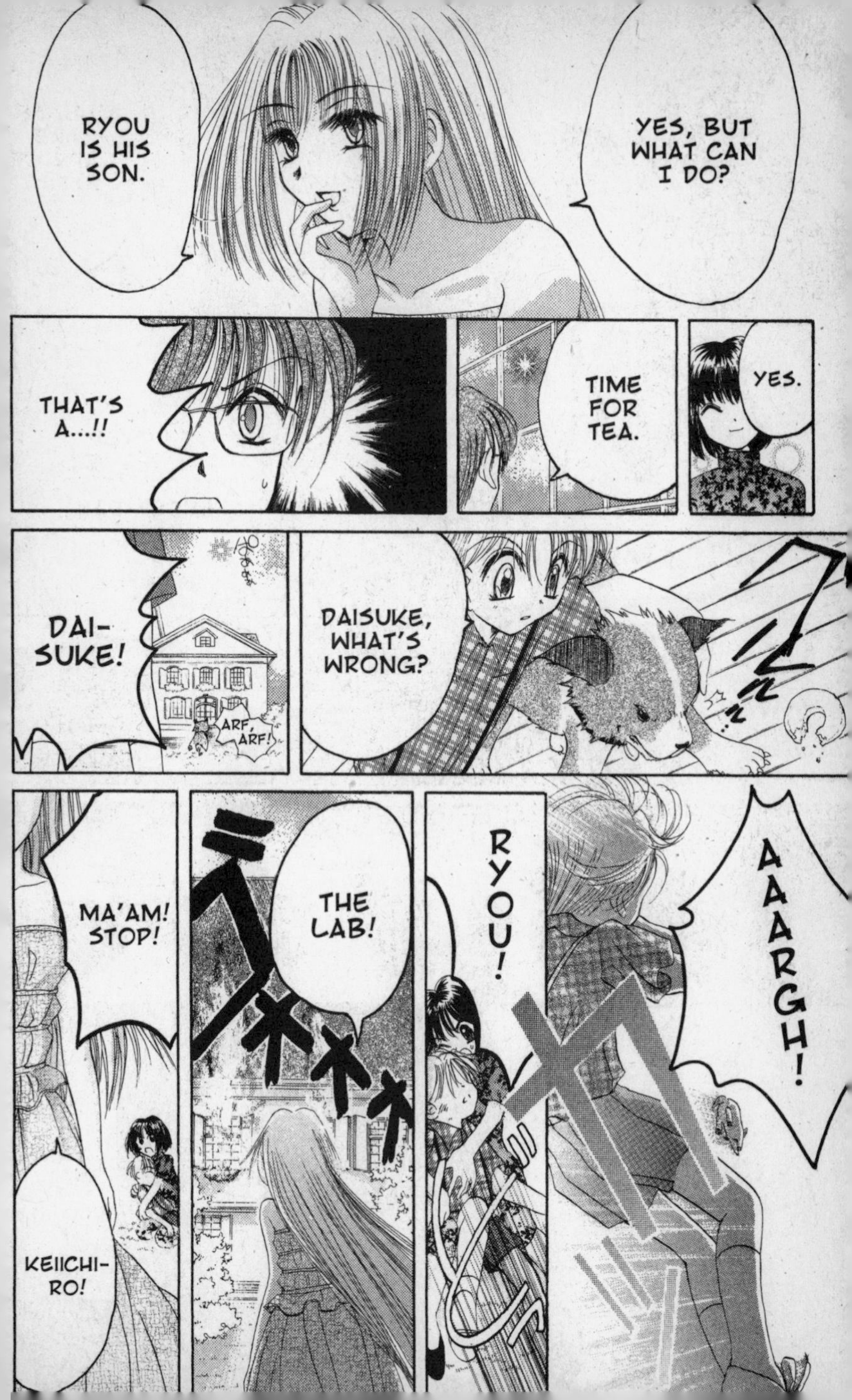
YES, BUT WHAT CAN I DO?
RYOU IS HIS SON.
YES.
TIME FOR TEA.
THAT'S A...!!
DAISUKE, WHAT'S WRONG?
DAI-SUKE!
ARF, ARF!
AAARGH!
RYOU!
THE LAB!
MA'AM! STOP!
KEIICHI-RO!

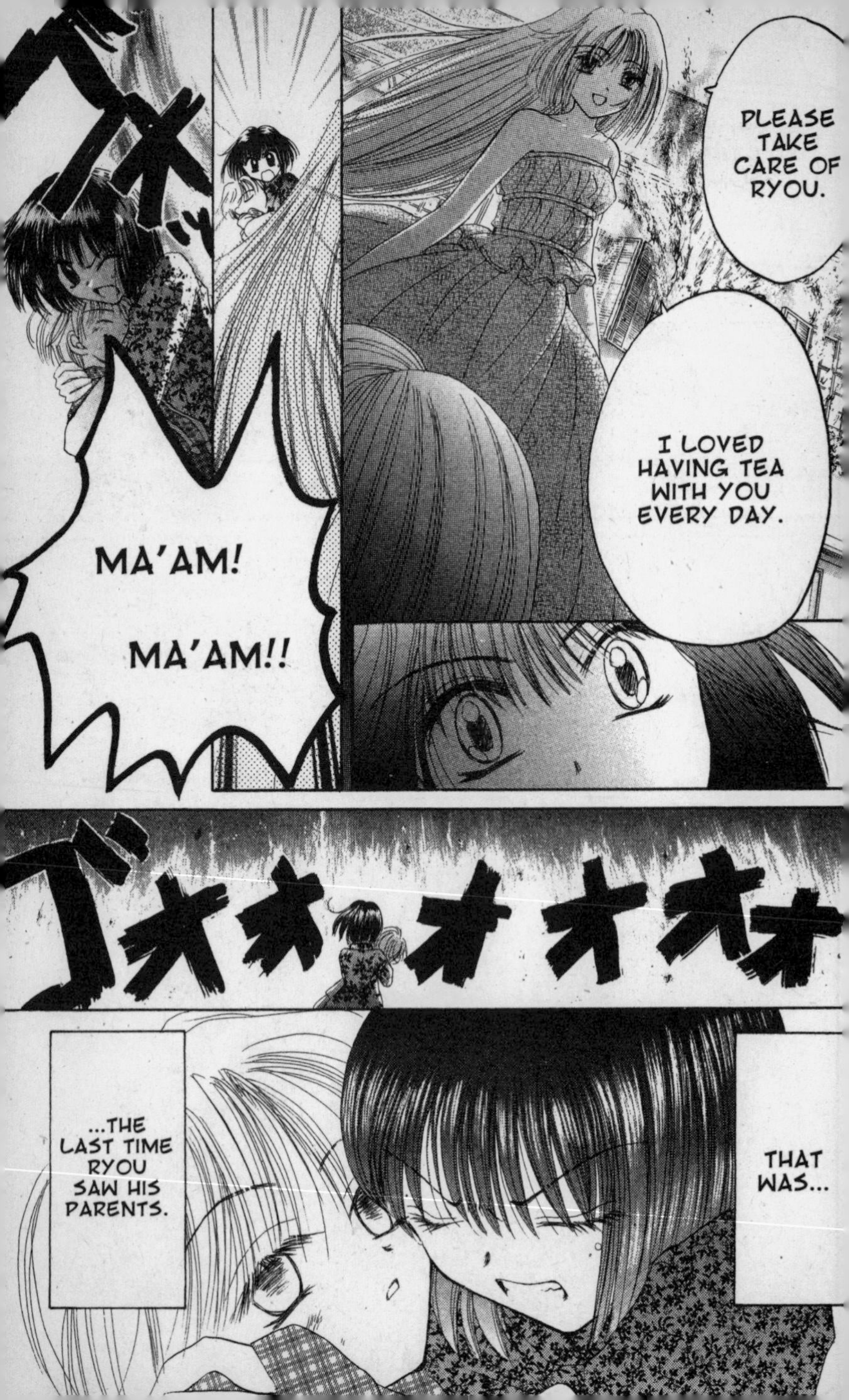
PLEASE TAKE CARE OF RYOU.
I LOVED HAVING TEA WITH YOU EVERY DAY.
MA'AM!
MA'AM!!
THAT WAS...
...THE LAST TIME RYOU SAW HIS PARENTS.

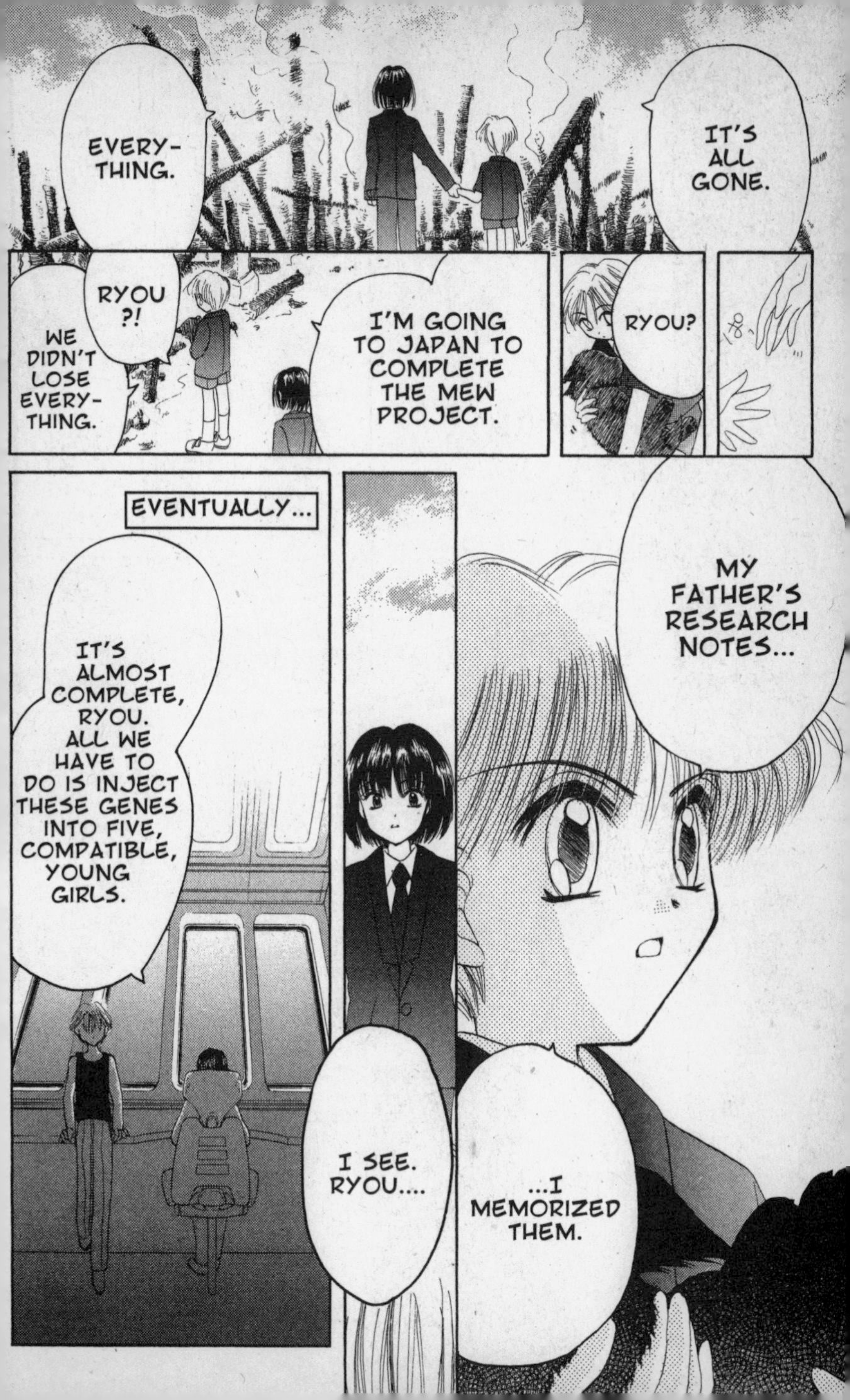
IT'S ALL GONE.
EVERYTHING.
RYOU?
RYOU?!
WE DIDN'T LOSE EVERYTHING.
I'M GOING TO JAPAN TO COMPLETE THE MEW PROJECT.
MY FATHER'S RESEARCH NOTES...
...I MEMORIZED THEM.
I SEE. RYOU....
EVENTUALLY...
IT'S ALMOST COMPLETE, RYOU. ALL WE HAVE TO DO IS INJECT THESE GENES INTO FIVE, COMPATIBLE, YOUNG GIRLS.

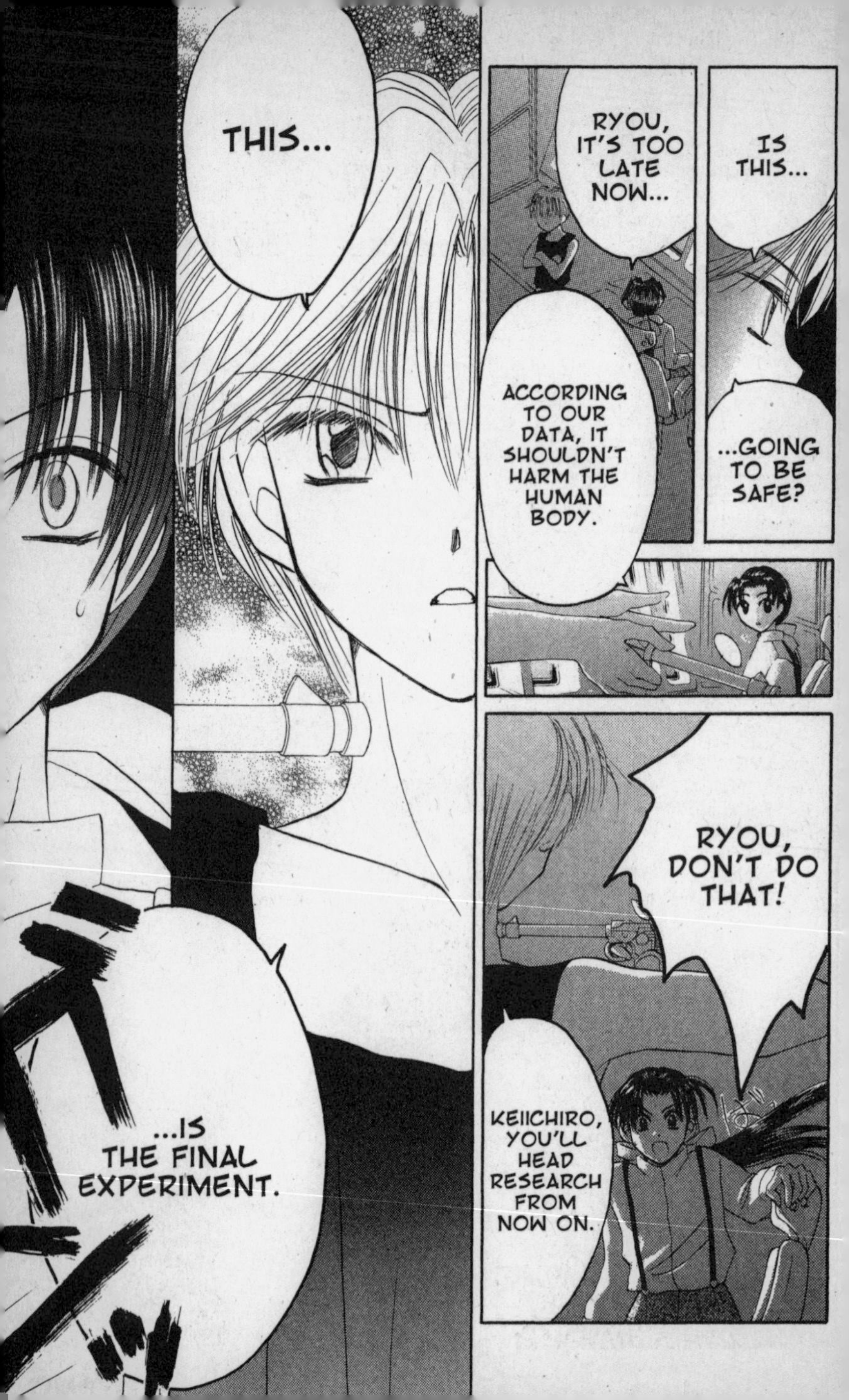
IS THIS...
...GOING TO BE SAFE?
RYOU, IT'S TOO LATE NOW...
ACCORDING TO OUR DATA, IT SHOULDN'T HARM THE HUMAN BODY.
RYOU, DON'T DO THAT!
KEIICHIRO, YOU'LL HEAD RESEARCH FROM NOW ON.
THIS...
...IS THE FINAL EXPERIMENT.

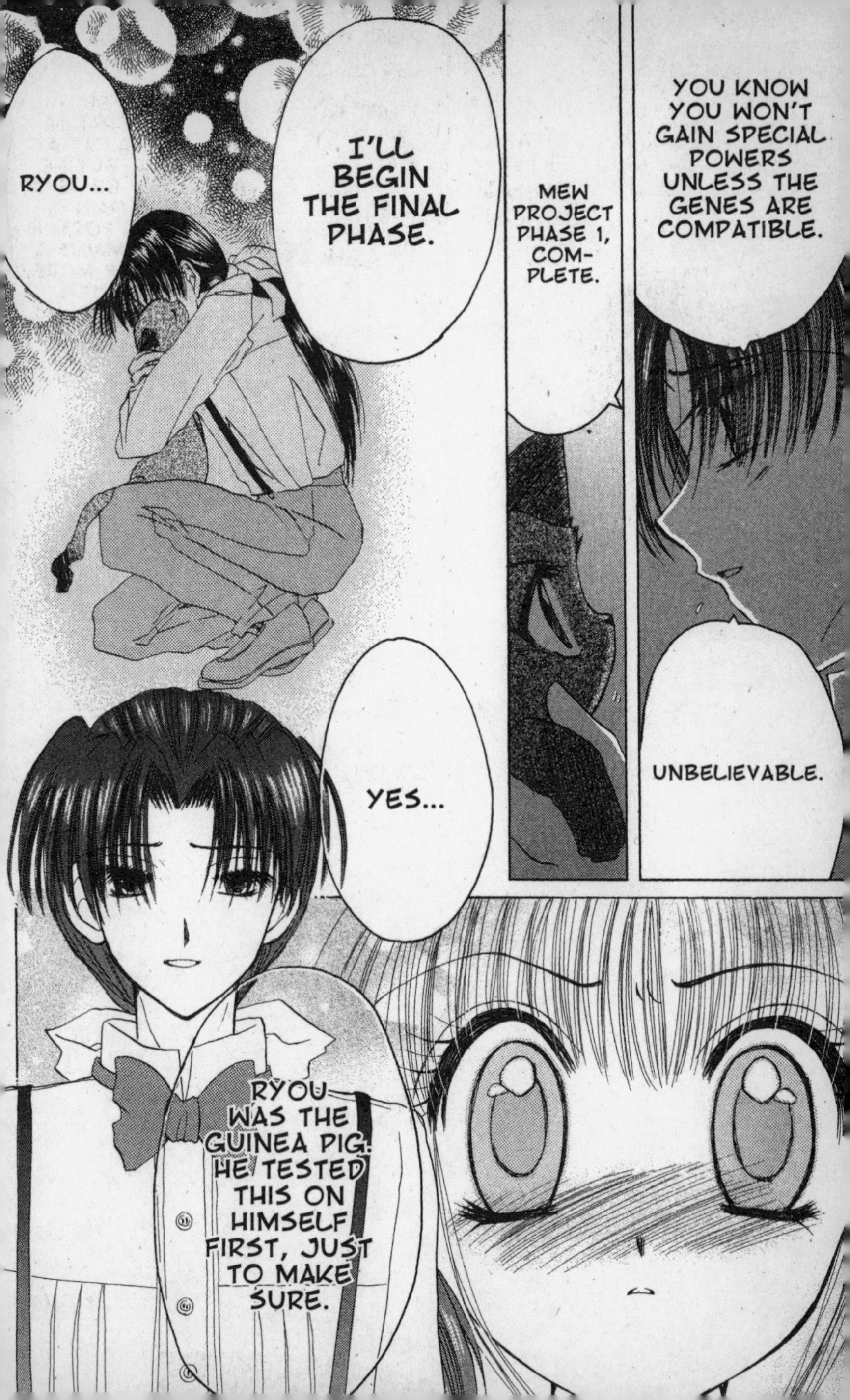
YOU KNOW YOU WON'T GAIN SPECIAL POWERS UNLESS THE GENES ARE COMPATIBLE.
UNBELIEVABLE.
MEW PROJECT PHASE 1, COM-PLETE.
I'LL BEGIN THE FINAL PHASE.
RYOU...
YES...
RYOU WAS THE GUINEA PIG. HE TESTED THIS ON HIMSELF FIRST, JUST TO MAKE SURE.

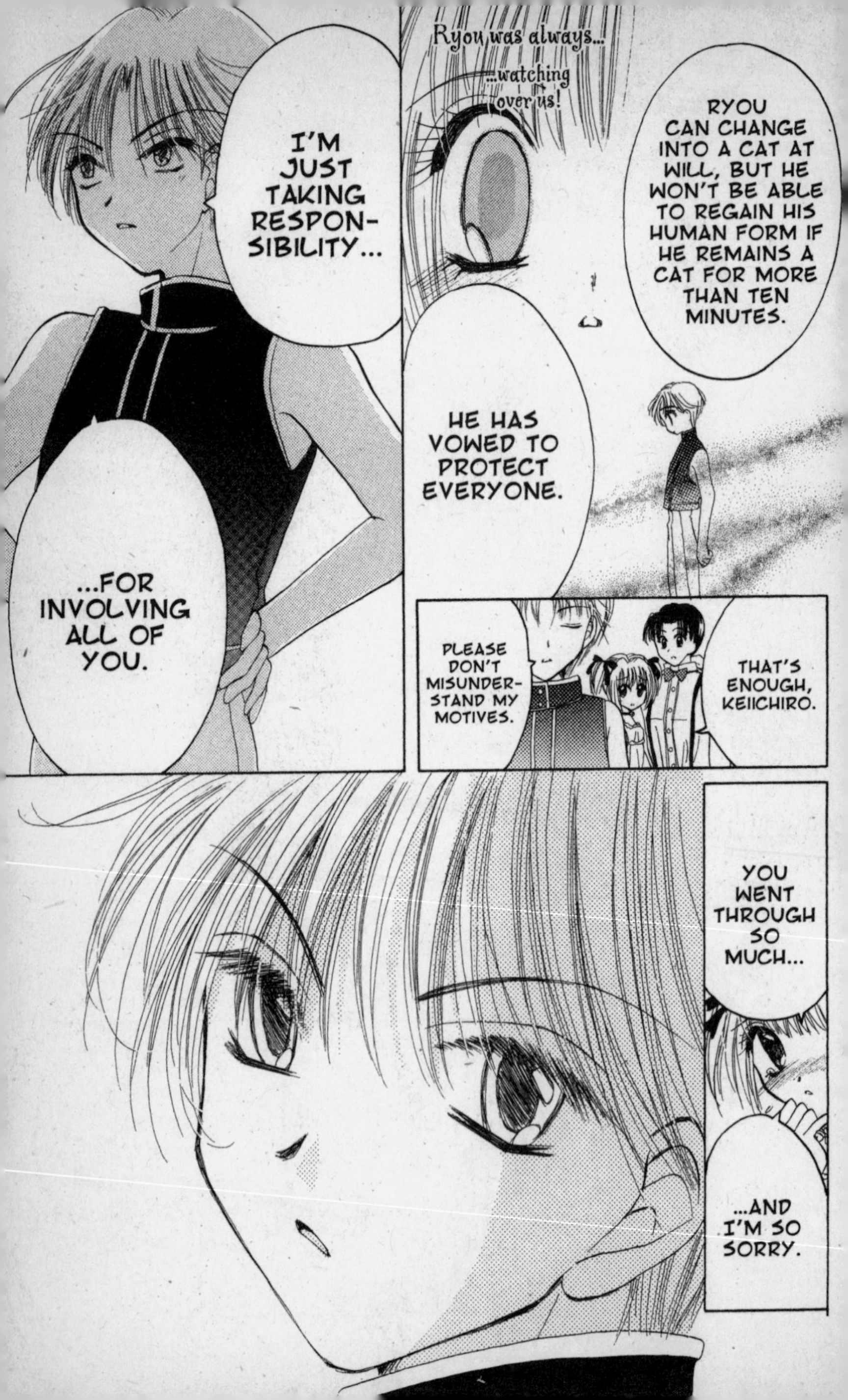
Ryou was always...
...watching over us!
RYOU CAN CHANGE INTO A CAT AT WILL, BUT HE WON'T BE ABLE TO REGAIN HIS HUMAN FORM IF HE REMAINS A CAT FOR MORE THAN TEN MINUTES.
HE HAS VOWED TO PROTECT EVERYONE.
THAT'S ENOUGH, KEIICHIRO.
PLEASE DON'T MISUNDERSTAND MY MOTIVES.
I'M JUST TAKING RESPON-SIBILITY...
...FOR INVOLVING ALL OF YOU.
YOU WENT THROUGH SO MUCH...
...AND I'M SO SORRY.

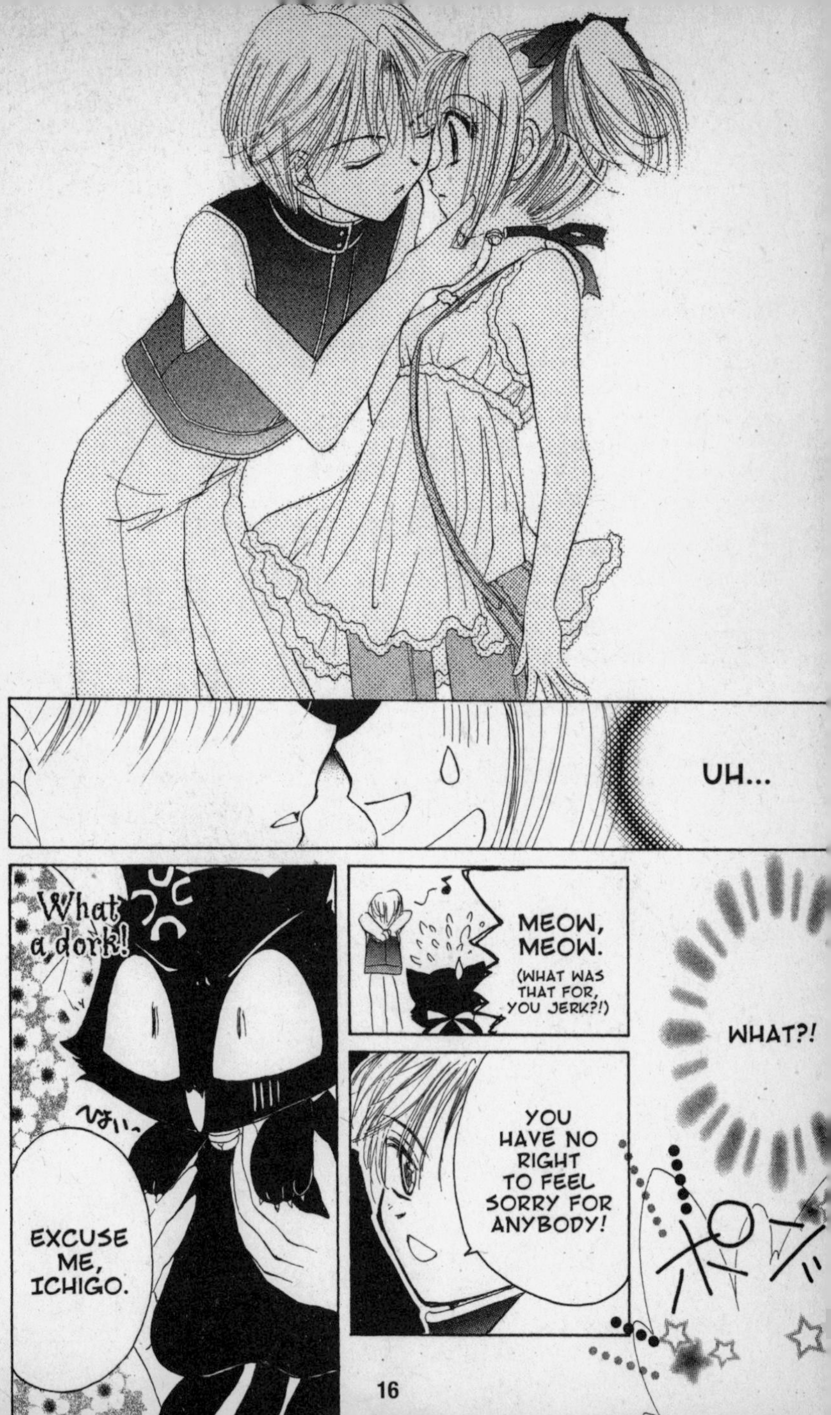

UH...
WHAT?!
MEOW, MEOW.
(WHAT WAS THAT FOR, YOU JERK?!)
YOU HAVE NO RIGHT TO FEEL SORRY FOR ANYBODY!
What a dork!
EXCUSE ME, ICHIGO.

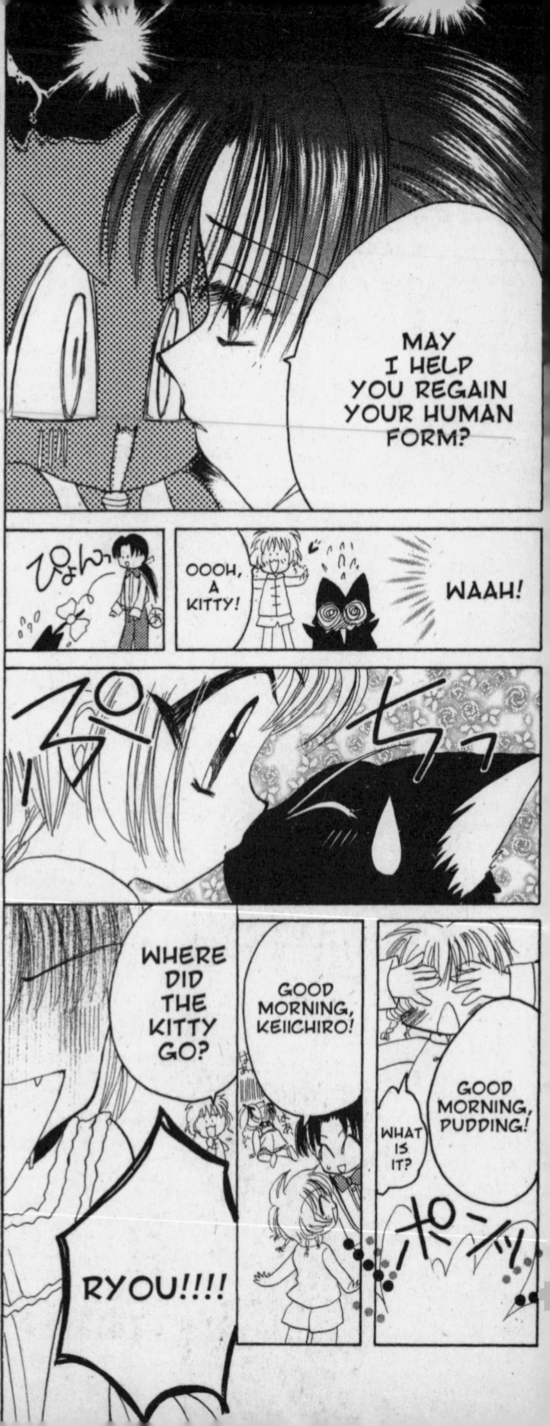

MAY I HELP YOU REGAIN YOUR HUMAN FORM?
WAAH!
OOOH, A KITTY!
ぴょんっ
GOOD MORNING, PUDDING!
WHAT IS IT?
ポーンッ
GOOD MORNING, KEIICHIRO!
WHERE DID THE KITTY GO?
RYOU!!!!

Tokyo Mew Mew

Ichigo's Costume Designs Wanted!!

Usually, I would have a little side comic here. However, we received a lot of entries when we held the "Design Ichigo's Costume Contest"! The winning design by Kanako Kozuki was used on a cover! I thought one wasn't enough, so I decided to pick six more designs to use in an illustration, instead of the usual side comics.

I would have picked more entries, but due to a lack of space, I just couldn't! I chose the designs of both Junior Grand Prix winners, two of the five Idea Award winners, and two of the Cute Award winners. Enjoy Ichigo's fashion show!!

Grand Prix design.

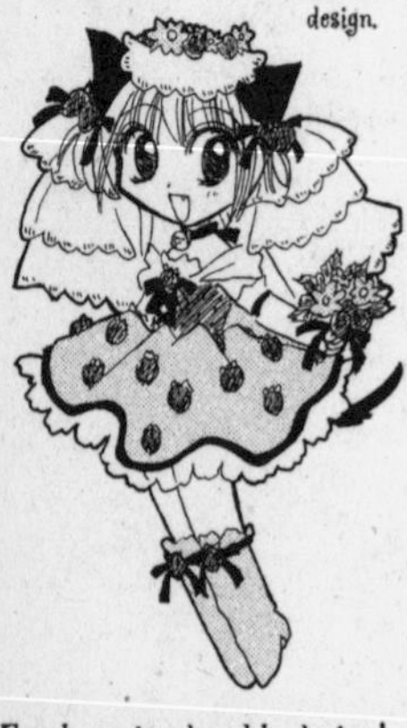

An elegant, adorable design! Perfect for the Grand Prix Award. I had a hard time coloring this one!

FYI: This contest is closed!

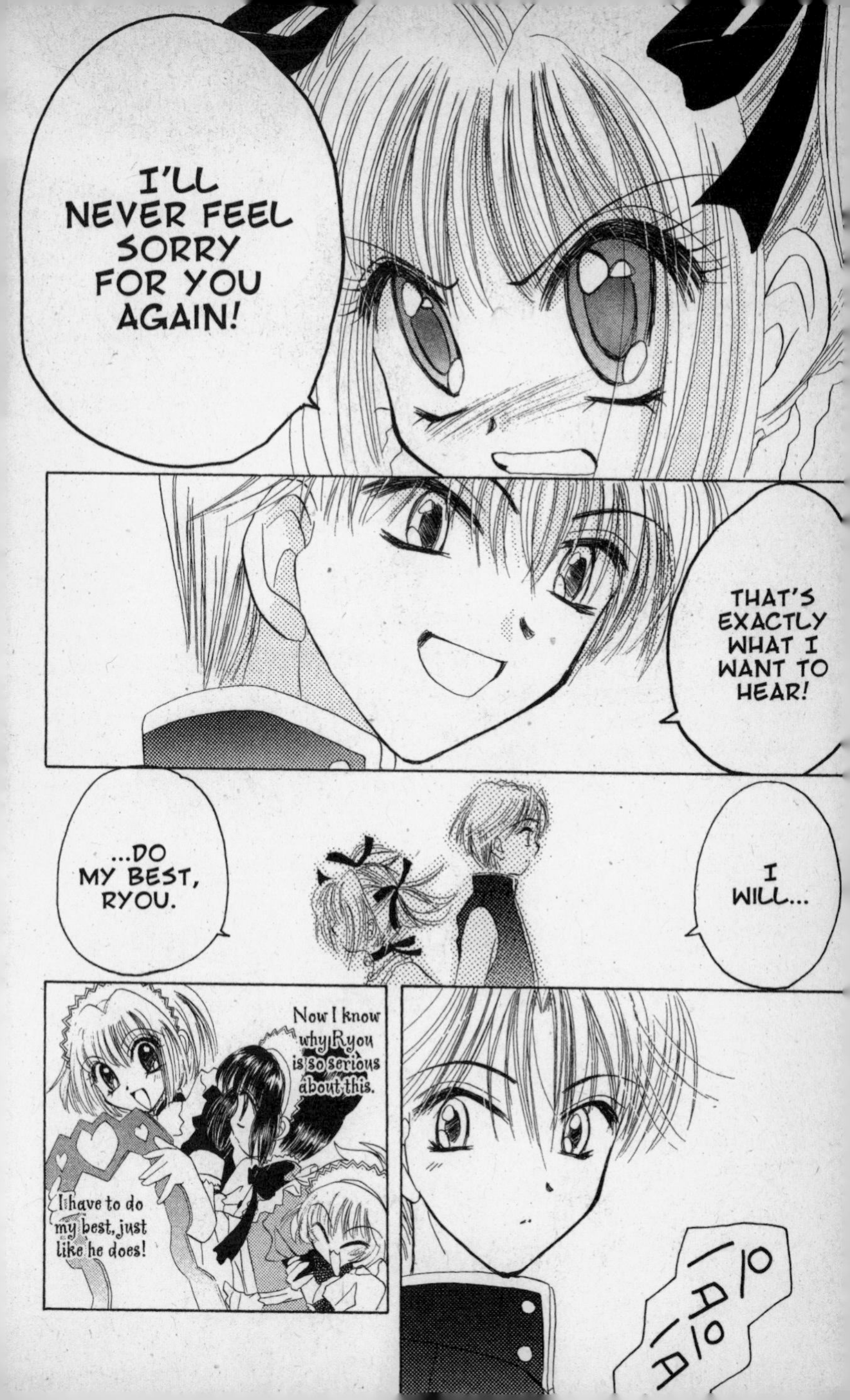
I'LL NEVER FEEL SORRY FOR YOU AGAIN!
THAT'S EXACTLY WHAT I WANT TO HEAR!
I WILL...
...DO MY BEST, RYOU.
Now I know why Ryou is so serious about this.
I have to do my best, just like he does!

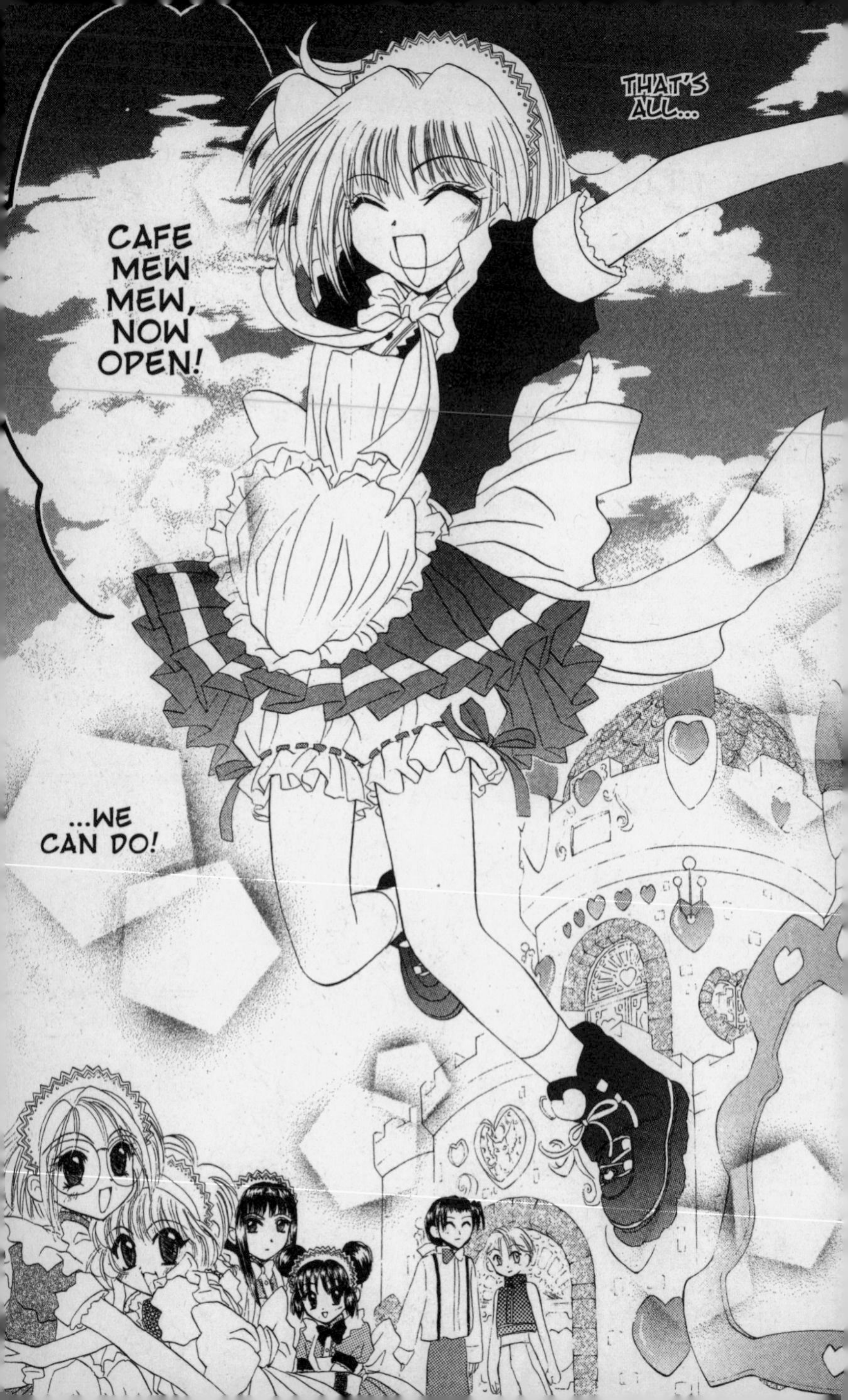

THAT'S ALL...
CAFE MEW MEW, NOW OPEN!
...WE CAN DO!

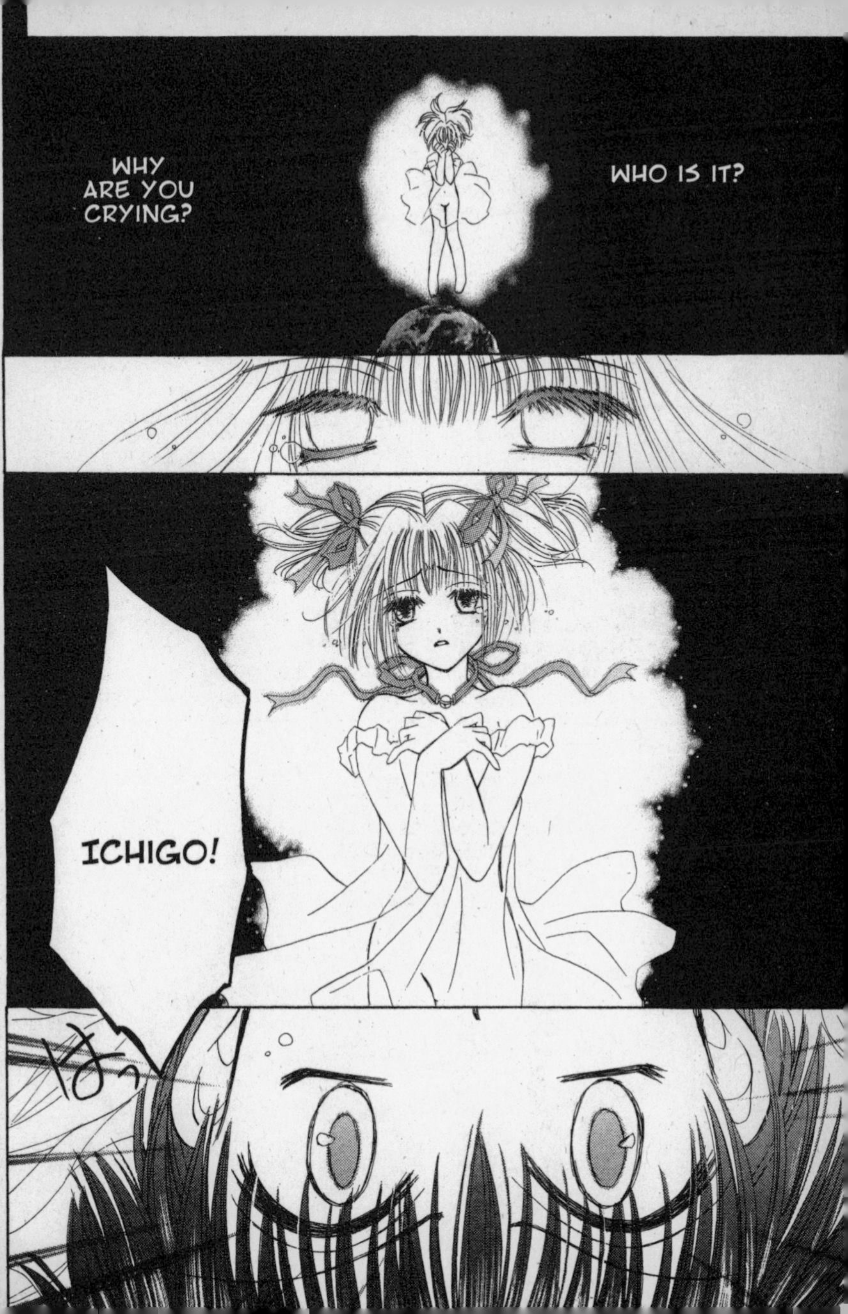
WHO IS IT?
WHY ARE YOU CRYING?
ICHIGO!
はっ

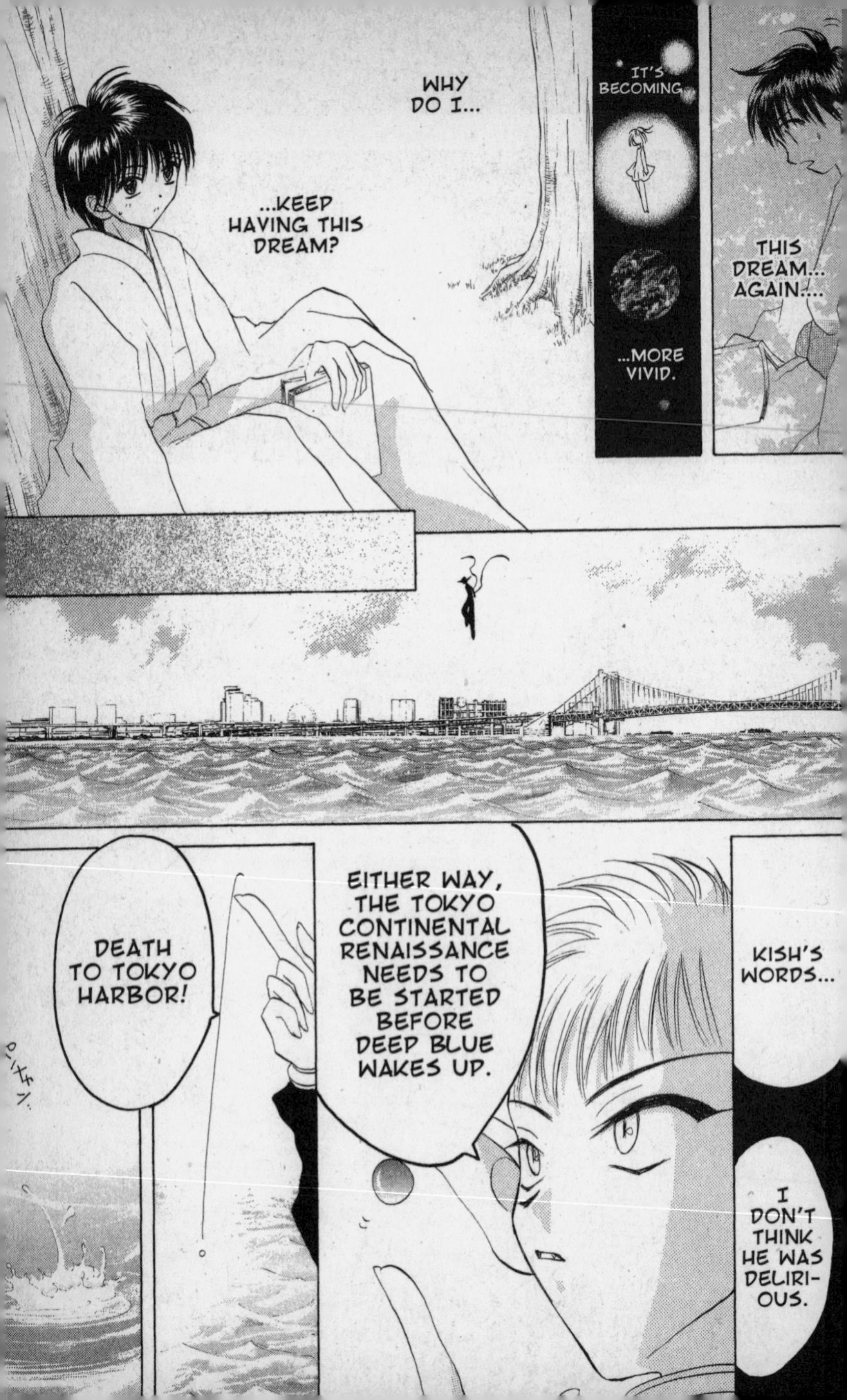
THIS DREAM... AGAIN....
IT'S BECOMING
...MORE VIVID.
WHY DO I...
...KEEP HAVING THIS DREAM?
KISH'S WORDS...
I DON'T THINK HE WAS DELIRI-OUS.
EITHER WAY, THE TOKYO CONTINENTAL RENAISSANCE NEEDS TO BE STARTED BEFORE DEEP BLUE WAKES UP.
DEATH TO TOKYO HARBOR!

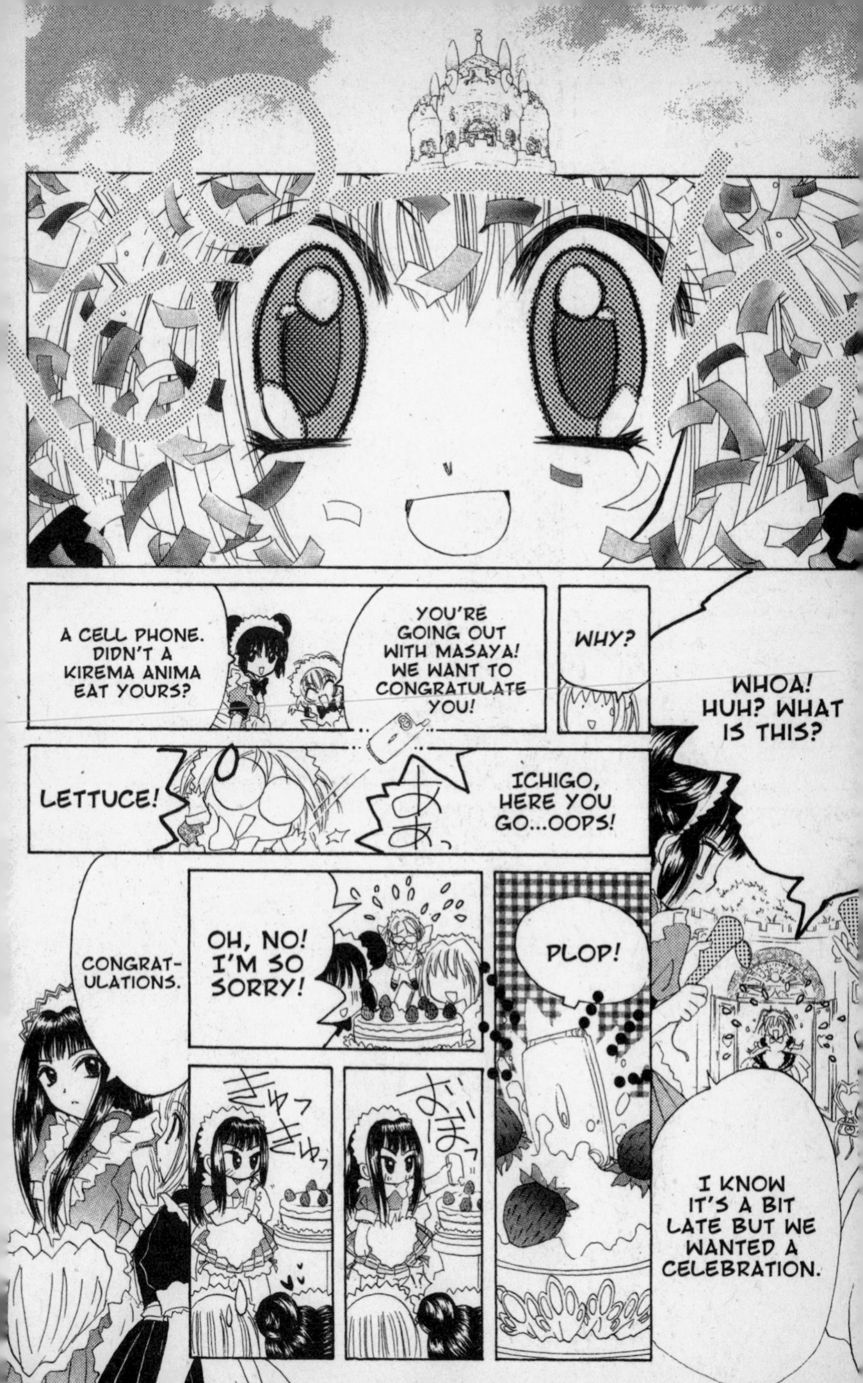
WHOA! HUH? WHAT IS THIS?
I KNOW IT'S A BIT LATE BUT WE WANTED A CELEBRATION.
WHY?
YOU'RE GOING OUT WITH MASAYA! WE WANT TO CONGRATULATE YOU!
A CELL PHONE. DIDN'T A KIREMA ANIMA EAT YOURS?
ICHIGO, HERE YOU GO...OOPS!
あっ
LETTUCE!
PLOP!
OH, NO! I'M SO SORRY!
CONGRAT-ULATIONS.
おぼっ
きゃっ きゃっ

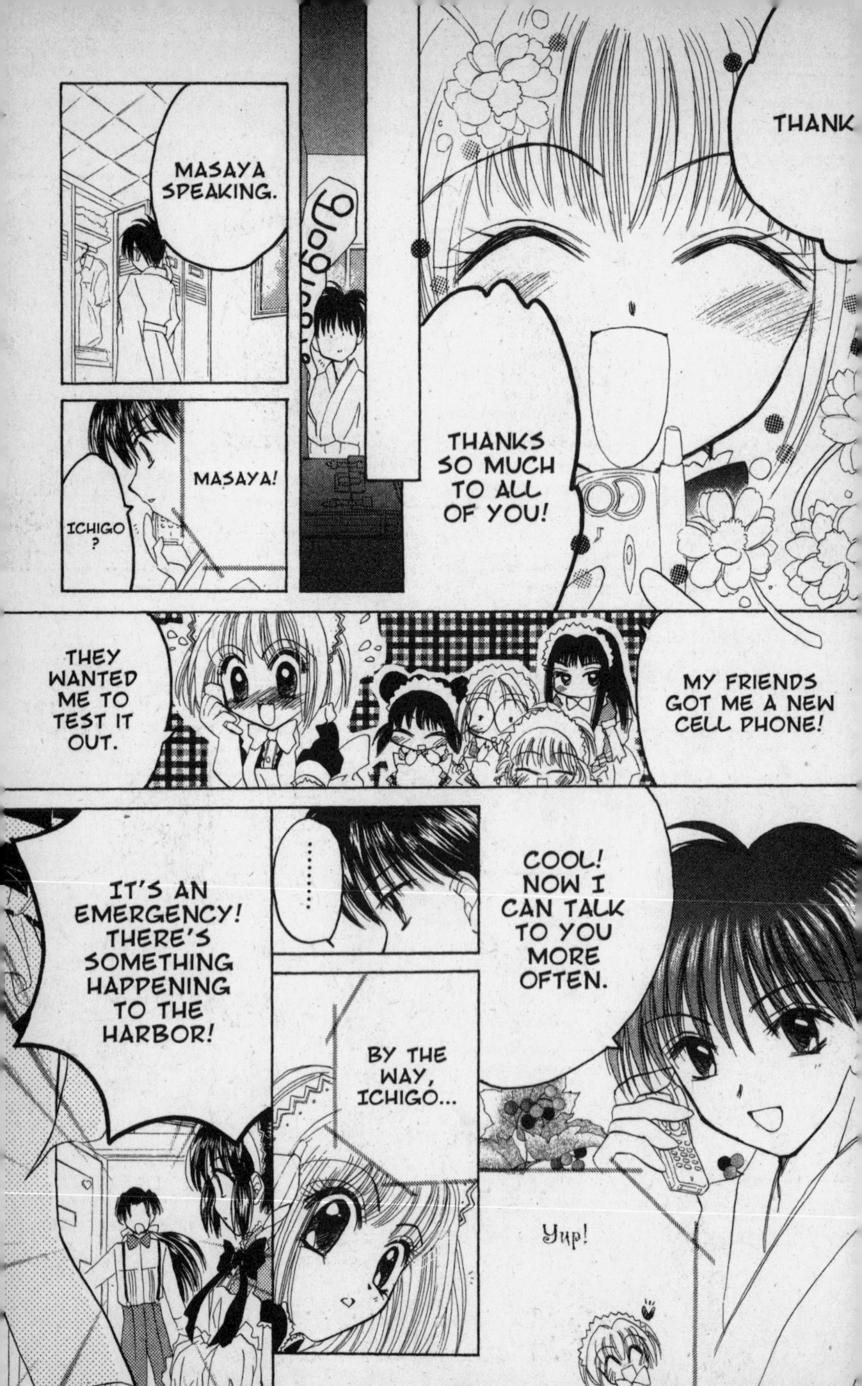
THANK
THANKS SO MUCH TO ALL OF YOU!
MASAYA SPEAKING.
MASAYA!
ICHIGO?
MY FRIENDS GOT ME A NEW CELL PHONE!
THEY WANTED ME TO TEST IT OUT.
COOL! NOW I CAN TALK TO YOU MORE OFTEN.
Yup!
......
BY THE WAY, ICHIGO...
IT'S AN EMERGENCY! THERE'S SOMETHING HAPPENING TO THE HARBOR!

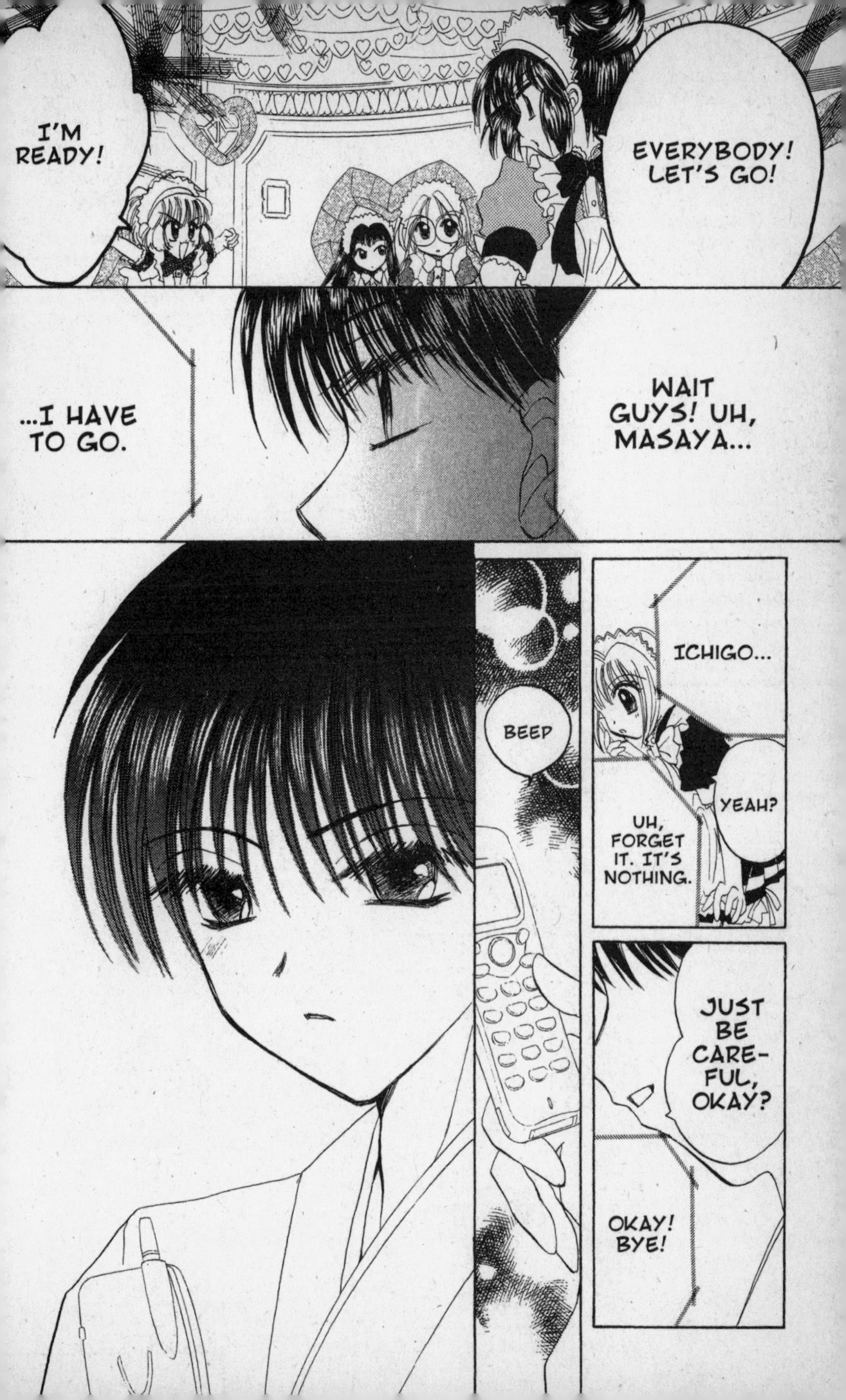
EVERYBODY! LET'S GO!
I'M READY!
WAIT GUYS! UH, MASAYA...
...I HAVE TO GO.
ICHIGO...
YEAH?
UH, FORGET IT. IT'S NOTHING.
JUST BE CARE-FUL, OKAY?
OKAY! BYE!
BEEP

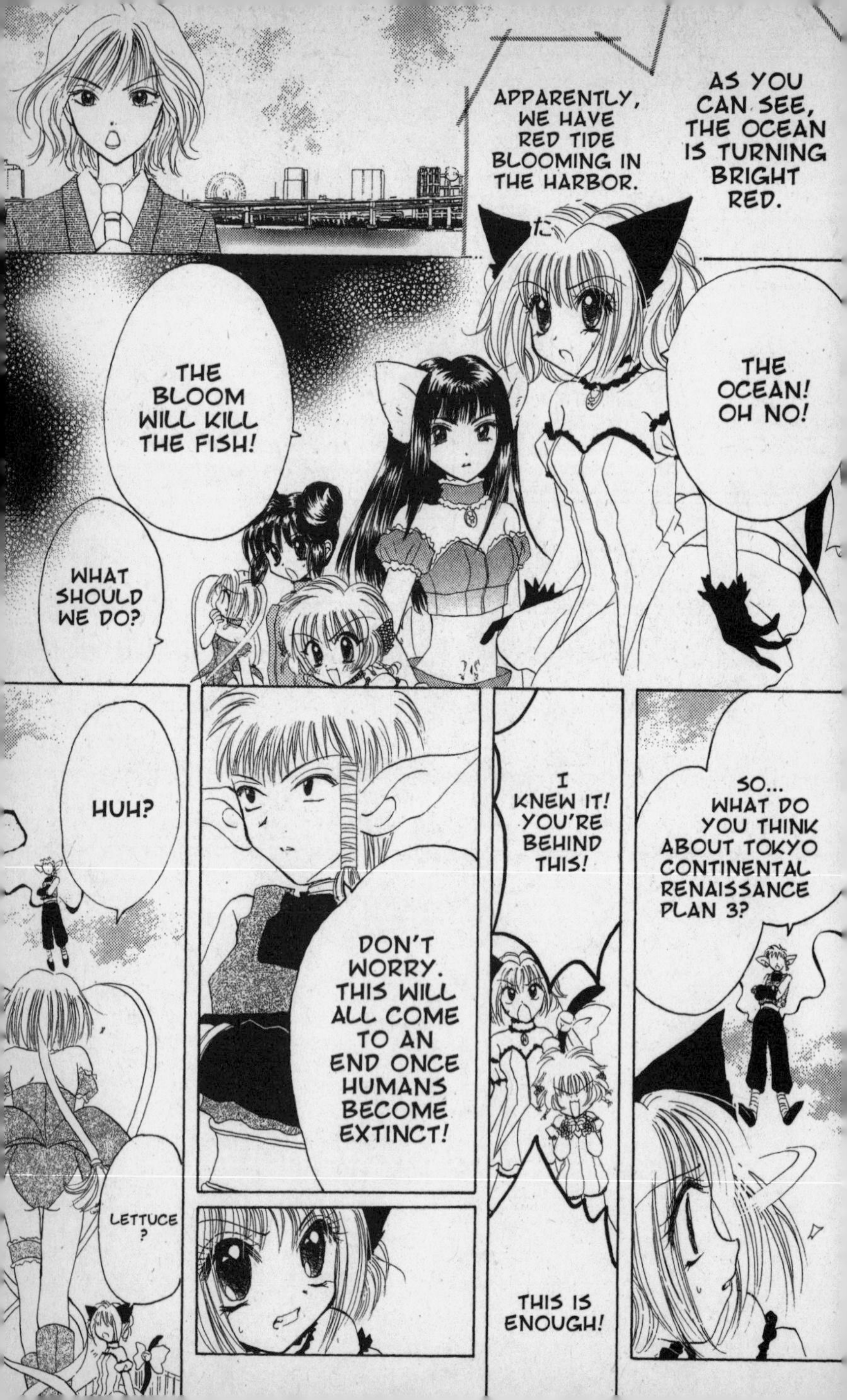
AS YOU CAN SEE, THE OCEAN IS TURNING BRIGHT RED.
APPARENTLY, WE HAVE RED TIDE BLOOMING IN THE HARBOR.
THE OCEAN! OH NO!
THE BLOOM WILL KILL THE FISH!
WHAT SHOULD WE DO?
SO... WHAT DO YOU THINK ABOUT TOKYO CONTINENTAL RENAISSANCE PLAN 3?
I KNEW IT! YOU'RE BEHIND THIS!
THIS IS ENOUGH!
DON'T WORRY. THIS WILL ALL COME TO AN END ONCE HUMANS BECOME EXTINCT!
HUH?
LETTUCE?

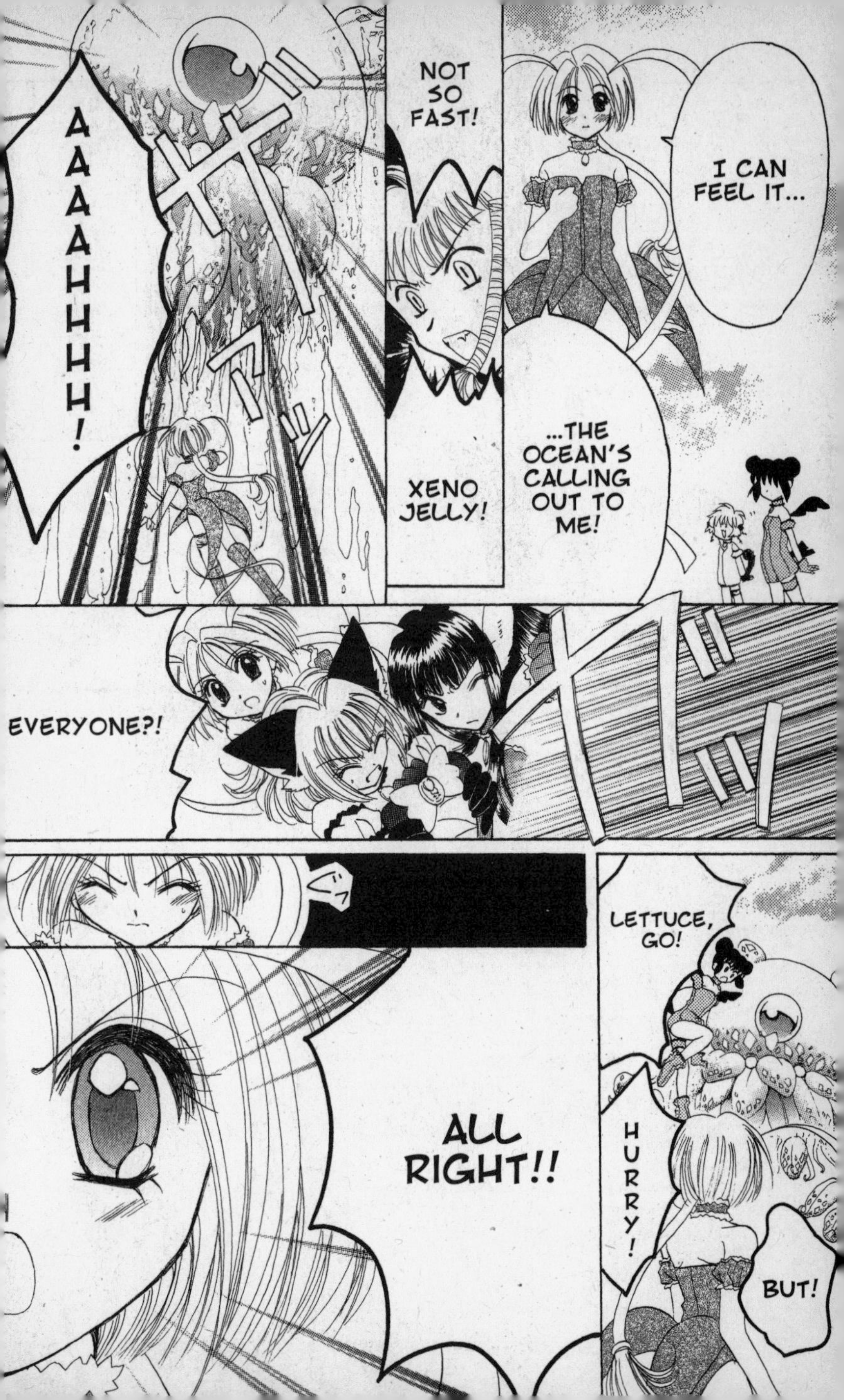
I CAN FEEL IT...
...THE OCEAN'S CALLING OUT TO ME!
NOT SO FAST!
XENO JELLY!
AAAAHHHH!
EVERYONE?!
LETTUCE, GO!
HURRY!
BUT!
ALL RIGHT!!

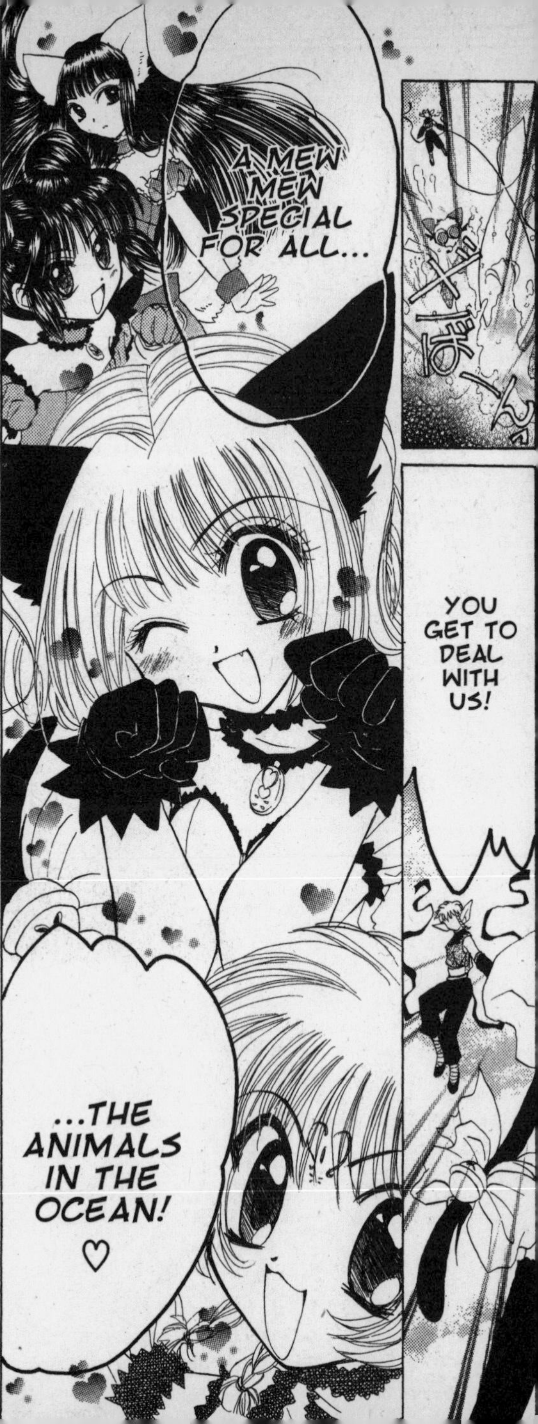
YOU GET TO DEAL WITH US!
A MEW MEW SPECIAL FOR ALL...
...THE ANIMALS IN THE OCEAN! ♡

Tokyo Mew Mew
Ichigo's Costume Designs Wanted!!

Junior Grand Prix

Ami Haganuma
Fukushima prefecture
5th grade

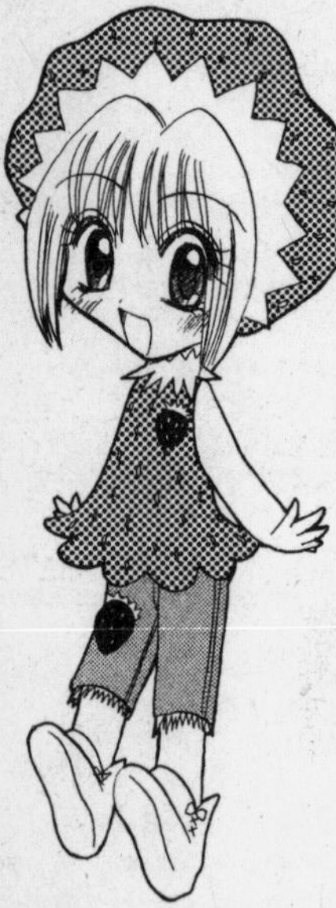

You can relax at home or go out for fun in this outfit! I like the casual feel of the design, and I totally wish I could buy it! It looks like something you could find at a store. It's a simple design, but very adorable!

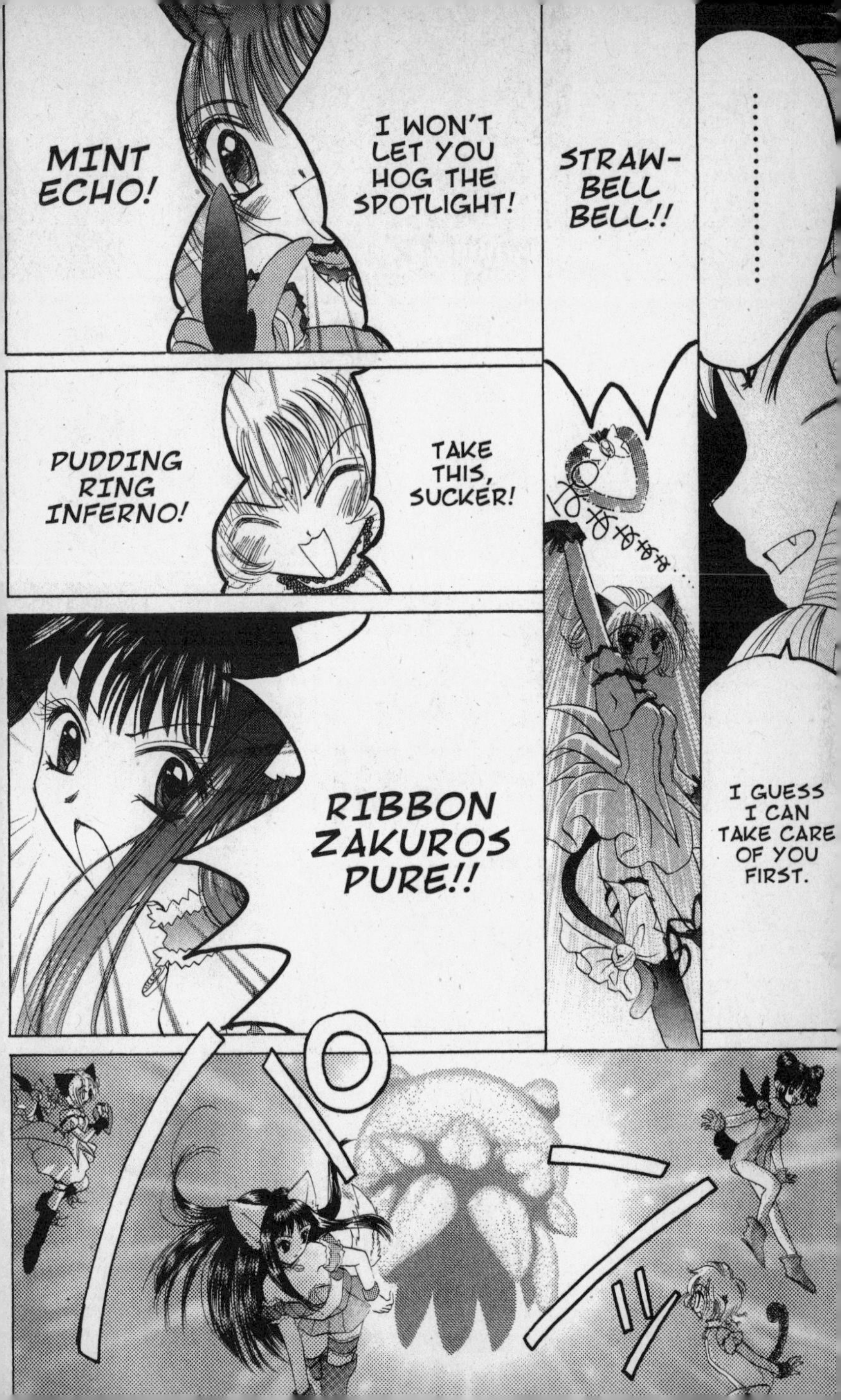
......
I GUESS I CAN TAKE CARE OF YOU FIRST.
STRAW-BELL BELL!!
I WON'T LET YOU HOG THE SPOTLIGHT!
MINT ECHO!
TAKE THIS, SUCKER!
PUDDING RING INFERNO!
RIBBON ZAKUROS PURE!!

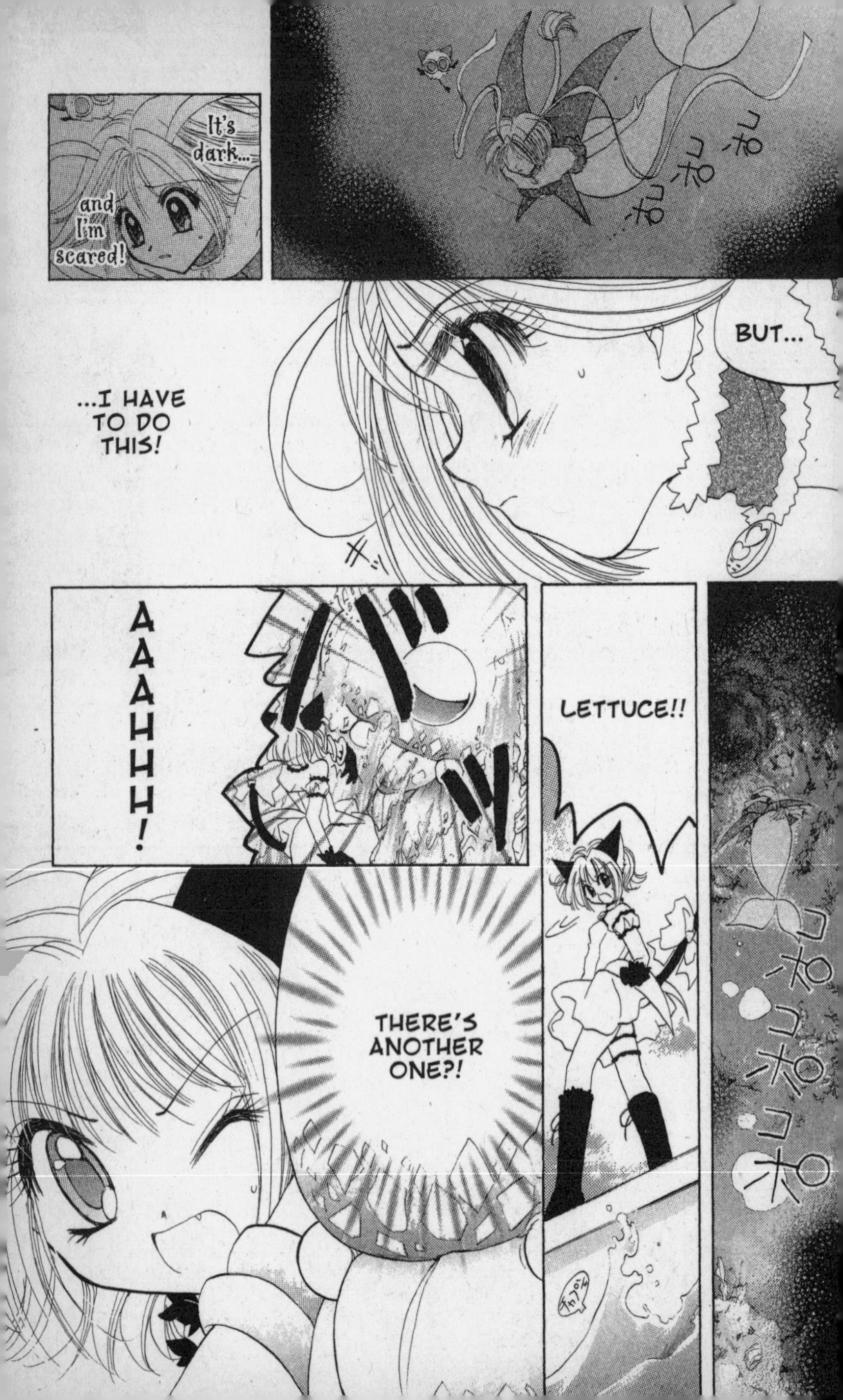
It's dark...
and I'm scared!
BUT...
...I HAVE TO DO THIS!
LETTUCE!!
AAAHHH!
THERE'S ANOTHER ONE?!

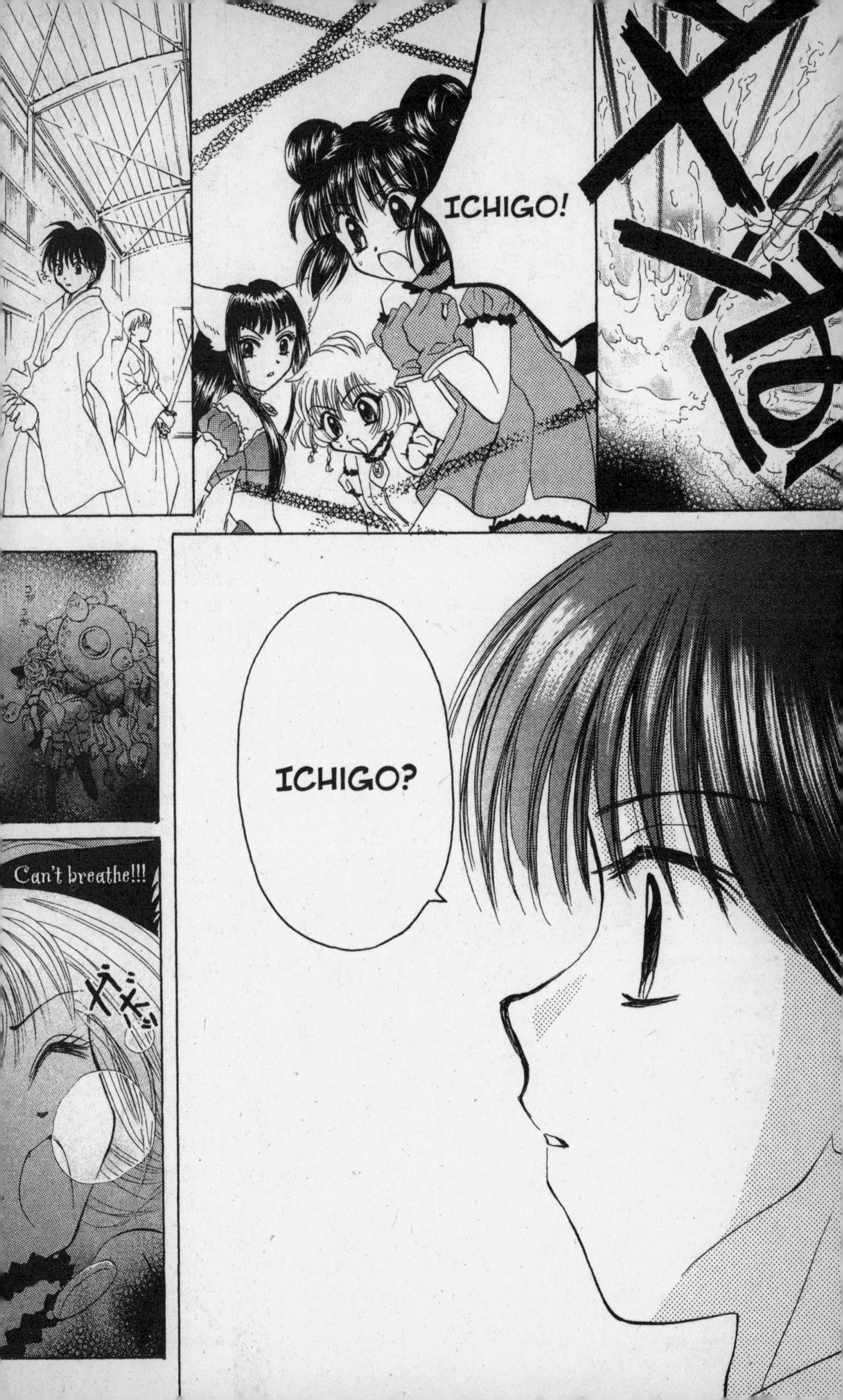
ICHIGO!
ICHIGO?
Can't breathe!!!

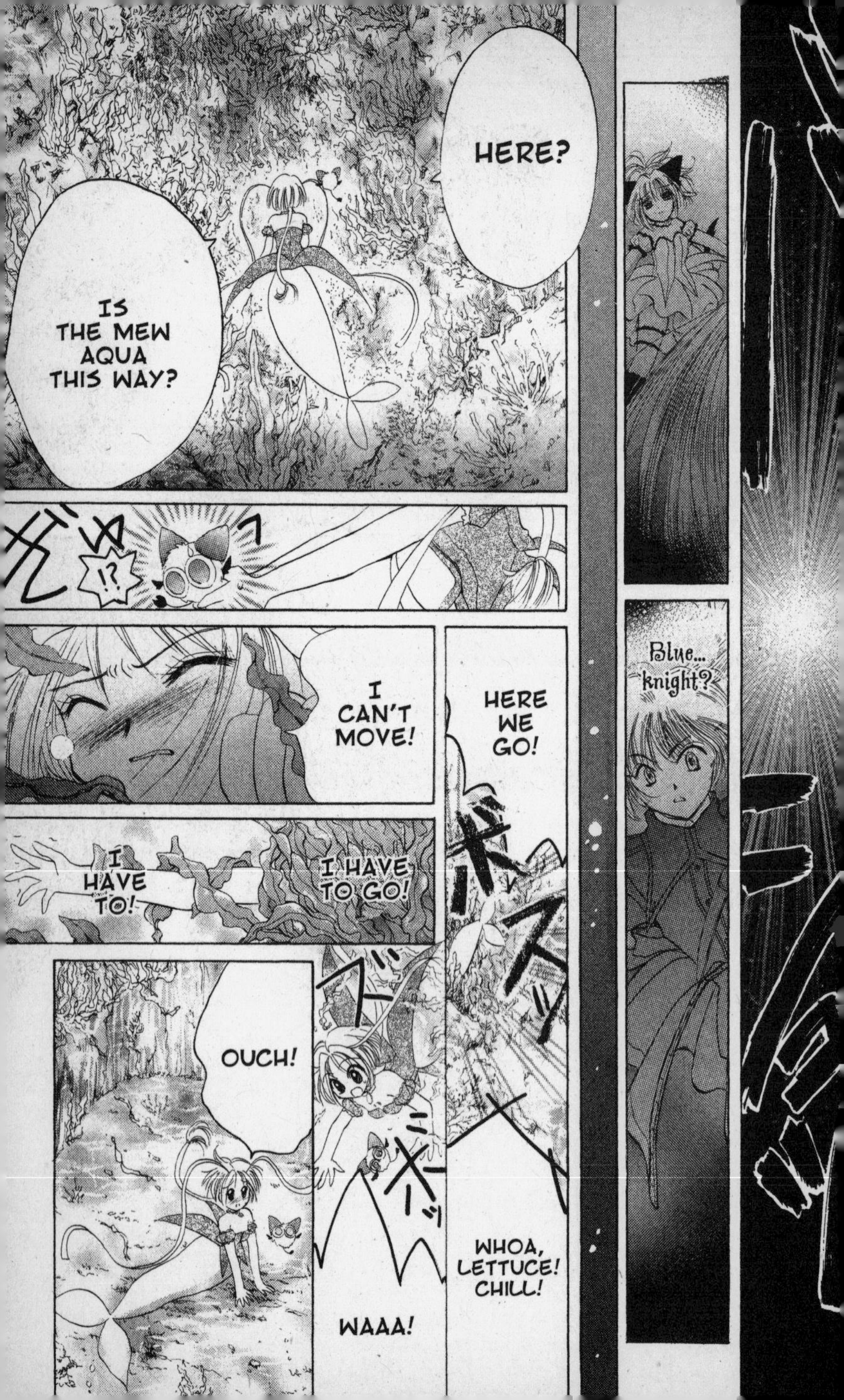
Blue... knight?
HERE?
IS THE MEW AQUA THIS WAY?
!?
HERE WE GO!
WHOA, LETTUCE! CHILL!
I CAN'T MOVE!
I HAVE TO GO!
I HAVE TO!
WAAA!
OUCH!

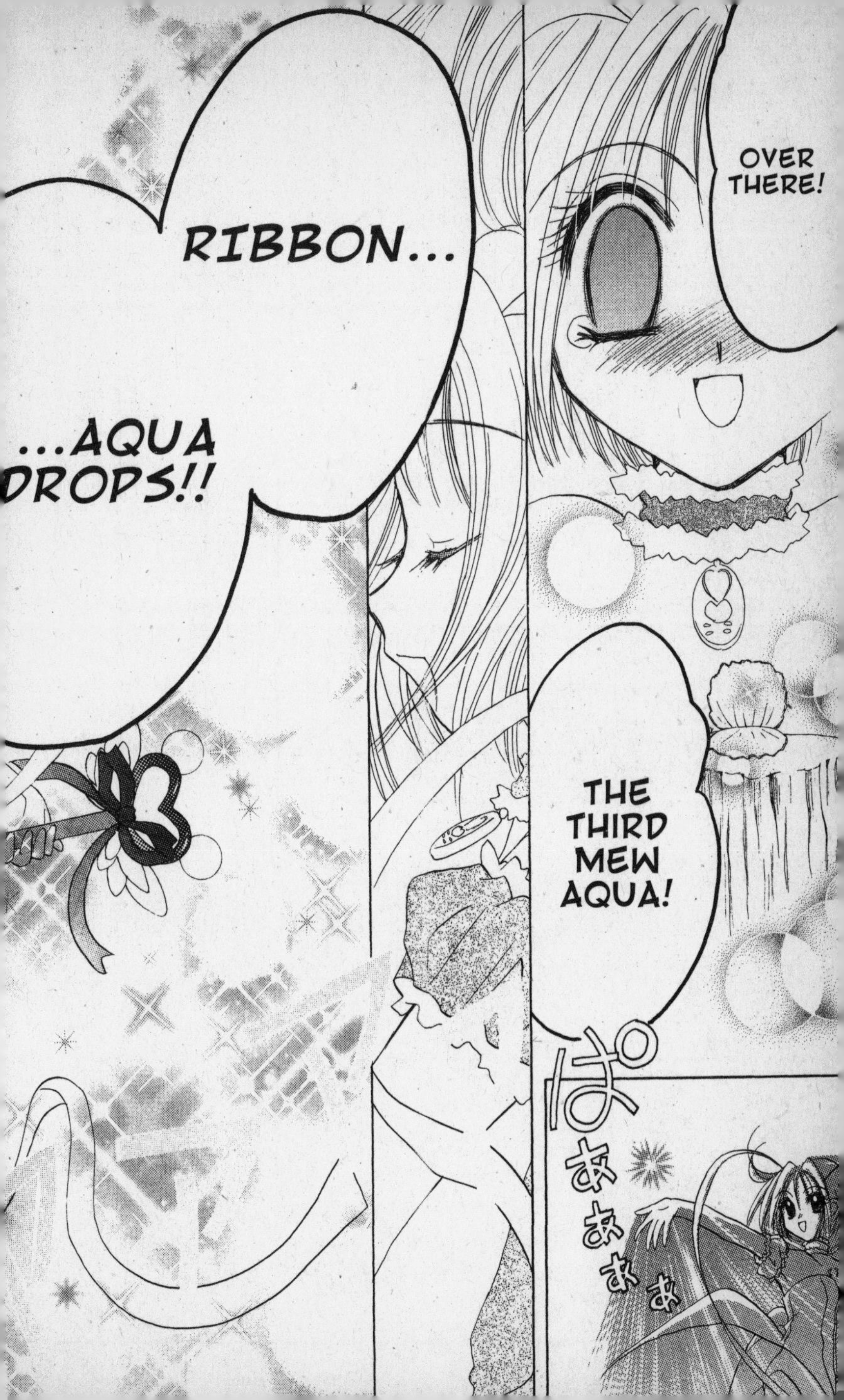
OVER THERE!
THE THIRD MEW AQUA!
ぱああああ
RIBBON...
...AQUA DROPS!!

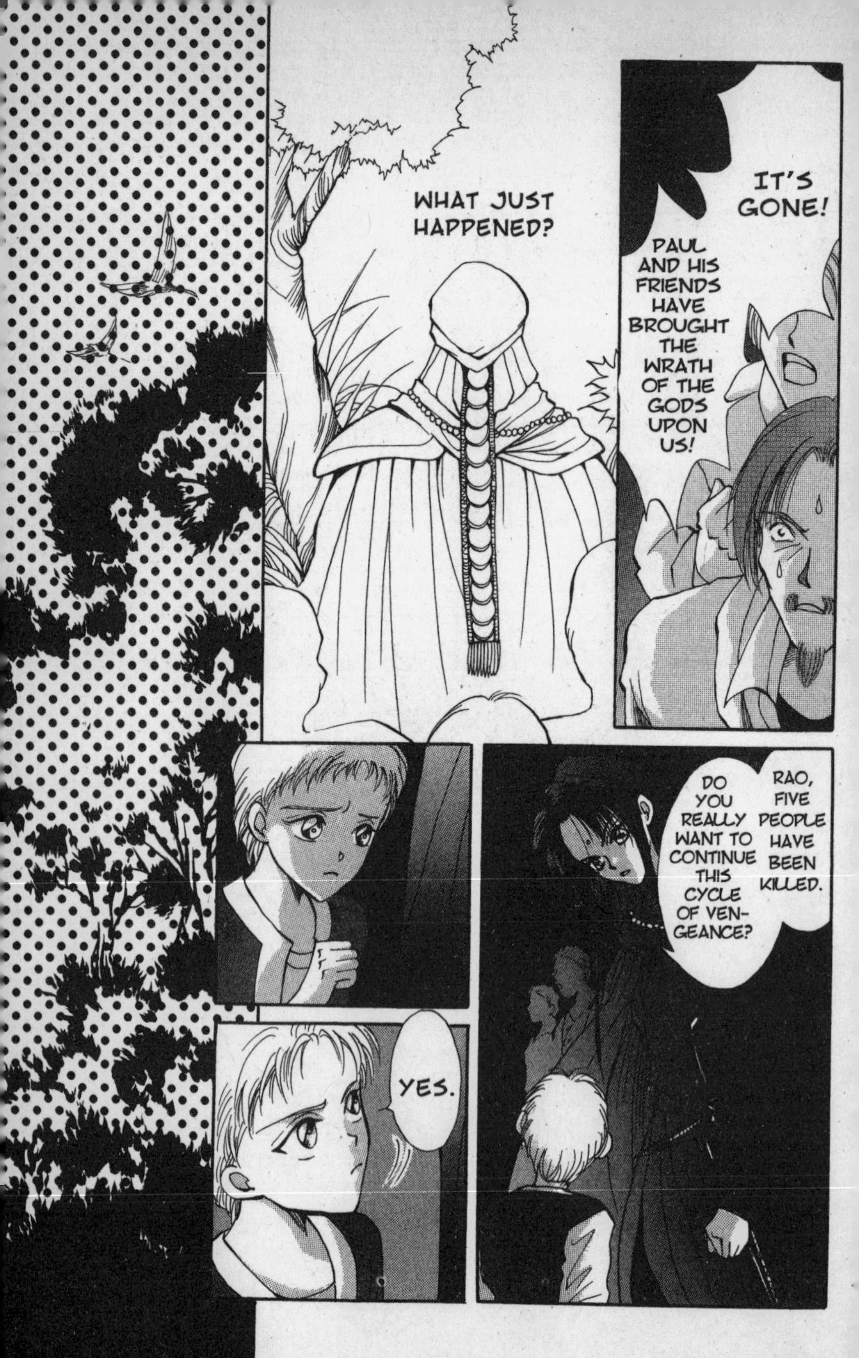
IT'S GONE!
PAUL AND HIS FRIENDS HAVE BROUGHT THE WRATH OF THE GODS UPON US!
WHAT JUST HAPPENED?
RAO, FIVE PEOPLE HAVE BEEN KILLED.
DO YOU REALLY WANT TO CONTINUE THIS CYCLE OF VEN-GEANCE?
YES.

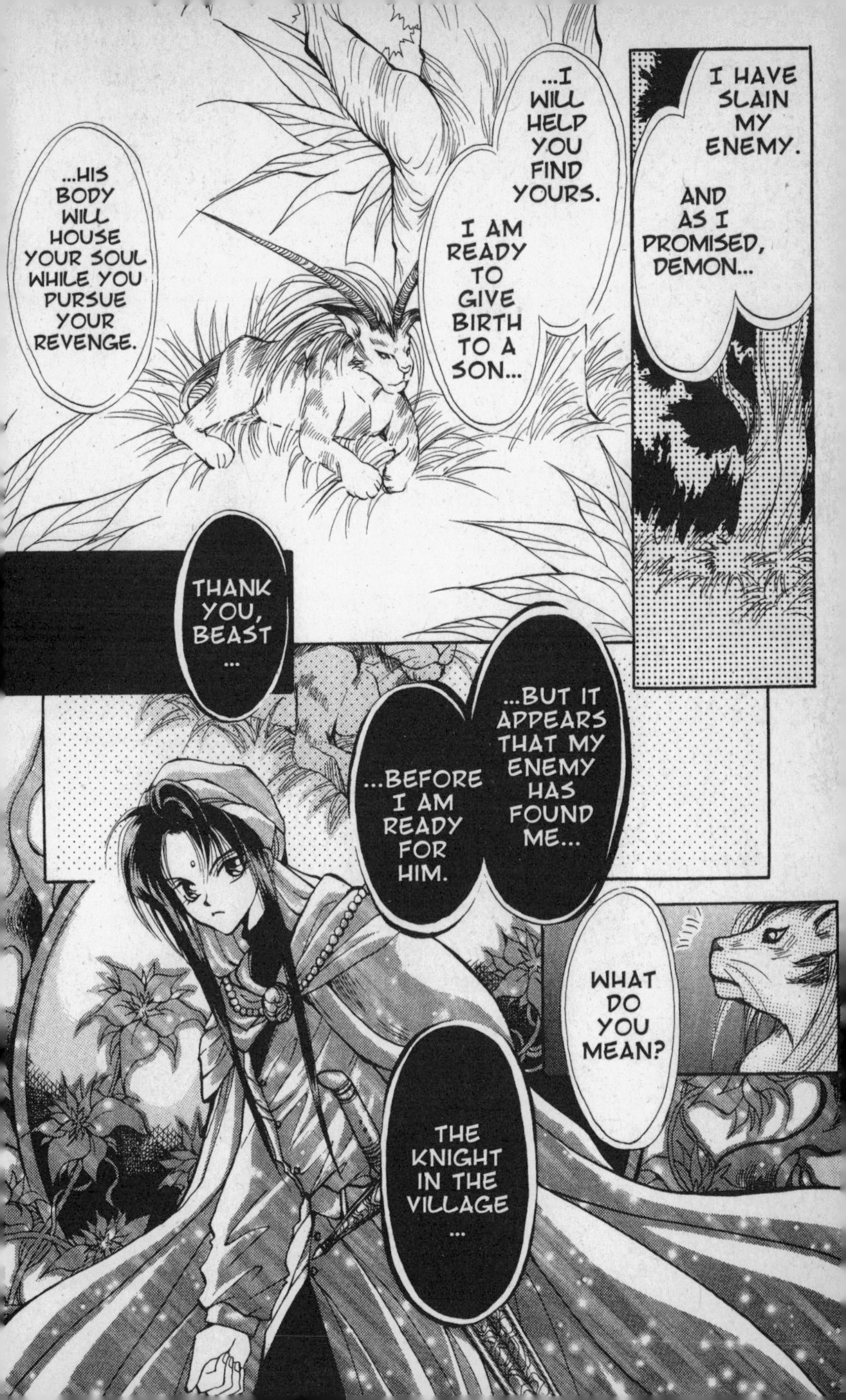
I HAVE SLAIN MY ENEMY.
AND AS I PROMISED, DEMON...
...I WILL HELP YOU FIND YOURS.
I AM READY TO GIVE BIRTH TO A SON...
...HIS BODY WILL HOUSE YOUR SOUL WHILE YOU PURSUE YOUR REVENGE.
THANK YOU, BEAST...
...BUT IT APPEARS THAT MY ENEMY HAS FOUND ME...
...BEFORE I AM READY FOR HIM.
WHAT DO YOU MEAN?
THE KNIGHT IN THE VILLAGE...

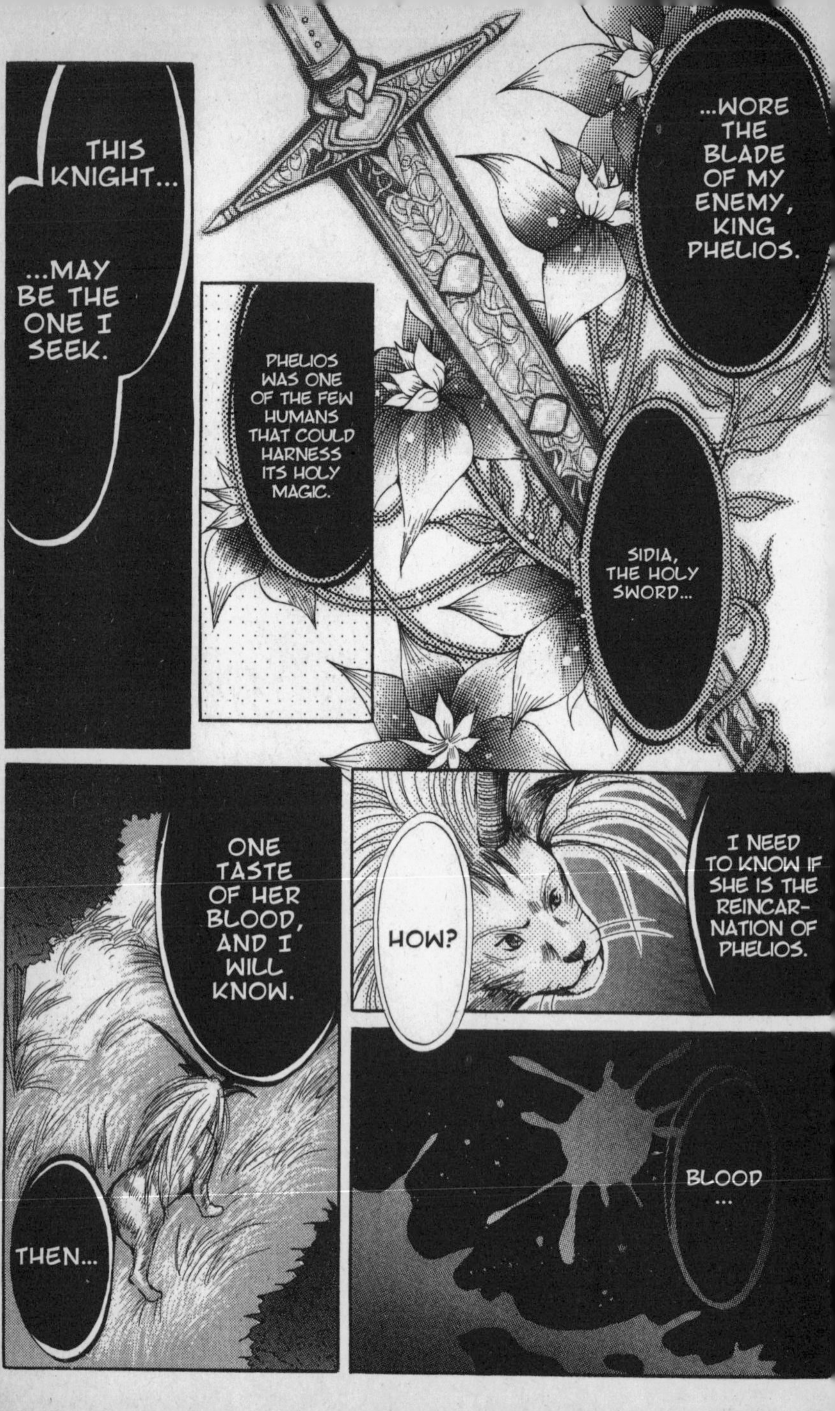
...WORE THE BLADE OF MY ENEMY, KING PHELIOS.
SIDIA, THE HOLY SWORD...
PHELIOS WAS ONE OF THE FEW HUMANS THAT COULD HARNESS ITS HOLY MAGIC.
THIS KNIGHT...
...MAY BE THE ONE I SEEK.
I NEED TO KNOW IF SHE IS THE REINCARNATION OF PHELIOS.
HOW?
BLOOD...
ONE TASTE OF HER BLOOD, AND I WILL KNOW.
THEN...

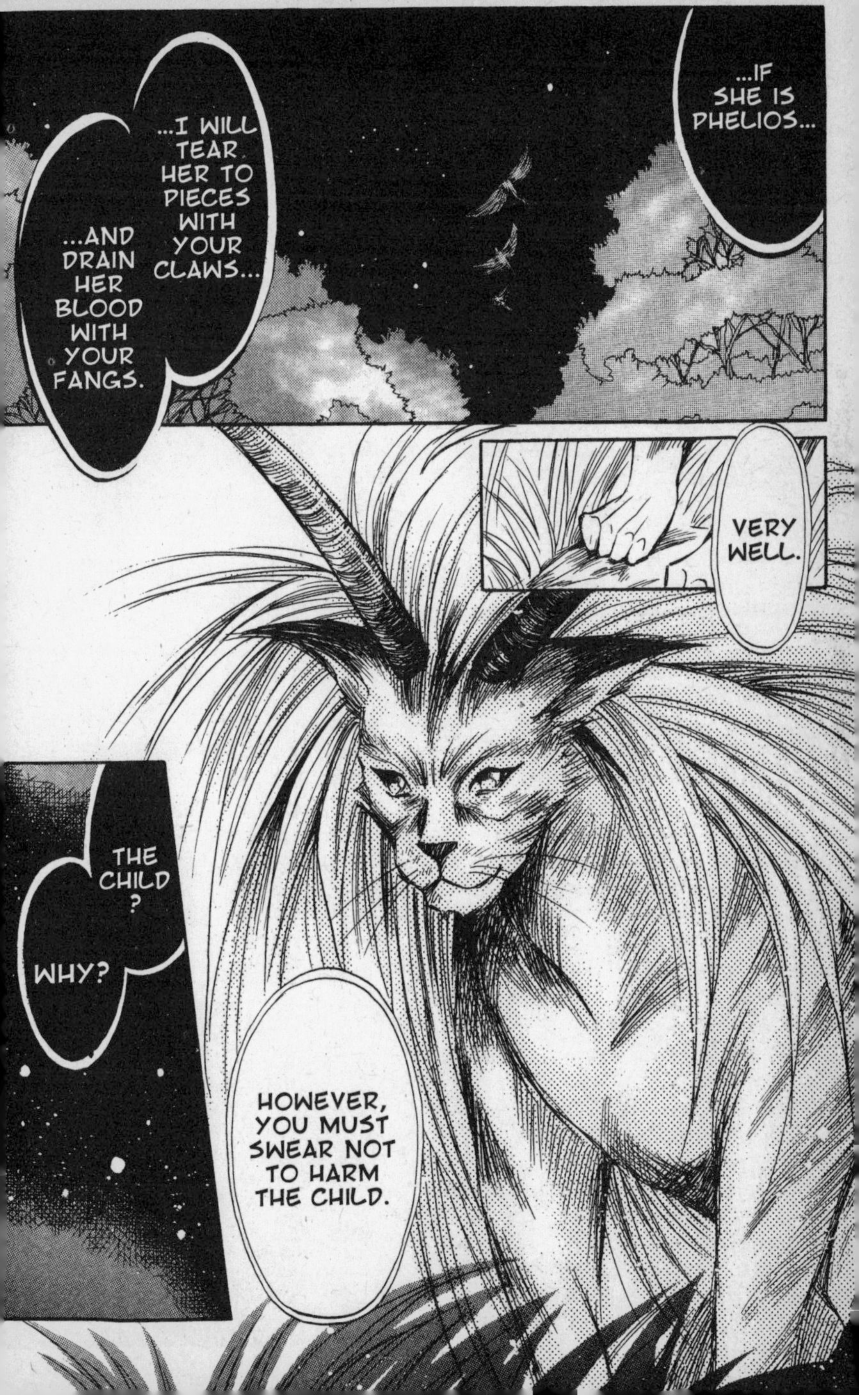
...IF SHE IS PHELIOS...
...I WILL TEAR HER TO PIECES WITH YOUR CLAWS...
...AND DRAIN HER BLOOD WITH YOUR FANGS.
VERY WELL.
HOWEVER, YOU MUST SWEAR NOT TO HARM THE CHILD.
THE CHILD?
WHY?

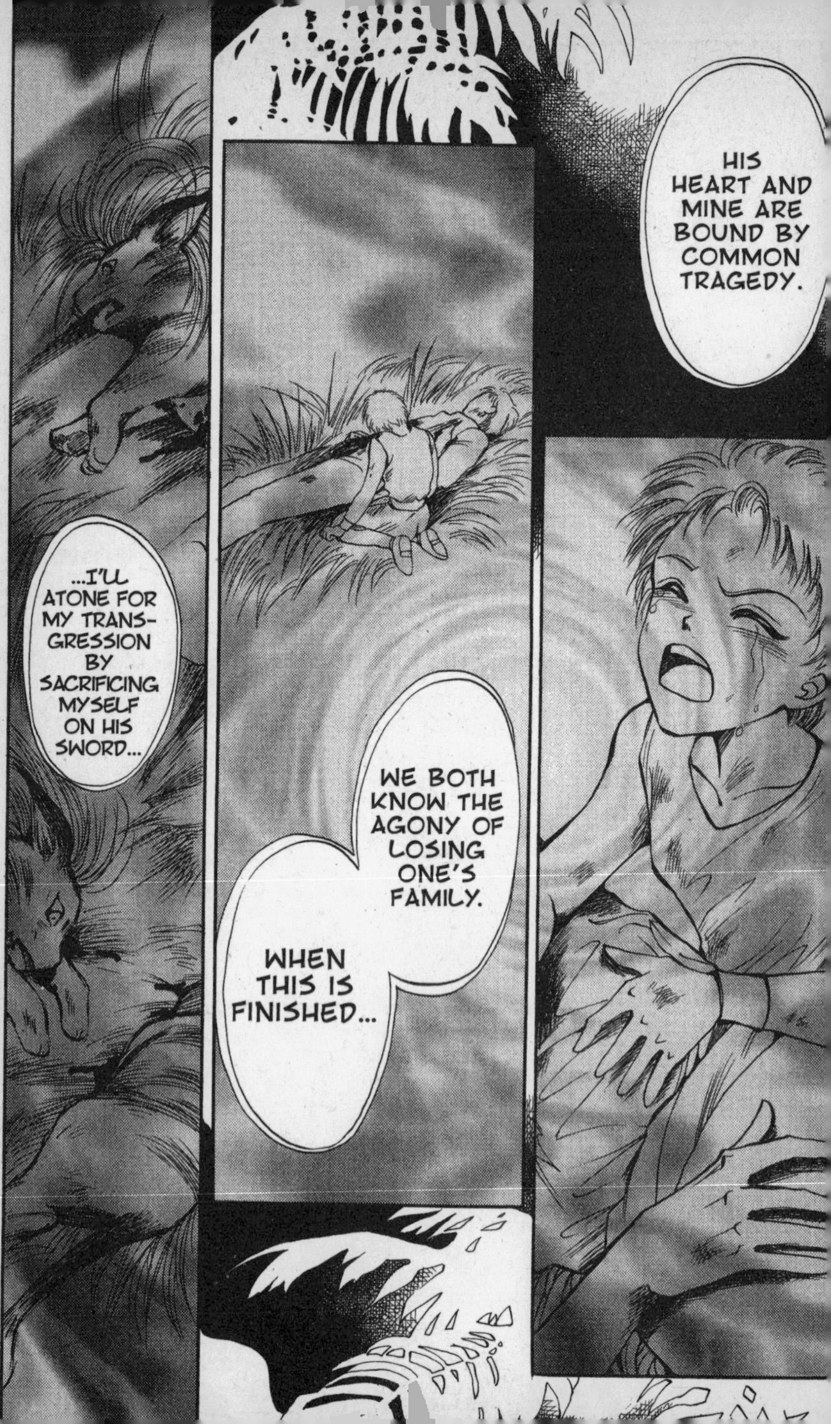
HIS HEART AND MINE ARE BOUND BY COMMON TRAGEDY.
WE BOTH KNOW THE AGONY OF LOSING ONE'S FAMILY.
WHEN THIS IS FINISHED...
...I'LL ATONE FOR MY TRANSGRESSION BY SACRIFICING MYSELF ON HIS SWORD...

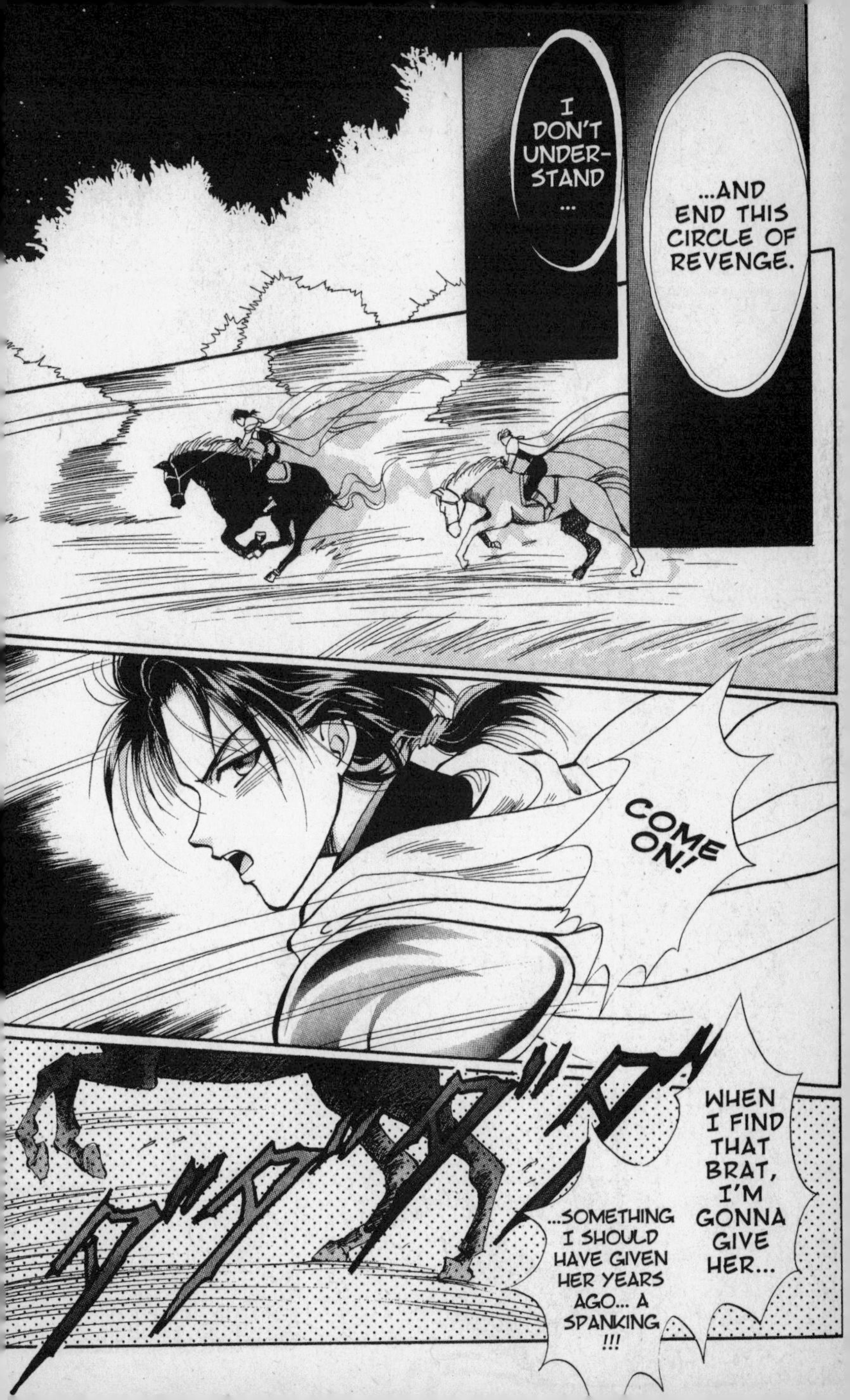
...AND END THIS CIRCLE OF REVENGE.
I DON'T UNDER-STAND ...
COME ON!
WHEN I FIND THAT BRAT, I'M GONNA GIVE HER...
...SOMETHING I SHOULD HAVE GIVEN HER YEARS AGO... A SPANKING !!!

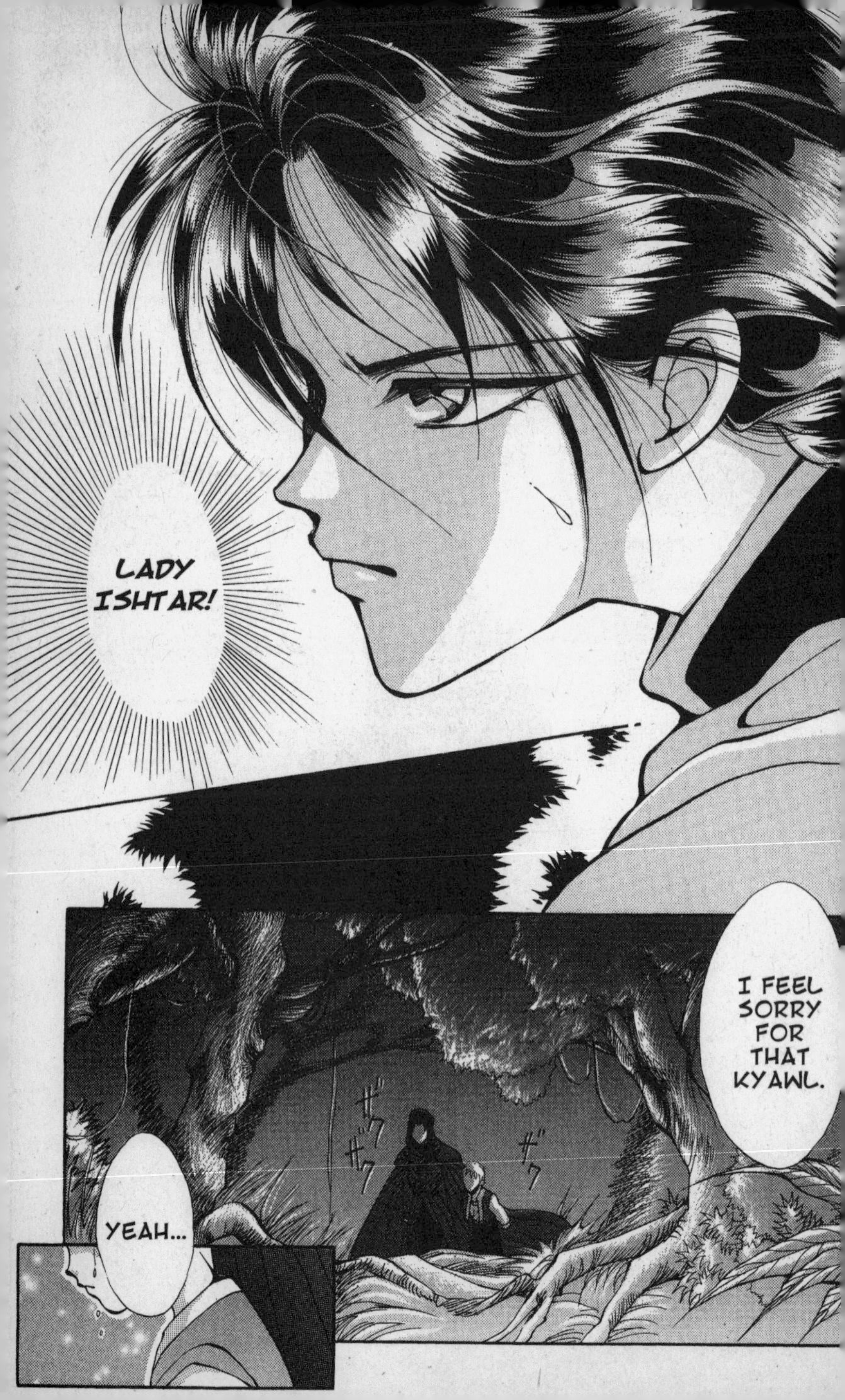
LADY ISHTAR!
I FEEL SORRY FOR THAT KYAWL.
YEAH...

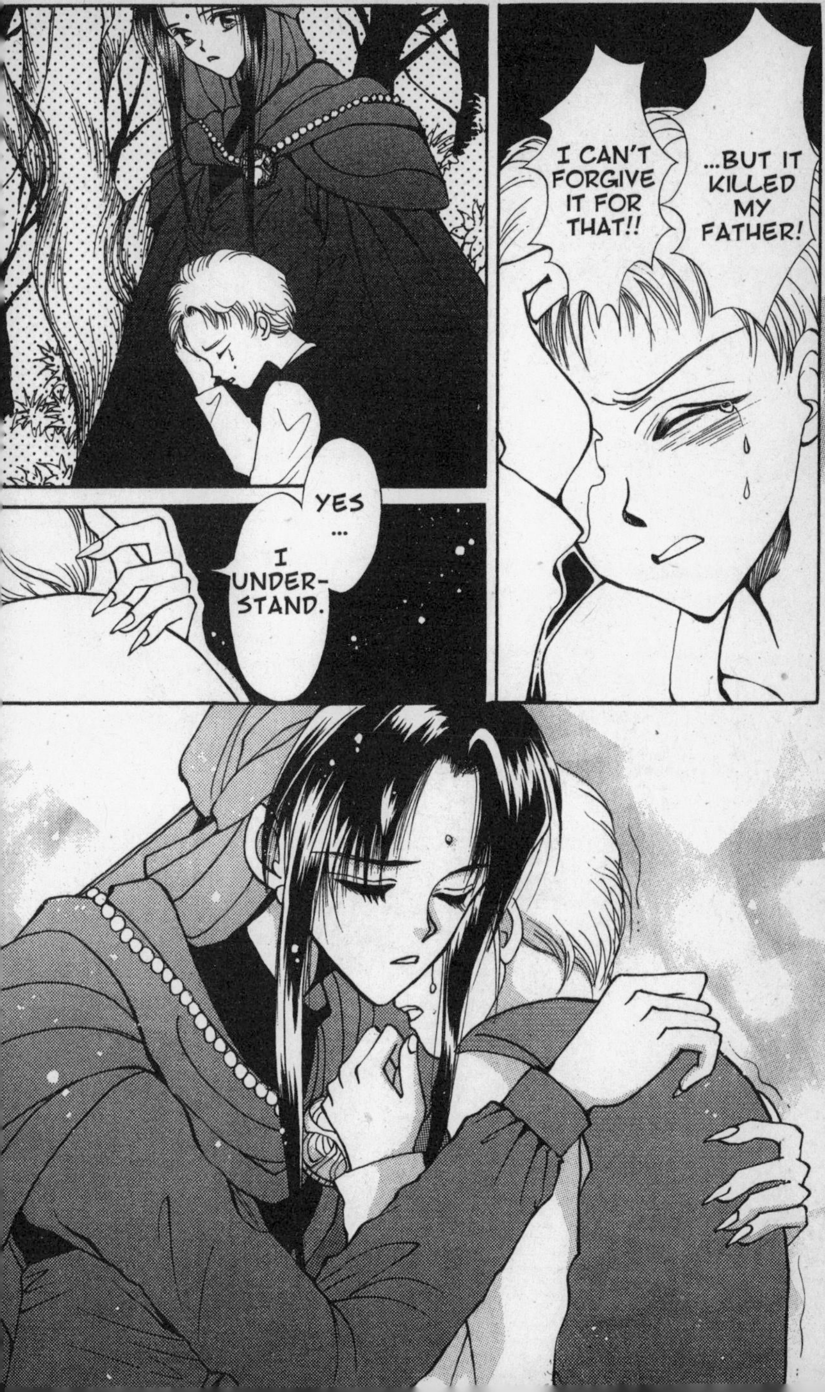
...BUT IT KILLED MY FATHER!
I CAN'T FORGIVE IT FOR THAT!!
YES ... I UNDERSTAND.

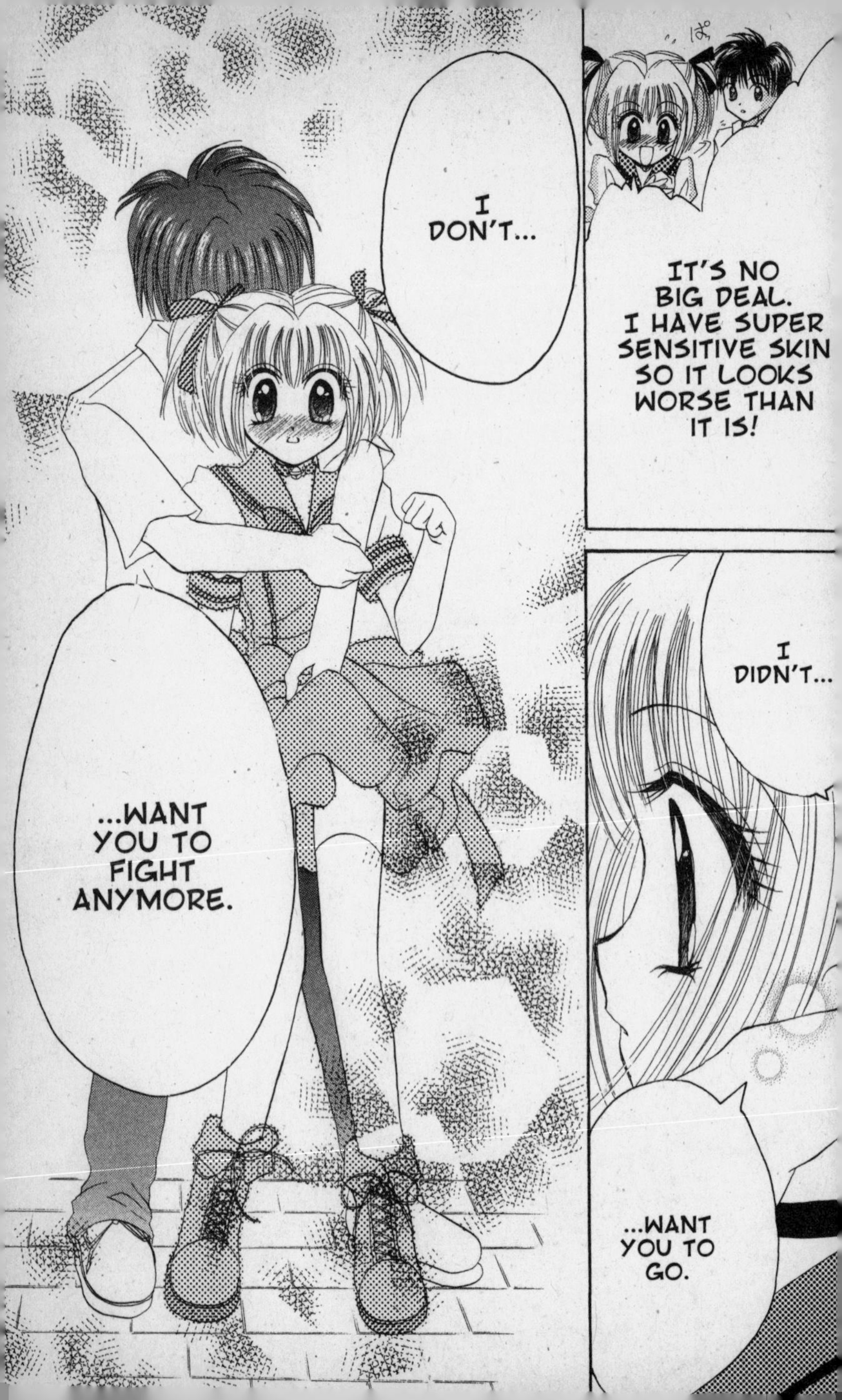
ぱ
IT'S NO BIG DEAL. I HAVE SUPER SENSITIVE SKIN SO IT LOOKS WORSE THAN IT IS!
I DIDN'T...
...WANT YOU TO GO.
I DON'T...
...WANT YOU TO FIGHT ANYMORE.

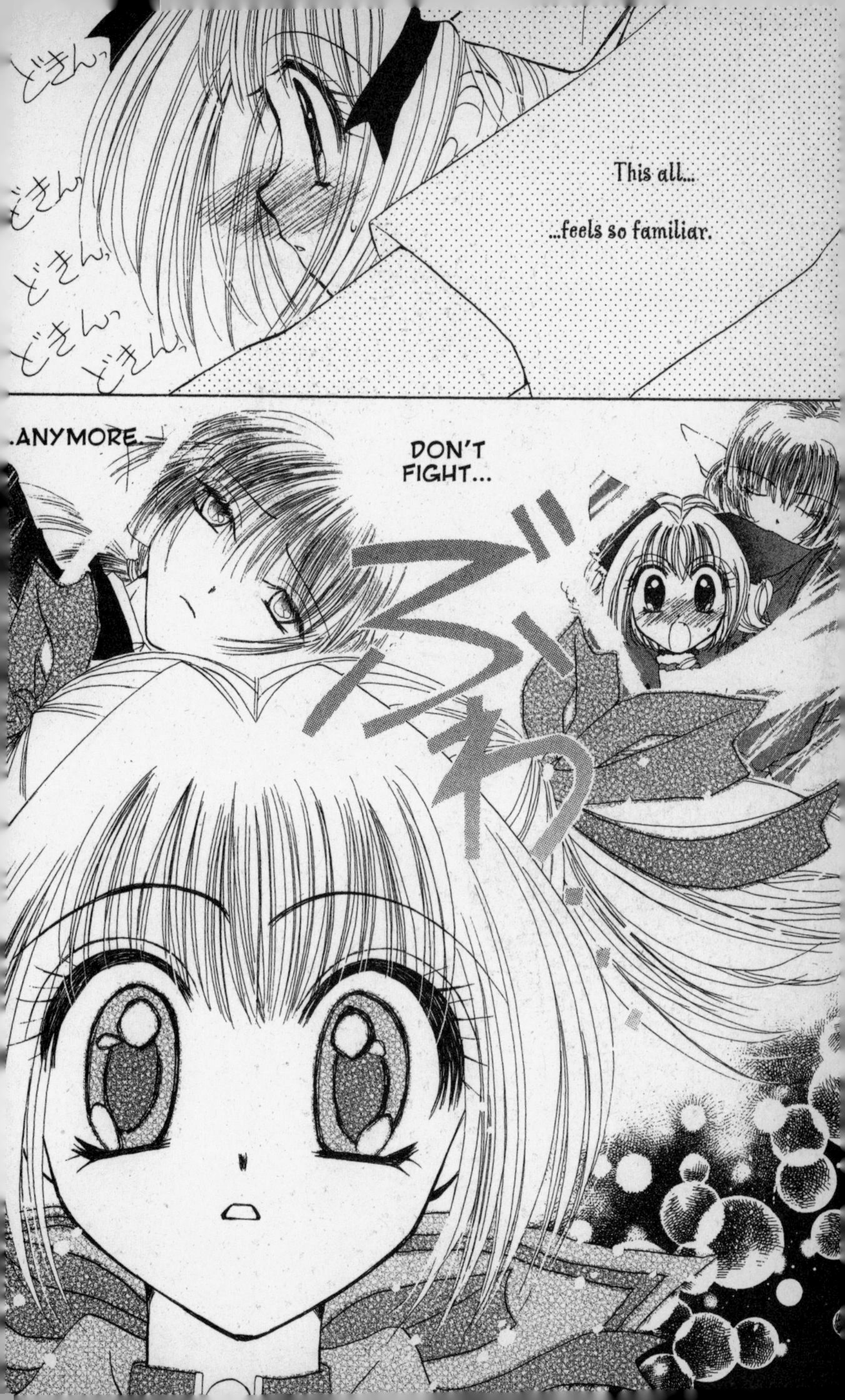
This all...
...feels so familiar.
どきんっ
どきんっ
どきんっ
どきんっ
どきんっ
DON'T FIGHT...
..ANYMORE.
ざわっ

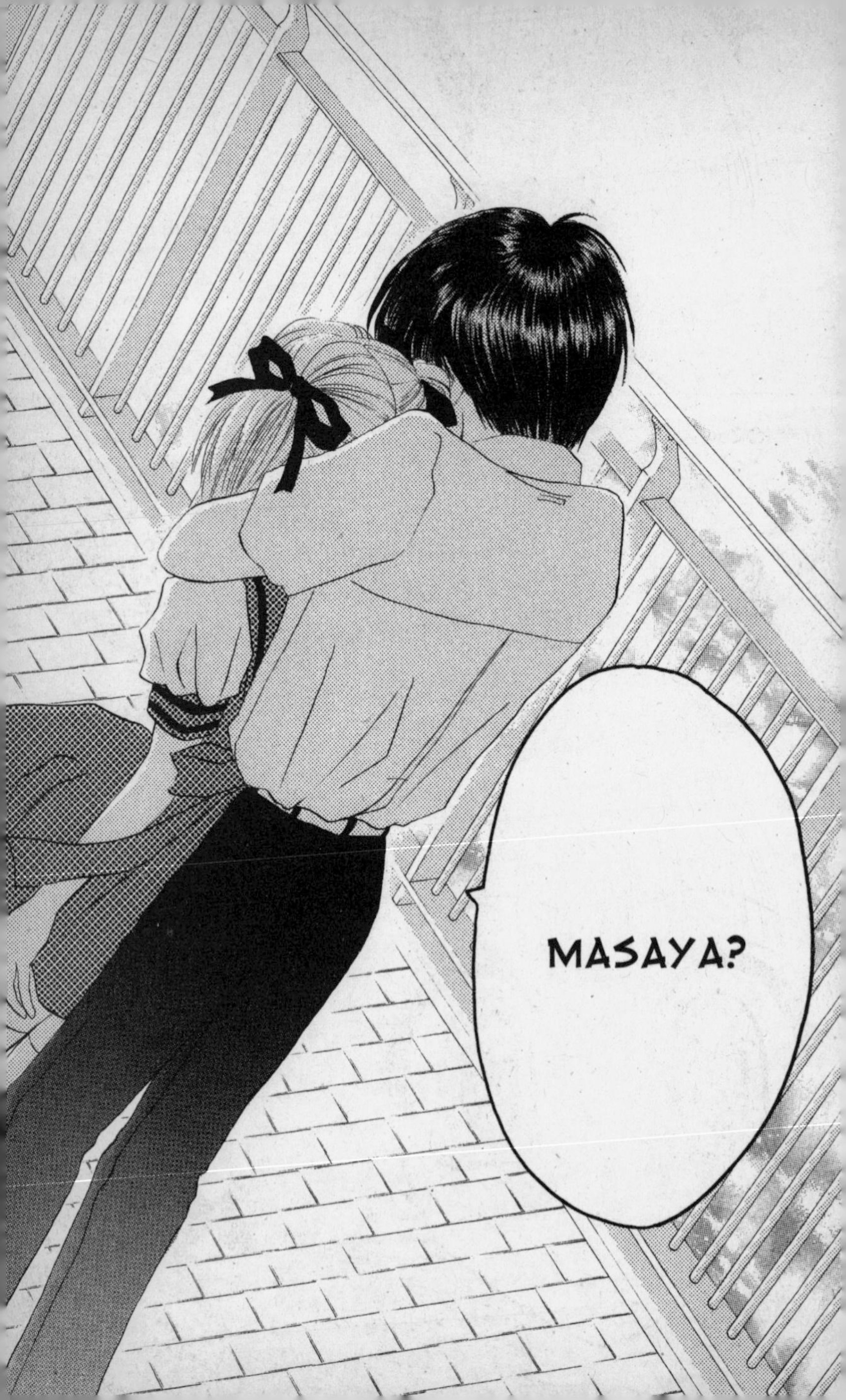
MASAYA?

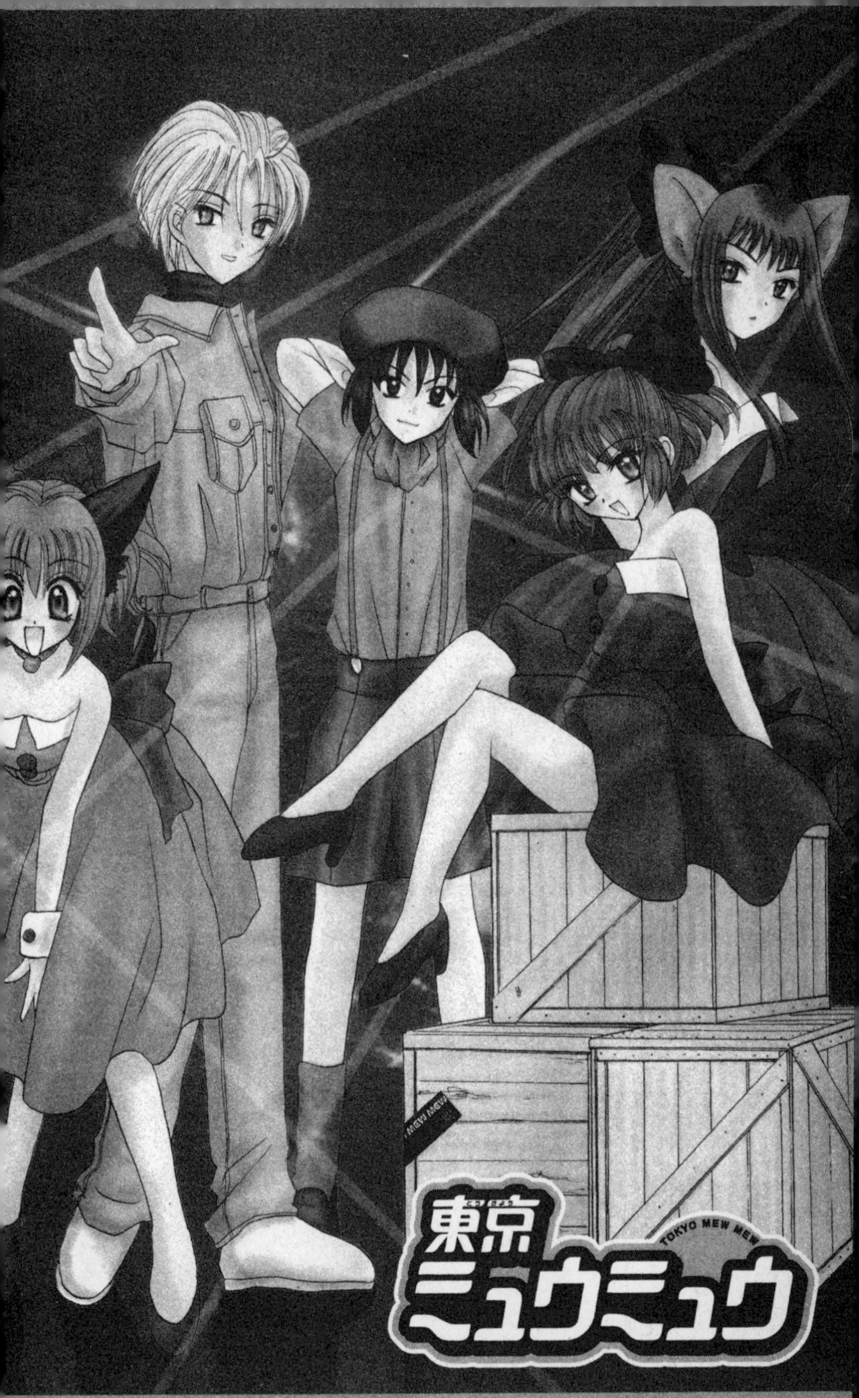
東京ミュウミュウ
TOKYO MEW MEW

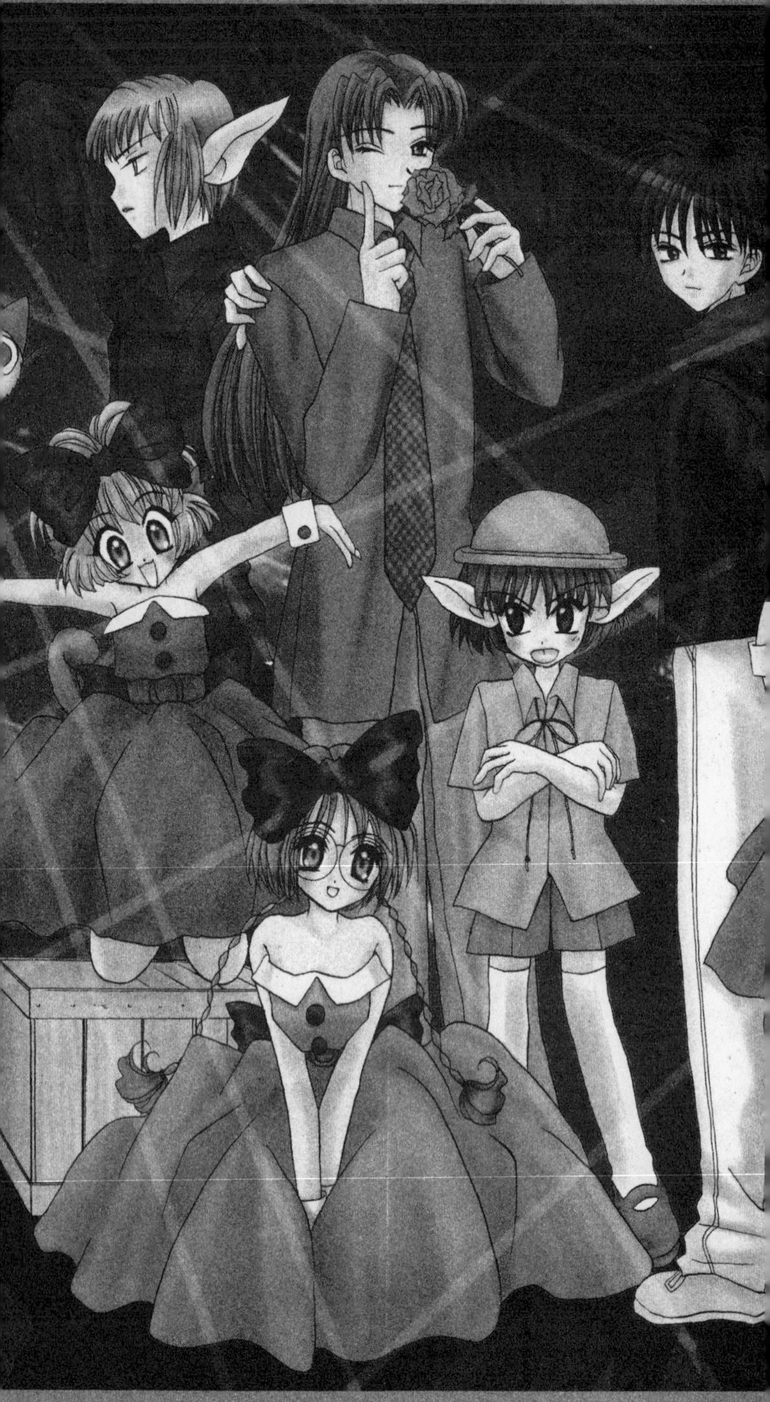

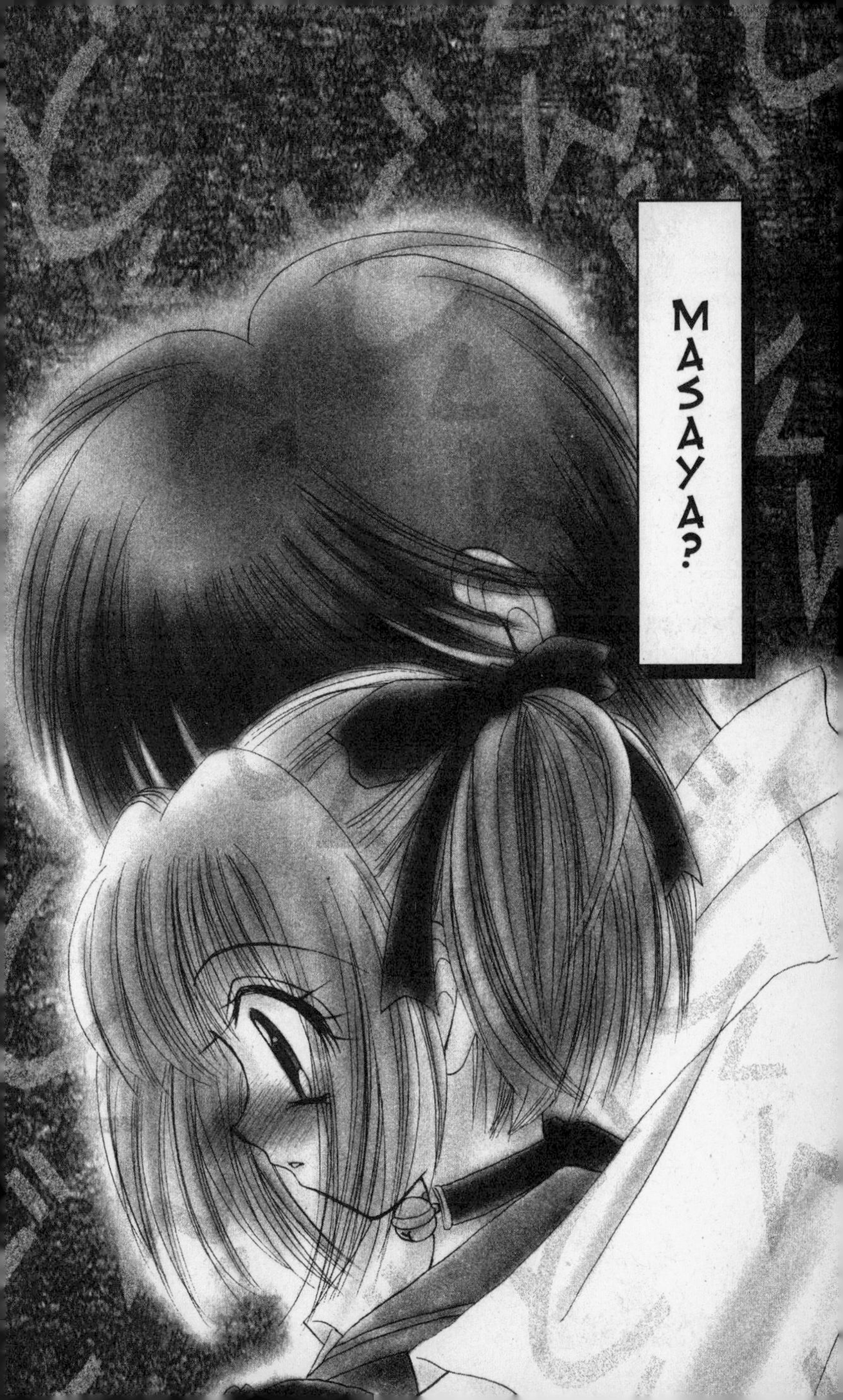
MASAYA?

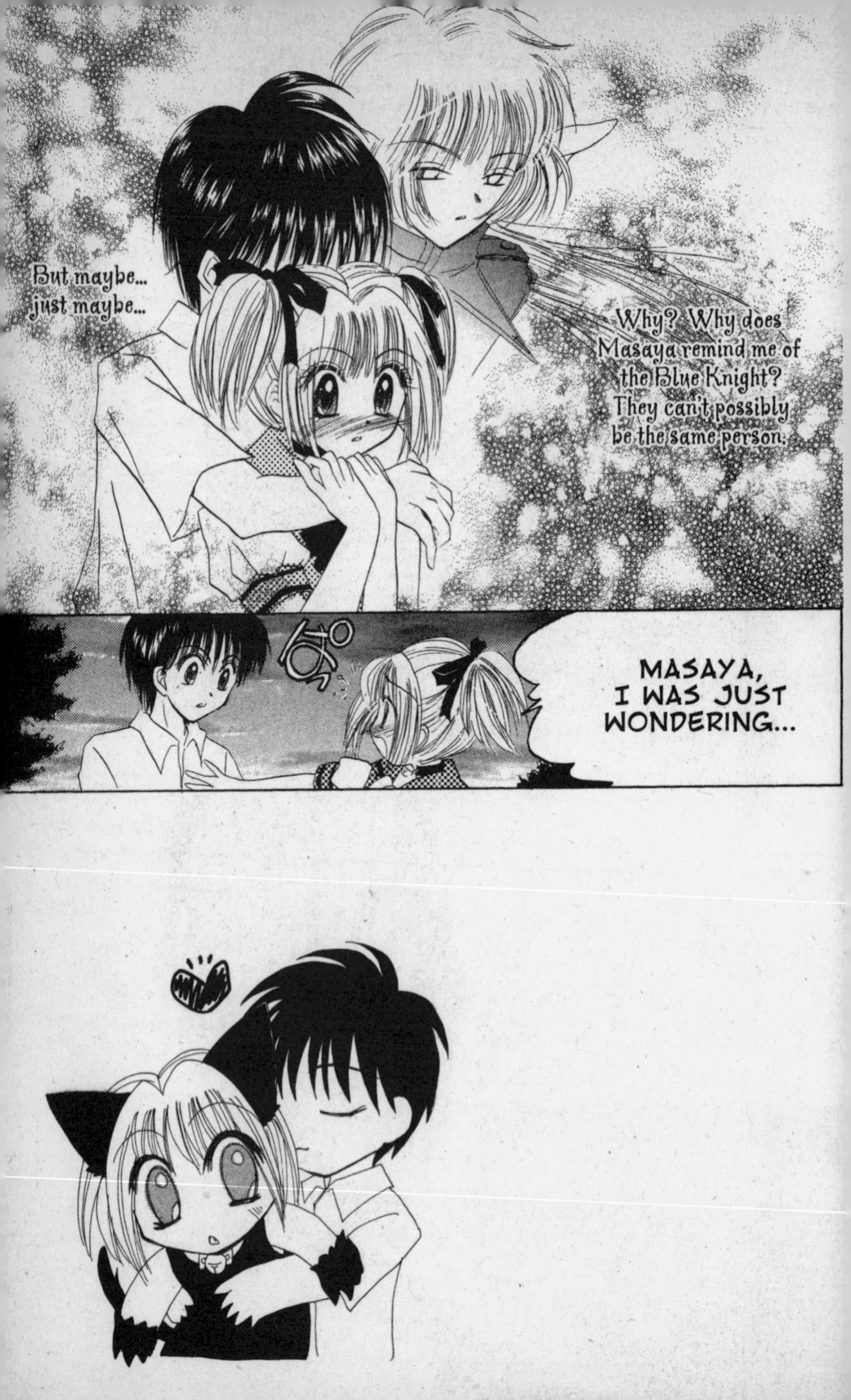
Why? Why does Masaya remind me of the Blue Knight? They can't possibly be the same person.
But maybe... just maybe...
MASAYA, I WAS JUST WONDERING...

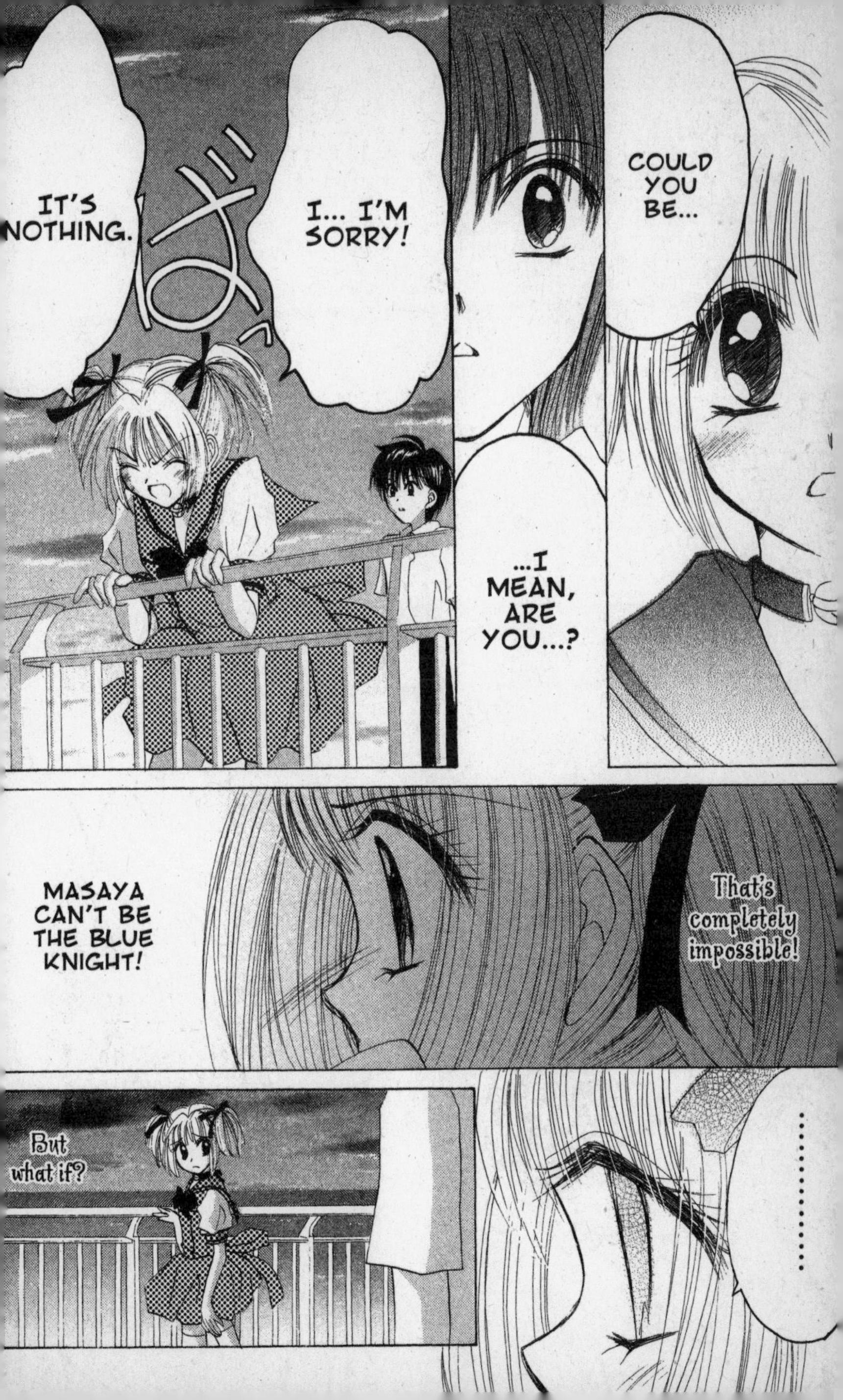
COULD YOU BE...
...I MEAN, ARE YOU...?
I... I'M SORRY!
ばっ
IT'S NOTHING.
That's completely impossible!
MASAYA CAN'T BE THE BLUE KNIGHT!
....
But what if?

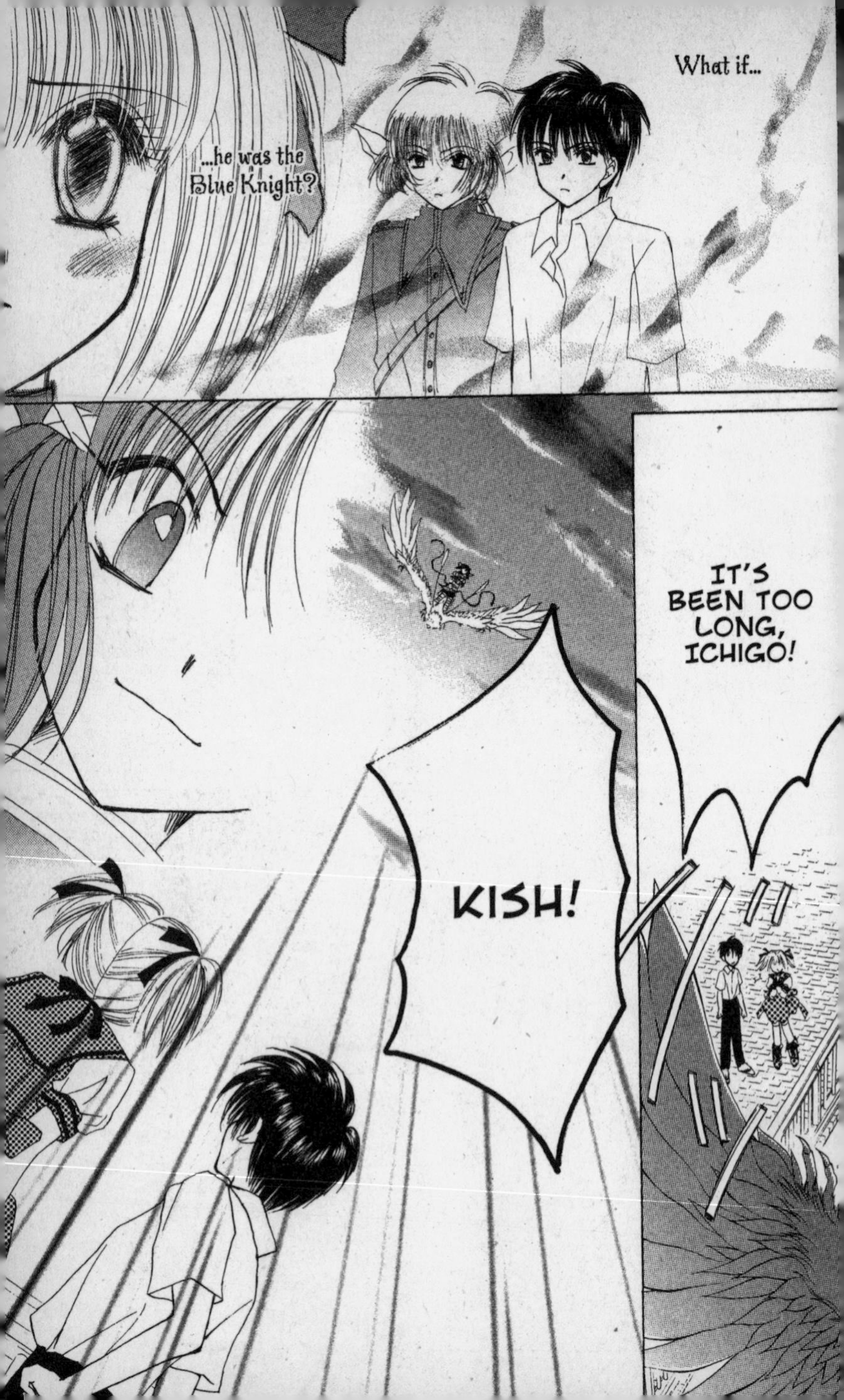
What if...
...he was the Blue Knight?
IT'S BEEN TOO LONG, ICHIGO!
KISH!

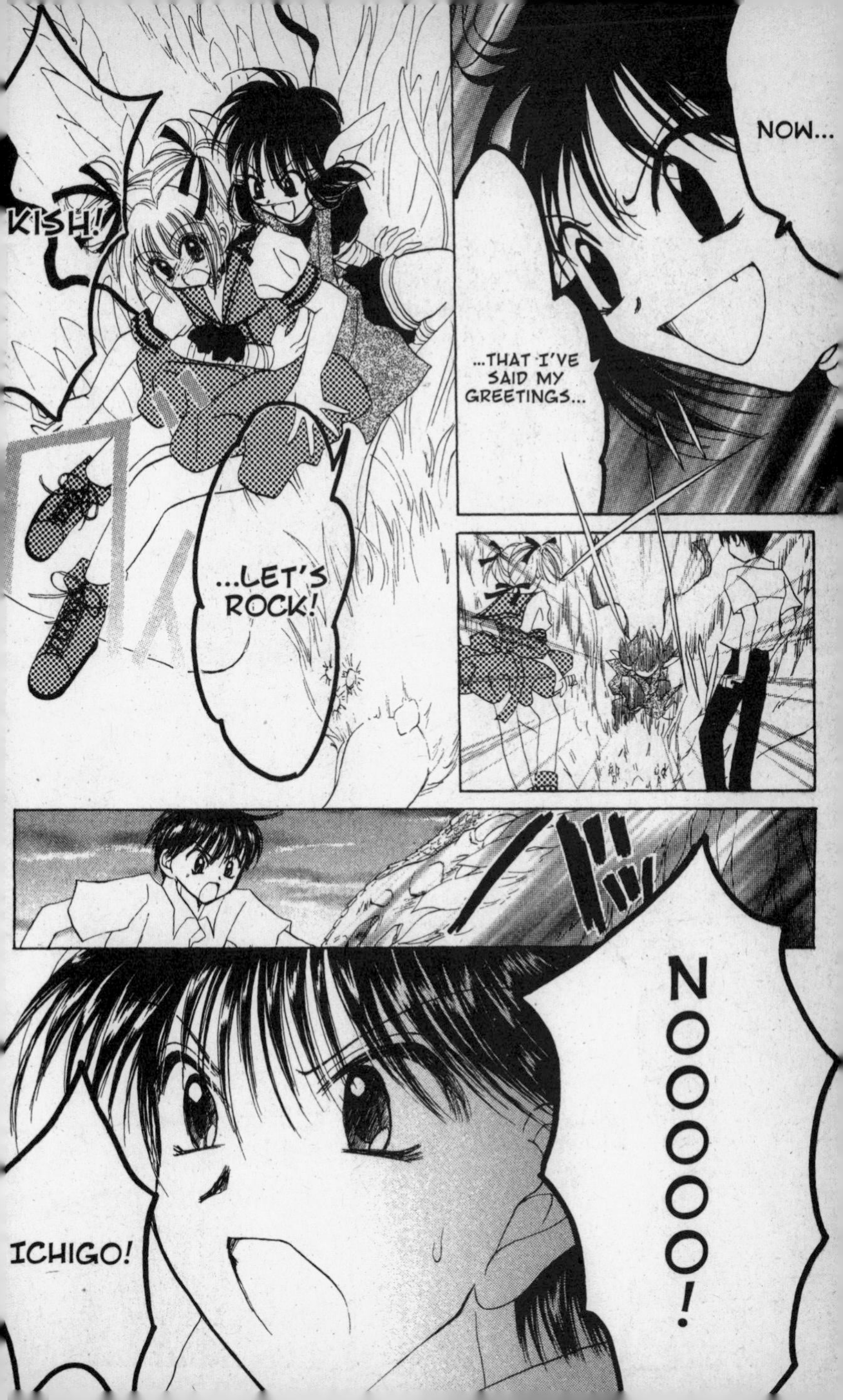
NOW...
...THAT I'VE SAID MY GREETINGS...
KISH!
...LET'S ROCK!
NOOOOOO!
ICHIGO!

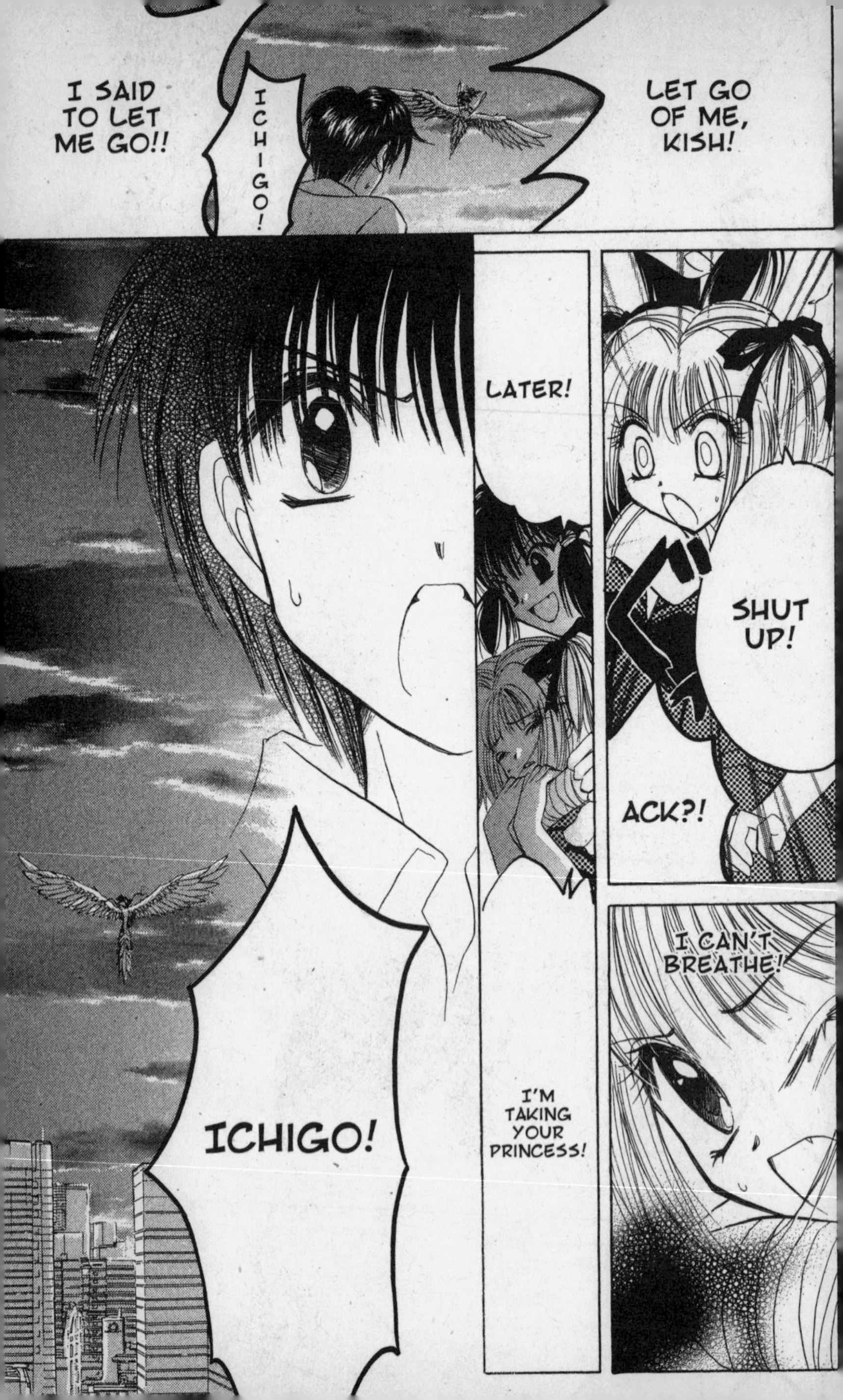
LET GO OF ME, KISH!
ICHIGO!
I SAID TO LET ME GO!!
SHUT UP!
ACK?!
I CAN'T BREATHE!
LATER!
I'M TAKING YOUR PRINCESS!
ICHIGO!

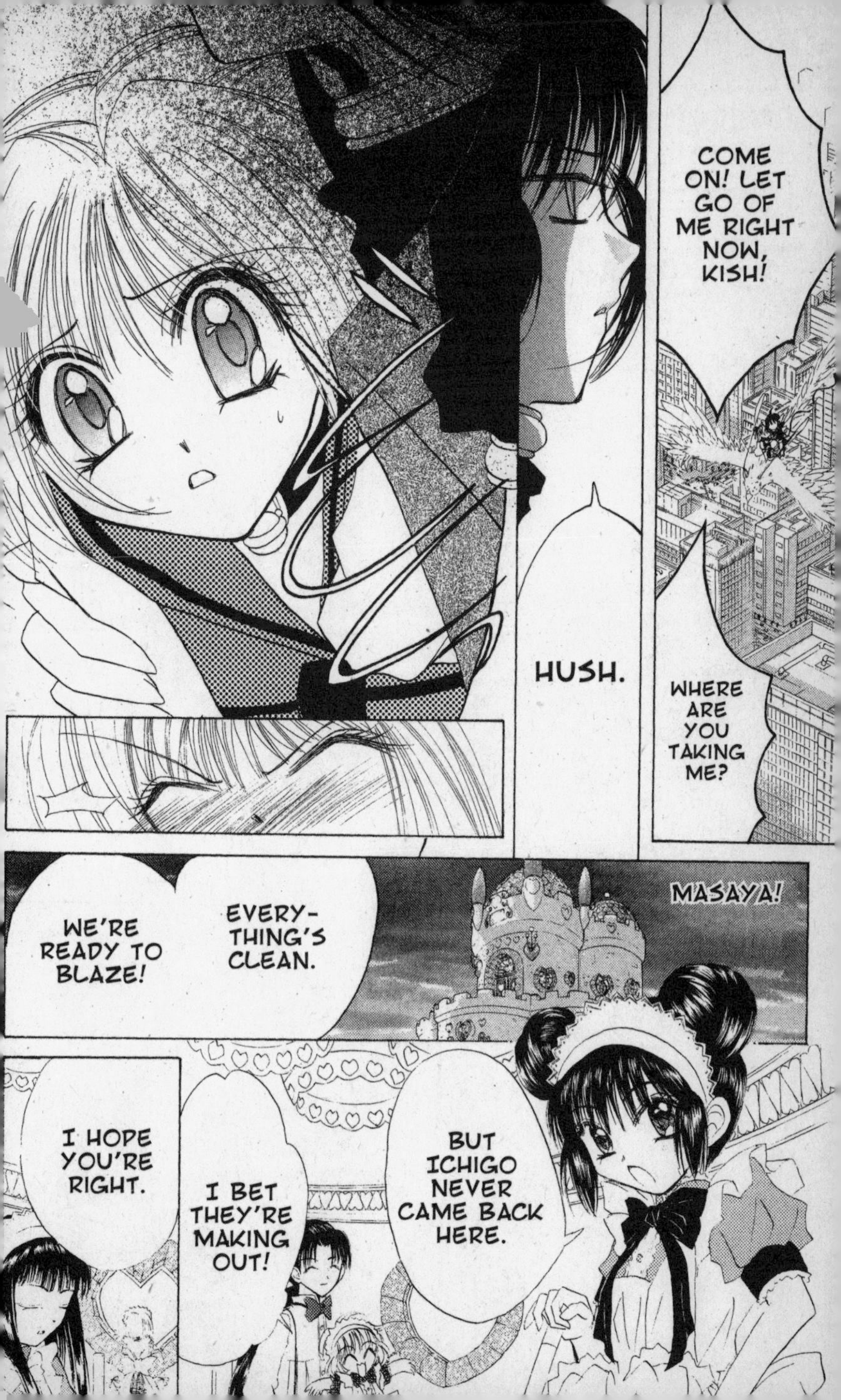
COME ON! LET GO OF ME RIGHT NOW, KISH!
WHERE ARE YOU TAKING ME?
HUSH.
MASAYA!
EVERY-THING'S CLEAN.
WE'RE READY TO BLAZE!
BUT ICHIGO NEVER CAME BACK HERE.
I BET THEY'RE MAKING OUT!
I HOPE YOU'RE RIGHT.

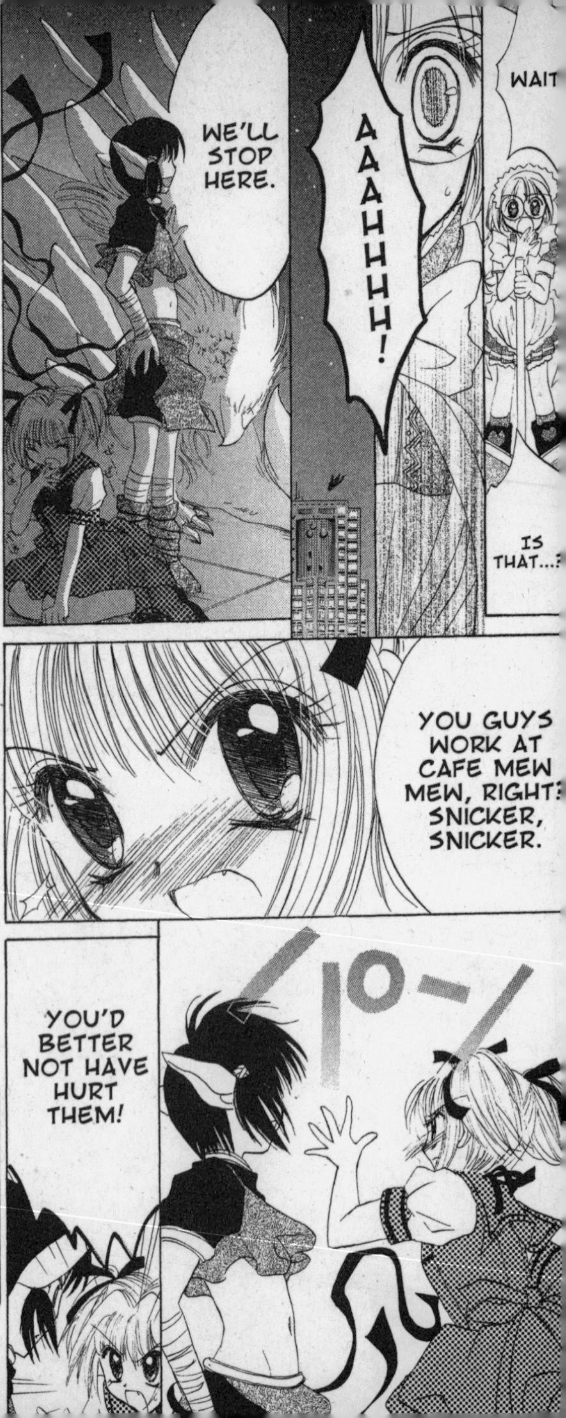
WAIT
IS THAT...?
AAAHHHH!
WE'LL STOP HERE.
YOU GUYS WORK AT CAFE MEW MEW, RIGHT? SNICKER, SNICKER.
YOU'D BETTER NOT HAVE HURT THEM!

Tokyo Mew Mew
Ichigo's Costume Designs Wanted!!

Junior Grand Prix

Mari Muraoka
Tochigi Prefecture
Sixth Grade

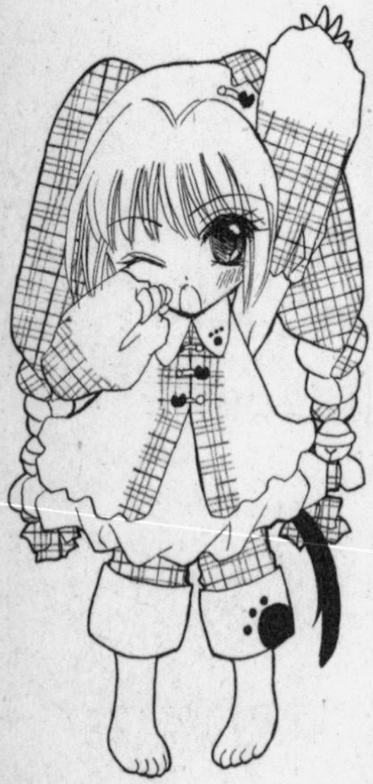

I told my co-workers, "I want this pajama set," to which my assistant replied, "I'll have one made!" Thanks so much! By the time this volume is published, I'll be wearing PJs to work! Ha, ha! A lovely design!

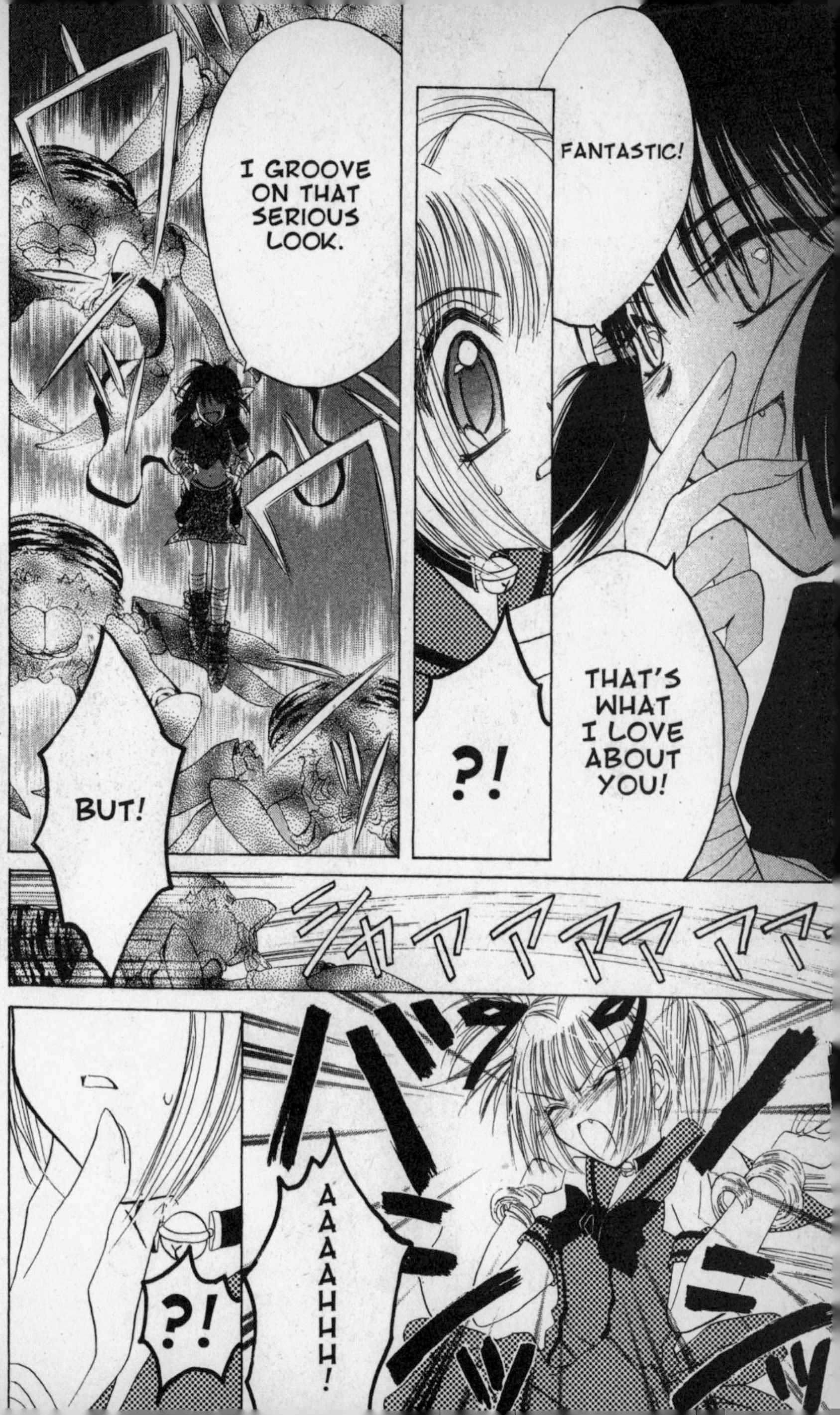
FANTASTIC!
THAT'S WHAT I LOVE ABOUT YOU!
?!
I GROOVE ON THAT SERIOUS LOOK.
BUT!
シャアアアアアア
バッ
AAAAHHH!
?!

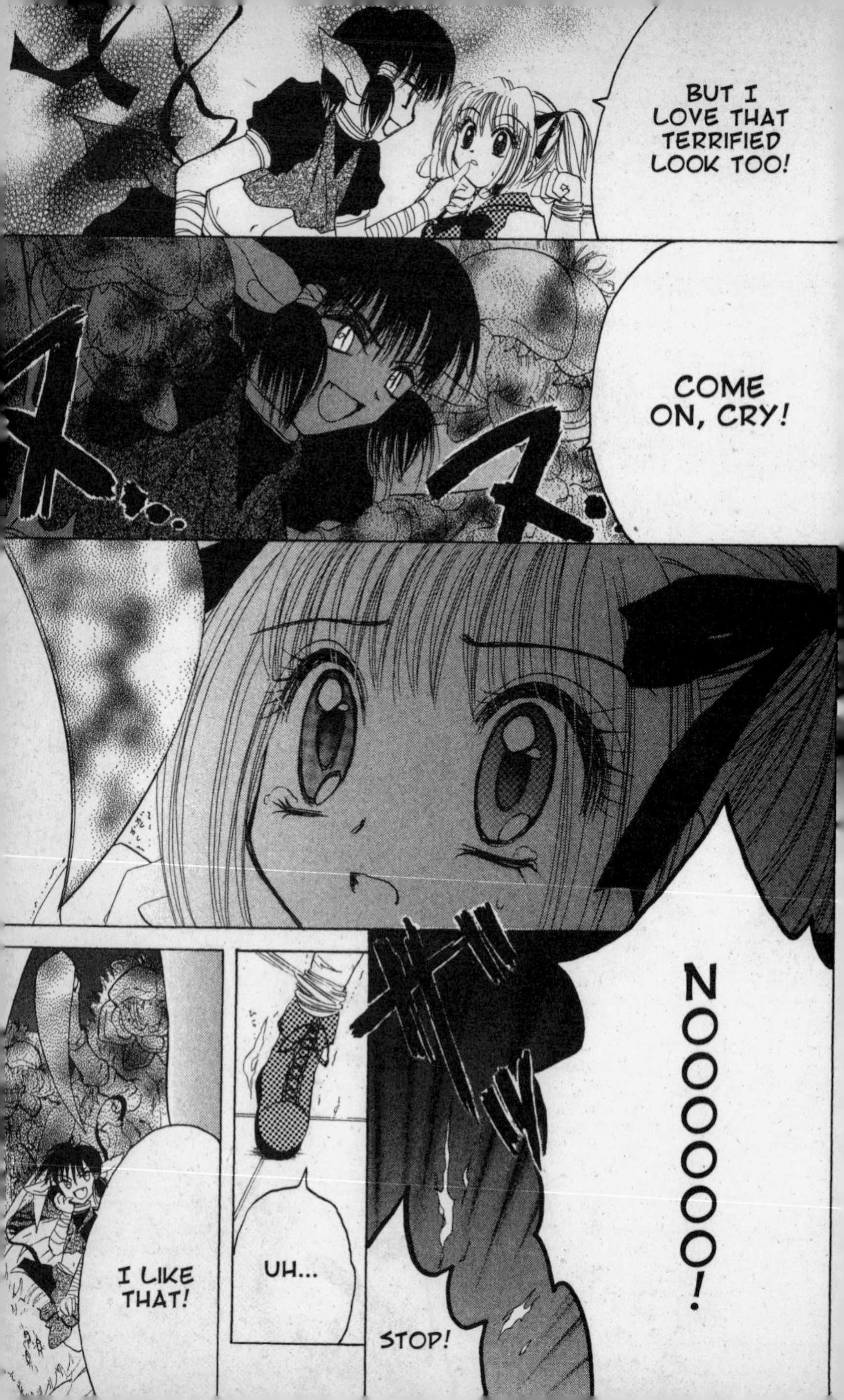
BUT I LOVE THAT TERRIFIED LOOK TOO!
COME ON, CRY!
NOOOOOOO!
STOP!
UH...
I LIKE THAT!

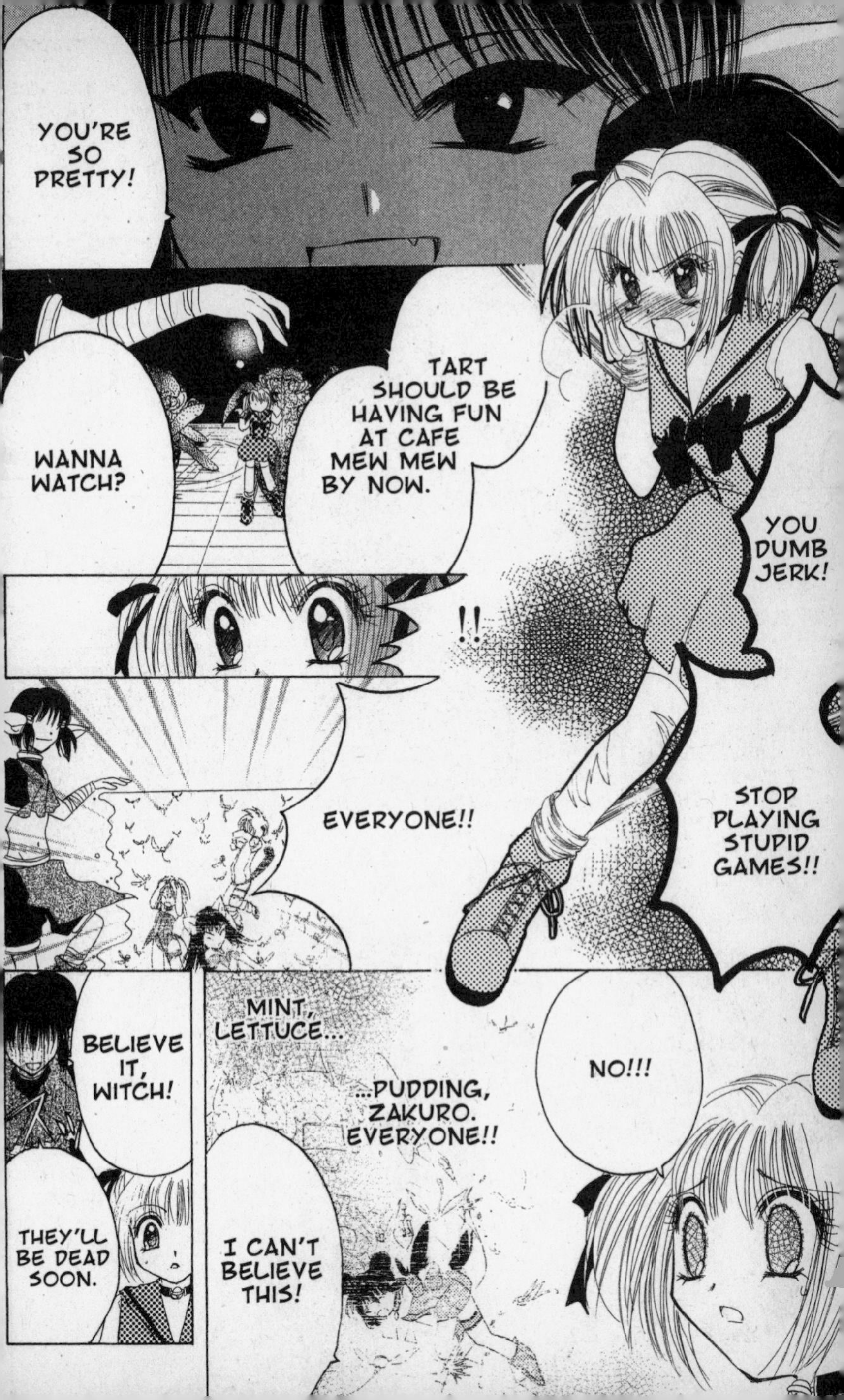
YOU'RE SO PRETTY!
YOU DUMB JERK!
STOP PLAYING STUPID GAMES!!
TART SHOULD BE HAVING FUN AT CAFE MEW MEW BY NOW.
WANNA WATCH?
!!
EVERYONE!!
NO!!!
MINT, LETTUCE...
...PUDDING, ZAKURO. EVERYONE!!
I CAN'T BELIEVE THIS!
BELIEVE IT, WITCH!
THEY'LL BE DEAD SOON.

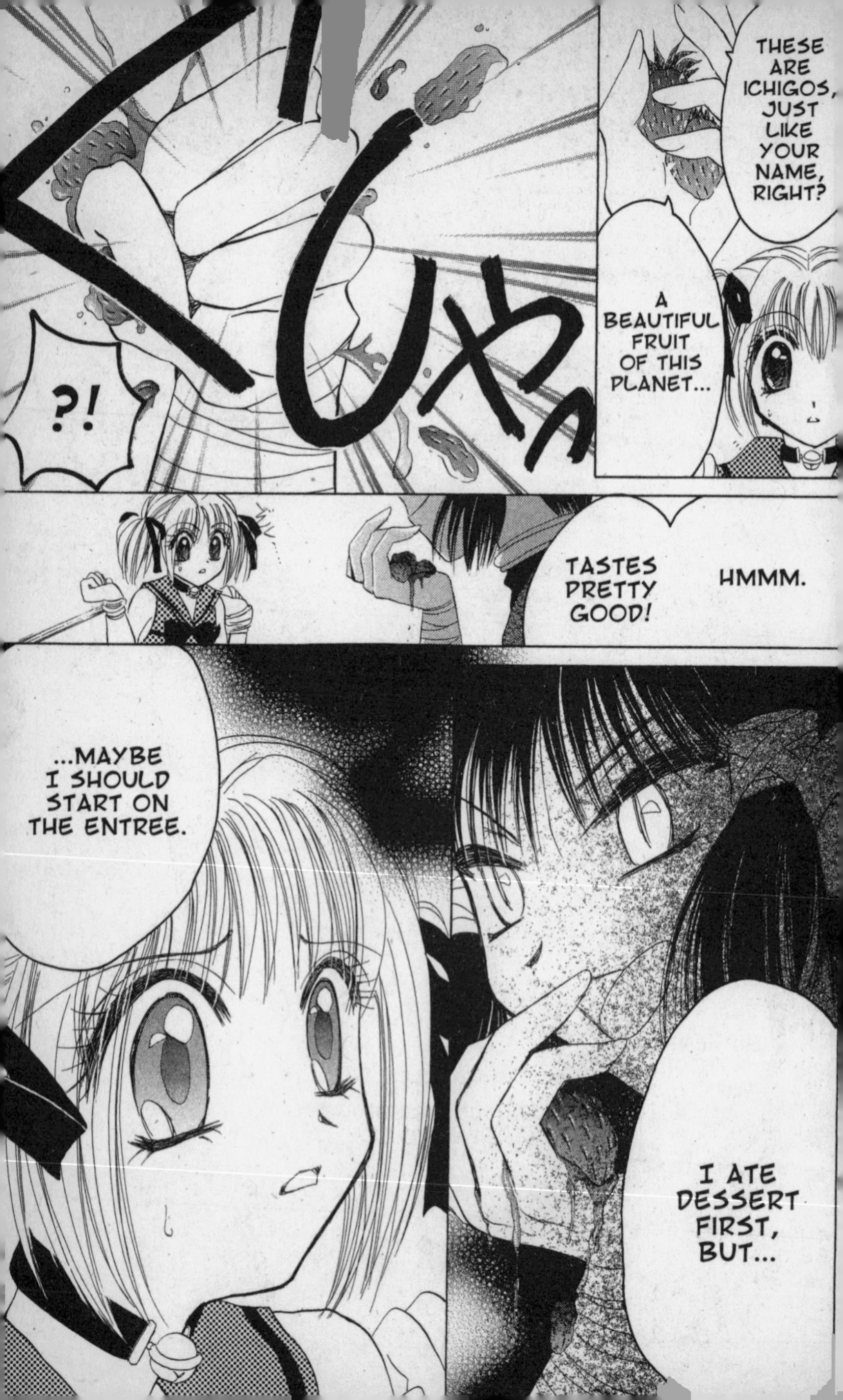
THESE ARE ICHIGOS, JUST LIKE YOUR NAME, RIGHT?
A BEAUTIFUL FRUIT OF THIS PLANET...
?!
HMMM.
TASTES PRETTY GOOD!
I ATE DESSERT FIRST, BUT...
...MAYBE I SHOULD START ON THE ENTREE.

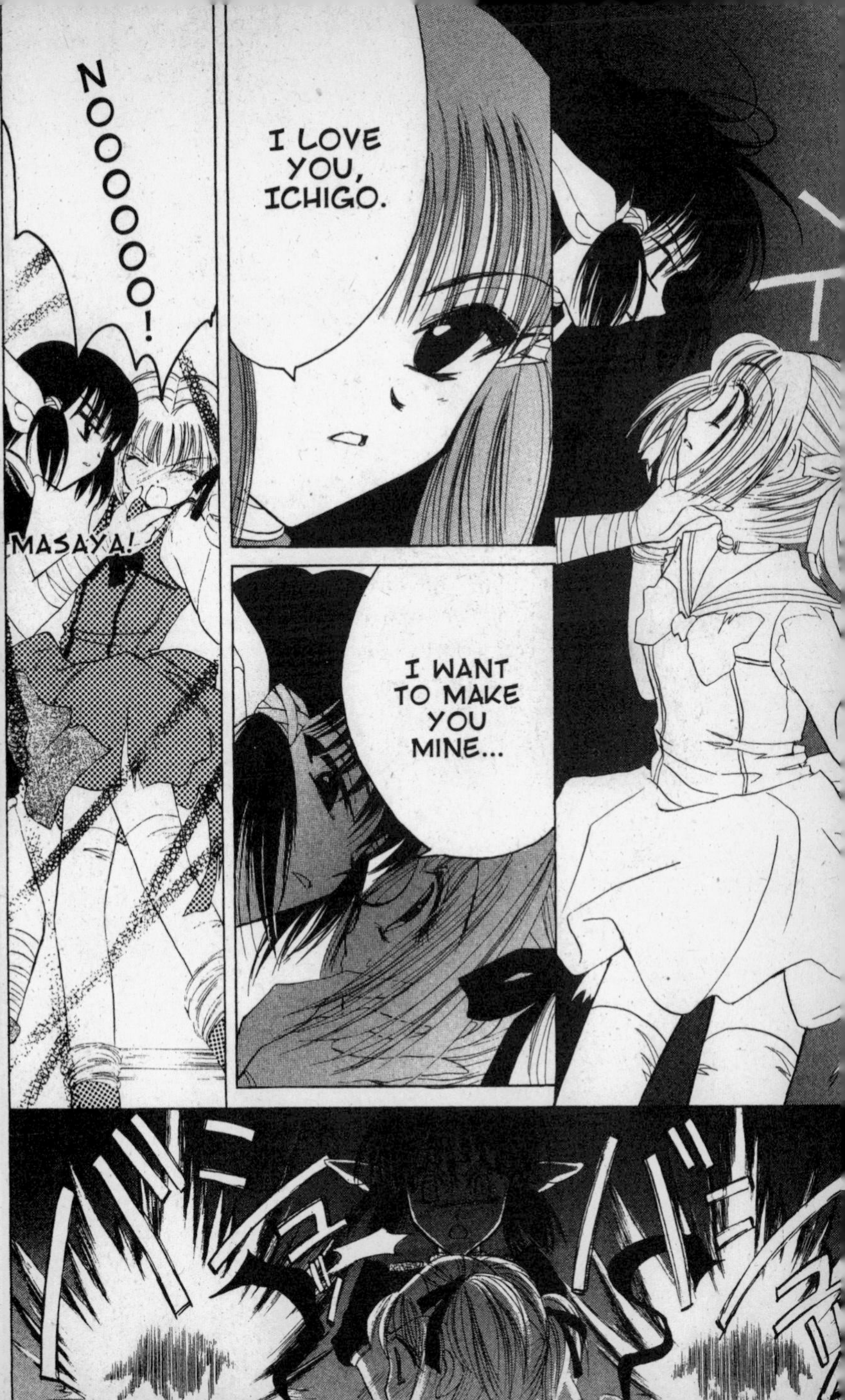
I LOVE YOU, ICHIGO.
I WANT TO MAKE YOU MINE...
NOOOOOOO!
MASAYA!

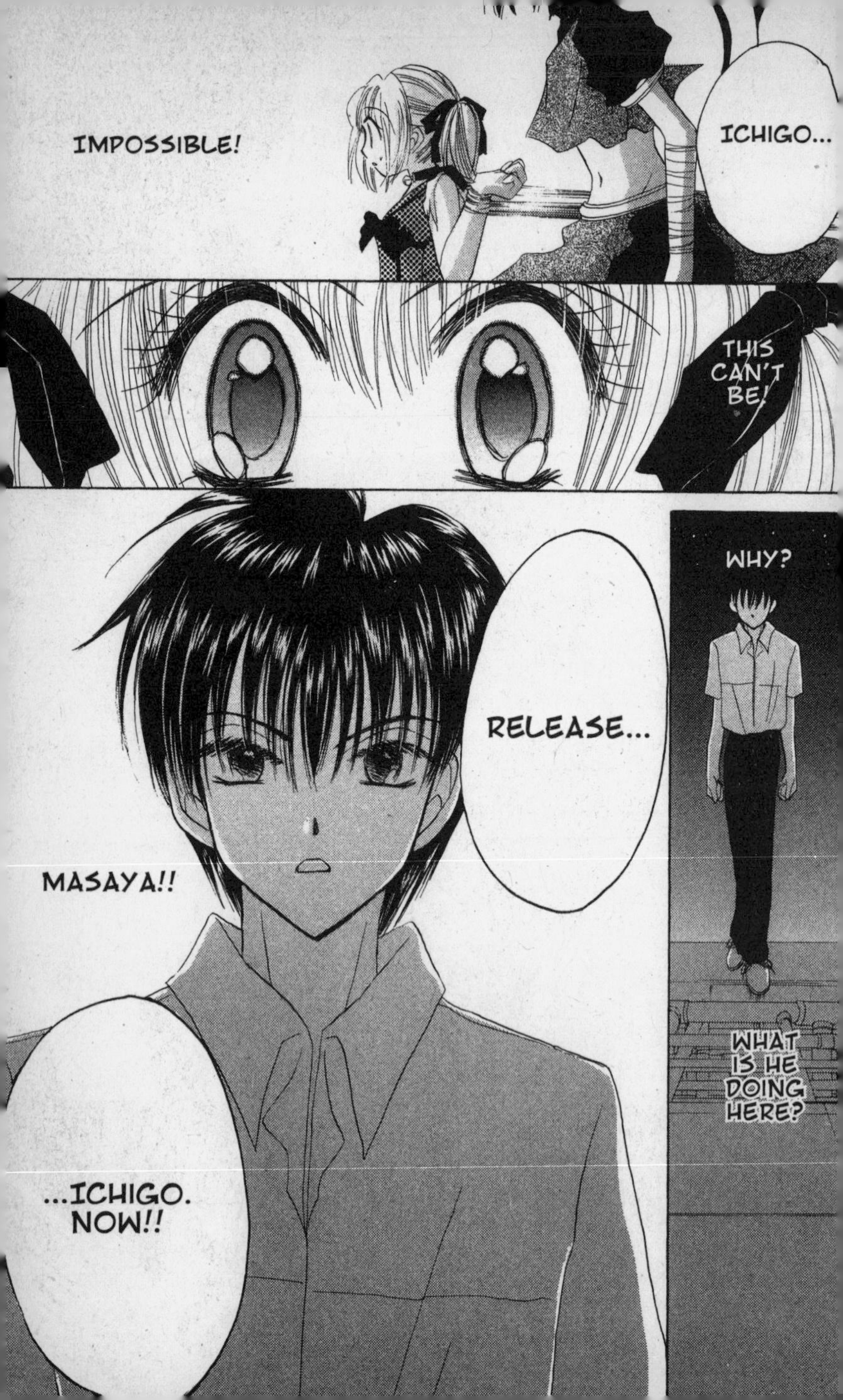
ICHIGO...
IMPOSSIBLE!
THIS CAN'T BE!
WHY?
WHAT IS HE DOING HERE?
RELEASE...
MASAYA!!
...ICHIGO. NOW!!

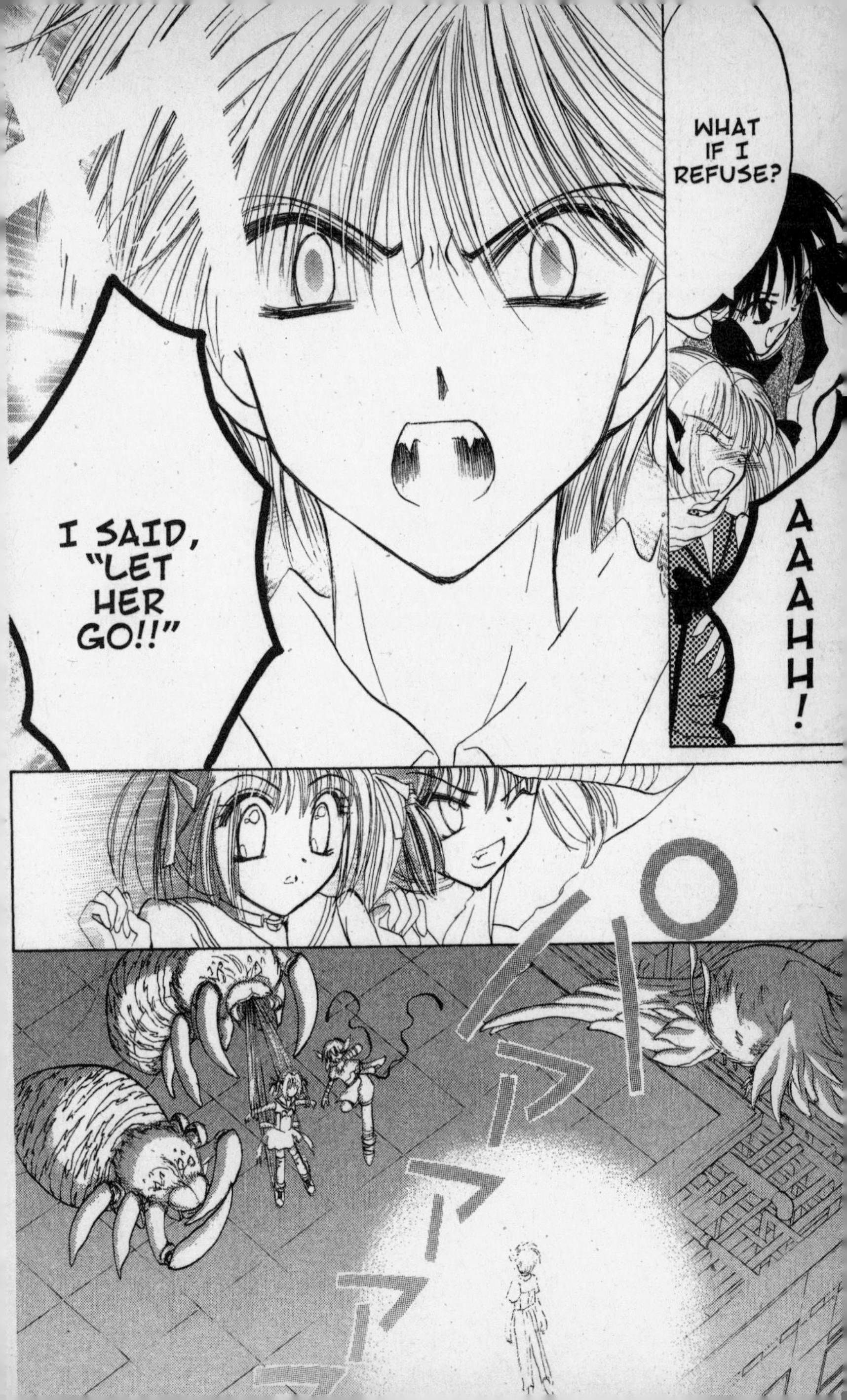
WHAT IF I REFUSE?
AAAHH!
I SAID, "LET HER GO!!"
パァァァァ

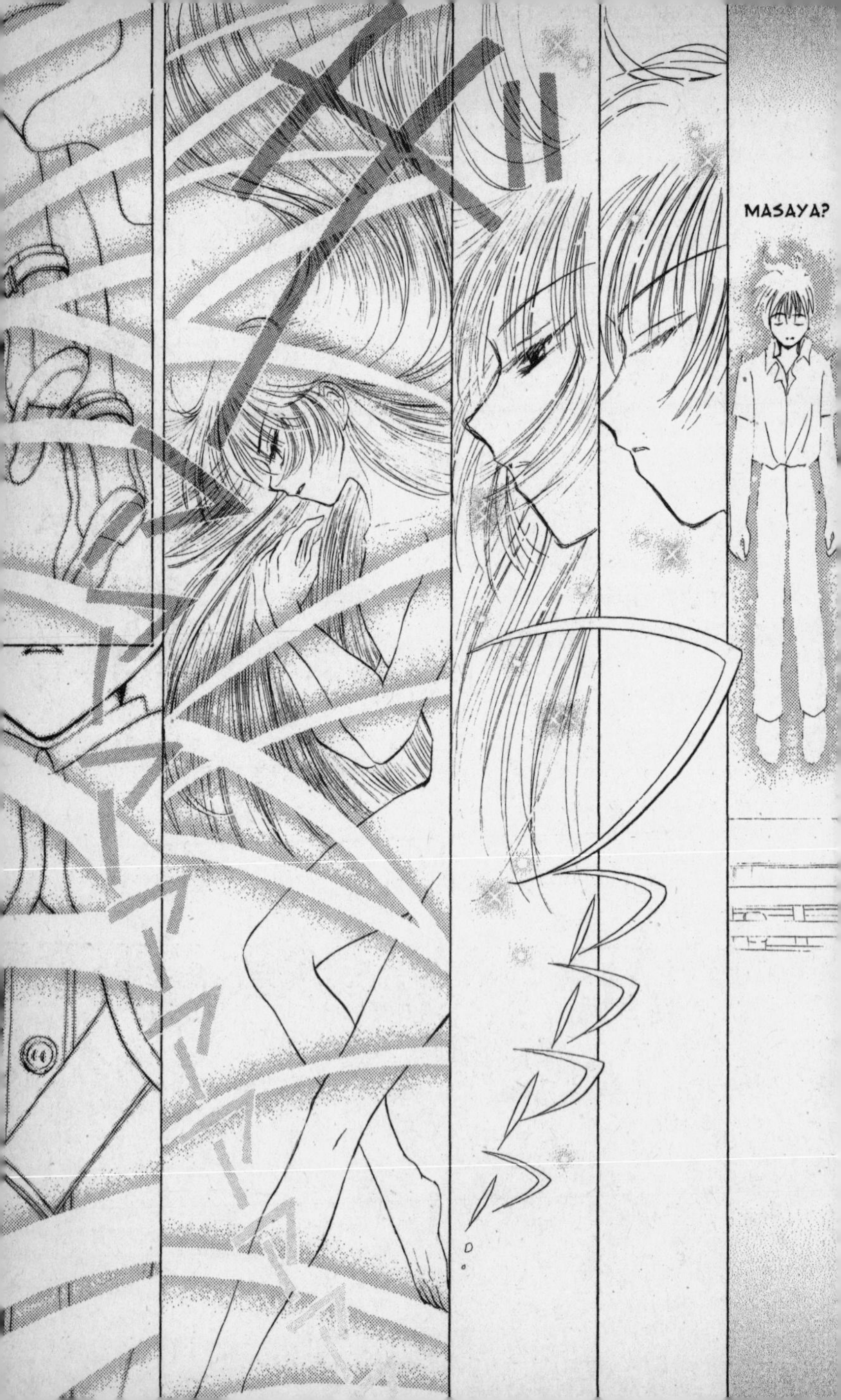
MASAYA?

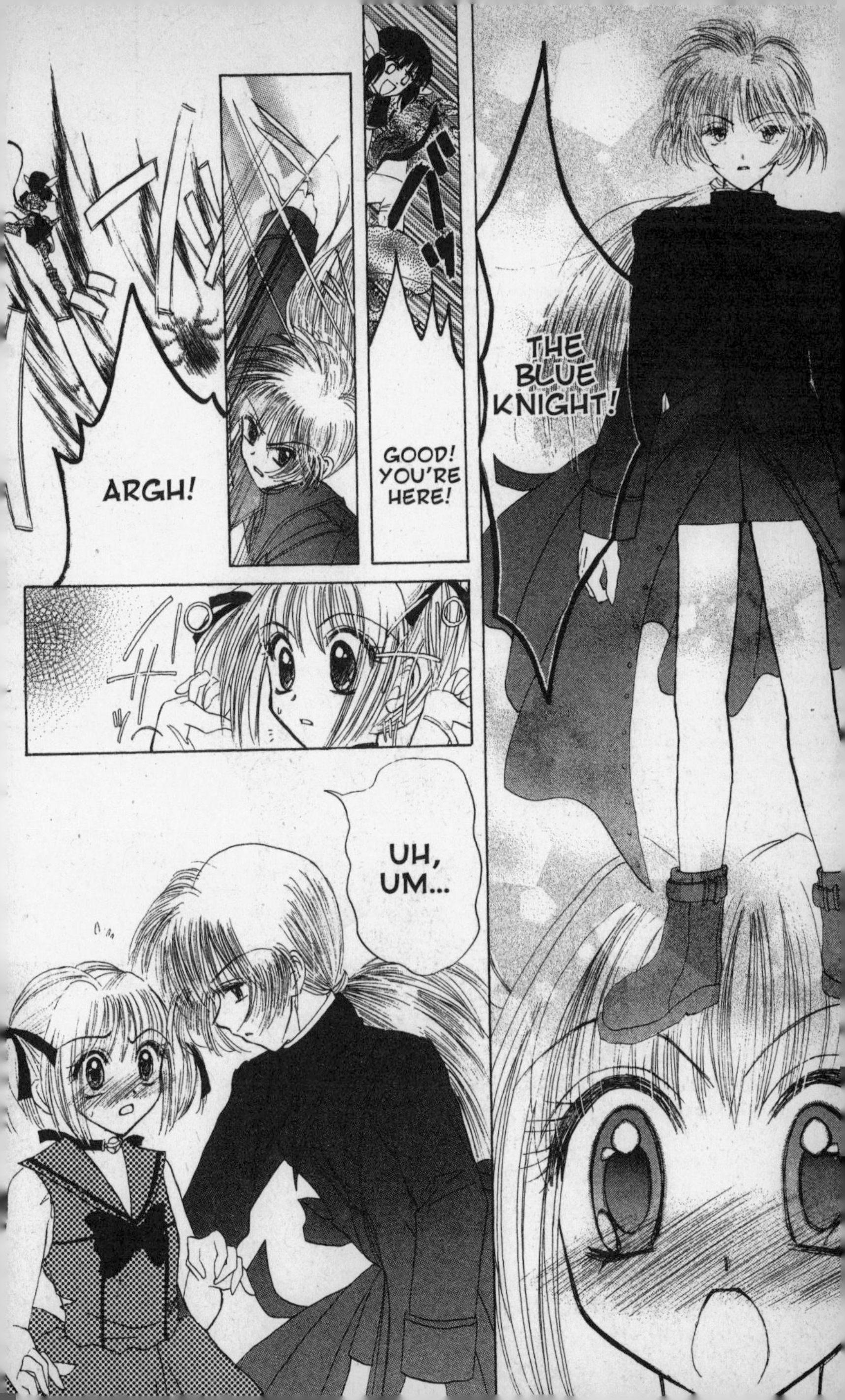
THE BLUE KNIGHT!
GOOD! YOU'RE HERE!
ARGH!
UH, UM...

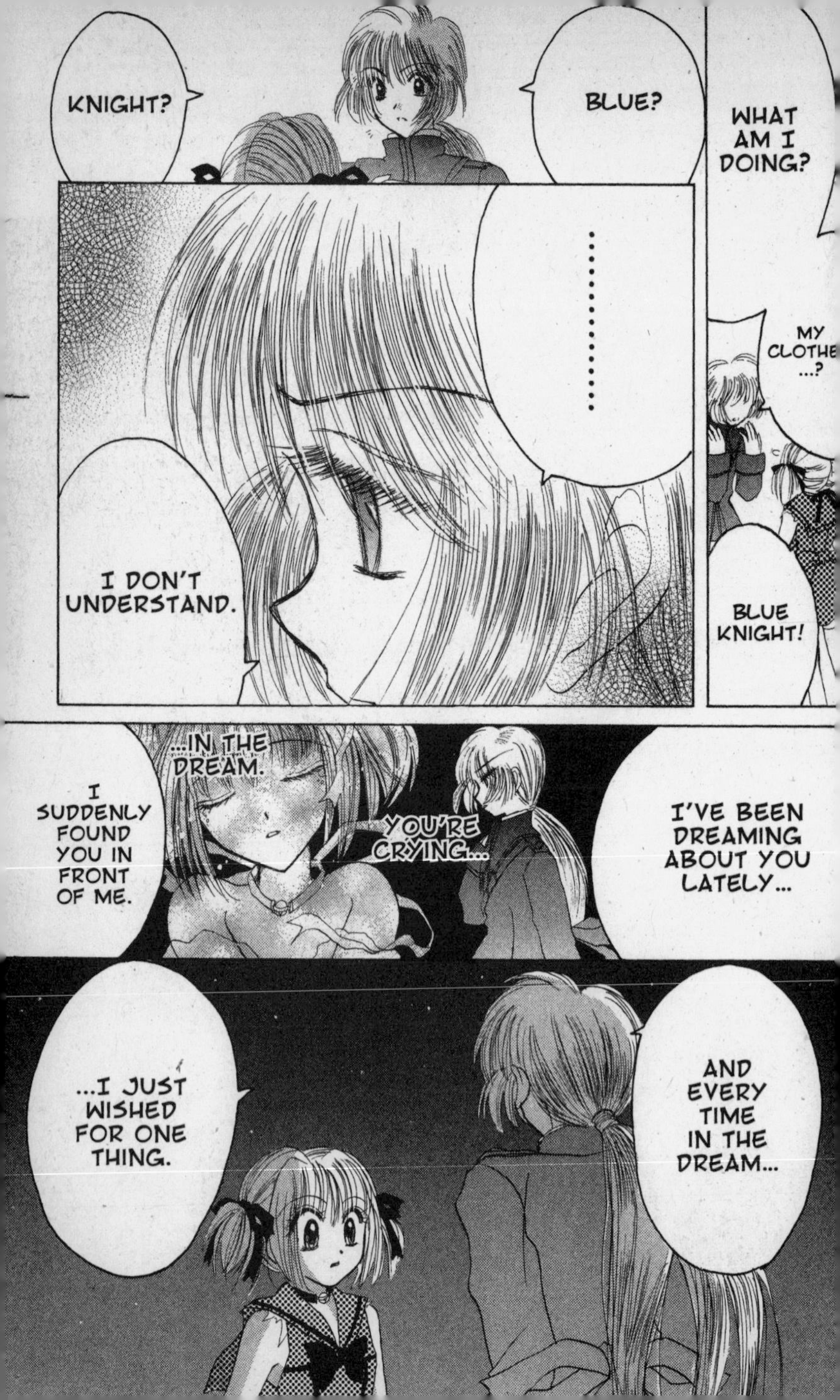
WHAT AM I DOING?
MY CLOTHE ...?
BLUE KNIGHT!
BLUE?
KNIGHT?
......
I DON'T UNDERSTAND.
I'VE BEEN DREAMING ABOUT YOU LATELY...
...IN THE DREAM.
YOU'RE CRYING...
I SUDDENLY FOUND YOU IN FRONT OF ME.
AND EVERY TIME IN THE DREAM...
...I JUST WISHED FOR ONE THING.

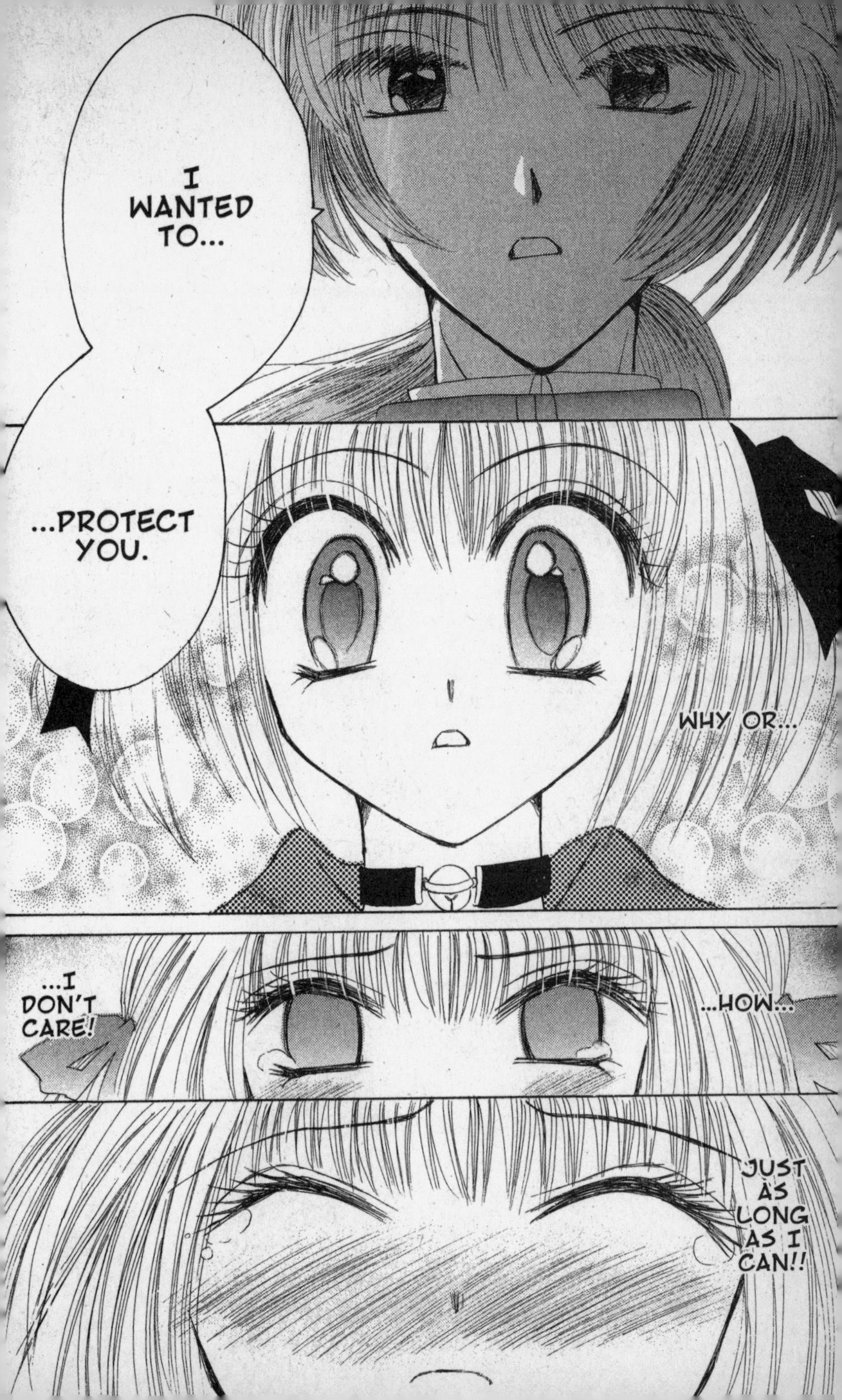

I WANTED TO...
...PROTECT YOU.
WHY OR...
...HOW...
...I DON'T CARE!
JUST AS LONG AS I CAN!!

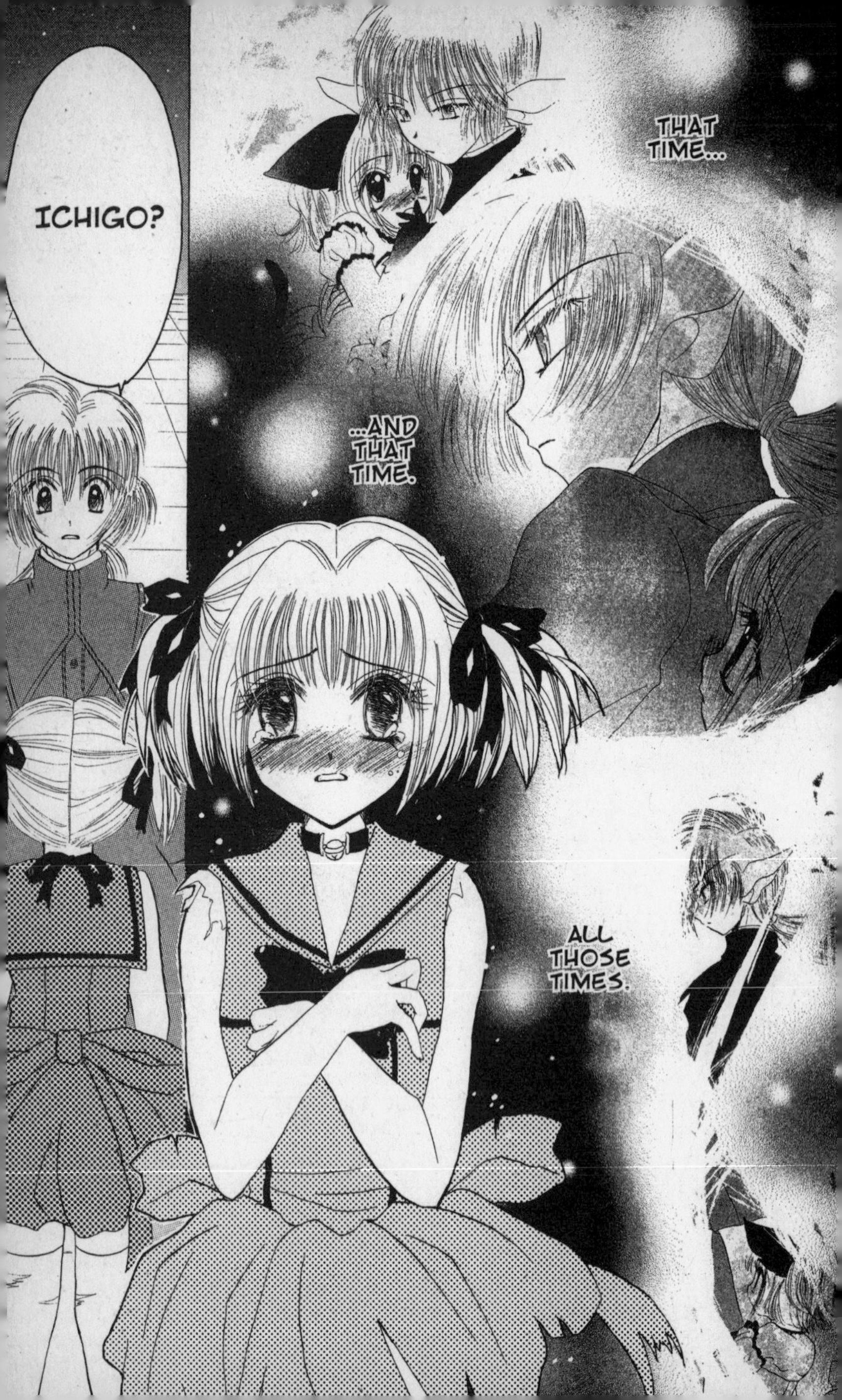
THAT TIME...
...AND THAT TIME.
ALL THOSE TIMES.
ICHIGO?

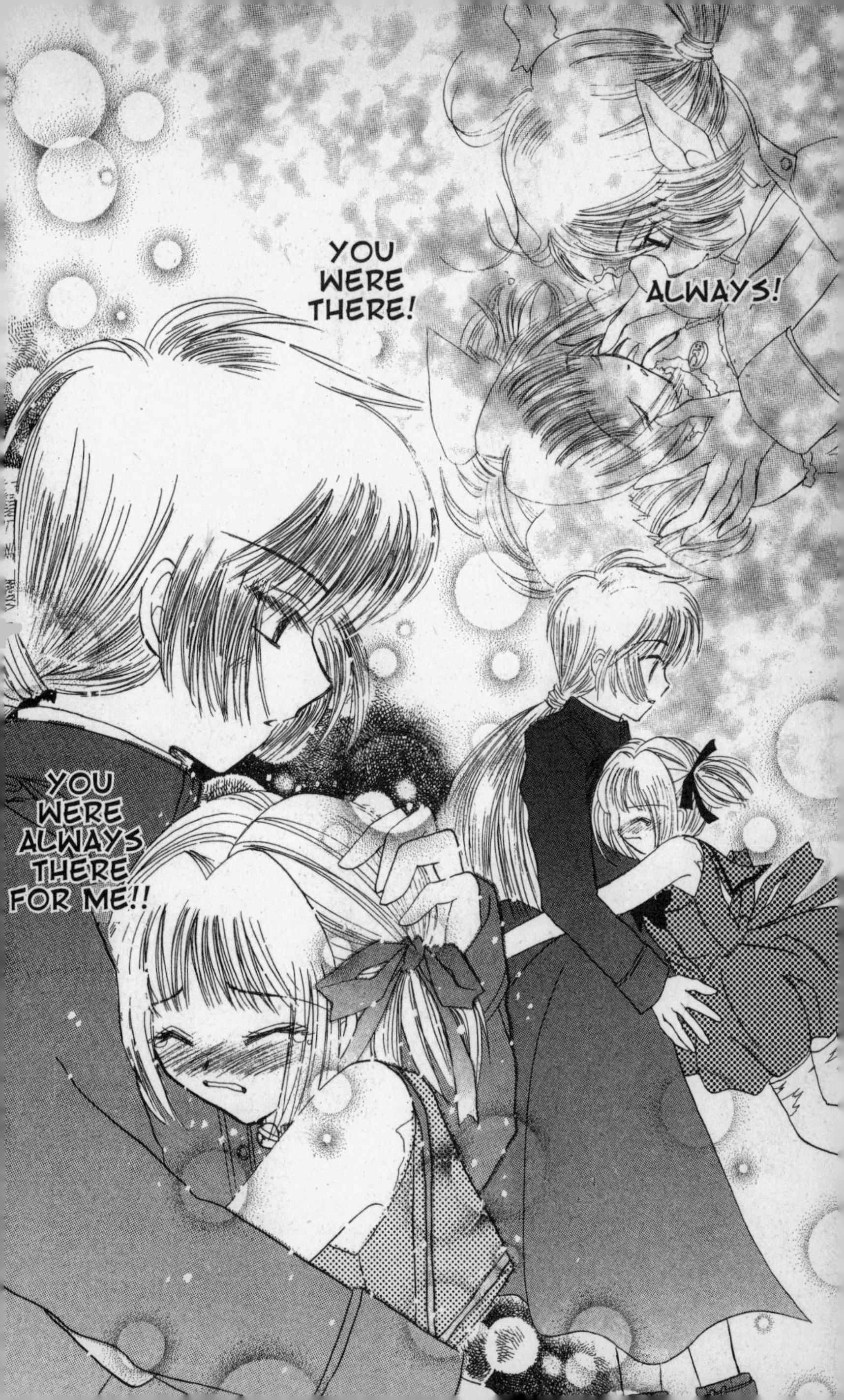
YOU WERE THERE!
ALWAYS!
YOU WERE ALWAYS THERE FOR ME!!

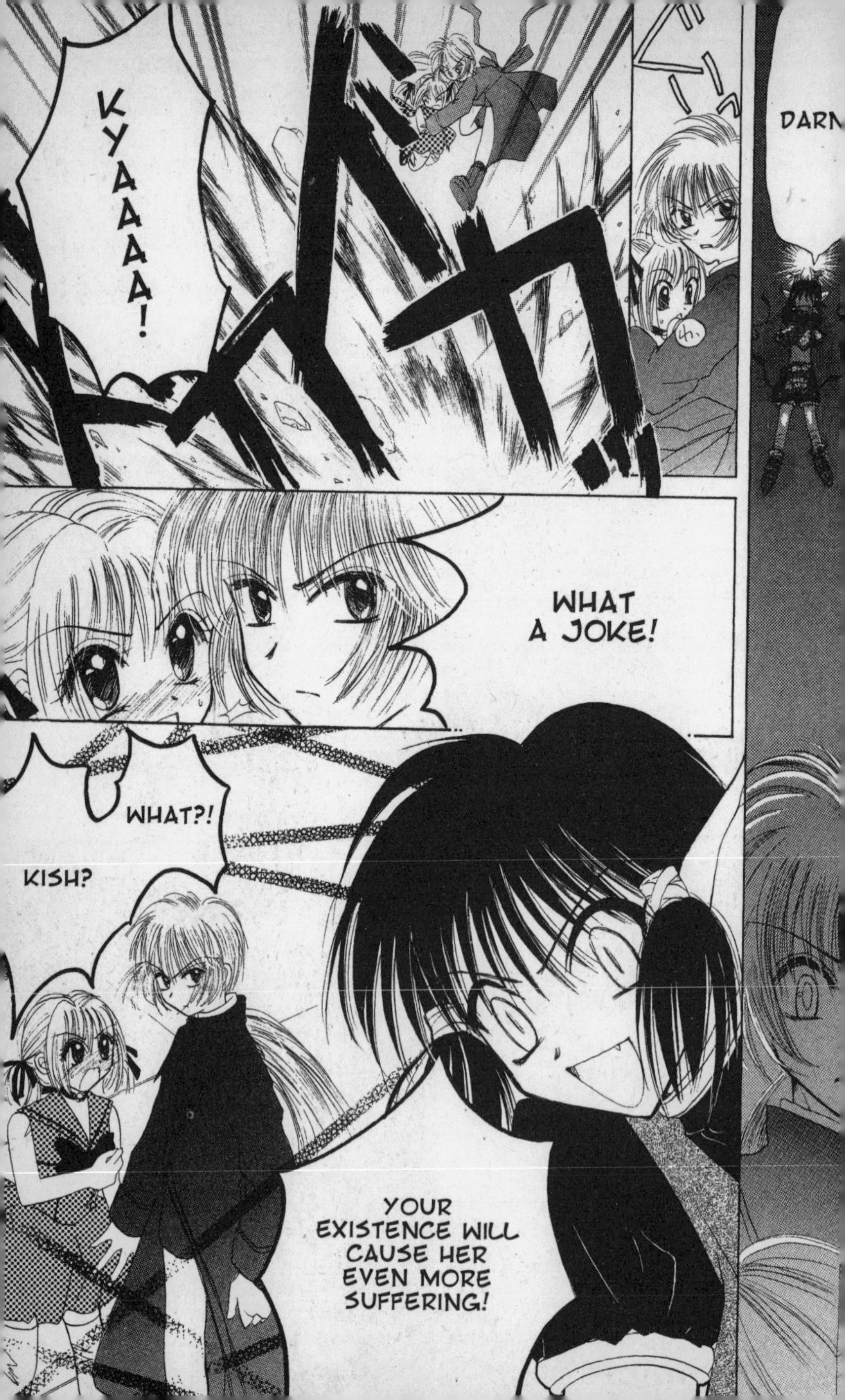

DARN
KYAAAA!
WHAT A JOKE!
WHAT?!
KISH?
YOUR EXISTENCE WILL CAUSE HER EVEN MORE SUFFERING!

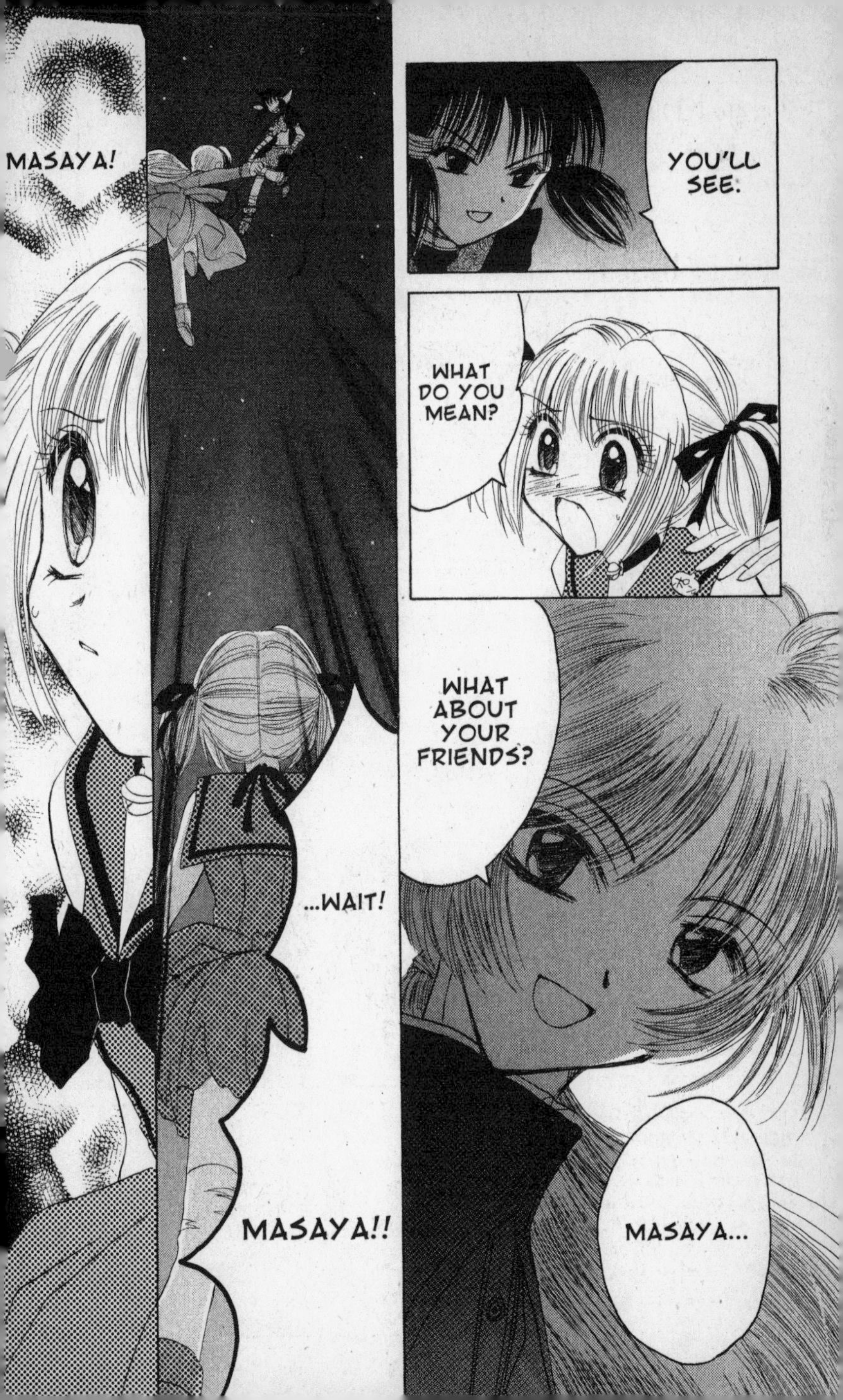
YOU'LL SEE.
WHAT DO YOU MEAN?
WHAT ABOUT YOUR FRIENDS?
MASAYA...
...WAIT!
MASAYA!!
MASAYA!

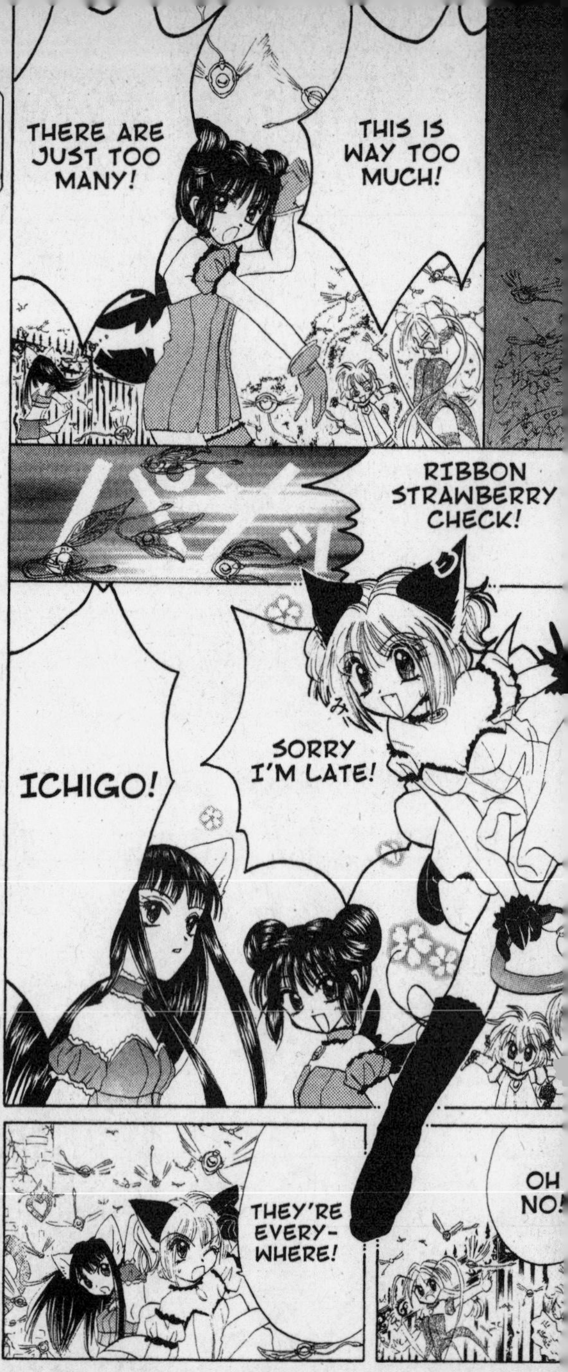
THIS IS WAY TOO MUCH!
THERE ARE JUST TOO MANY!
RIBBON STRAWBERRY CHECK!
SORRY I'M LATE!
ICHIGO!
OH NO!
THEY'RE EVERY-WHERE!

Tokyo Mew Mew

Ichigo's Costume Designs Wanted!!

Idea Award

Haruko Kuno
Hokkaido Prefecture
Seventh Grade

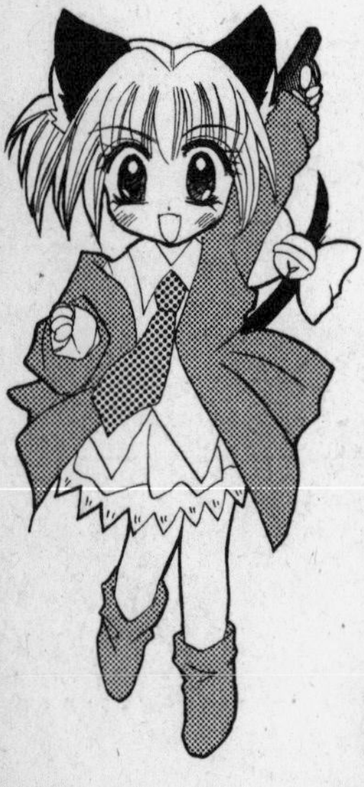

I totally love baggy clothes! The baggy boy's jacket in this design is a nice touch. I especially like how the jacket is off the shoulder on one side. It looks kind of simple, until you see the special details, like lace underneath the skirt. A too-cool design!

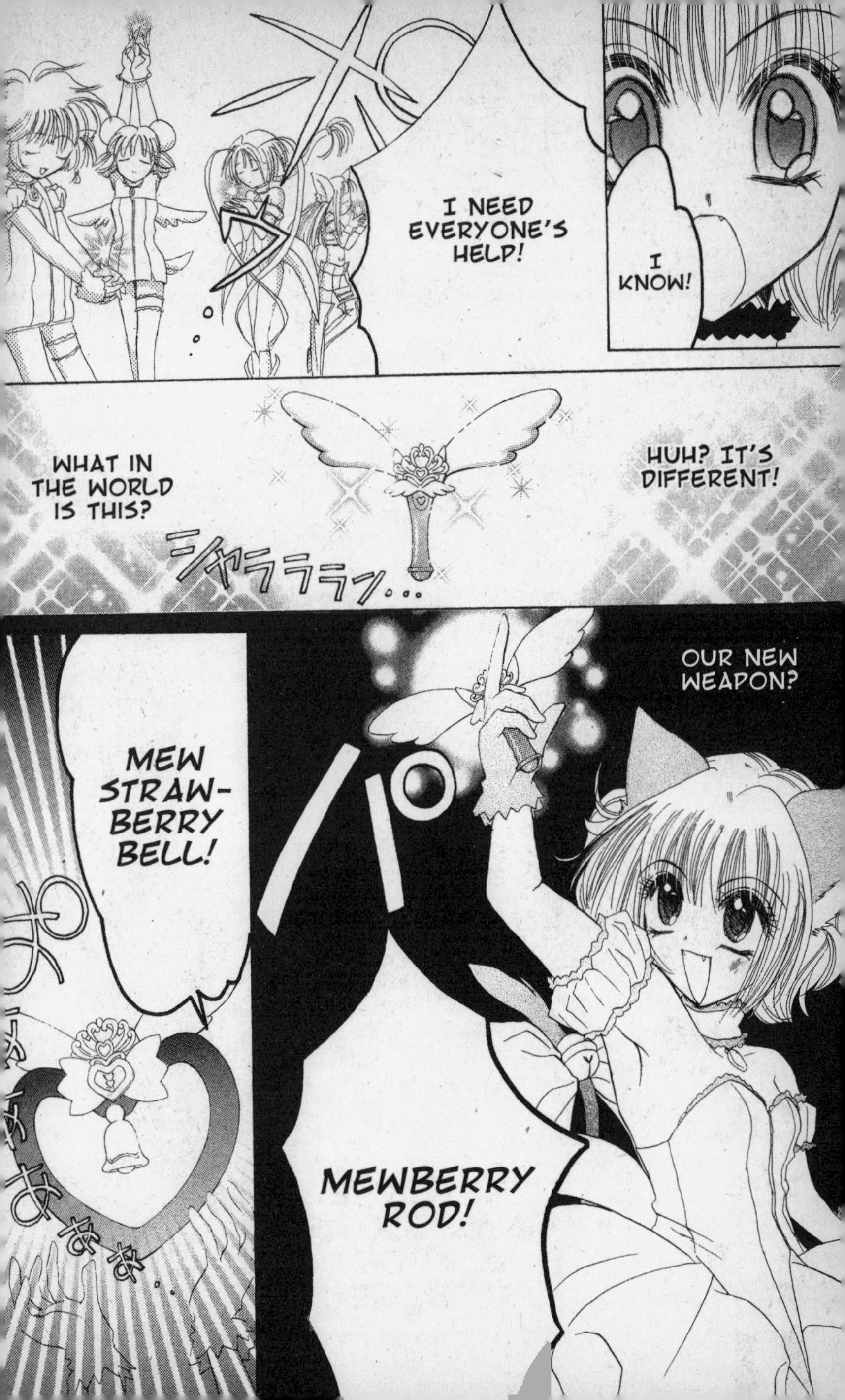
I KNOW!
I NEED EVERYONE'S HELP!
HUH? IT'S DIFFERENT!
WHAT IN THE WORLD IS THIS?
シャラララン…
OUR NEW WEAPON?
MEWBERRY ROD!
MEW STRAWBERRY BELL!

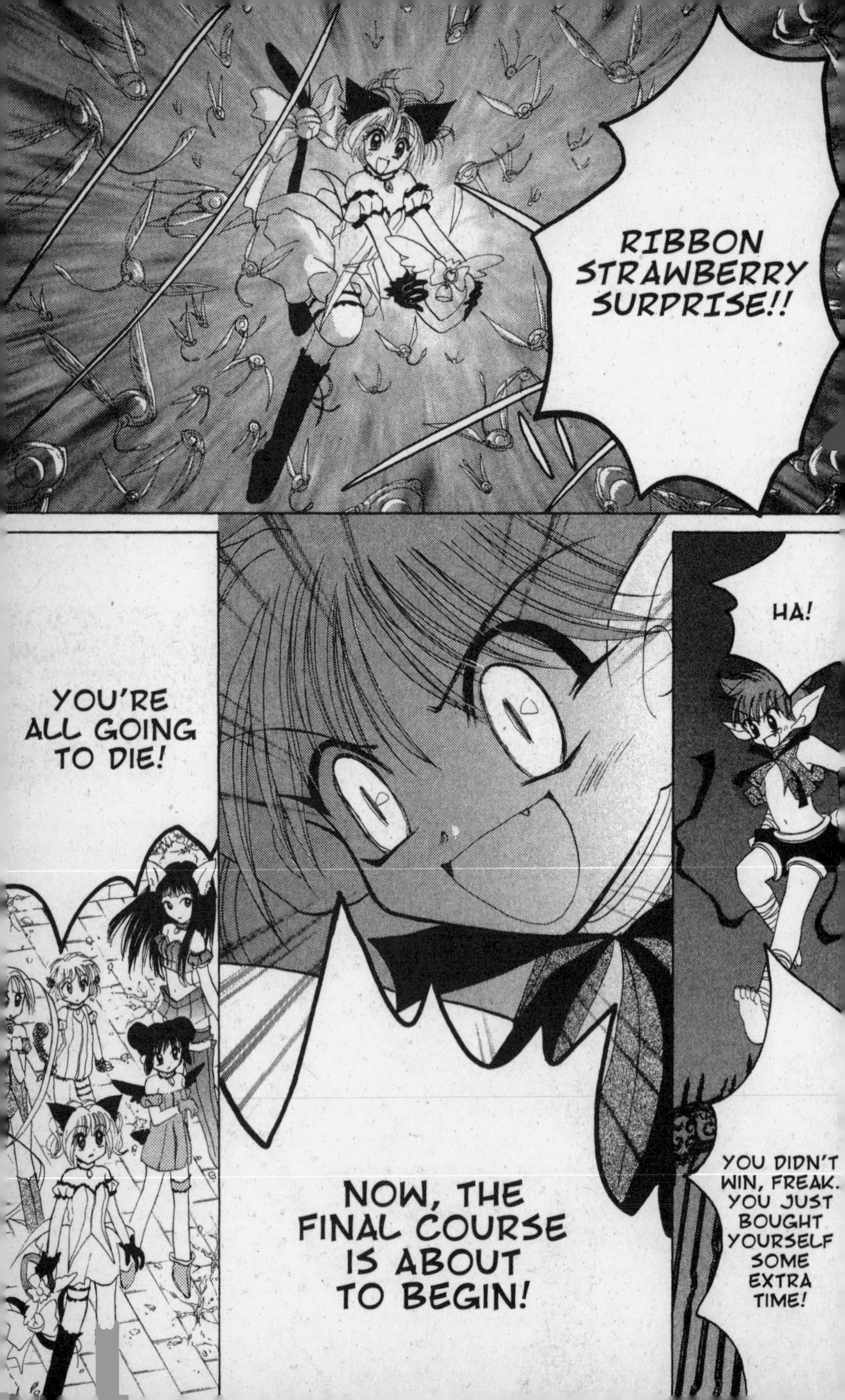
RIBBON STRAWBERRY SURPRISE!!
HA!
YOU DIDN'T WIN, FREAK. YOU JUST BOUGHT YOURSELF SOME EXTRA TIME!
NOW, THE FINAL COURSE IS ABOUT TO BEGIN!
YOU'RE ALL GOING TO DIE!

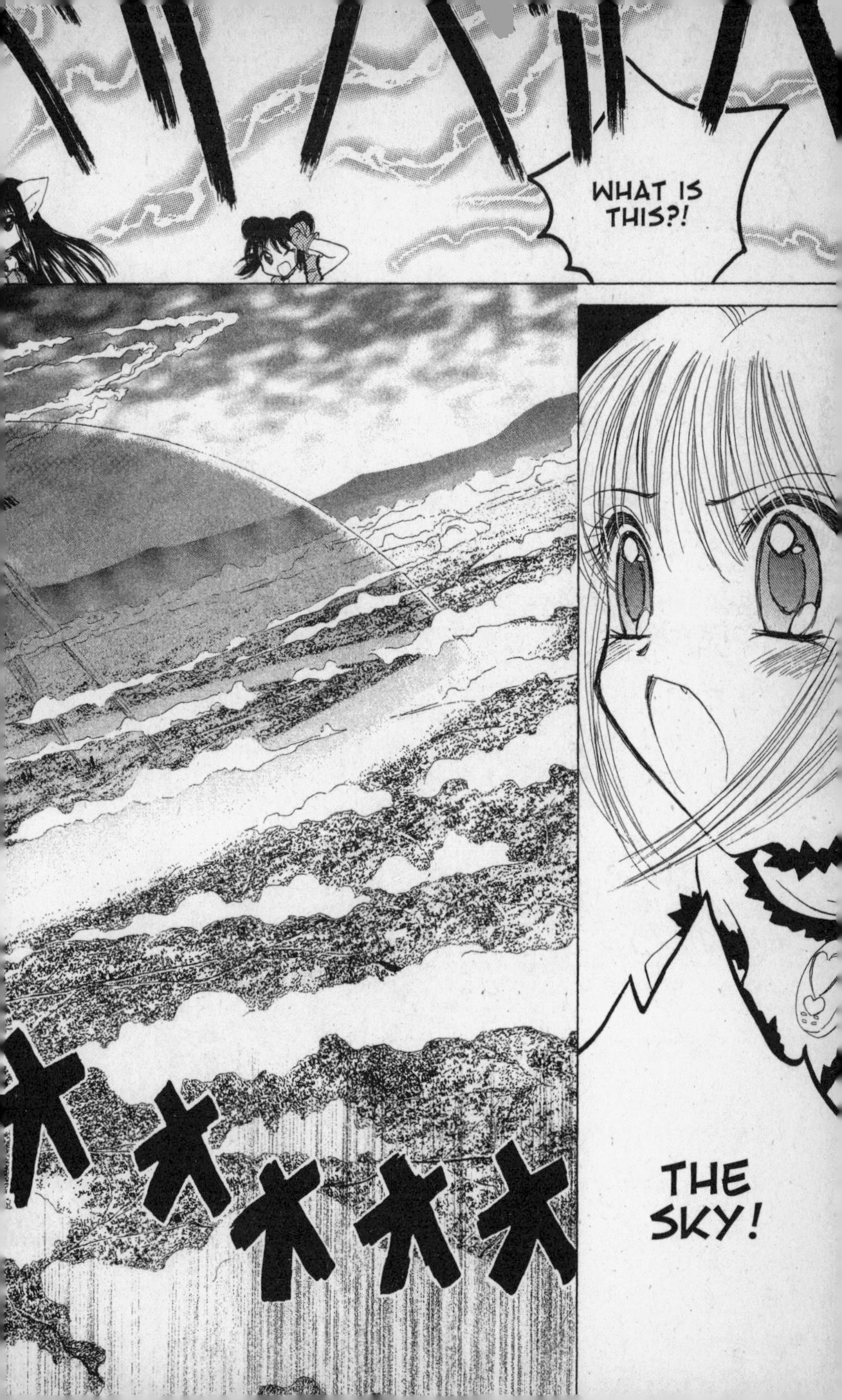
WHAT IS THIS?!
THE SKY!

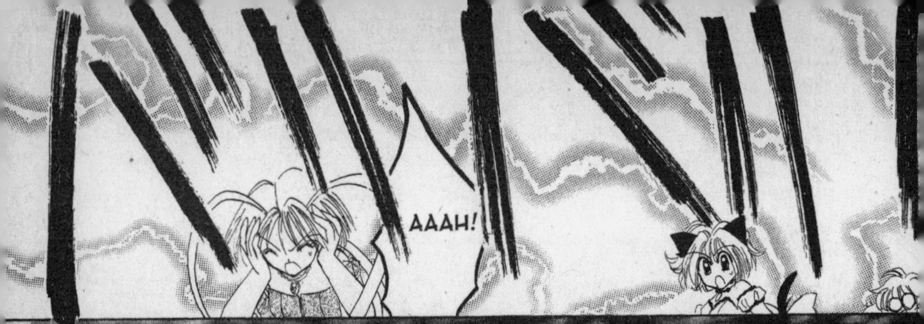
AAAH!

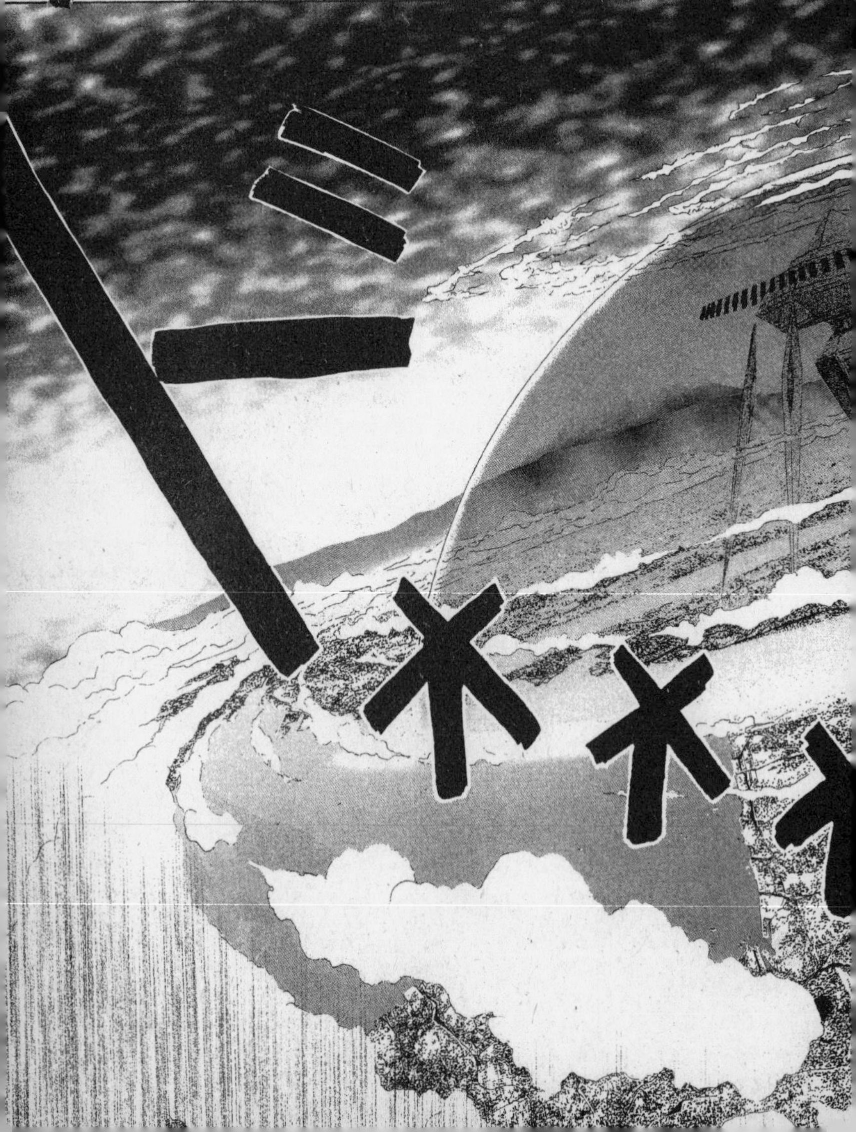

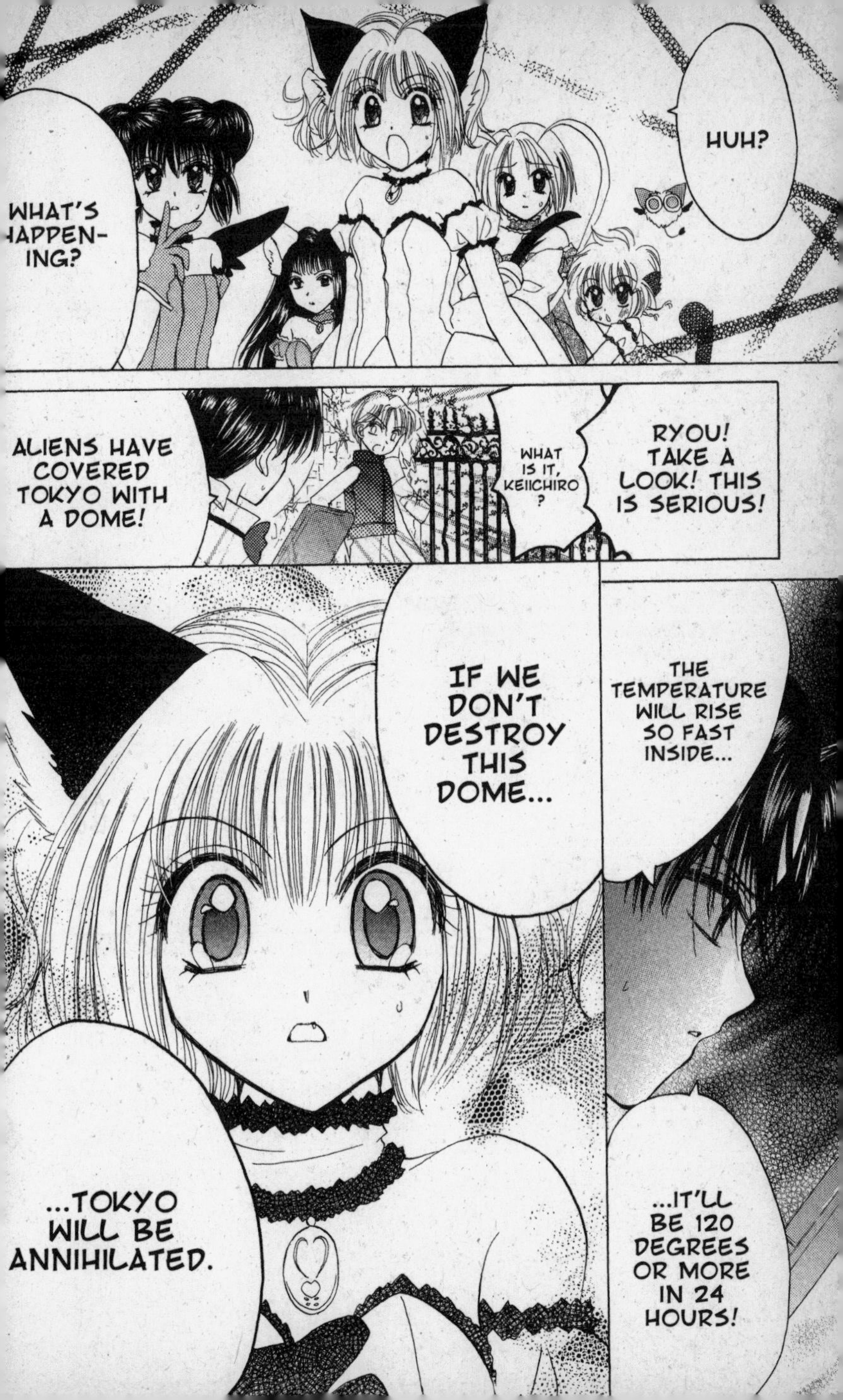
HUH?
WHAT'S HAPPEN-ING?
RYOU! TAKE A LOOK! THIS IS SERIOUS!
WHAT IS IT, KEIICHIRO?
ALIENS HAVE COVERED TOKYO WITH A DOME!
THE TEMPERATURE WILL RISE SO FAST INSIDE...
...IT'LL BE 120 DEGREES OR MORE IN 24 HOURS!
IF WE DON'T DESTROY THIS DOME...
...TOKYO WILL BE ANNIHILATED.

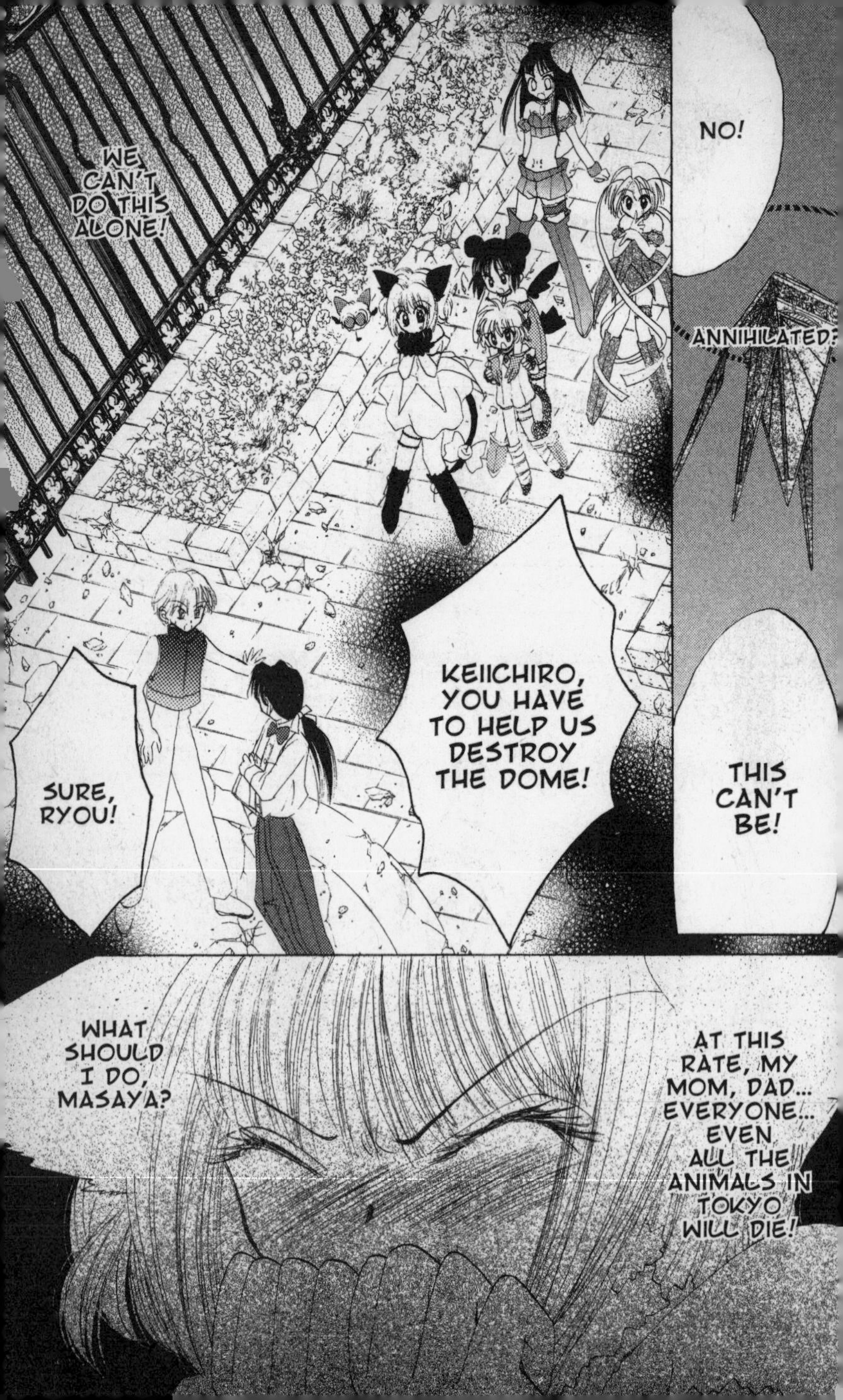
NO!
ANNIHILATED?
THIS CAN'T BE!
WE CAN'T DO THIS ALONE!
KEIICHIRO, YOU HAVE TO HELP US DESTROY THE DOME!
SURE, RYOU!
AT THIS RATE, MY MOM, DAD... EVERYONE... EVEN ALL THE ANIMALS IN TOKYO WILL DIE!
WHAT SHOULD I DO, MASAYA?

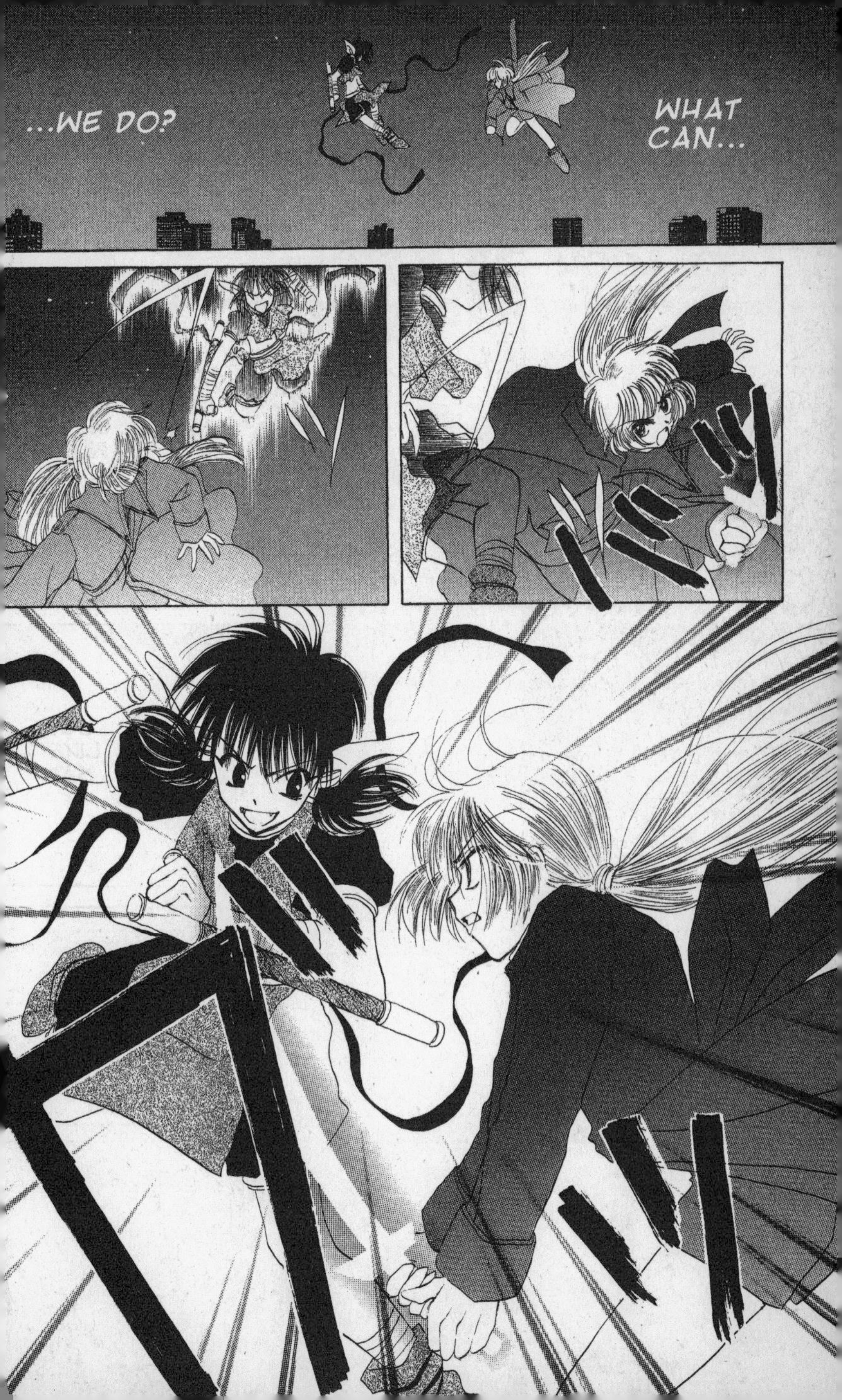
WHAT CAN...
...WE DO?

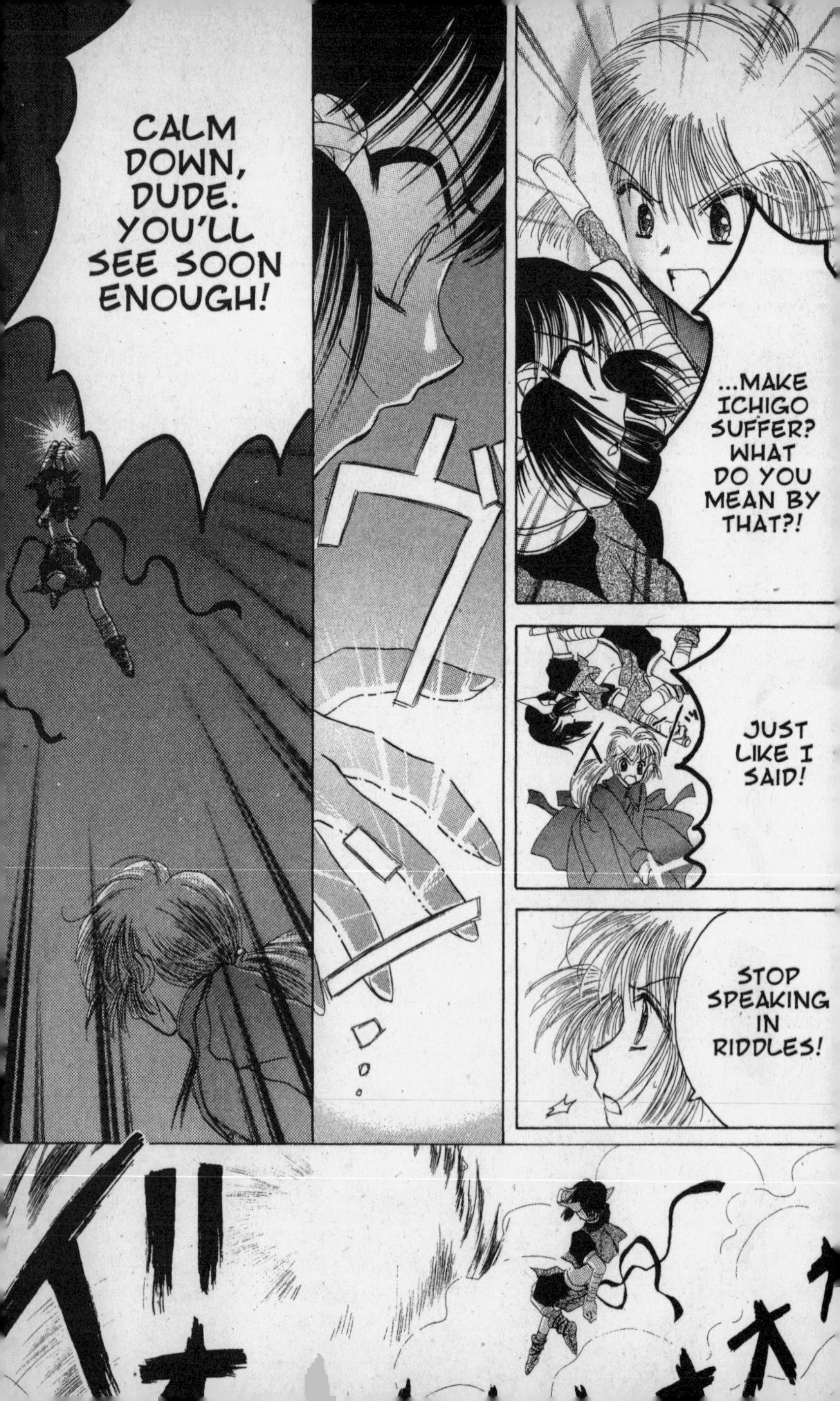
...MAKE ICHIGO SUFFER? WHAT DO YOU MEAN BY THAT?!
JUST LIKE I SAID!
STOP SPEAKING IN RIDDLES!
CALM DOWN, DUDE. YOU'LL SEE SOON ENOUGH!

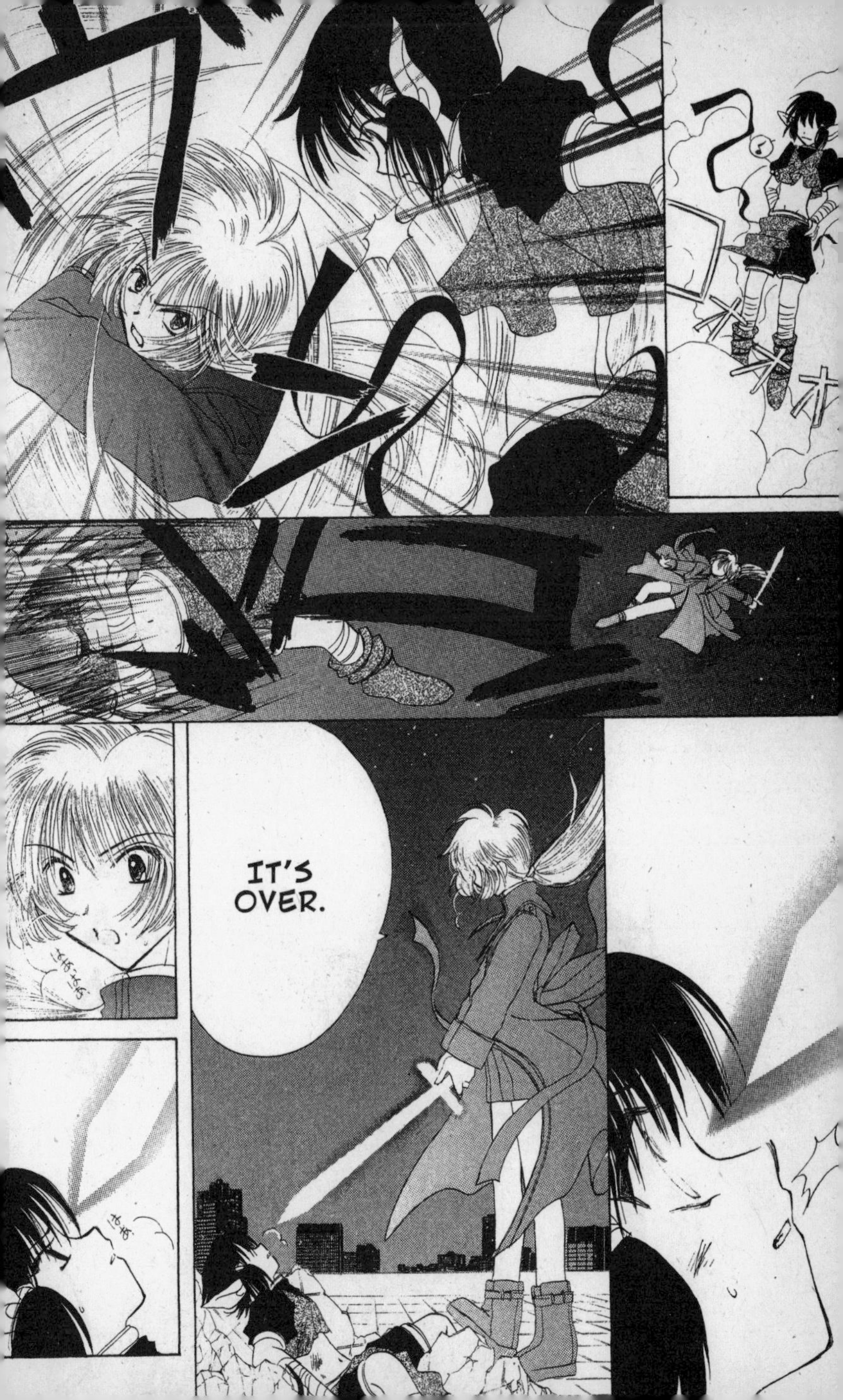
IT'S OVER.

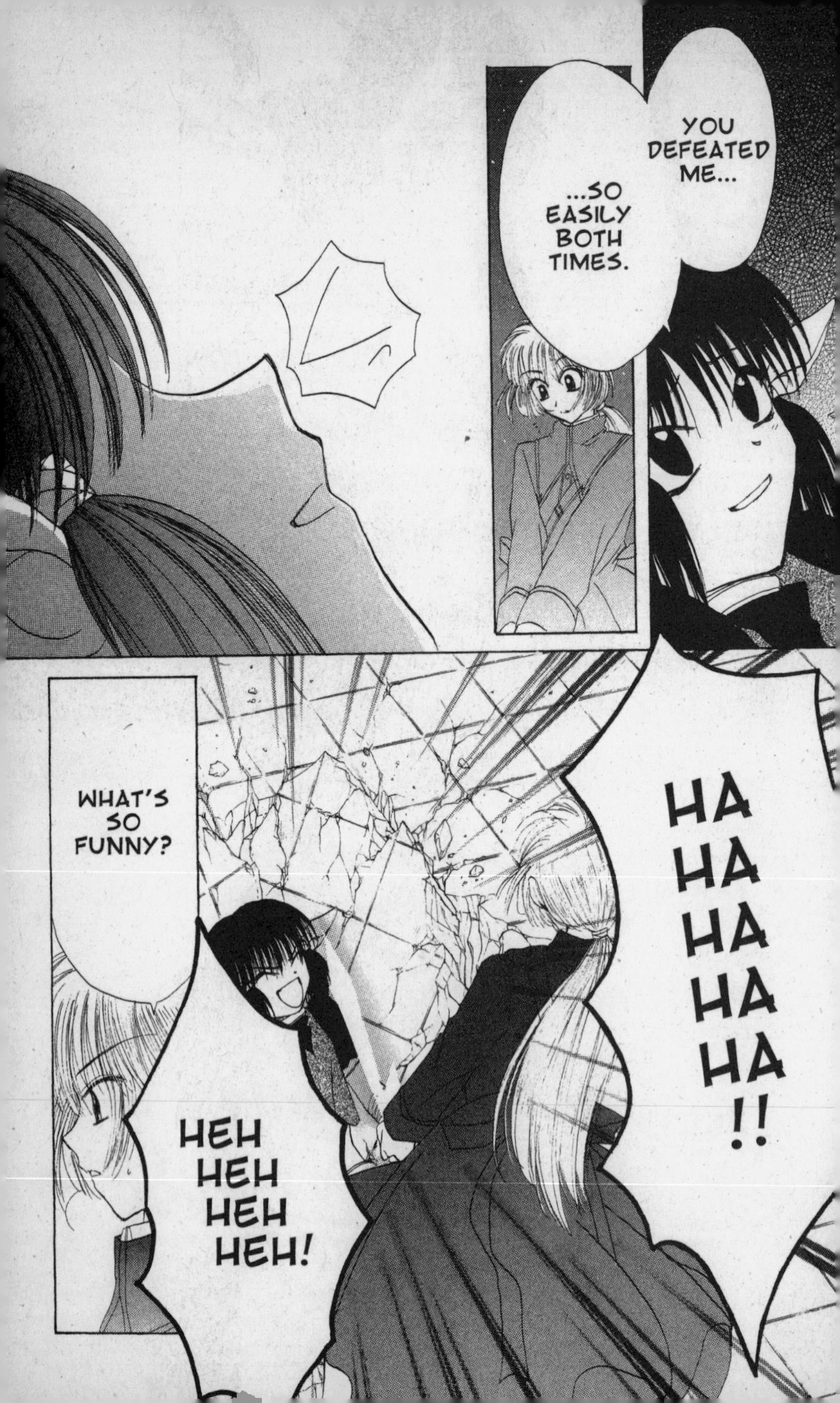

YOU DEFEATED ME...
...SO EASILY BOTH TIMES.
HA HA HA HA HA HA!!
WHAT'S SO FUNNY?
HEH HEH HEH HEH!

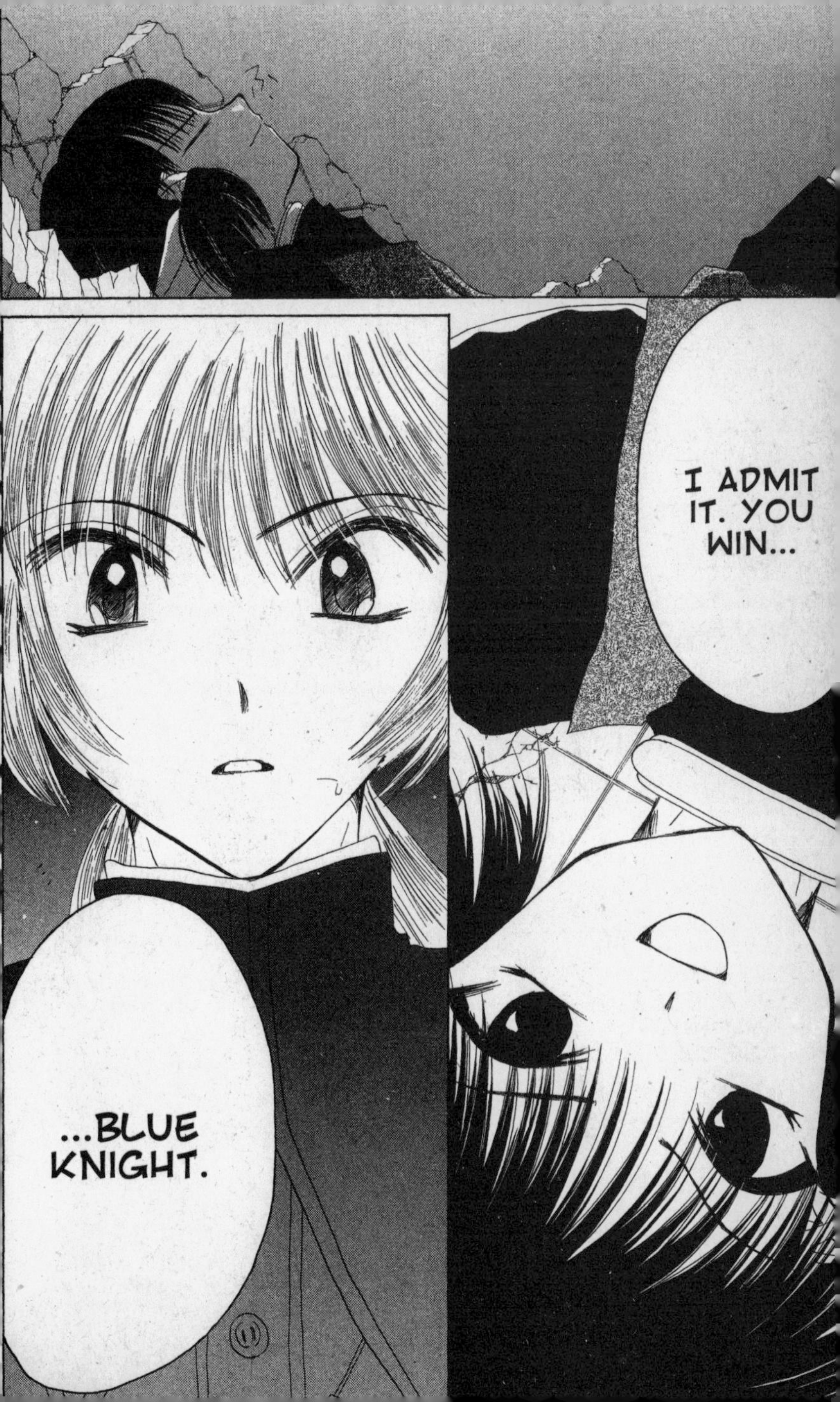
I ADMIT IT. YOU WIN...
...BLUE KNIGHT.

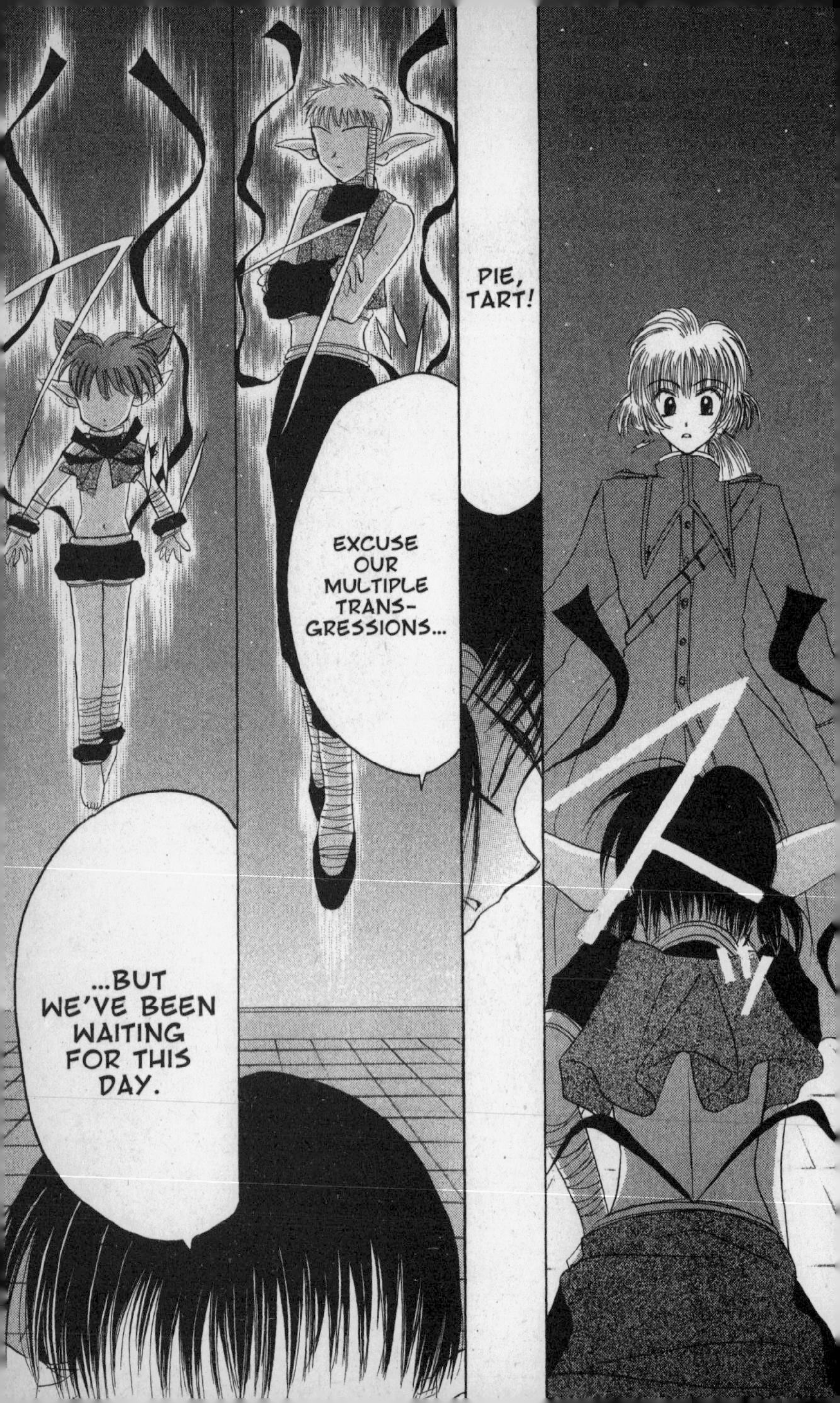
PIE, TART!
EXCUSE OUR MULTIPLE TRANS-GRESSIONS...
...BUT WE'VE BEEN WAITING FOR THIS DAY.

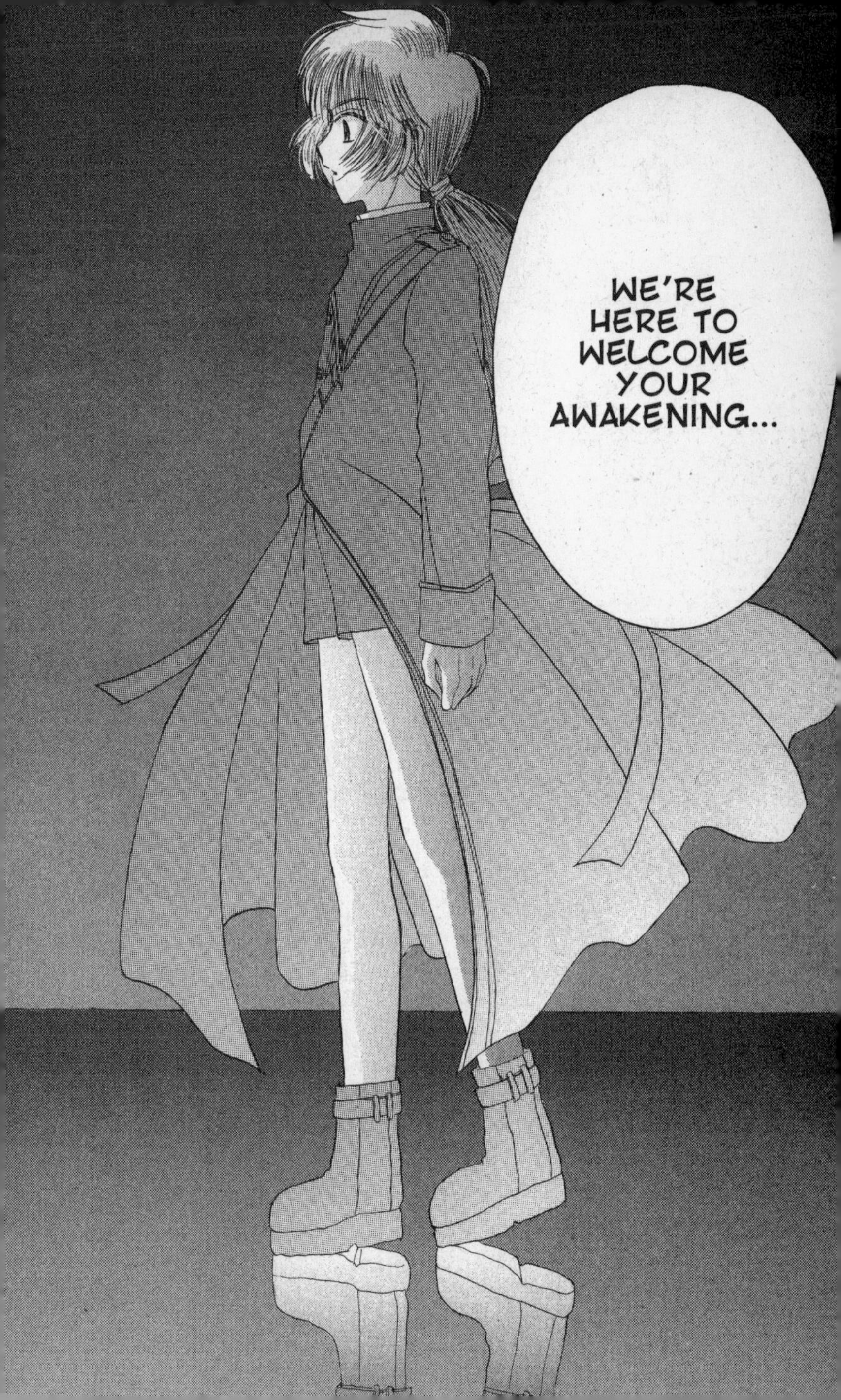
WE'RE HERE TO WELCOME YOUR AWAKENING...

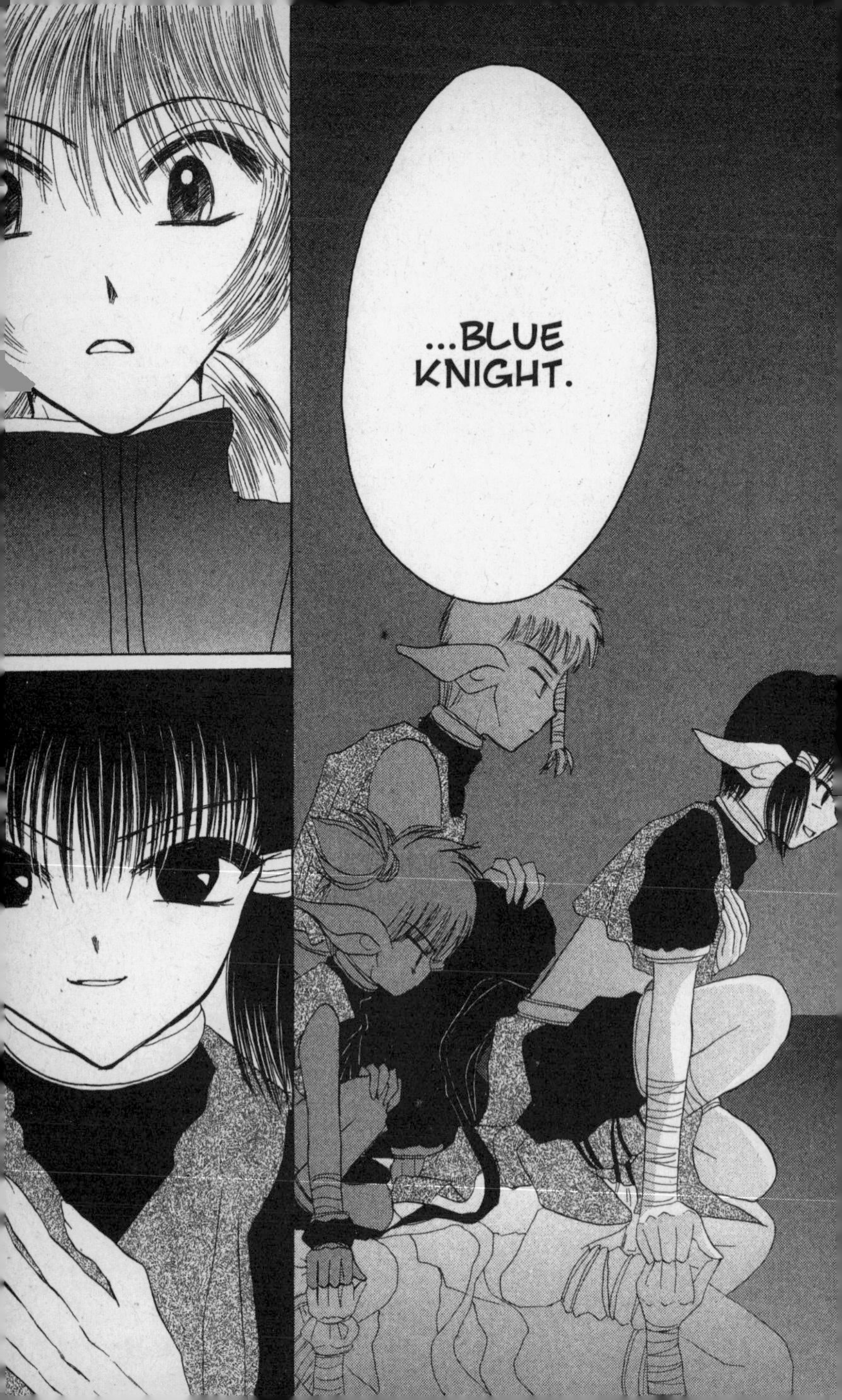
...BLUE
KNIGHT.

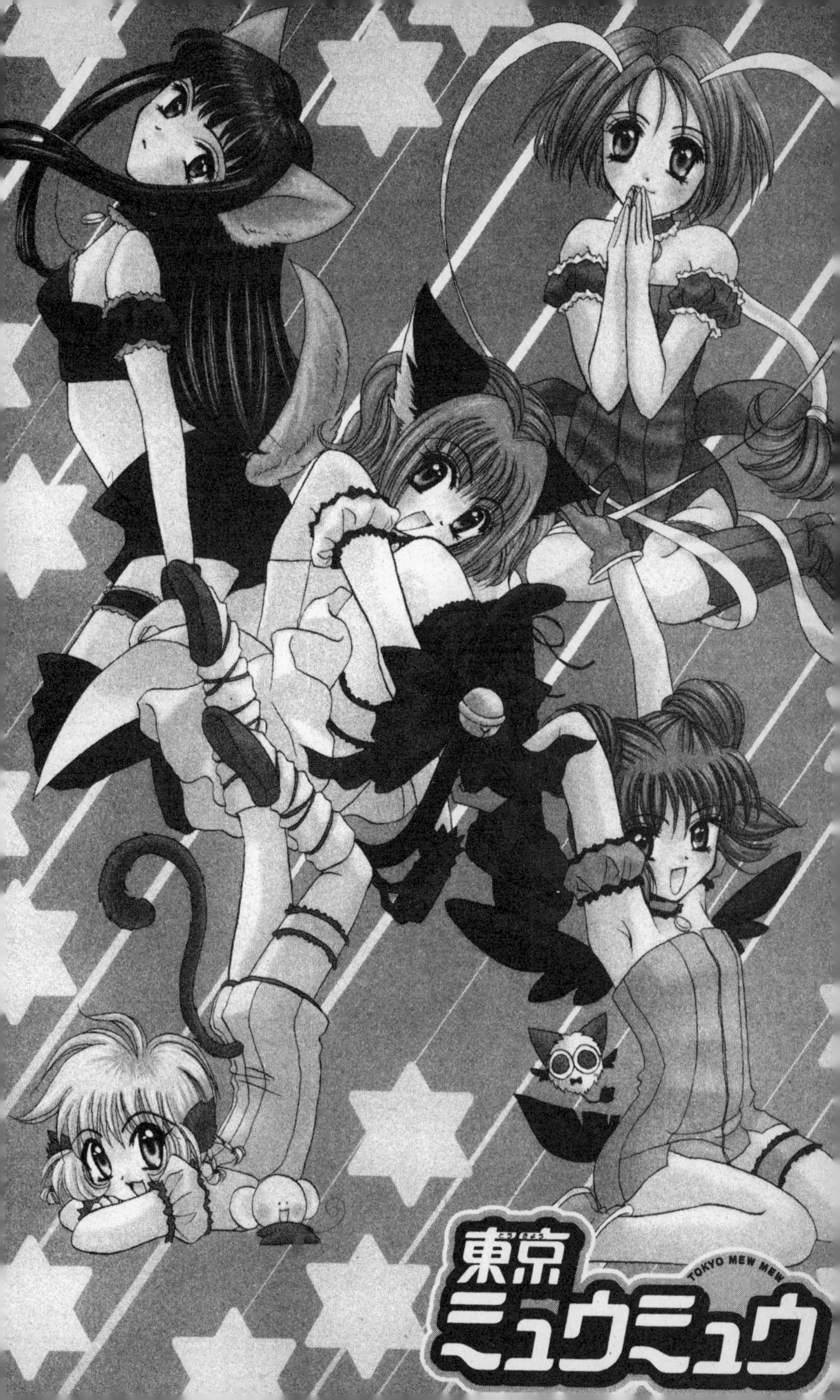
東京
ミュウミュウ
TOKYO MEW MEW

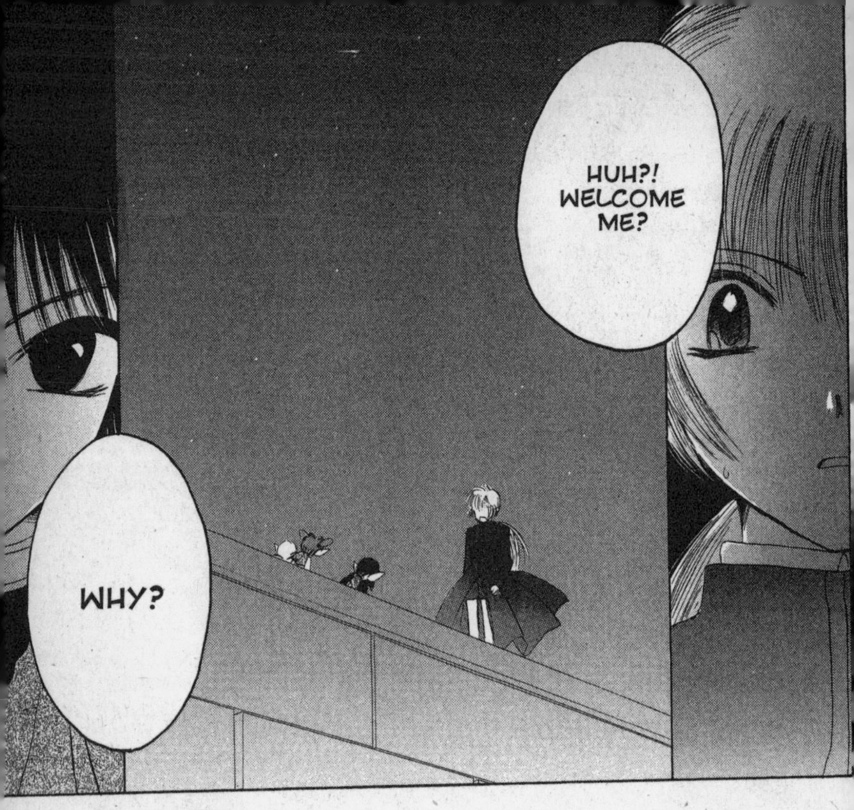
HUH?! WELCOME ME?
WHY?

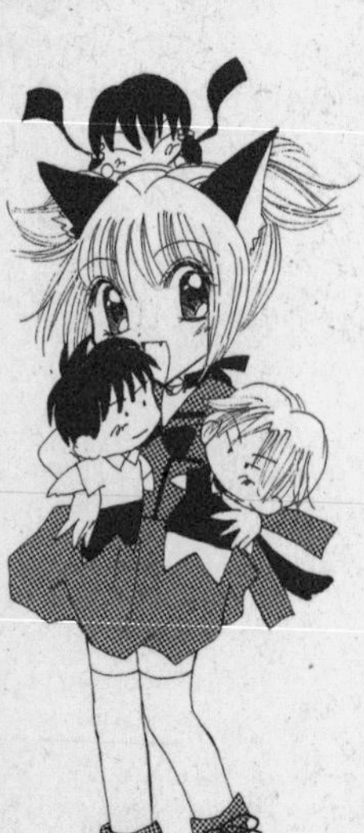

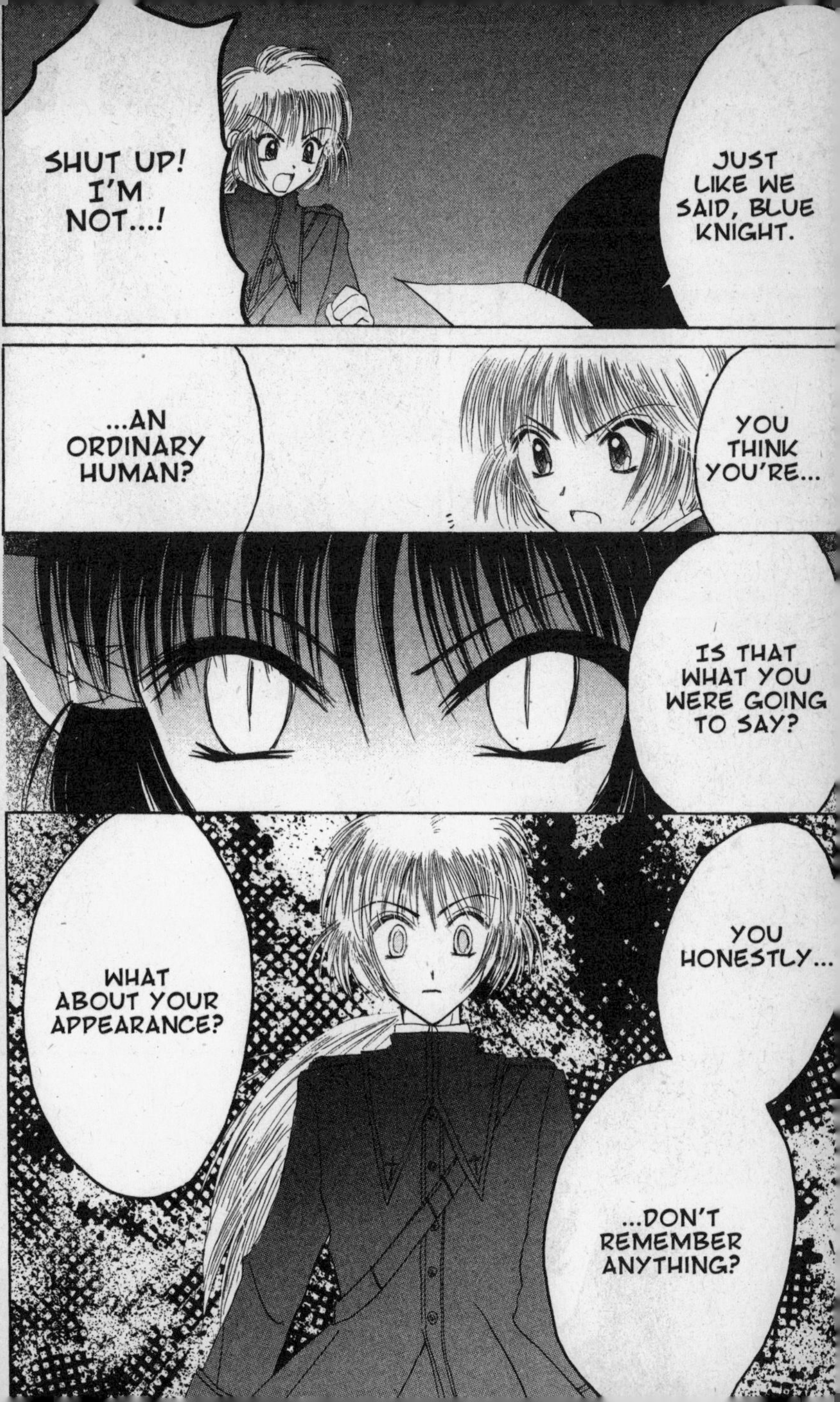
JUST LIKE WE SAID, BLUE KNIGHT.
SHUT UP! I'M NOT...!
YOU THINK YOU'RE...
...AN ORDINARY HUMAN?
IS THAT WHAT YOU WERE GOING TO SAY?
YOU HONESTLY...
...DON'T REMEMBER ANYTHING?
WHAT ABOUT YOUR APPEARANCE?

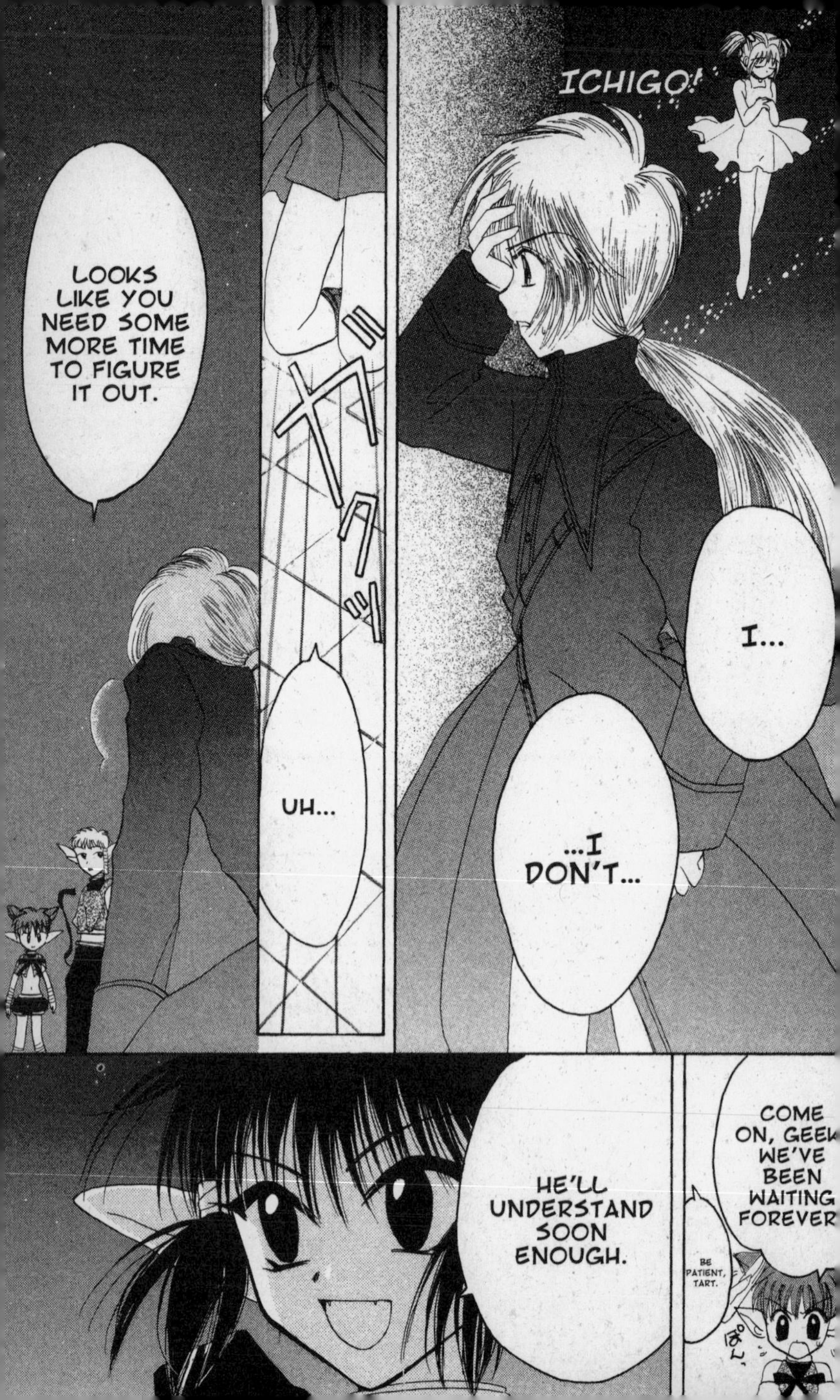

ICHIGO!
I...
...I DON'T...
UH...
LOOKS LIKE YOU NEED SOME MORE TIME TO FIGURE IT OUT.
COME ON, GEEK WE'VE BEEN WAITING FOREVER
BE PATIENT, TART.
HE'LL UNDERSTAND SOON ENOUGH.

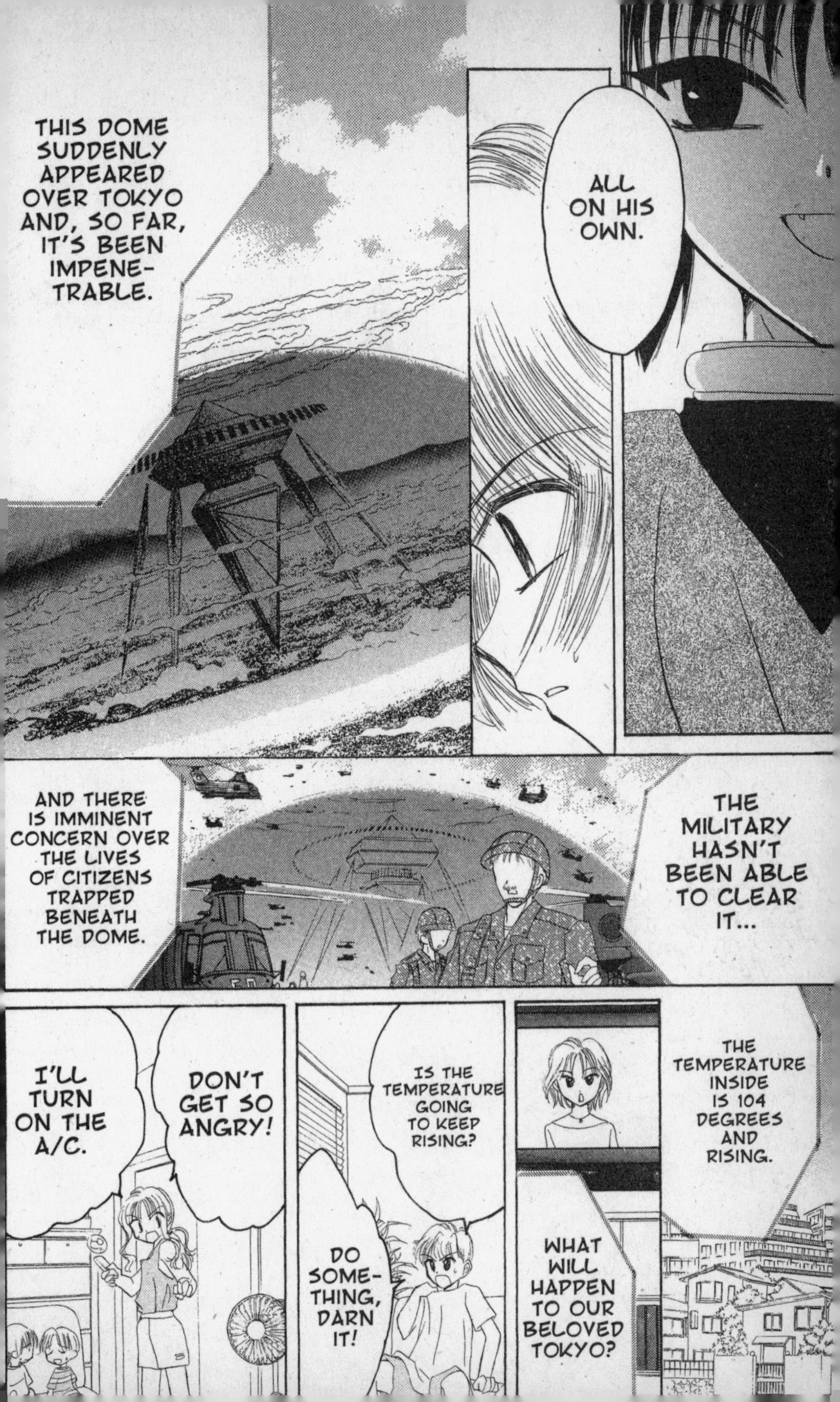
ALL ON HIS OWN.
THIS DOME SUDDENLY APPEARED OVER TOKYO AND, SO FAR, IT'S BEEN IMPENETRABLE.
THE MILITARY HASN'T BEEN ABLE TO CLEAR IT...
AND THERE IS IMMINENT CONCERN OVER THE LIVES OF CITIZENS TRAPPED BENEATH THE DOME.
THE TEMPERATURE INSIDE IS 104 DEGREES AND RISING.
WHAT WILL HAPPEN TO OUR BELOVED TOKYO?
IS THE TEMPERATURE GOING TO KEEP RISING?
DO SOMETHING, DARN IT!
DON'T GET SO ANGRY!
I'LL TURN ON THE A/C.

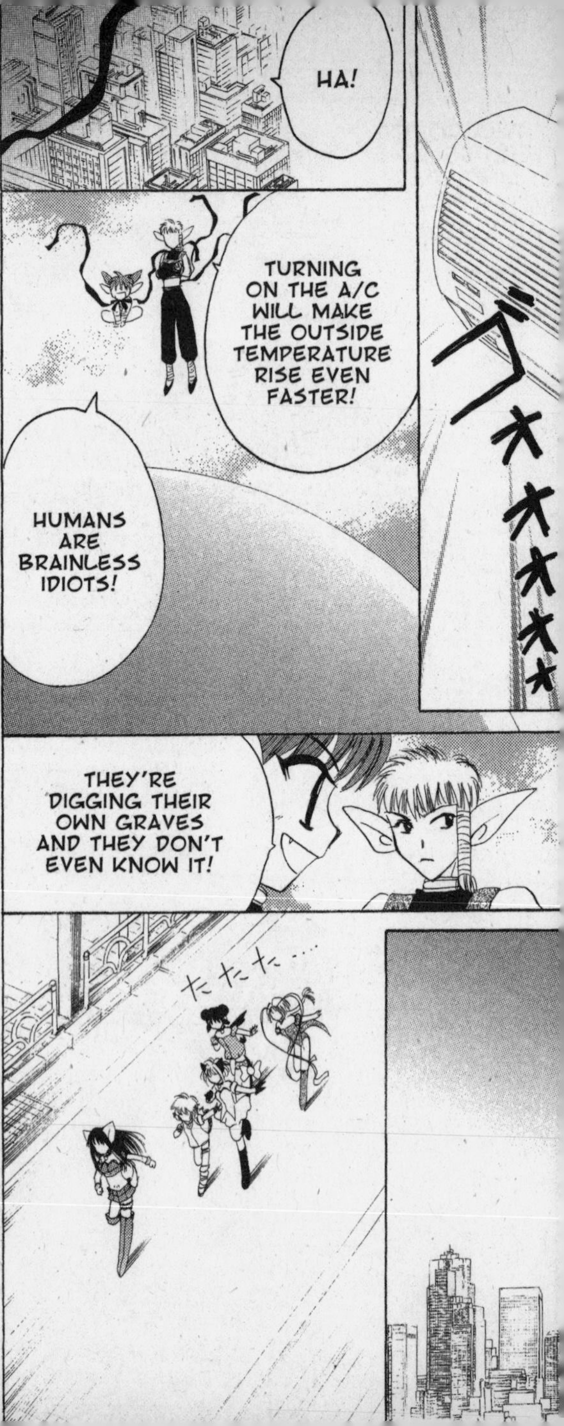
HA!
TURNING ON THE A/C WILL MAKE THE OUTSIDE TEMPERATURE RISE EVEN FASTER!
HUMANS ARE BRAINLESS IDIOTS!
THEY'RE DIGGING THEIR OWN GRAVES AND THEY DON'T EVEN KNOW IT!
たたた…

Tokyo Mew Mew
Ichigo's Costume Designs Wanted!!

Idea Award

Minako Tsuburaba
Aichi Prefecture
12th Grade

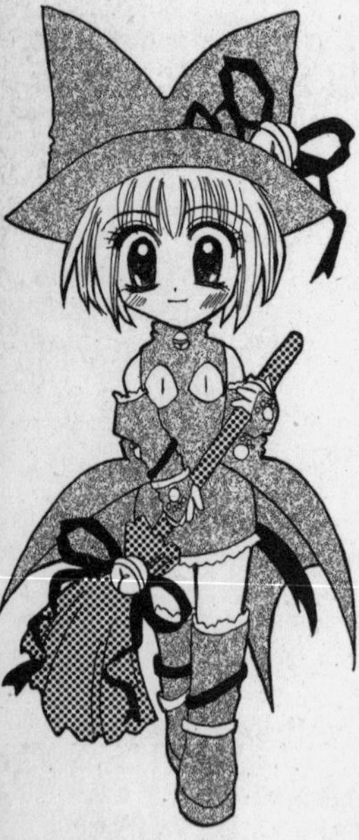

I liked this one because I thought it was the most playful design out of all the entries. Everything about the silhouette is very catlike! Gorgeous! I like the use of ribbons in the design too and I totally want the broom!

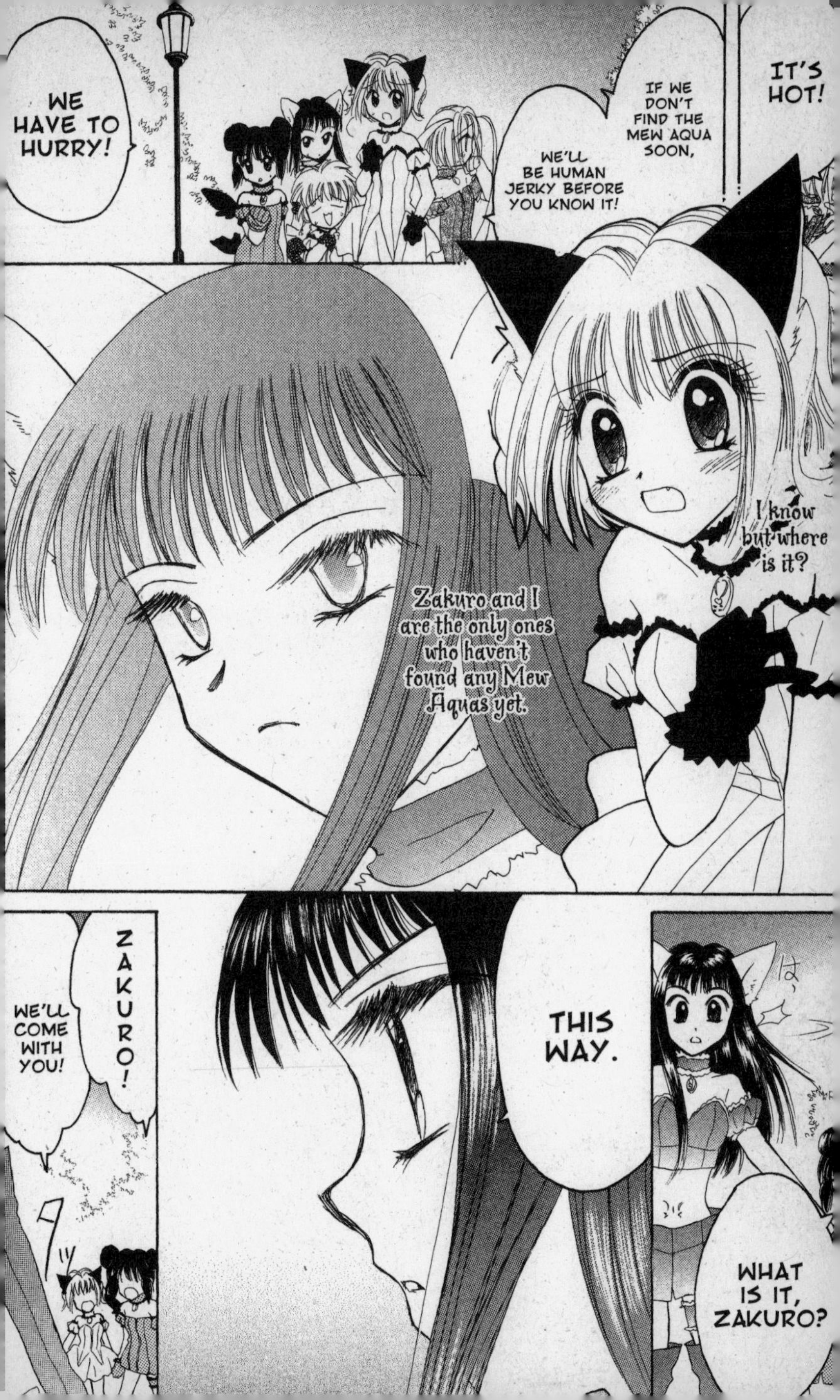
IT'S HOT!
IF WE DON'T FIND THE MEW AQUA SOON,
WE'LL BE HUMAN JERKY BEFORE YOU KNOW IT!
WE HAVE TO HURRY!
I know but where is it?
Zakuro and I are the only ones who haven't found any Mew Aquas yet.
は、
WHAT IS IT, ZAKURO?
THIS WAY.
ZAKURO!
WE'LL COME WITH YOU!

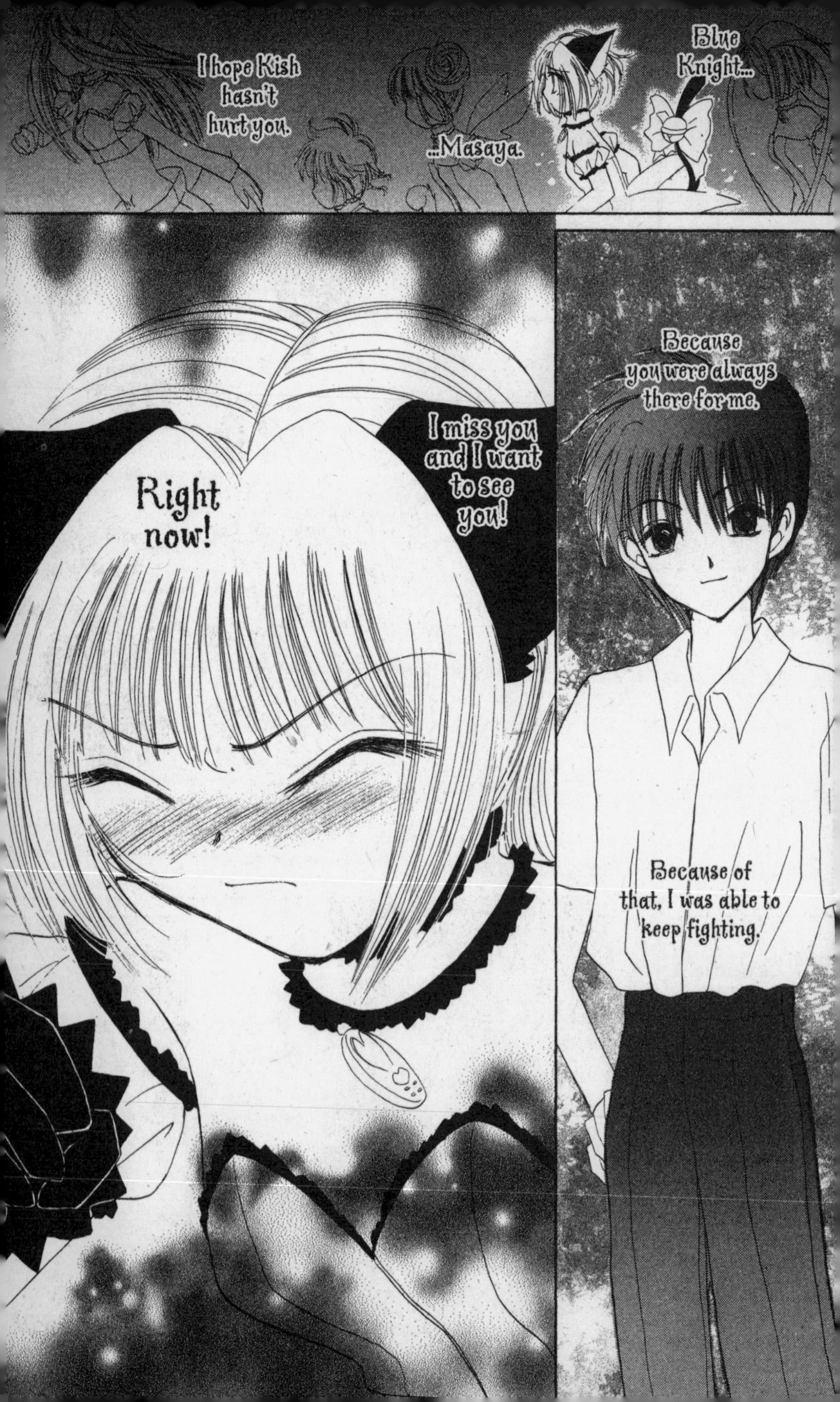
Blue Knight...
...Masaya.
I hope Kish hasn't hurt you.
Because you were always there for me.
Because of that, I was able to keep fighting.
I miss you and I want to see you!
Right now!

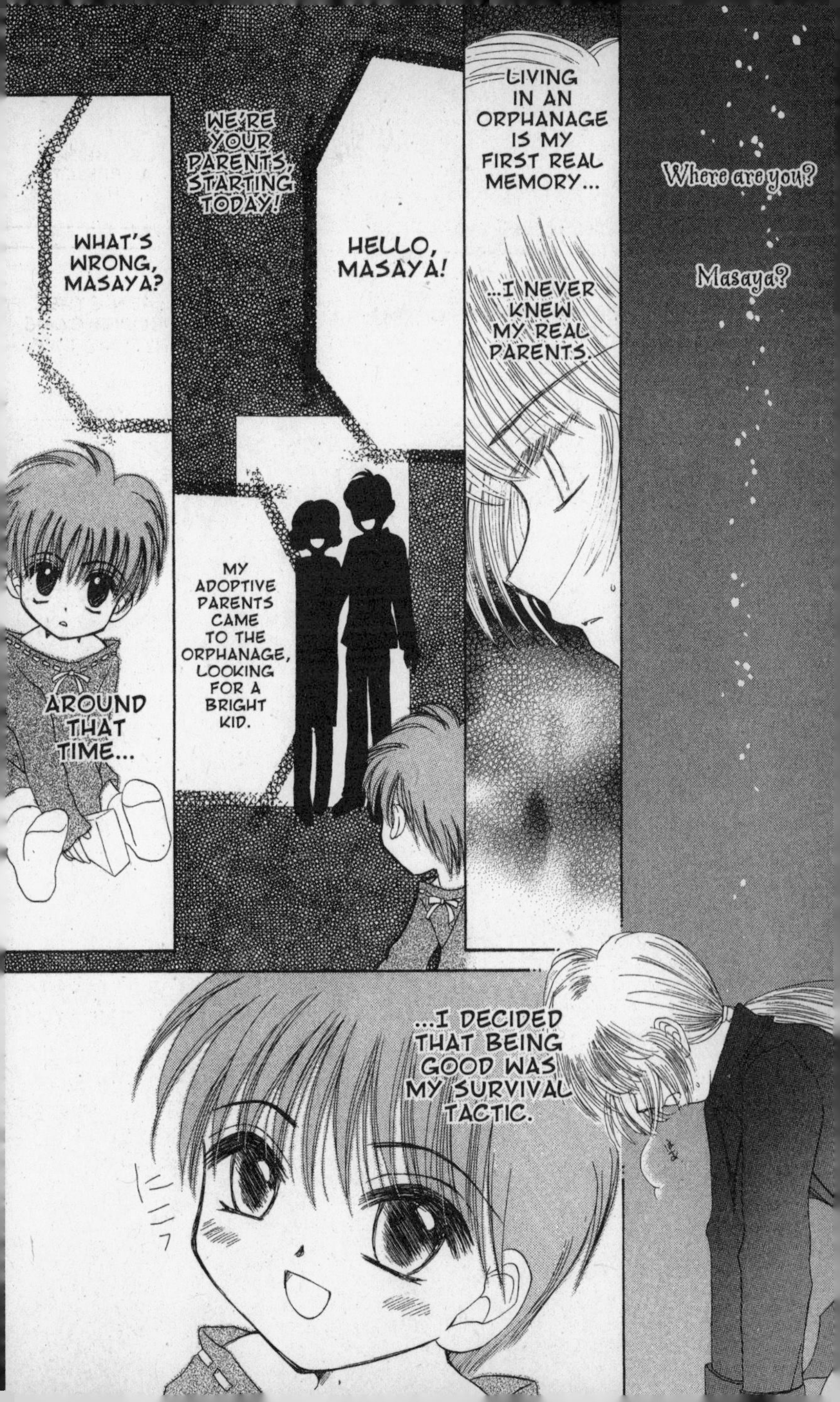
Where are you?
Masaya?
LIVING IN AN ORPHANAGE IS MY FIRST REAL MEMORY...
...I NEVER KNEW MY REAL PARENTS.
HELLO, MASAYA!
WE'RE YOUR PARENTS, STARTING TODAY!
MY ADOPTIVE PARENTS CAME TO THE ORPHANAGE, LOOKING FOR A BRIGHT KID.
WHAT'S WRONG, MASAYA?
AROUND THAT TIME...
...I DECIDED THAT BEING GOOD WAS MY SURVIVAL TACTIC.

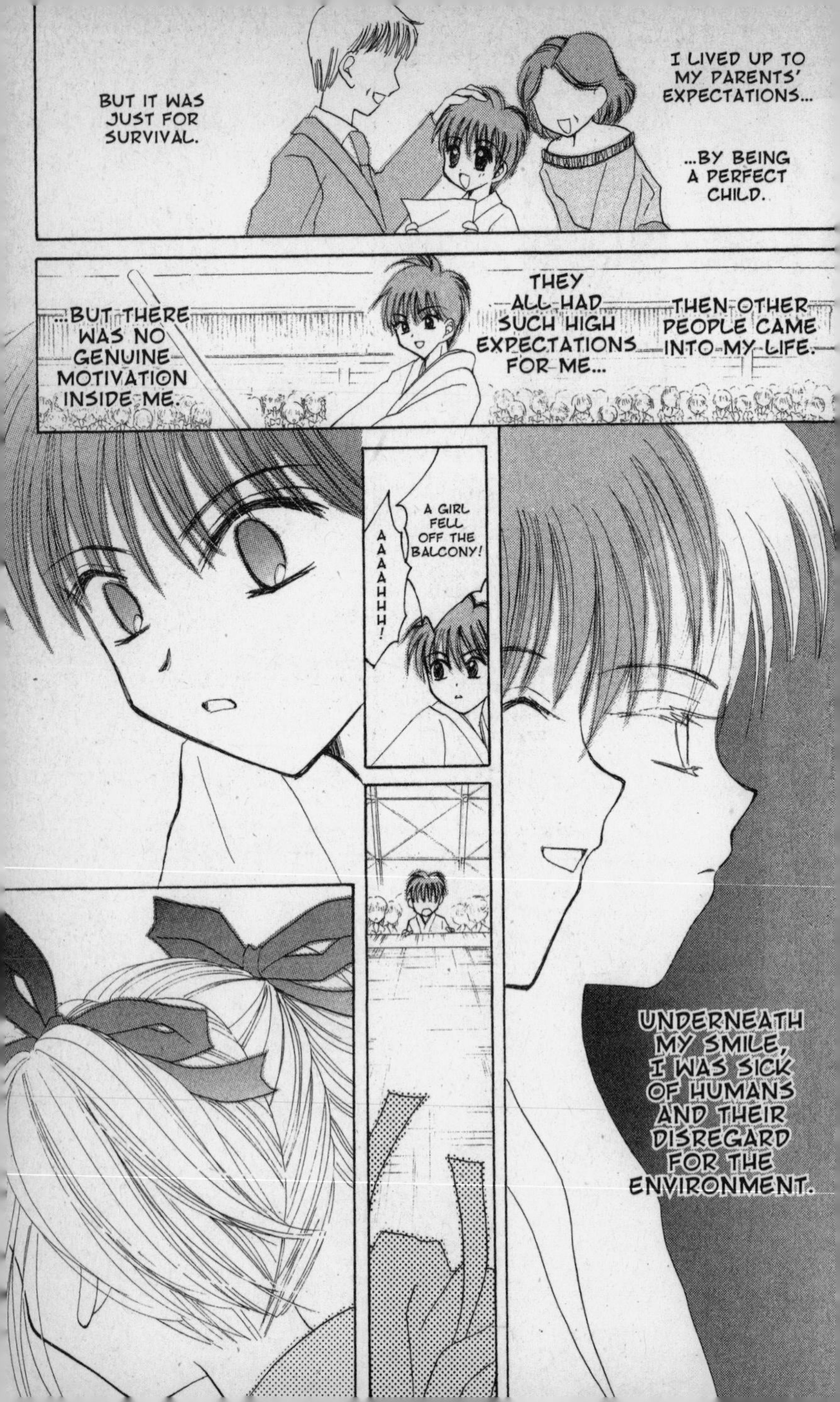

I LIVED UP TO MY PARENTS' EXPECTATIONS...
...BY BEING A PERFECT CHILD.
BUT IT WAS JUST FOR SURVIVAL.
THEN OTHER PEOPLE CAME INTO MY LIFE.
THEY ALL HAD SUCH HIGH EXPECTATIONS FOR ME...
...BUT THERE WAS NO GENUINE MOTIVATION INSIDE ME.
UNDERNEATH MY SMILE, I WAS SICK OF HUMANS AND THEIR DISREGARD FOR THE ENVIRONMENT.
A GIRL FELL OFF THE BALCONY!
AAAAAHHH!

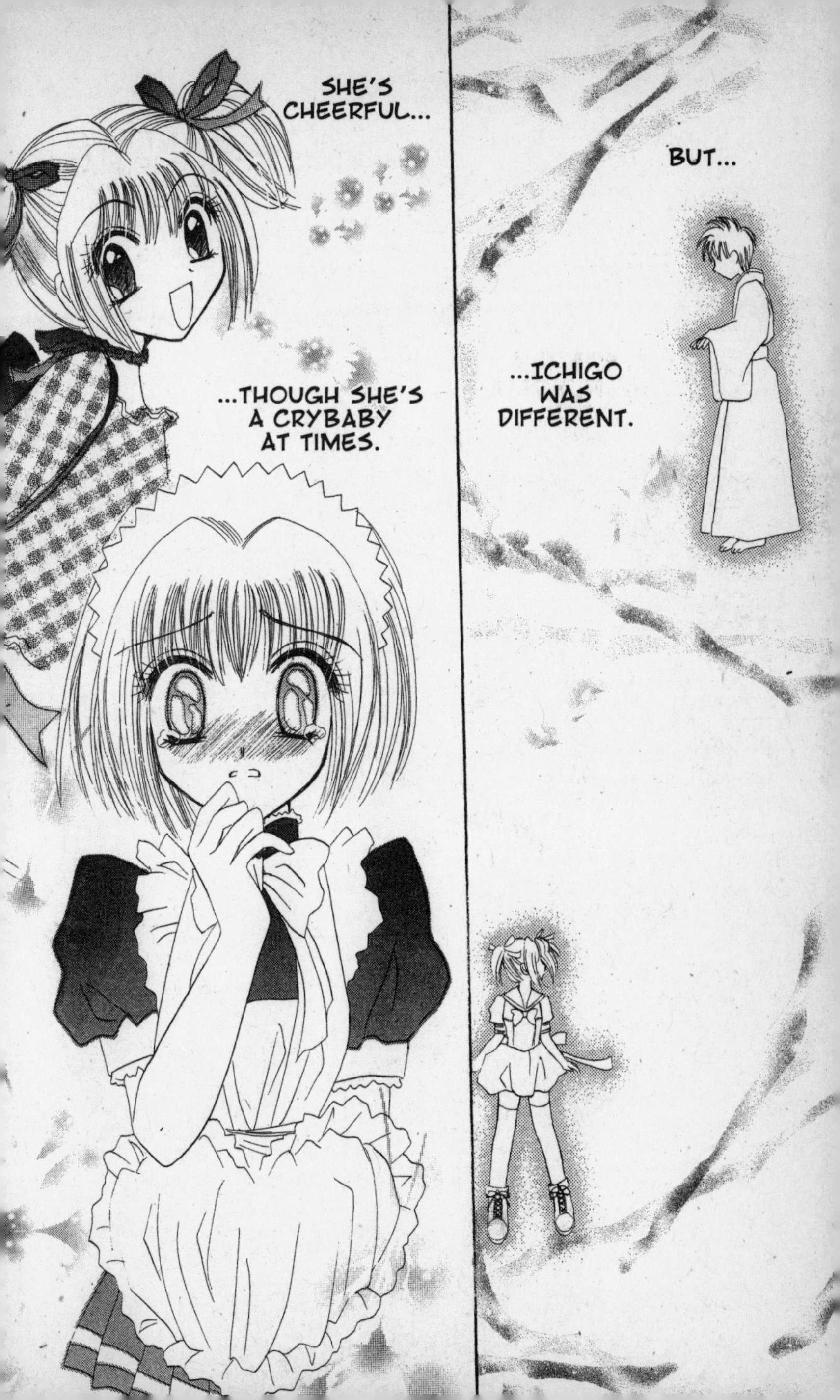
SHE'S CHEERFUL...
...THOUGH SHE'S A CRYBABY AT TIMES.
BUT...
...ICHIGO WAS DIFFERENT.

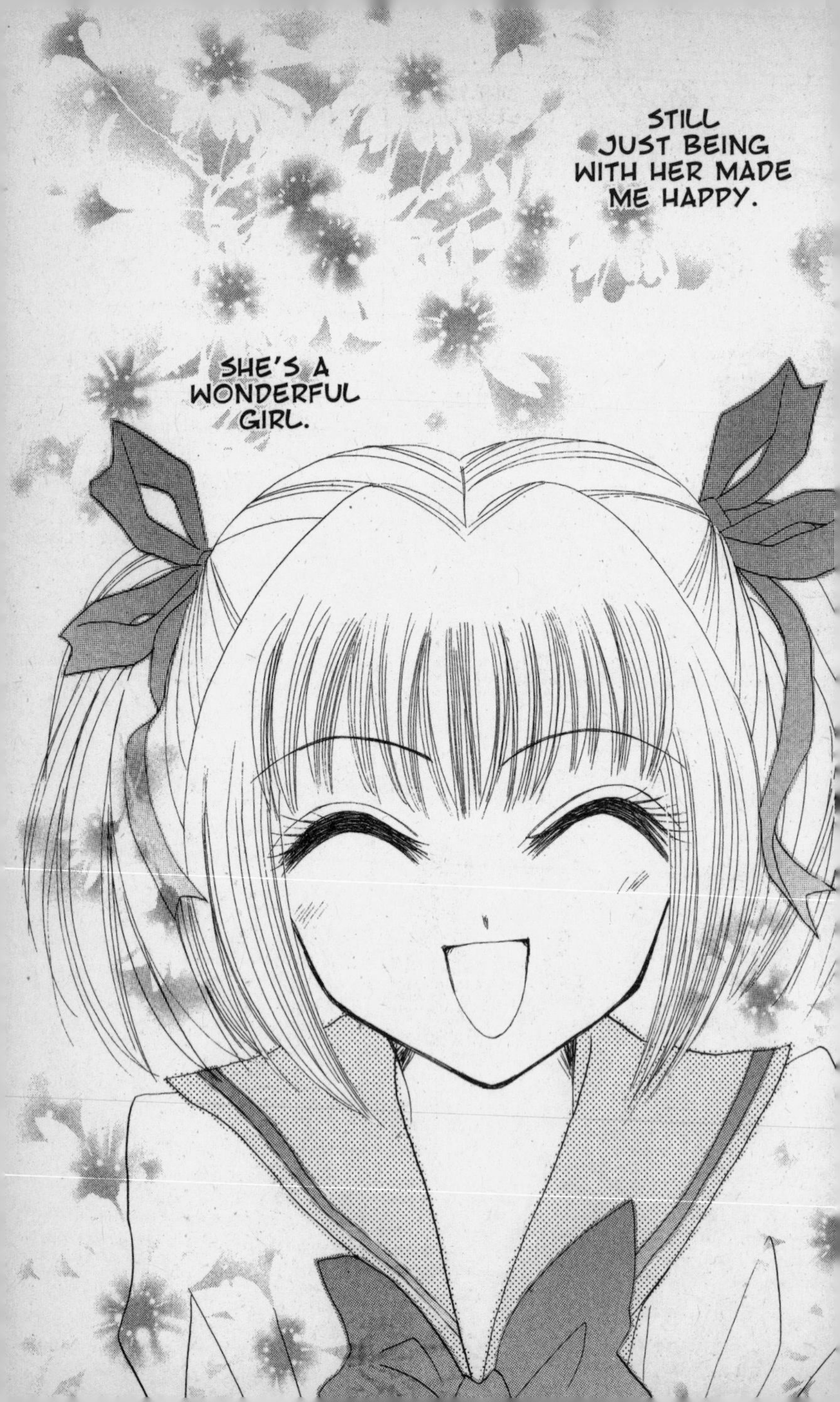
STILL JUST BEING WITH HER MADE ME HAPPY.
SHE'S A WONDERFUL GIRL.

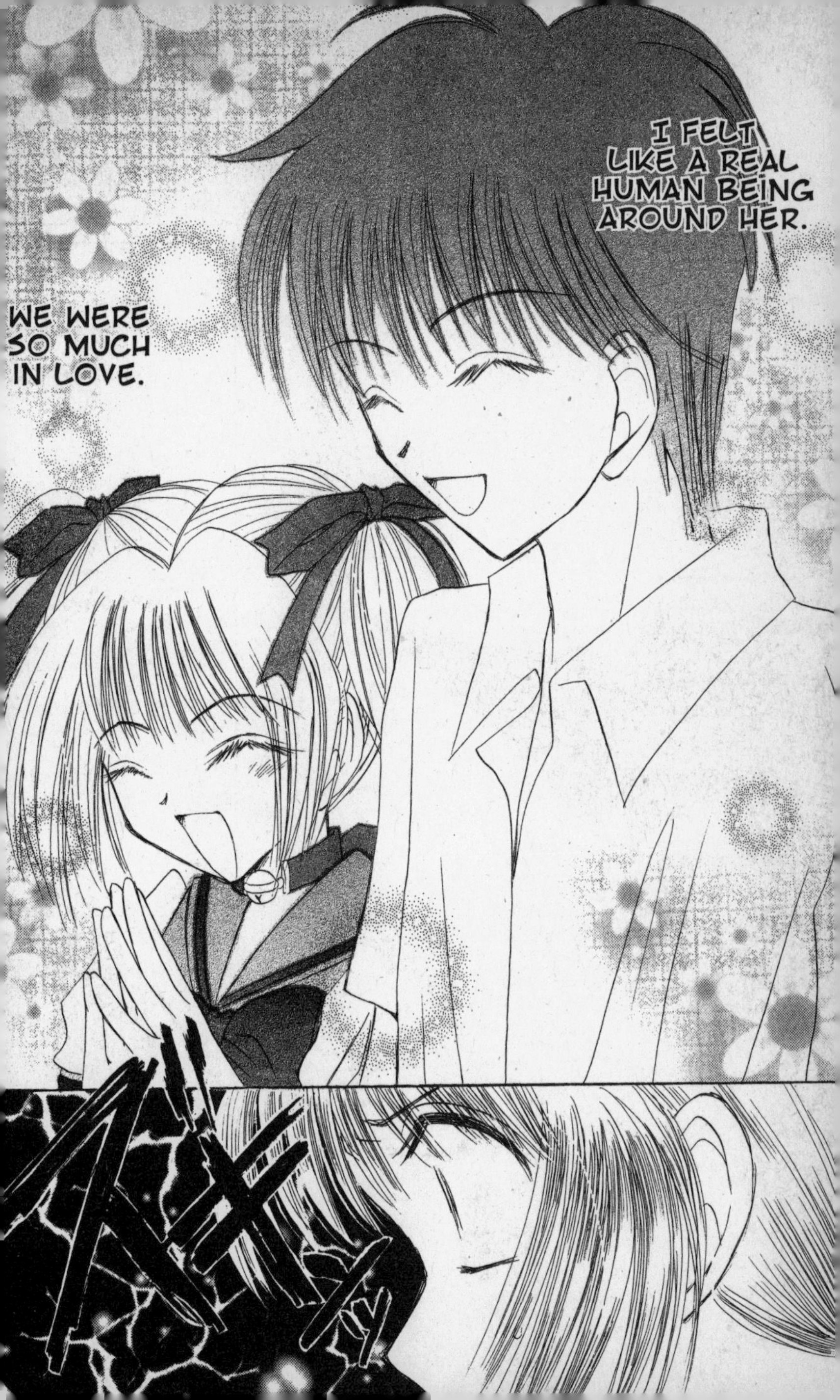
I FELT LIKE A REAL HUMAN BEING AROUND HER.
WE WERE SO MUCH IN LOVE.

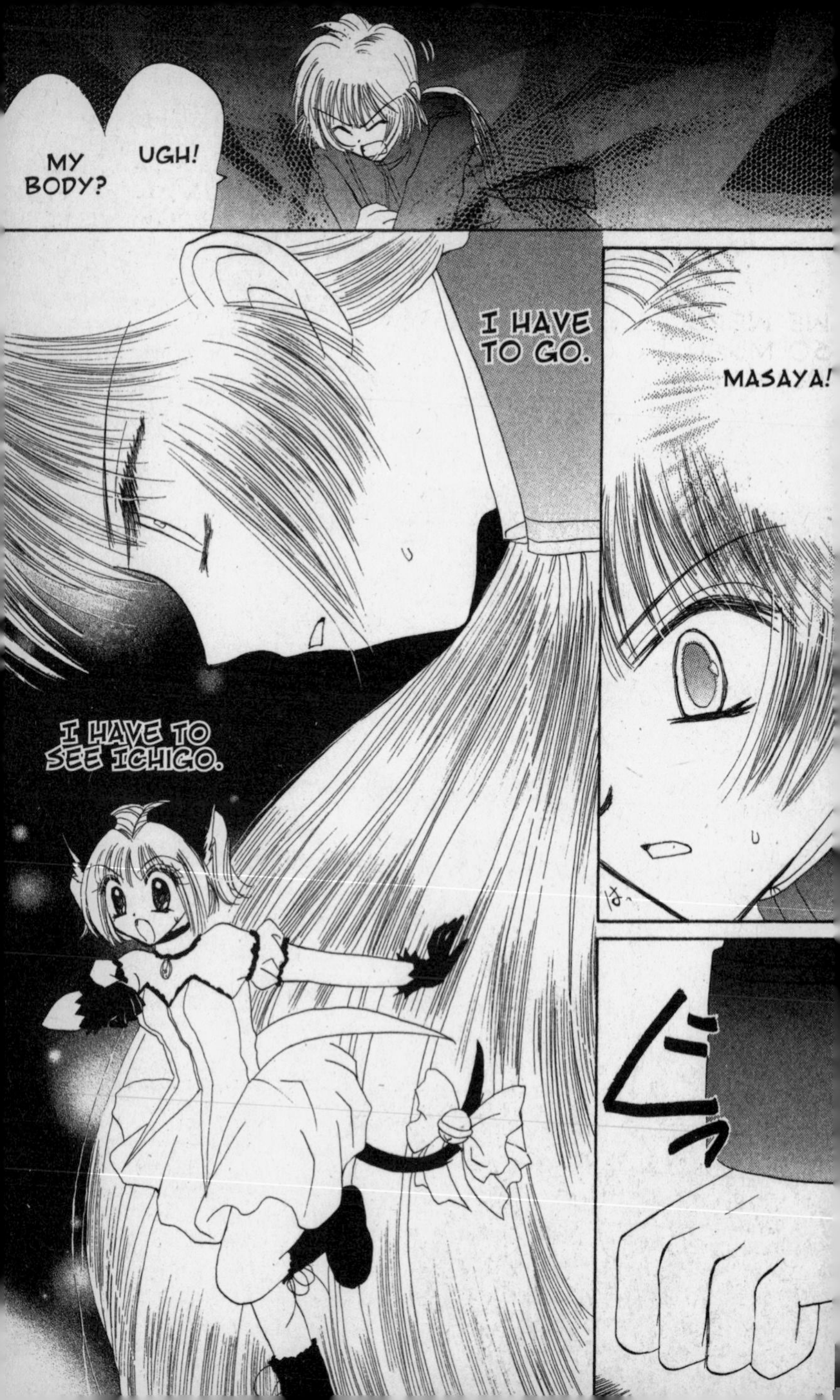
UGH!
MY BODY?
MASAYA!
は
ぐっ
I HAVE TO GO.
I HAVE TO SEE ICHIGO.

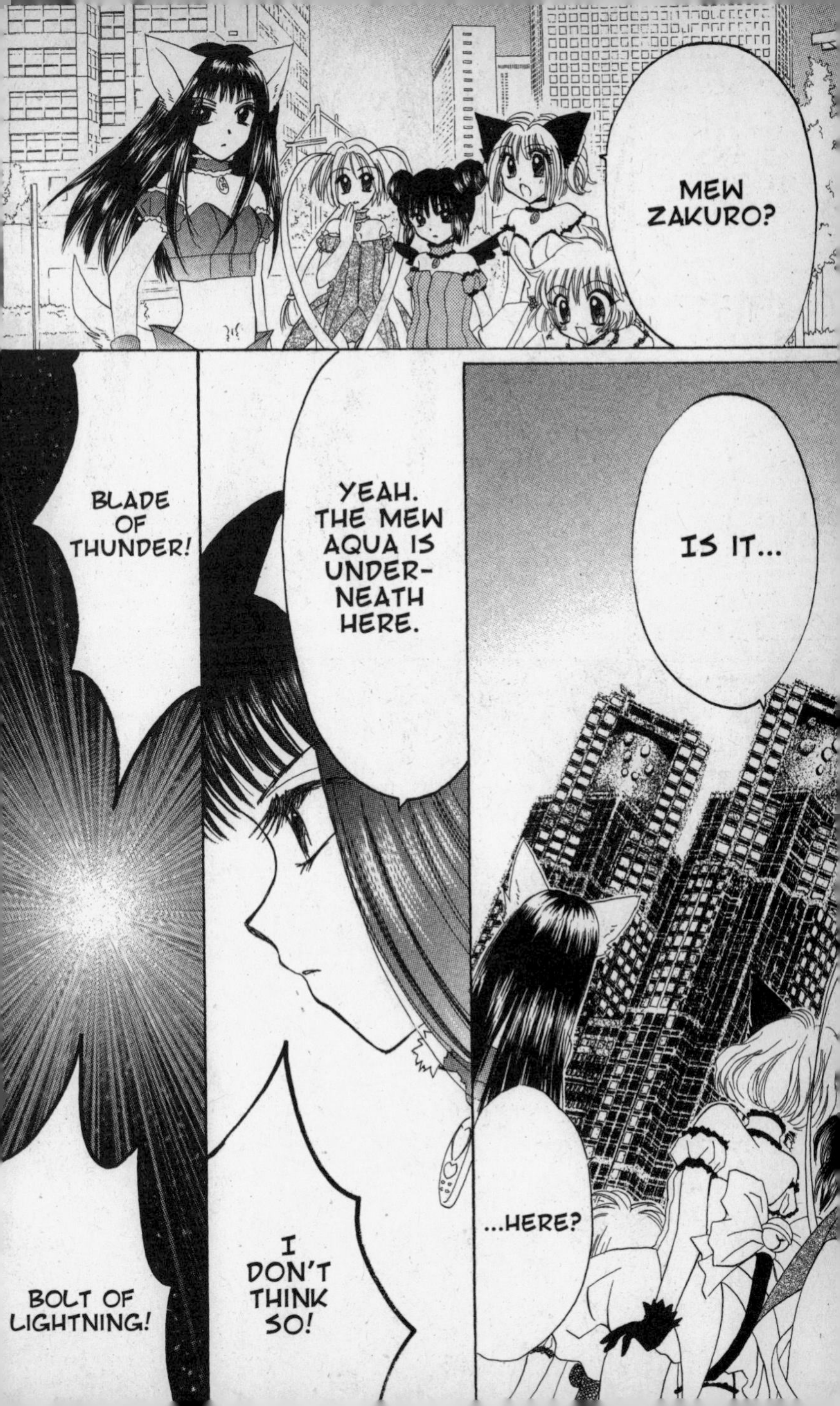
MEW ZAKURO?
IS IT...
...HERE?
YEAH. THE MEW AQUA IS UNDER-NEATH HERE.
I DON'T THINK SO!
BLADE OF THUNDER!
BOLT OF LIGHTNING!

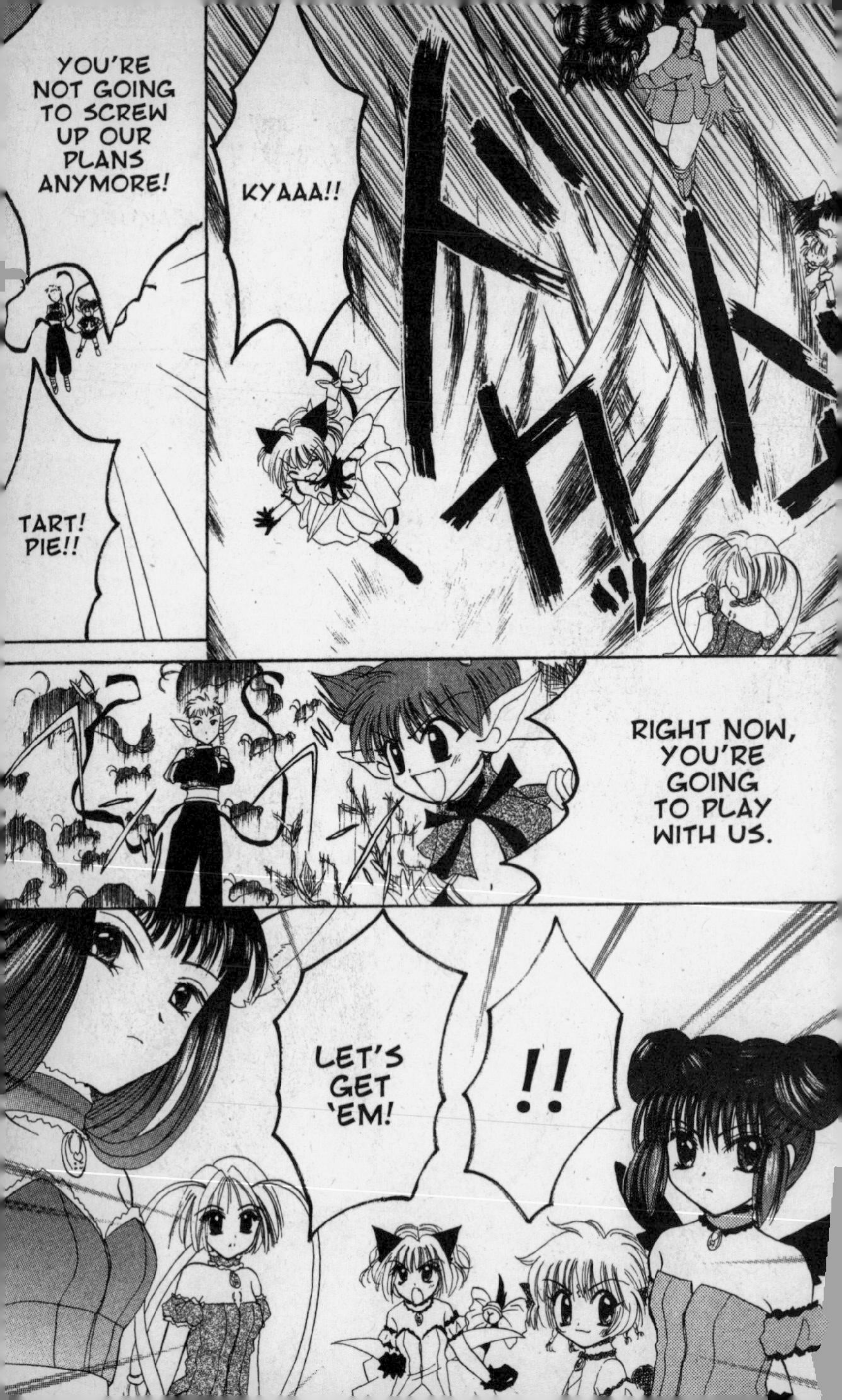
KYAAA!!
YOU'RE NOT GOING TO SCREW UP OUR PLANS ANYMORE!
TART! PIE!!
RIGHT NOW, YOU'RE GOING TO PLAY WITH US.
!!
LET'S GET 'EM!

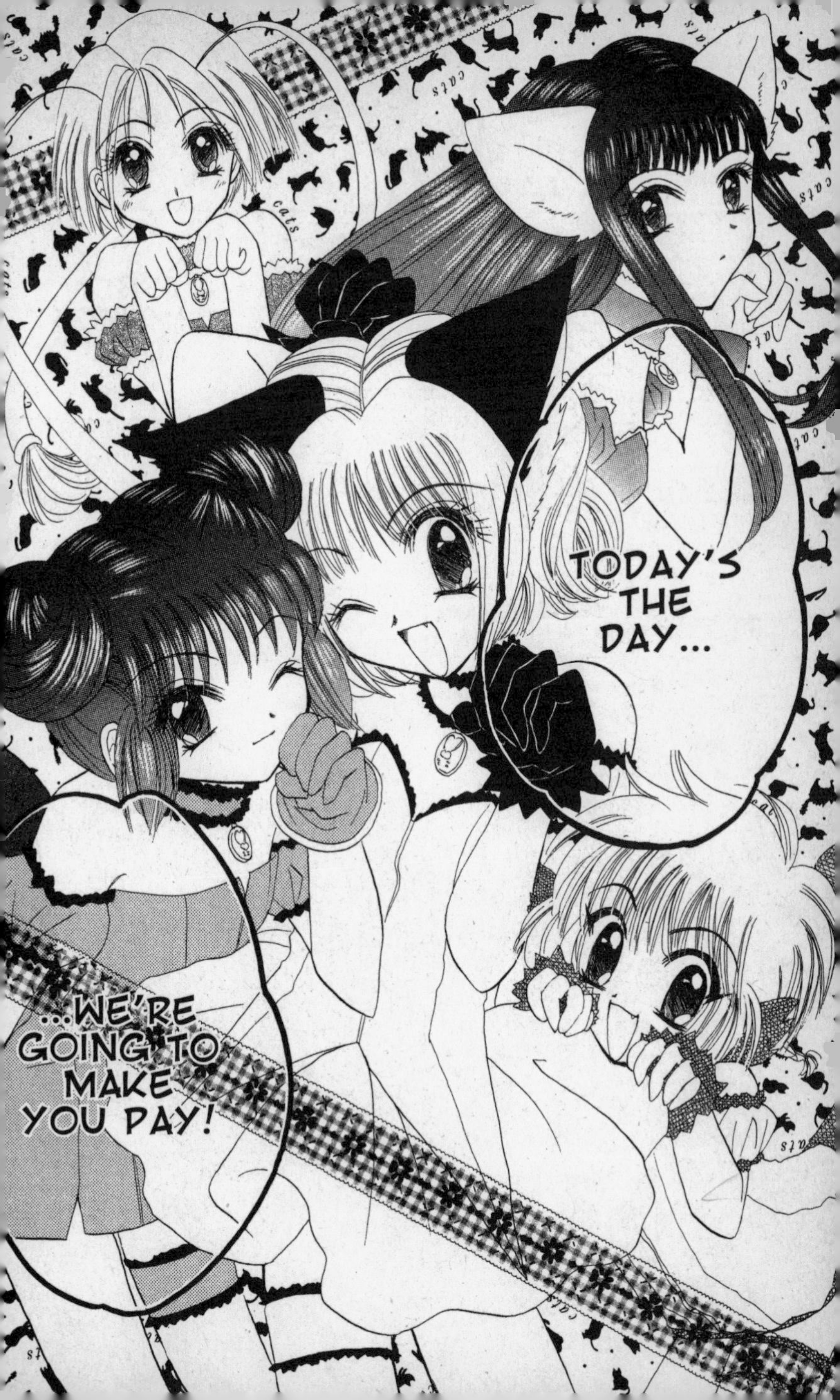
TODAY'S THE DAY...
...WE'RE GOING TO MAKE YOU PAY!

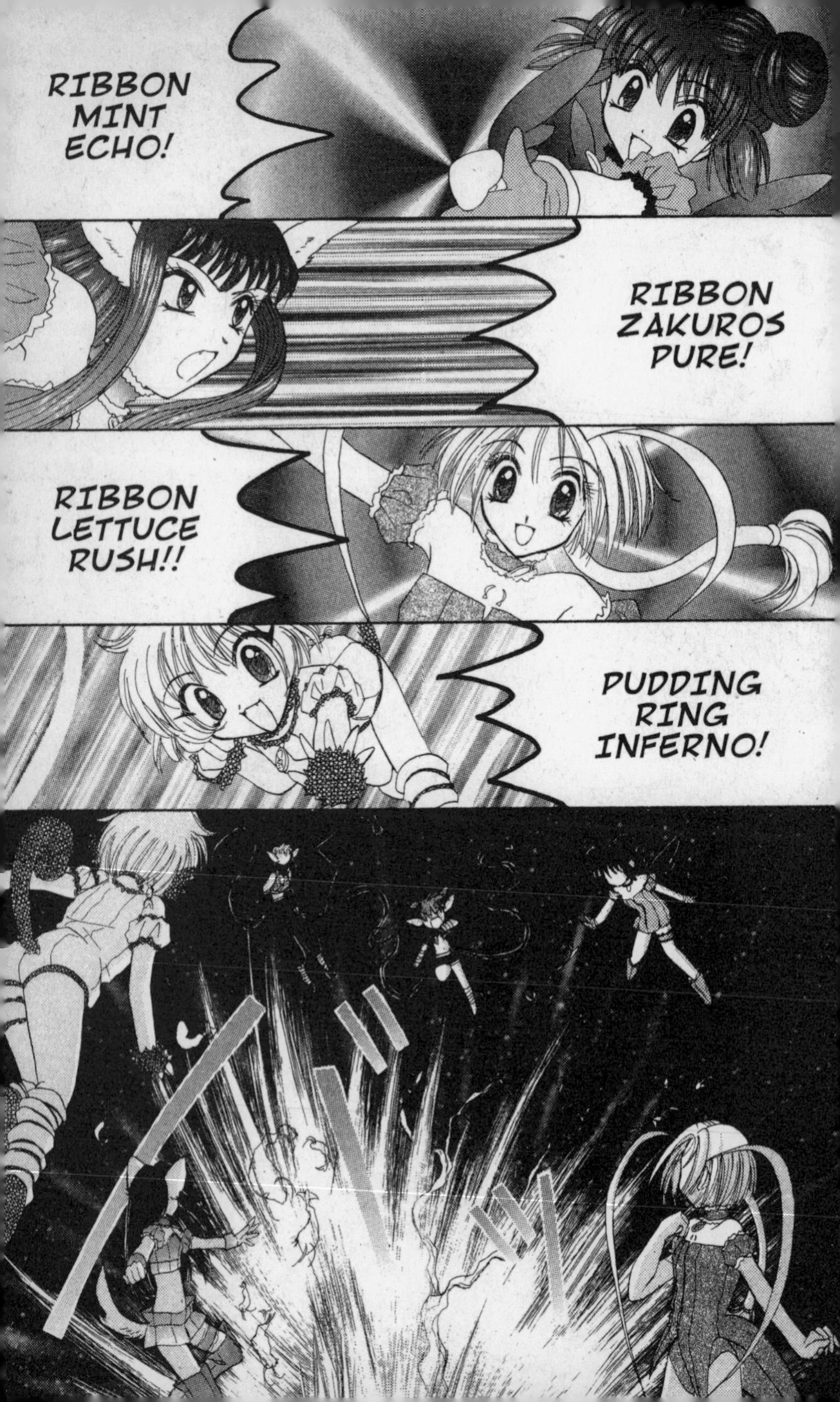
RIBBON MINT ECHO!
RIBBON ZAKUROS PURE!
RIBBON LETTUCE RUSH!!
PUDDING RING INFERNO!

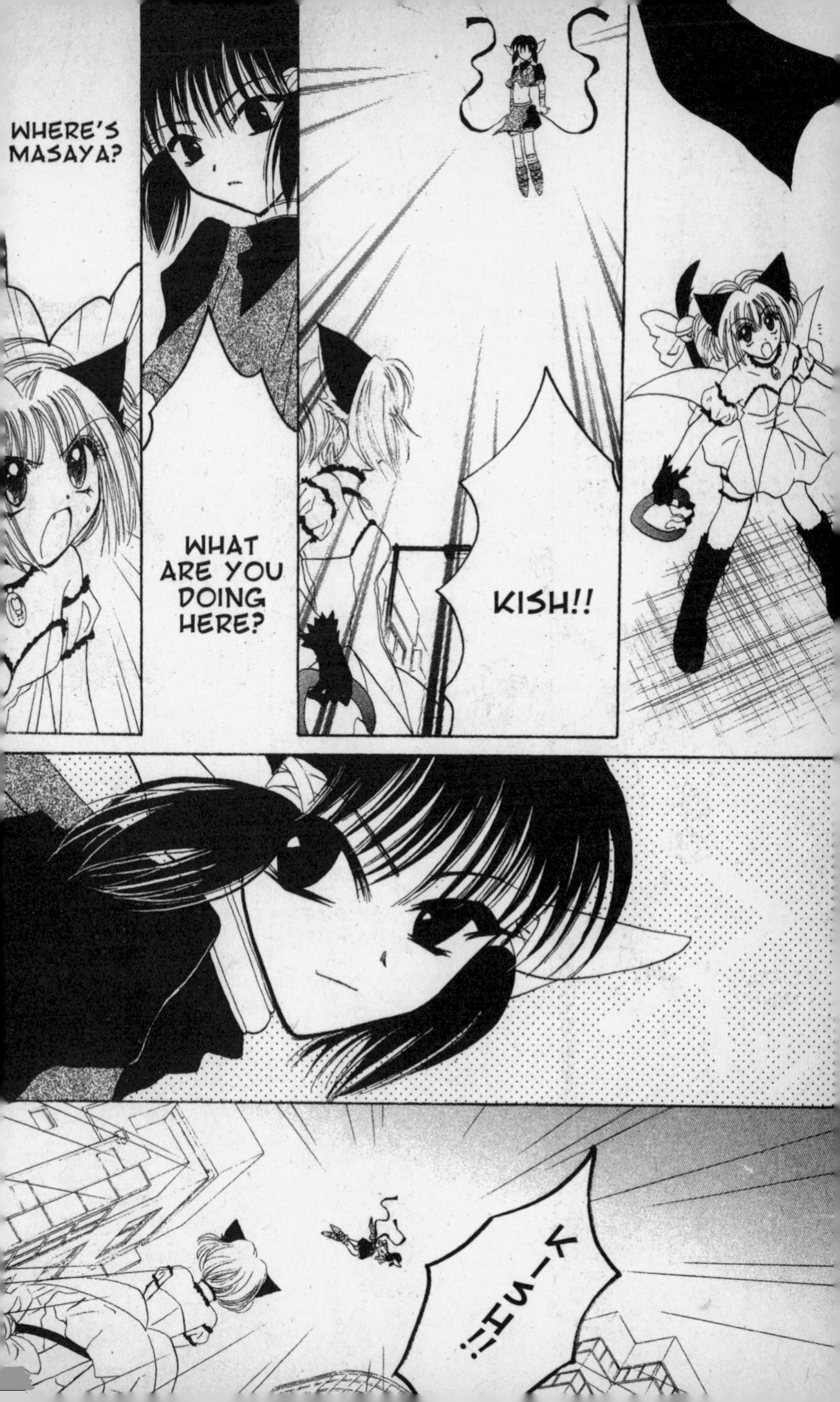
KISH!!
WHAT ARE YOU DOING HERE?
WHERE'S MASAYA?

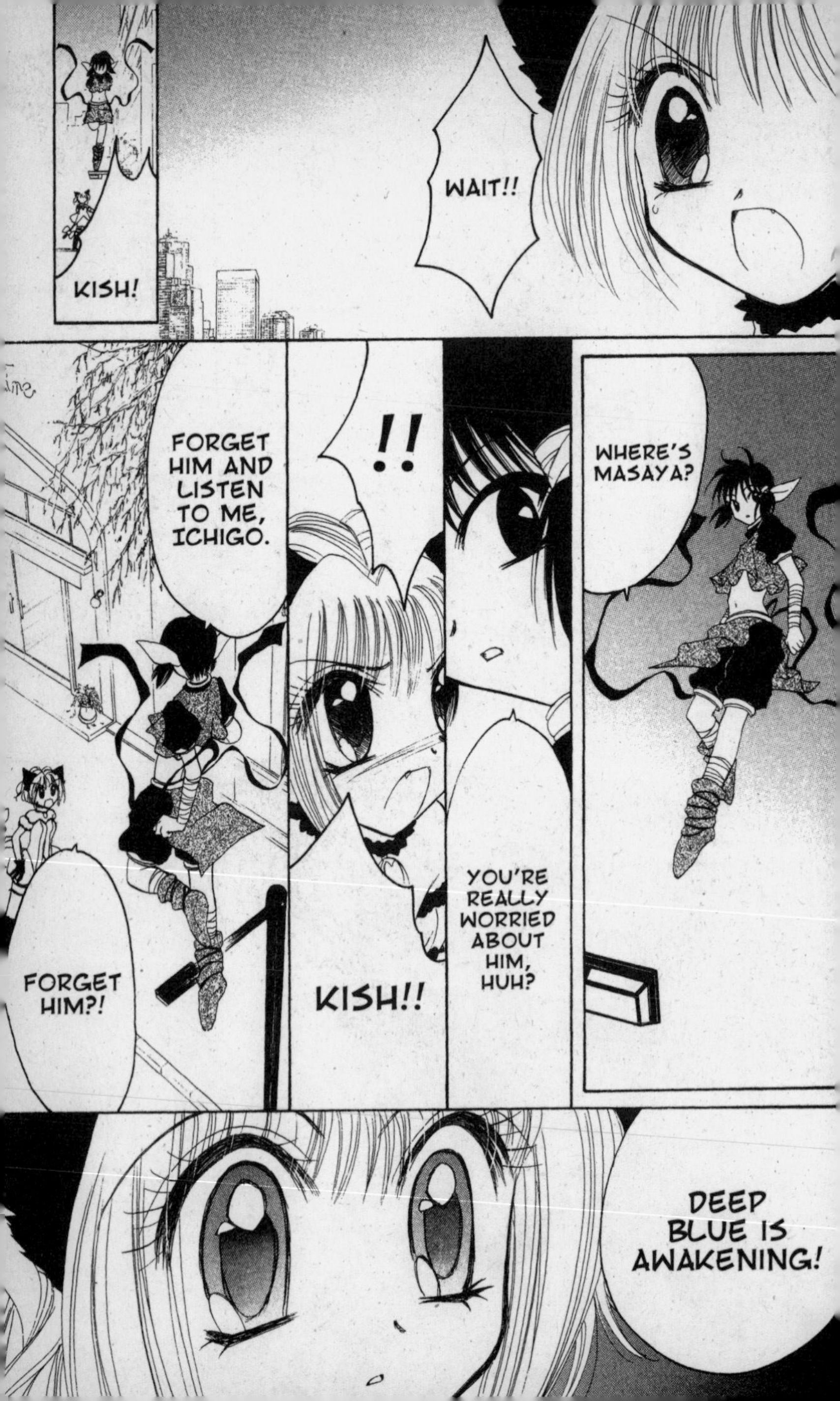
WAIT!!
KISH!
WHERE'S MASAYA?
YOU'RE REALLY WORRIED ABOUT HIM, HUH?
!!
KISH!!
FORGET HIM AND LISTEN TO ME, ICHIGO.
FORGET HIM?!
DEEP BLUE IS AWAKENING!

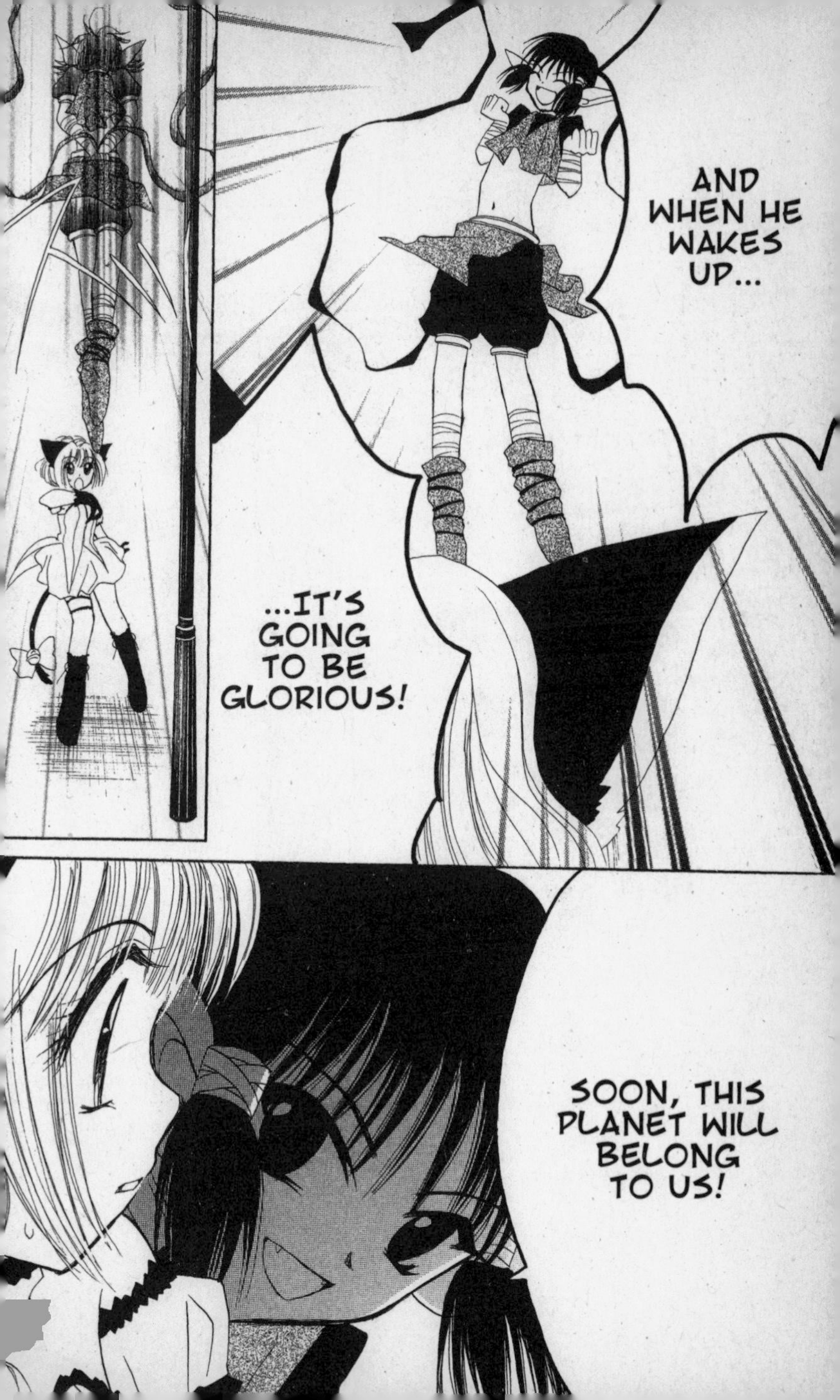
AND WHEN HE WAKES UP...
...IT'S GOING TO BE GLORIOUS!
SOON, THIS PLANET WILL BELONG TO US!

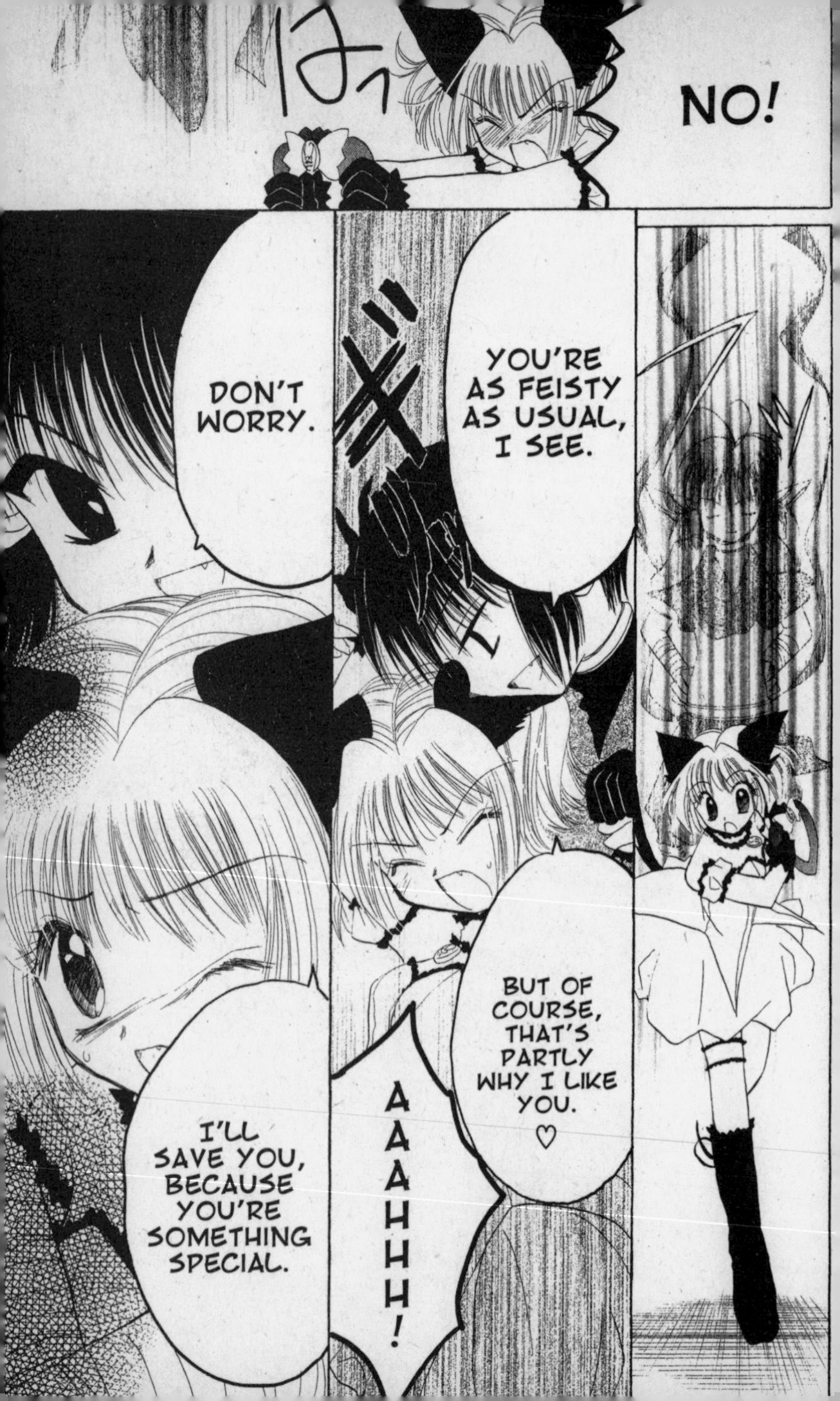
はっ
NO!
YOU'RE AS FEISTY AS USUAL, I SEE.
BUT OF COURSE, THAT'S PARTLY WHY I LIKE YOU. ♡
AAAHHH!
DON'T WORRY.
I'LL SAVE YOU, BECAUSE YOU'RE SOMETHING SPECIAL.

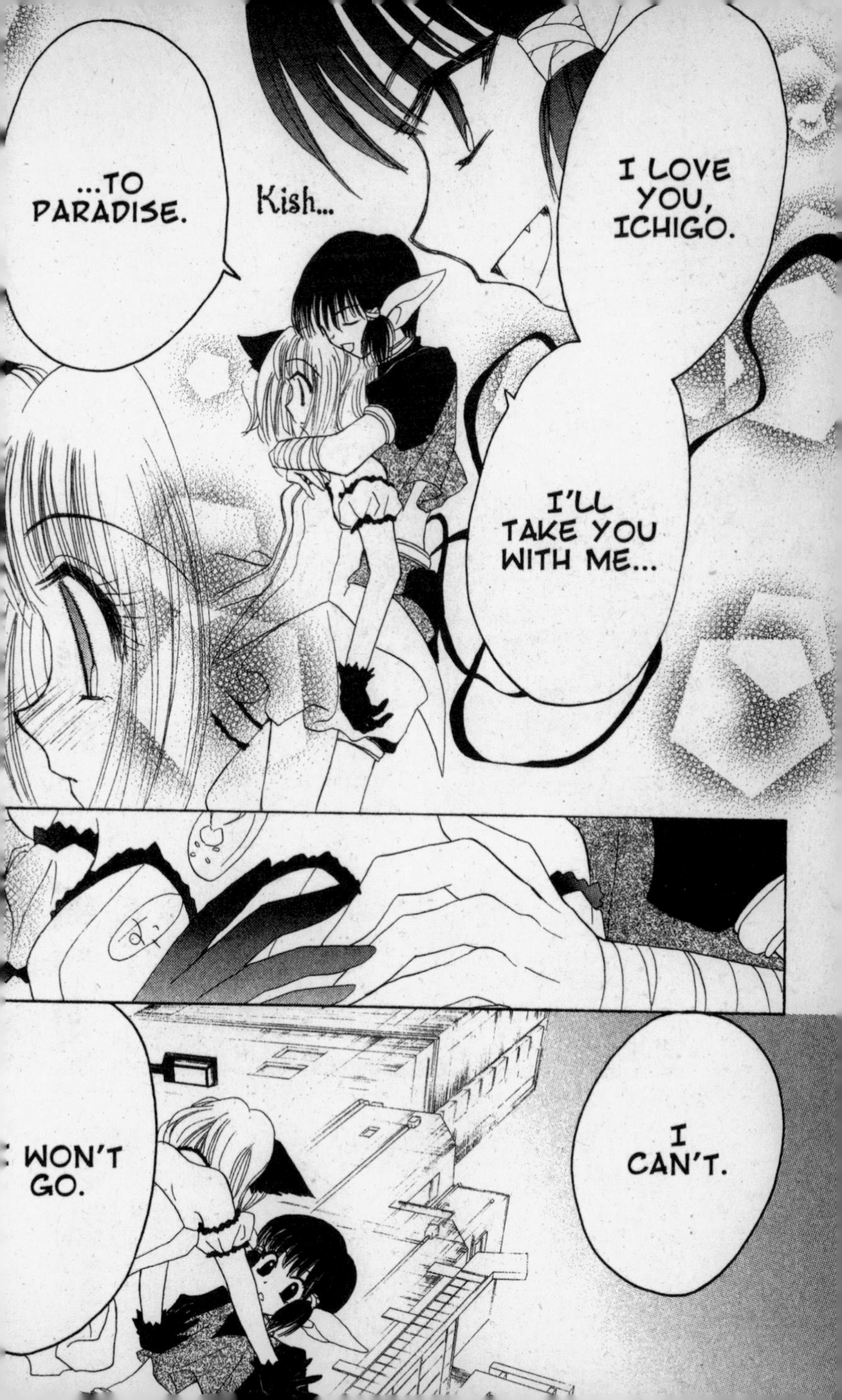
I LOVE YOU, ICHIGO.
I'LL TAKE YOU WITH ME...
...TO PARADISE.
Kish...
I CAN'T.
WON'T GO.

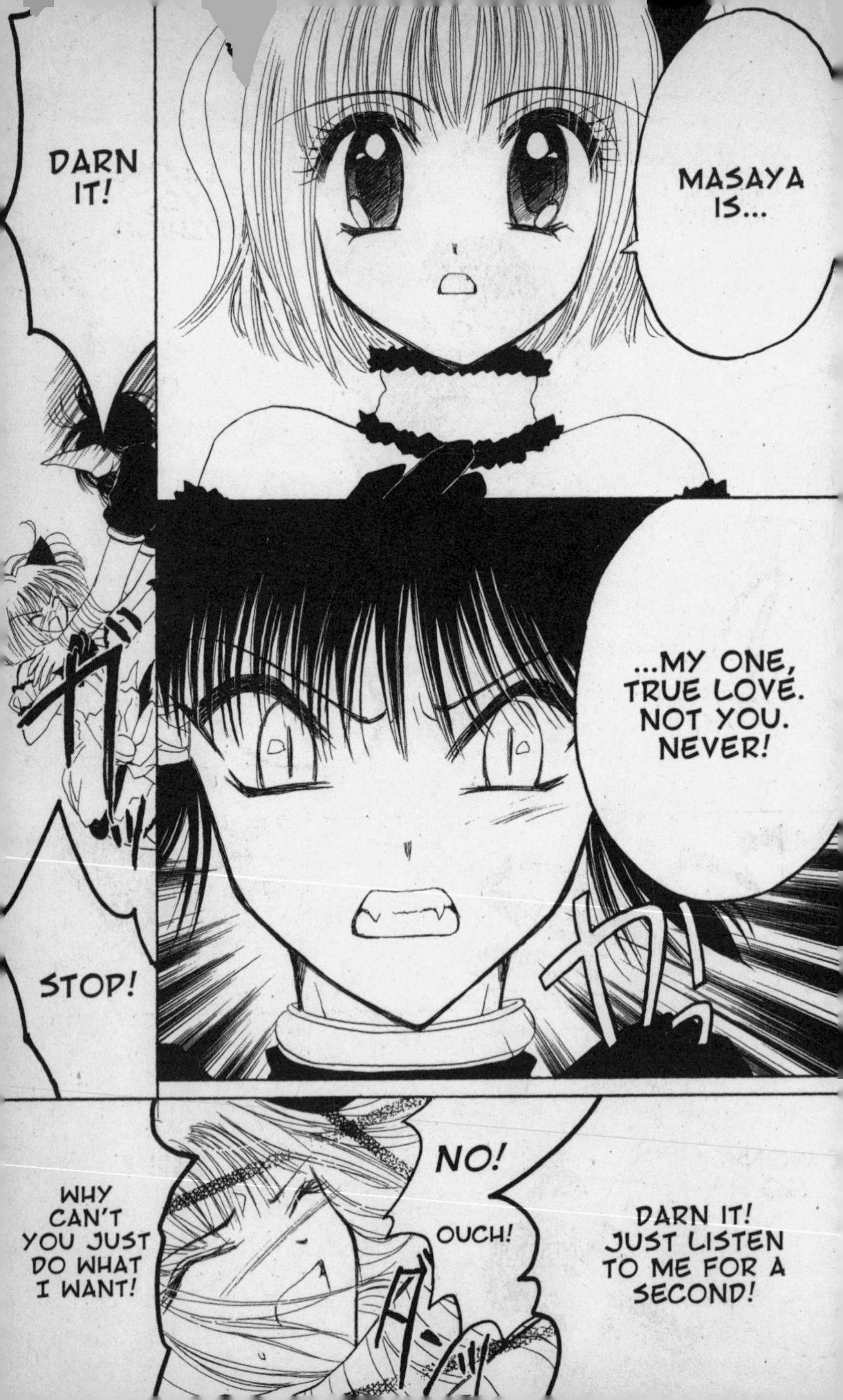
MASAYA IS...
...MY ONE, TRUE LOVE. NOT YOU. NEVER!
DARN IT!
STOP!
DARN IT! JUST LISTEN TO ME FOR A SECOND!
NO!
OUCH!
WHY CAN'T YOU JUST DO WHAT I WANT!

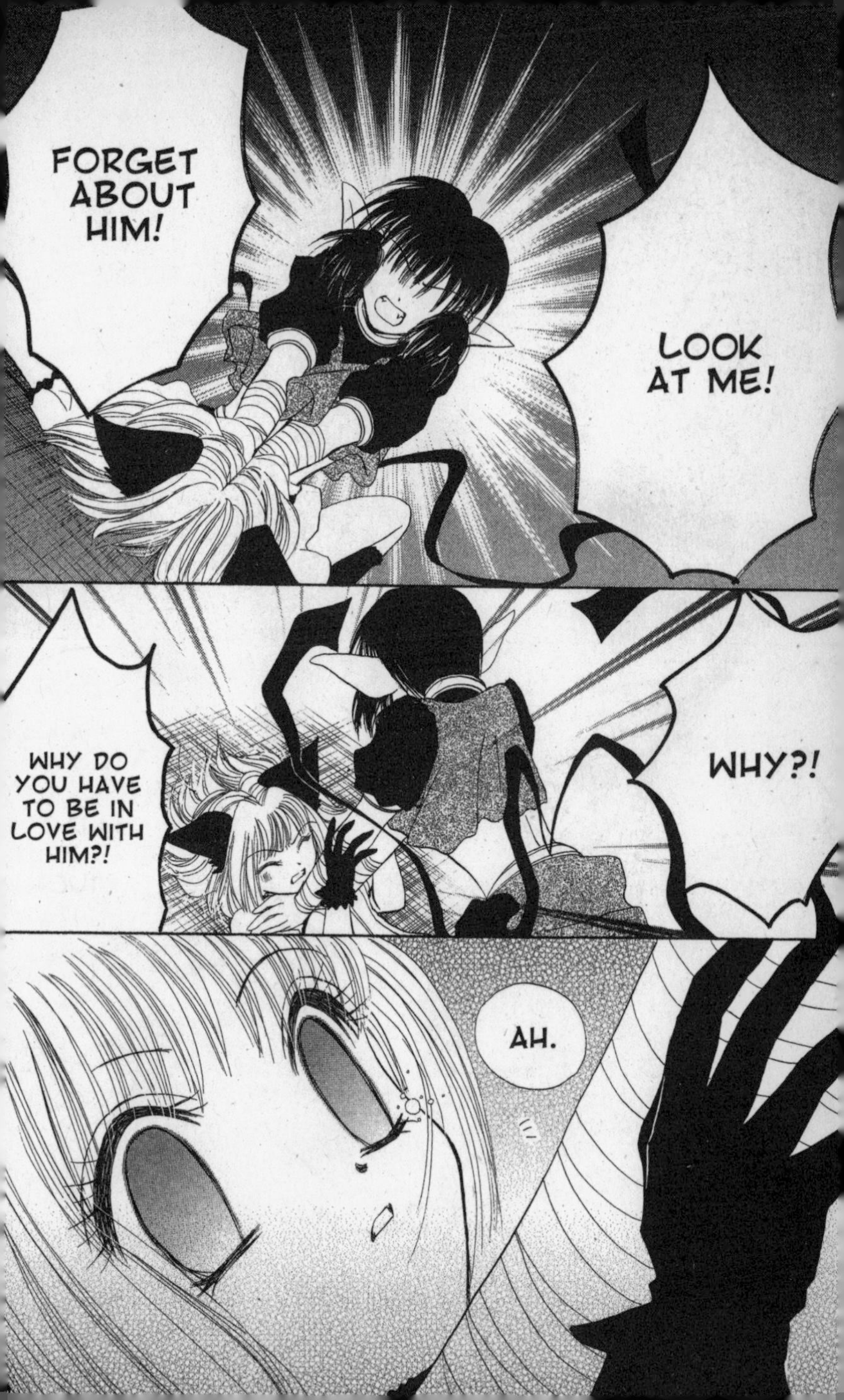
LOOK AT ME!
FORGET ABOUT HIM!
WHY?!
WHY DO YOU HAVE TO BE IN LOVE WITH HIM?!
AH.

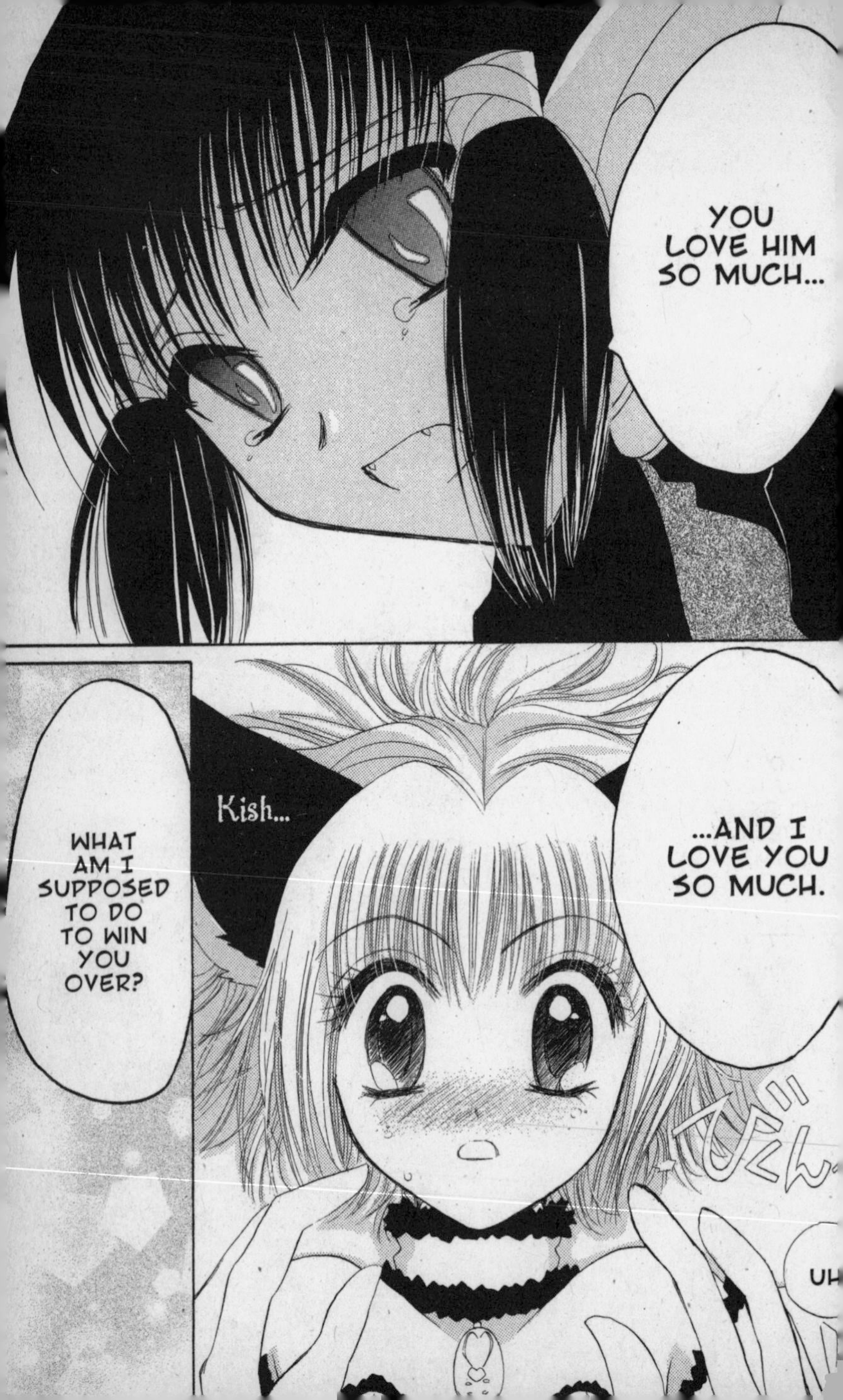
YOU LOVE HIM SO MUCH...
...AND I LOVE YOU SO MUCH.
Kish...
WHAT AM I SUPPOSED TO DO TO WIN YOU OVER?
UH

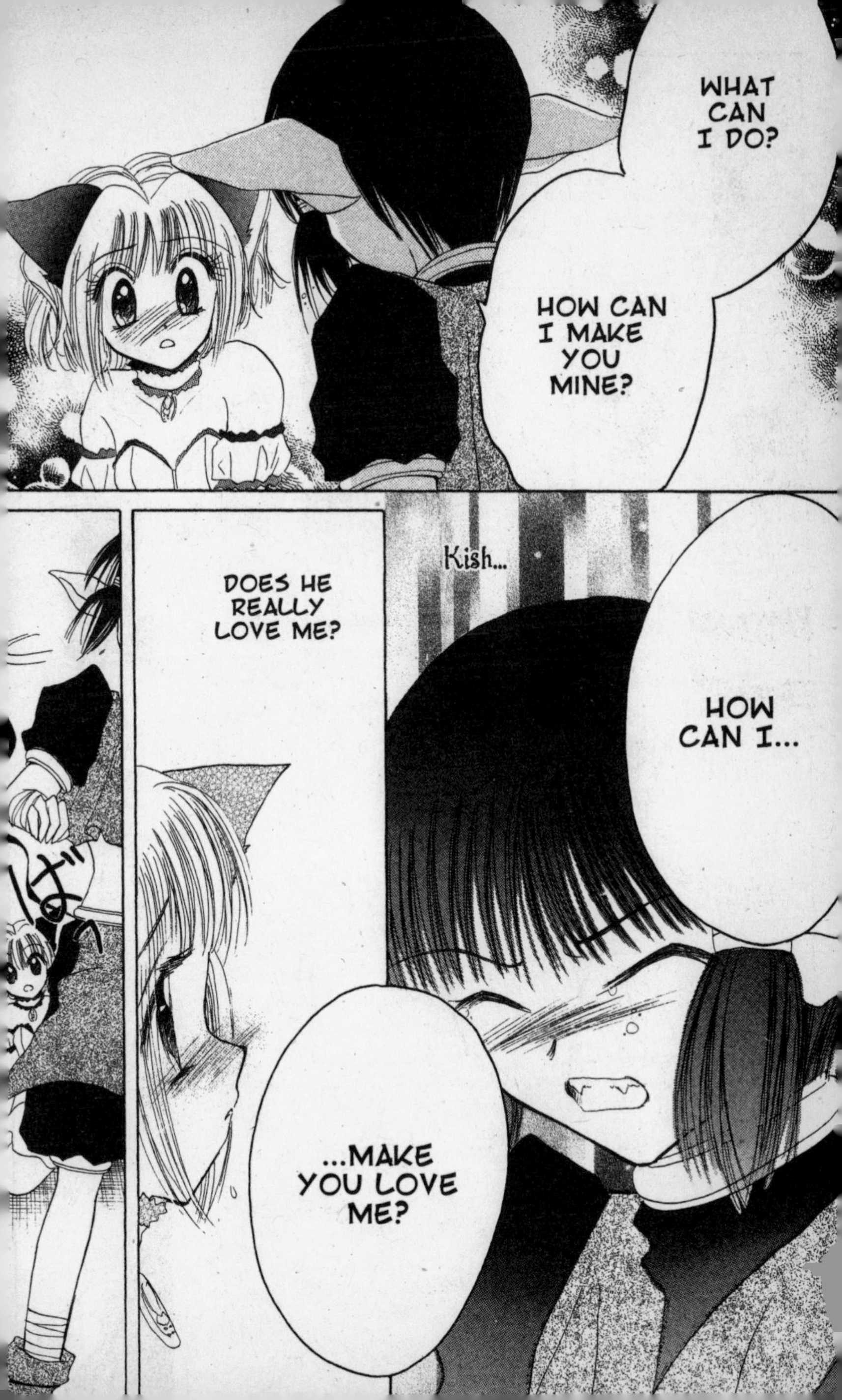
WHAT CAN I DO?
HOW CAN I MAKE YOU MINE?
Kish...
HOW CAN I...
...MAKE YOU LOVE ME?
DOES HE REALLY LOVE ME?
ば

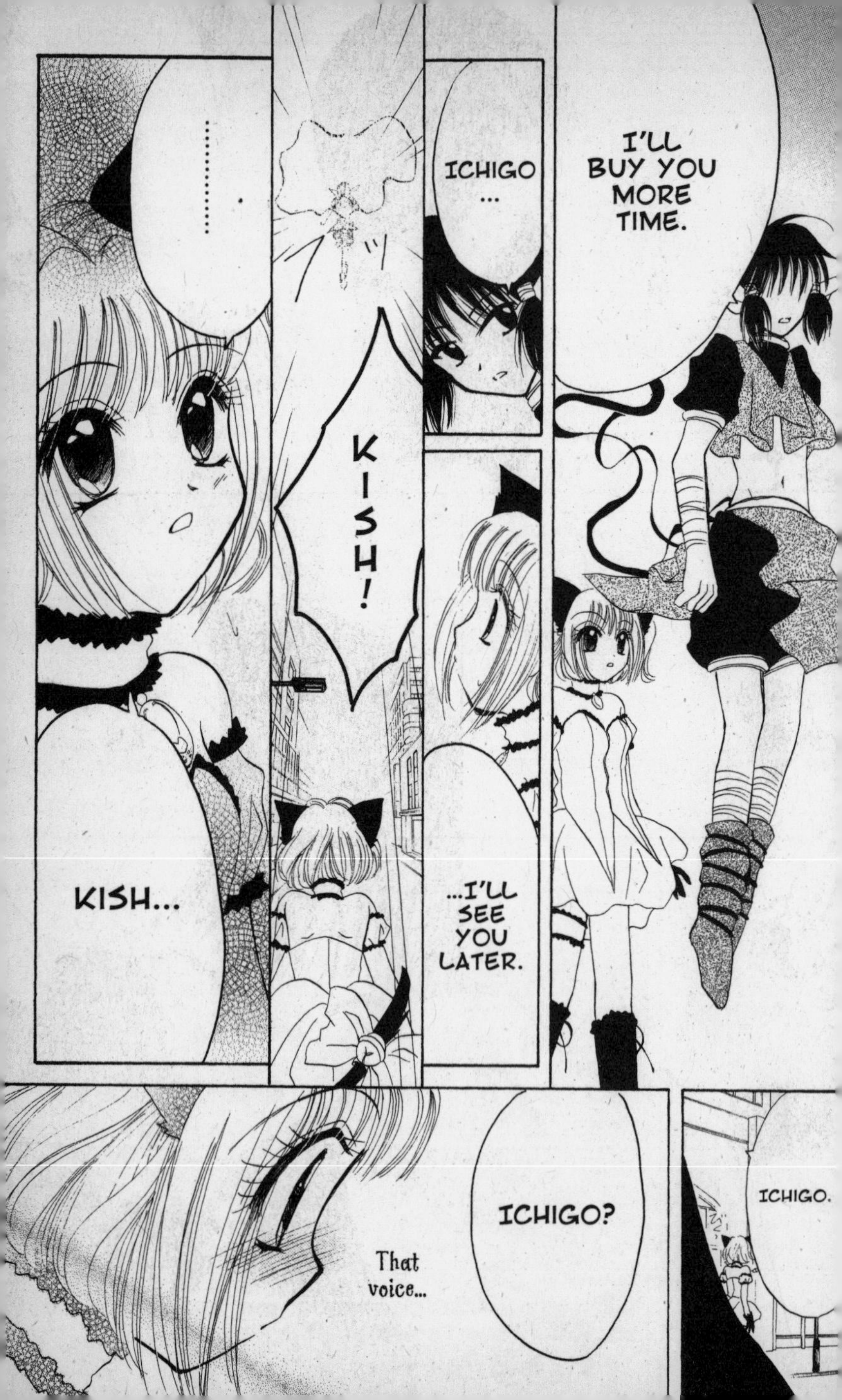
I'LL BUY YOU MORE TIME.
ICHIGO ...
...I'LL SEE YOU LATER.
KISH!
....
KISH...
ICHIGO.
ICHIGO?
That voice...

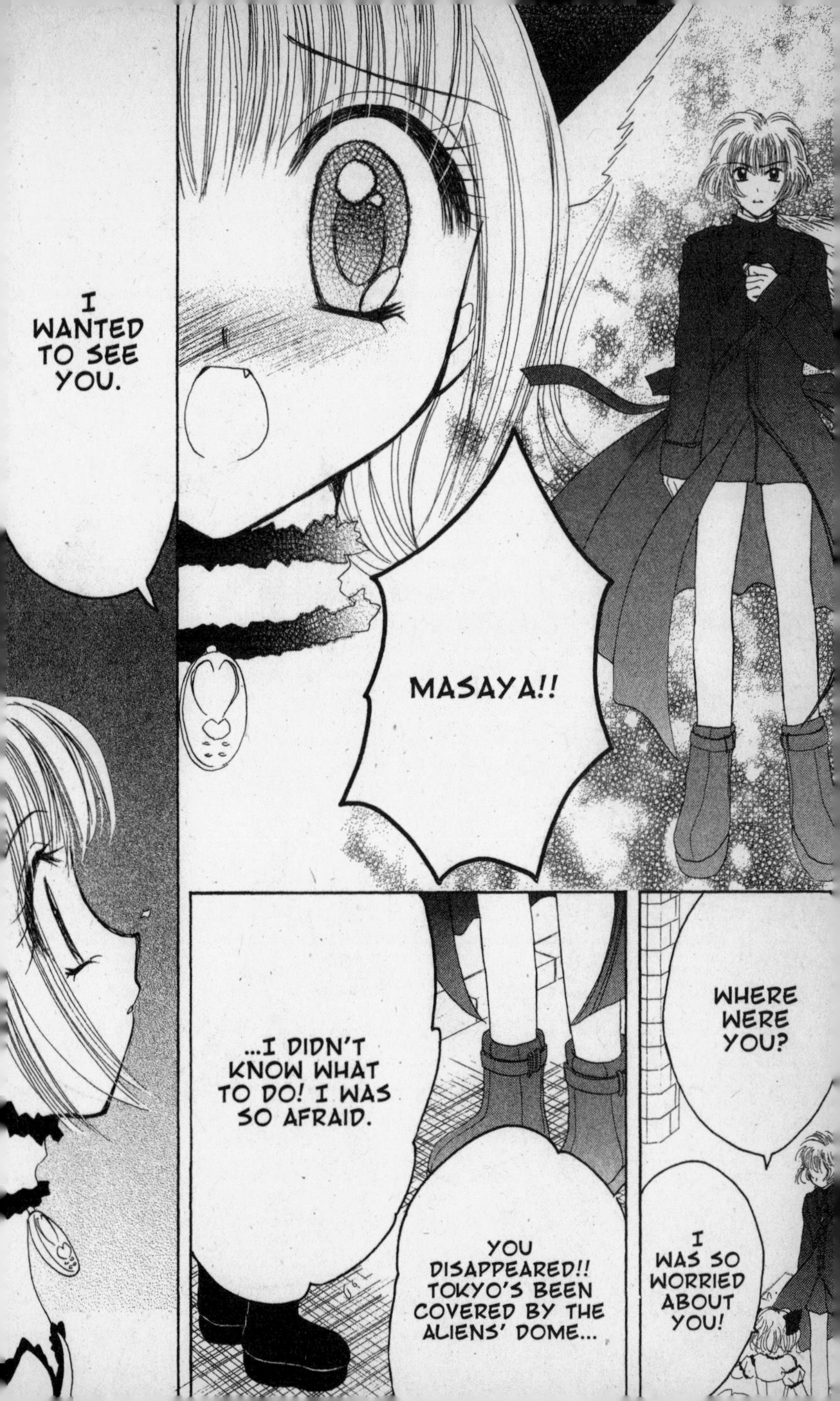
MASAYA!!
WHERE WERE YOU?
I WAS SO WORRIED ABOUT YOU!
YOU DISAPPEARED!! TOKYO'S BEEN COVERED BY THE ALIENS' DOME...
...I DIDN'T KNOW WHAT TO DO! I WAS SO AFRAID.
I WANTED TO SEE YOU.

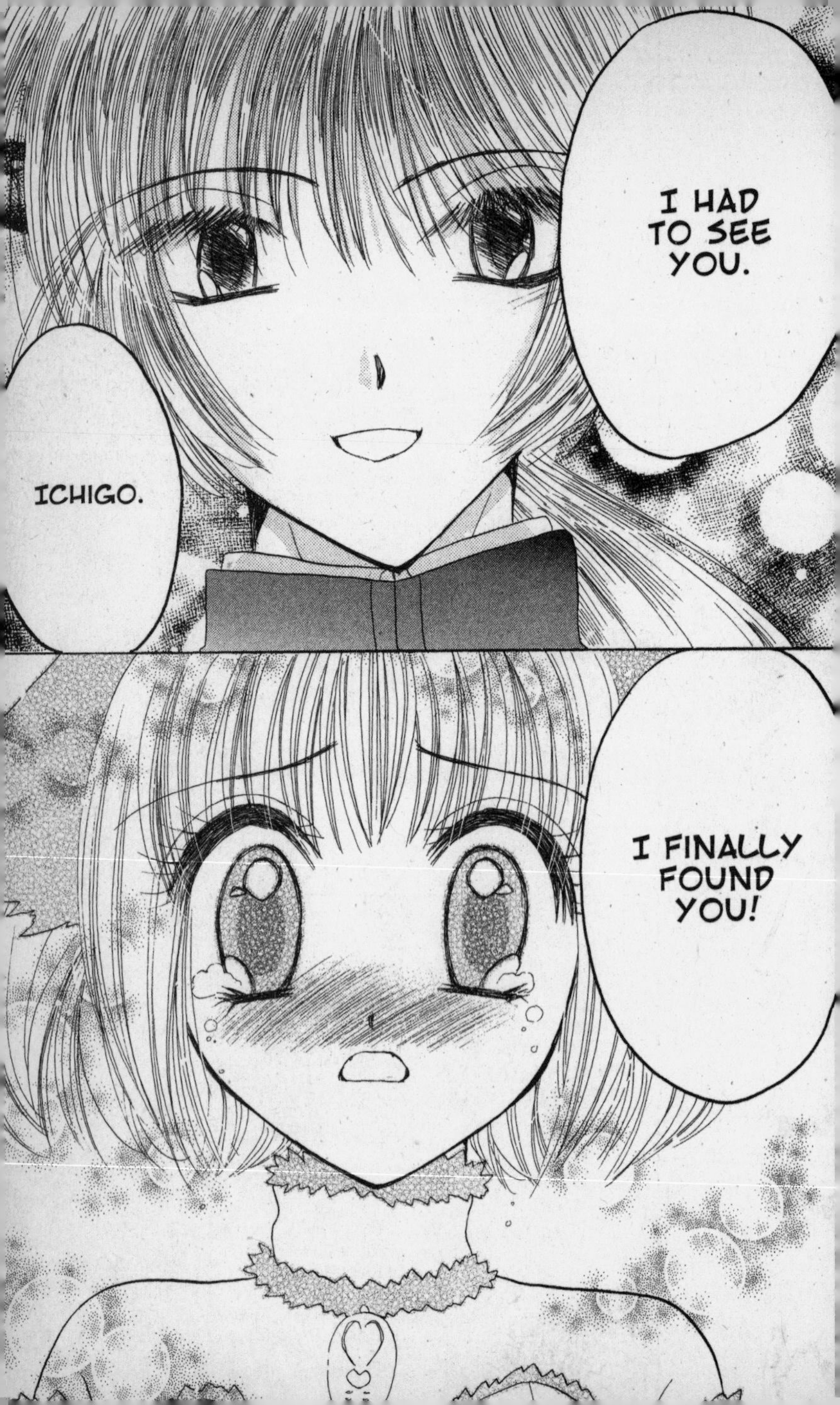
I HAD TO SEE YOU.
ICHIGO.
I FINALLY FOUND YOU!

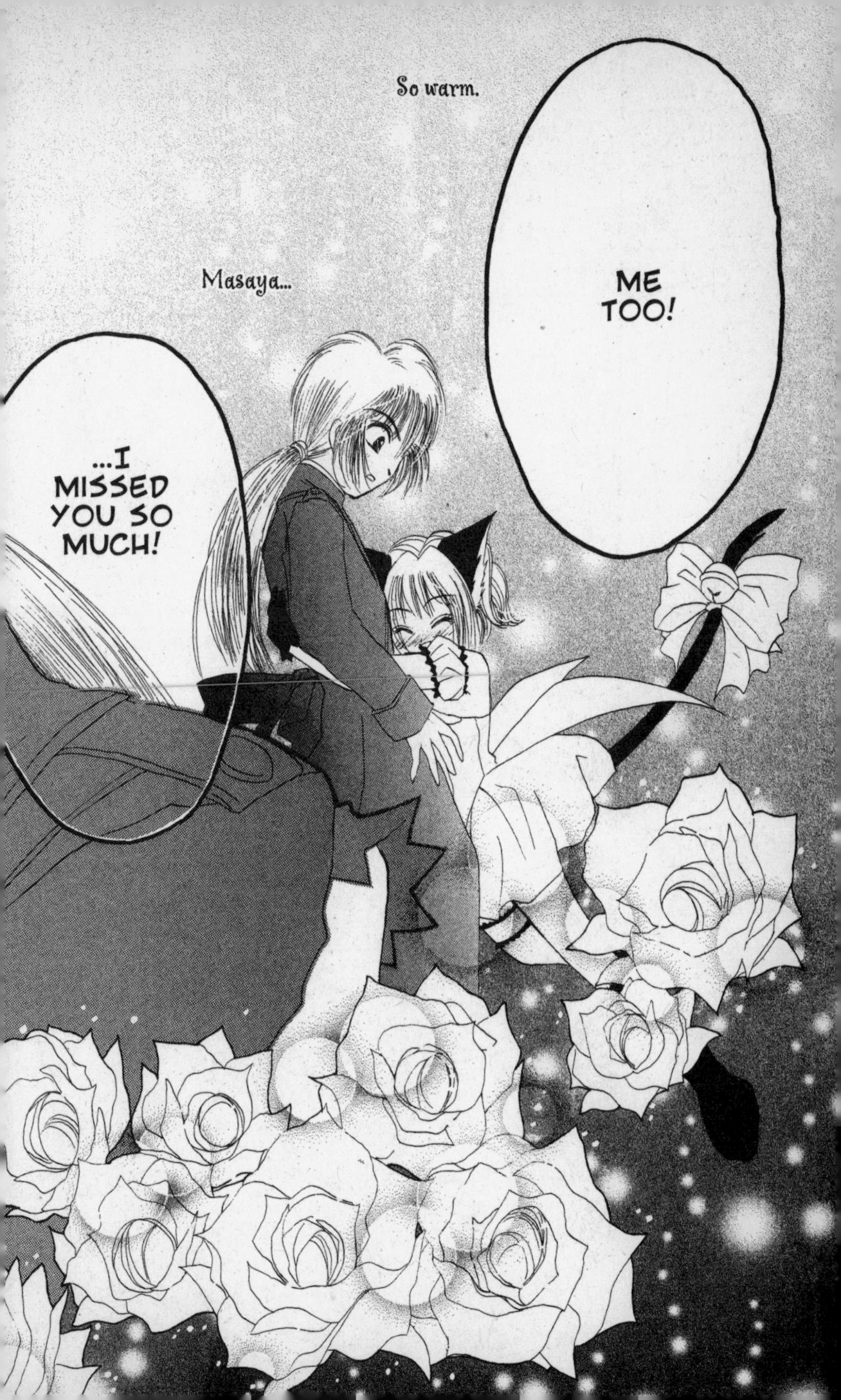
So warm.
ME TOO!
Masaya...
...I MISSED YOU SO MUCH!

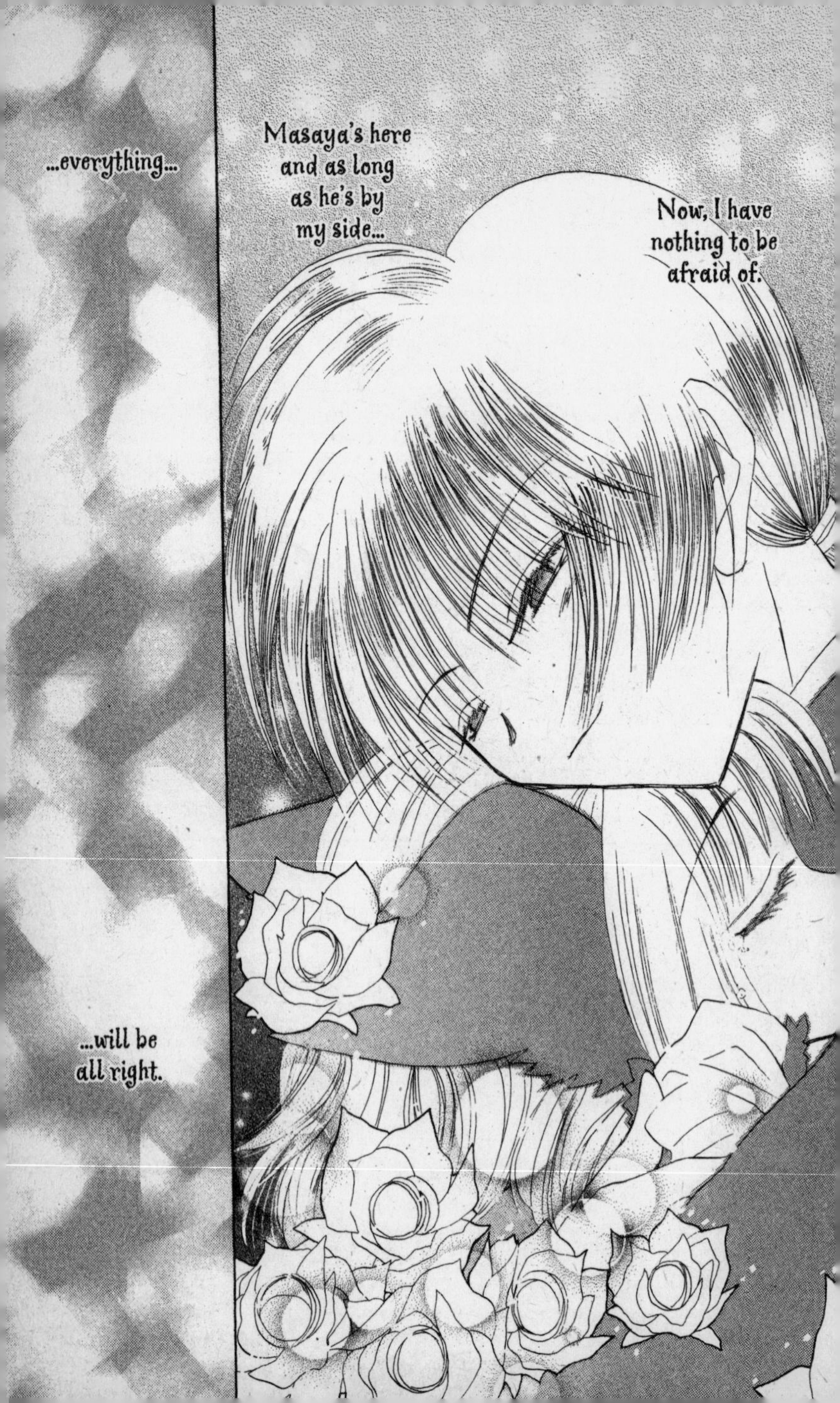
Now, I have nothing to be afraid of.
Masaya's here and as long as he's by my side...
...everything...
...will be all right.

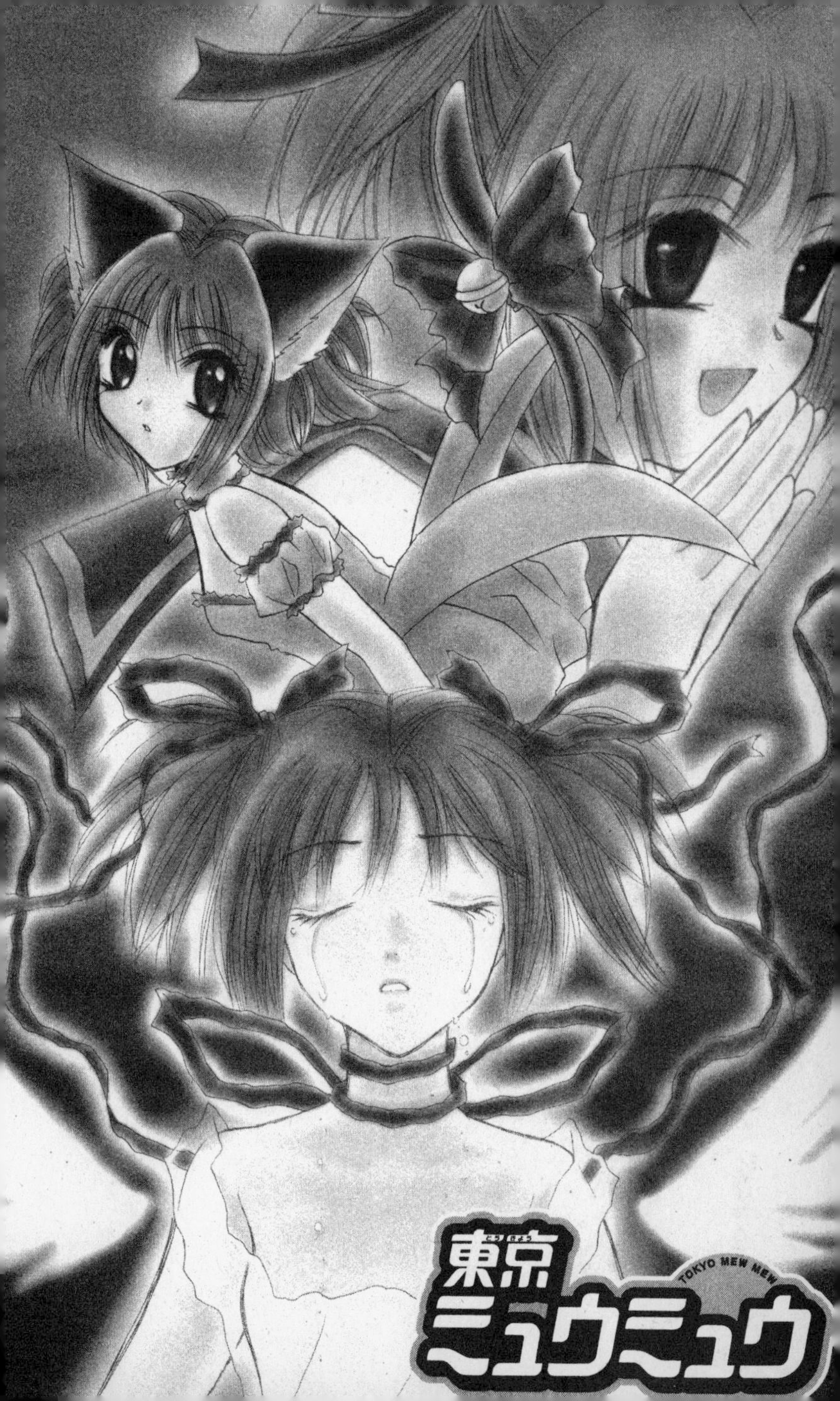
東京
TOKYO MEW MEW
ミュウミュウ

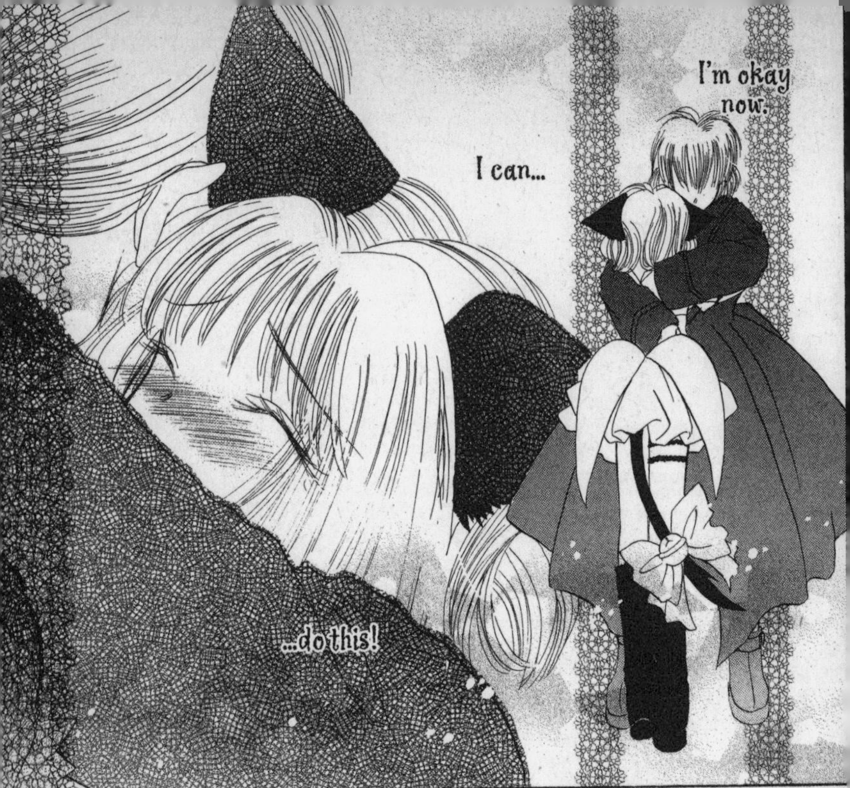
I'm okay now.
I can...
...do this!

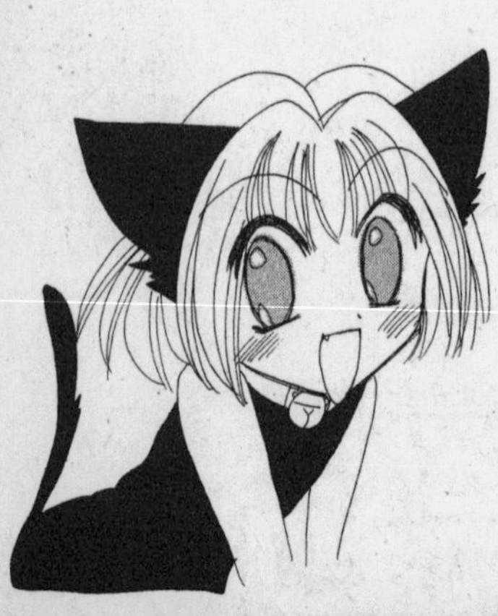

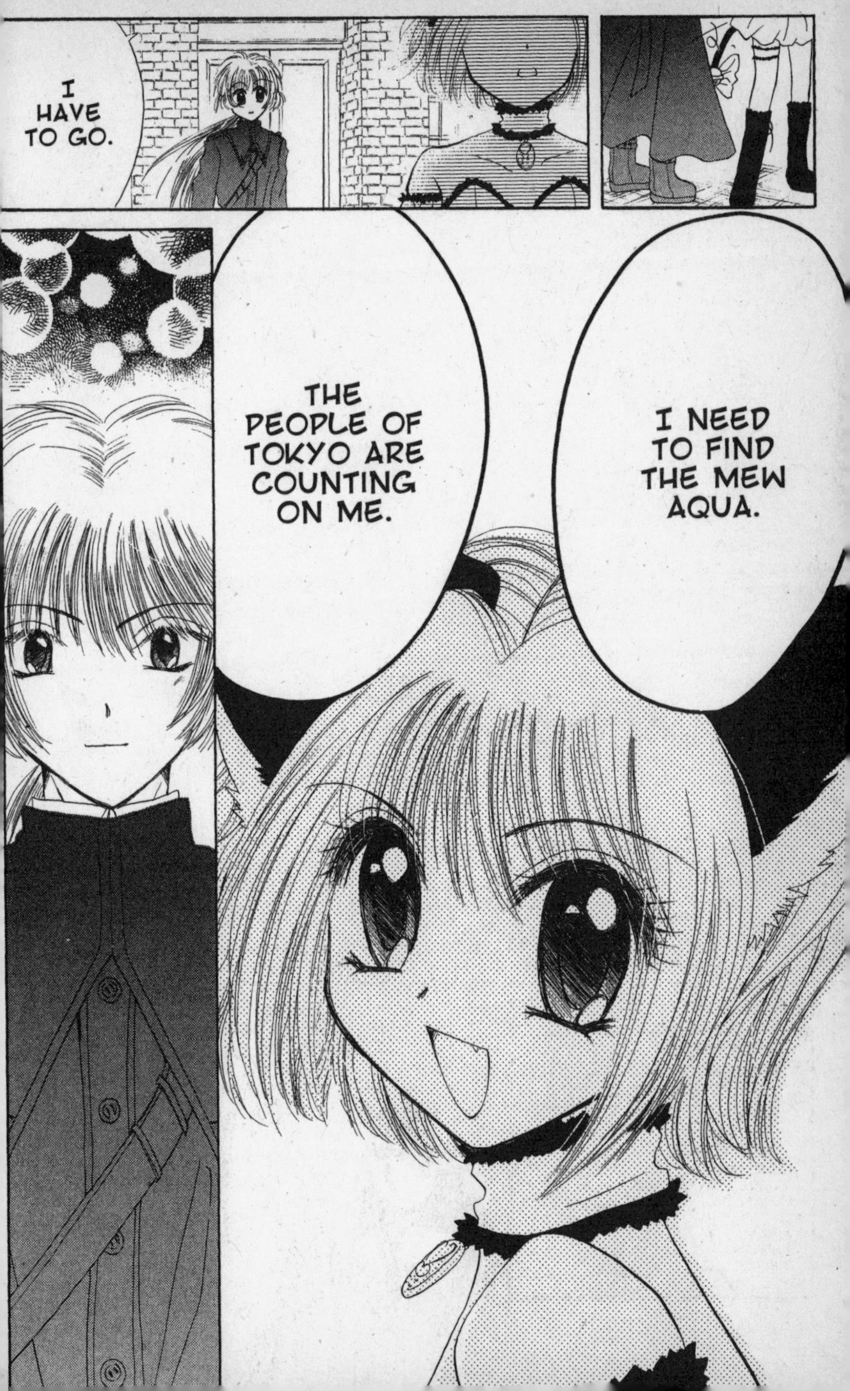
I HAVE TO GO.
I NEED TO FIND THE MEW AQUA.
THE PEOPLE OF TOKYO ARE COUNTING ON ME.

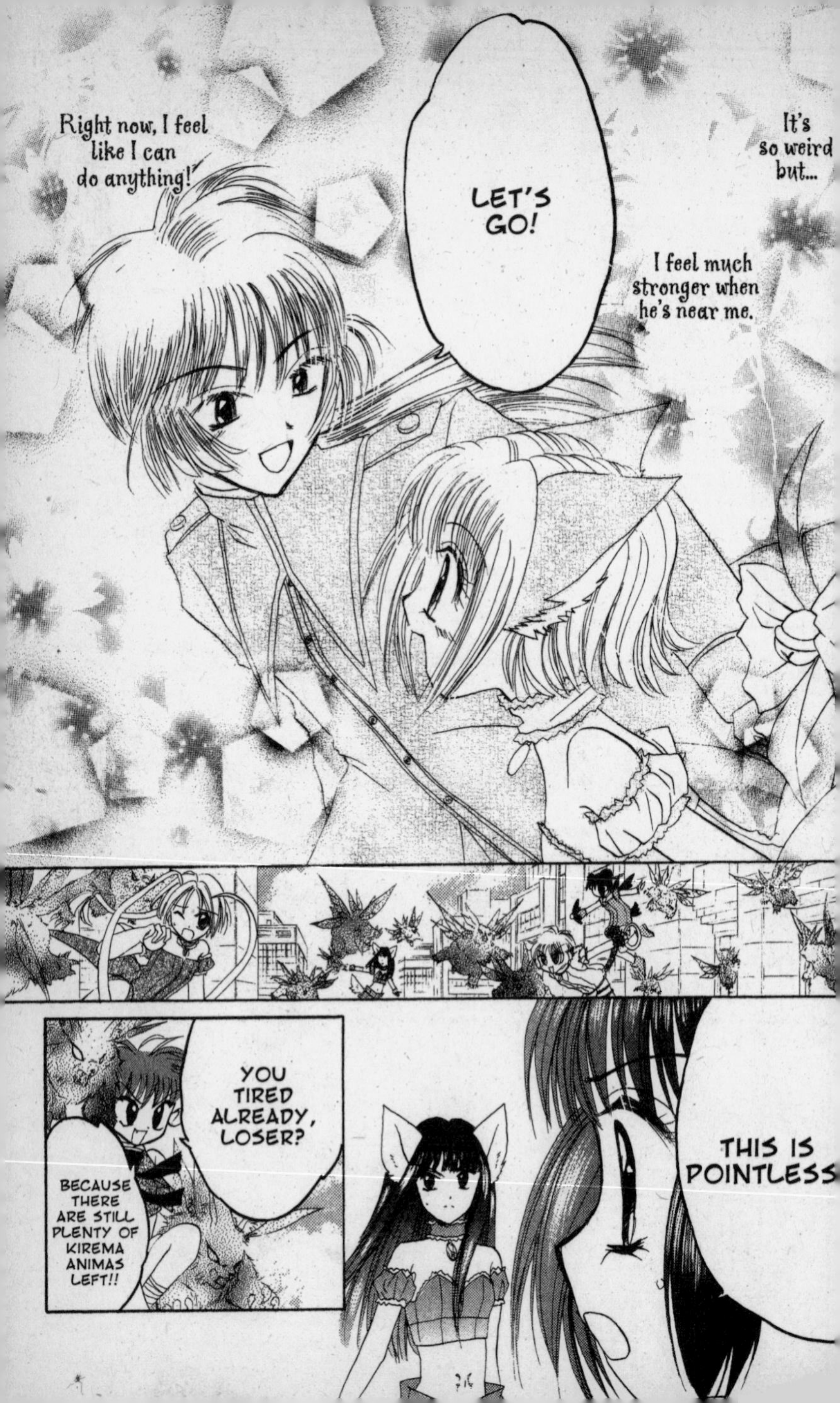
It's so weird but...
I feel much stronger when he's near me.
LET'S GO!
Right now, I feel like I can do anything!
THIS IS POINTLESS
YOU TIRED ALREADY, LOSER?
BECAUSE THERE ARE STILL PLENTY OF KIREMA ANIMAS LEFT!!

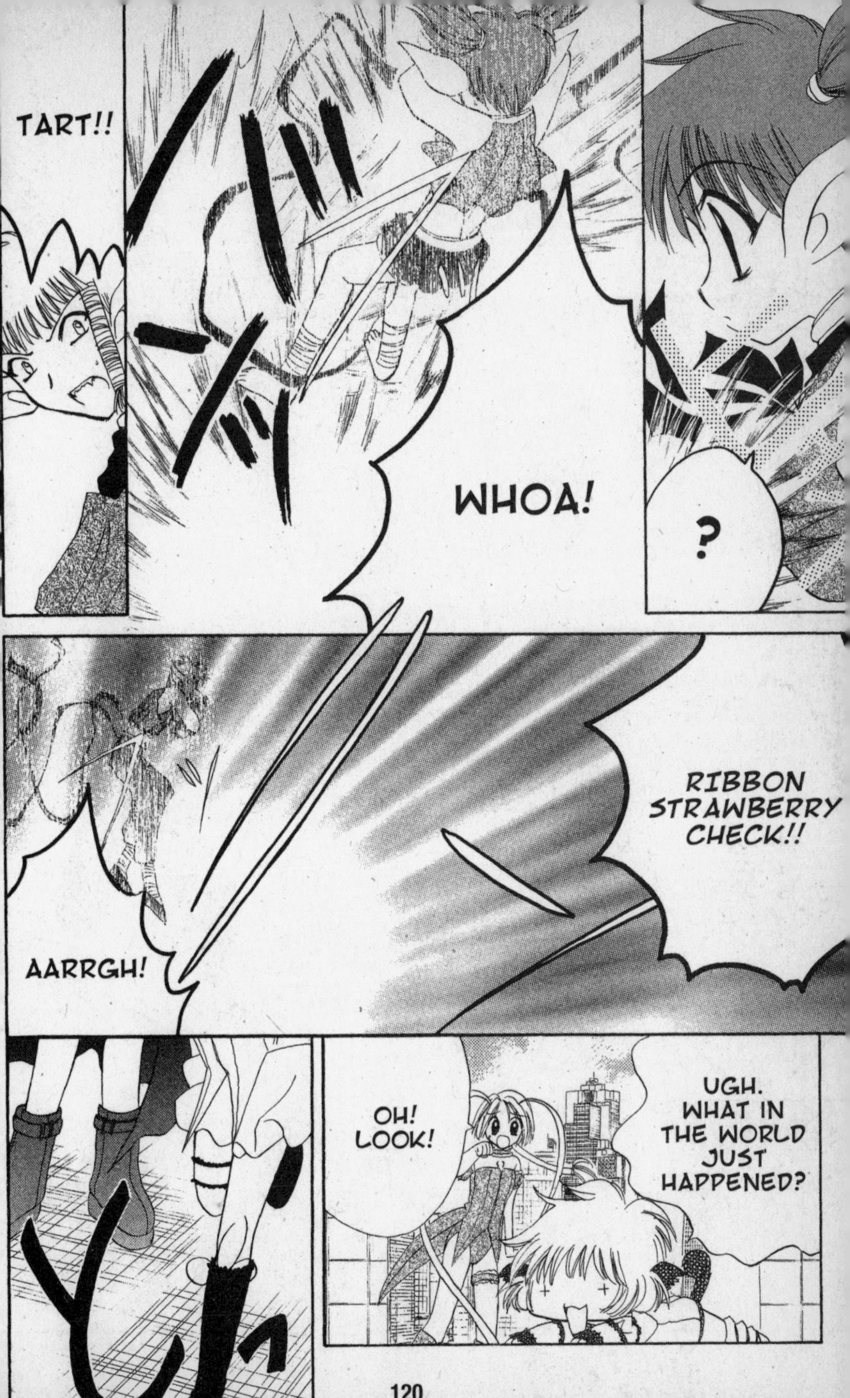
?
WHOA!
TART!!
RIBBON STRAWBERRY CHECK!!
AARRGH!
UGH. WHAT IN THE WORLD JUST HAPPENED?
OH! LOOK!

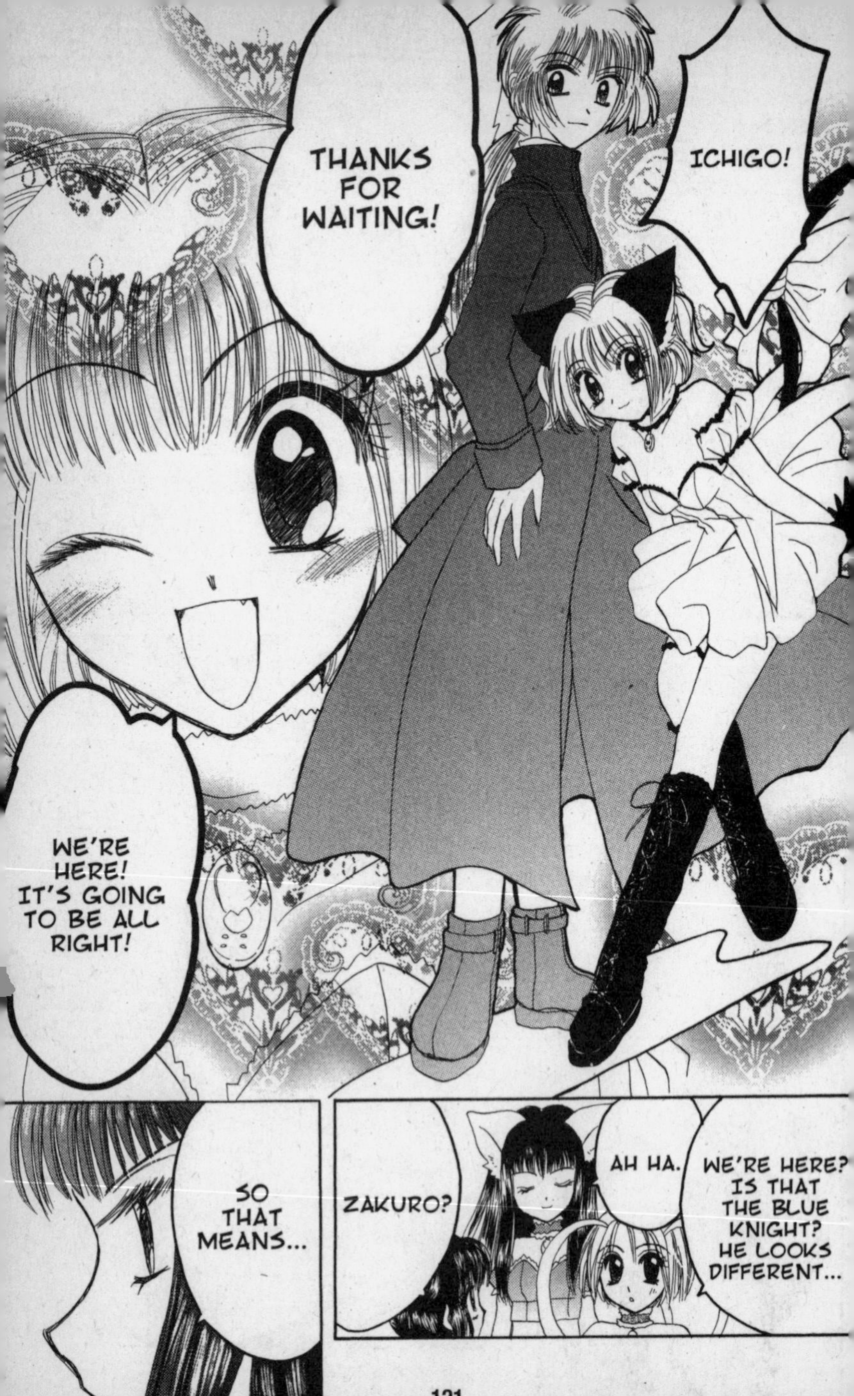
ICHIGO!
THANKS FOR WAITING!
WE'RE HERE! IT'S GOING TO BE ALL RIGHT!
WE'RE HERE? IS THAT THE BLUE KNIGHT? HE LOOKS DIFFERENT...
AH HA.
ZAKURO?
SO THAT MEANS...

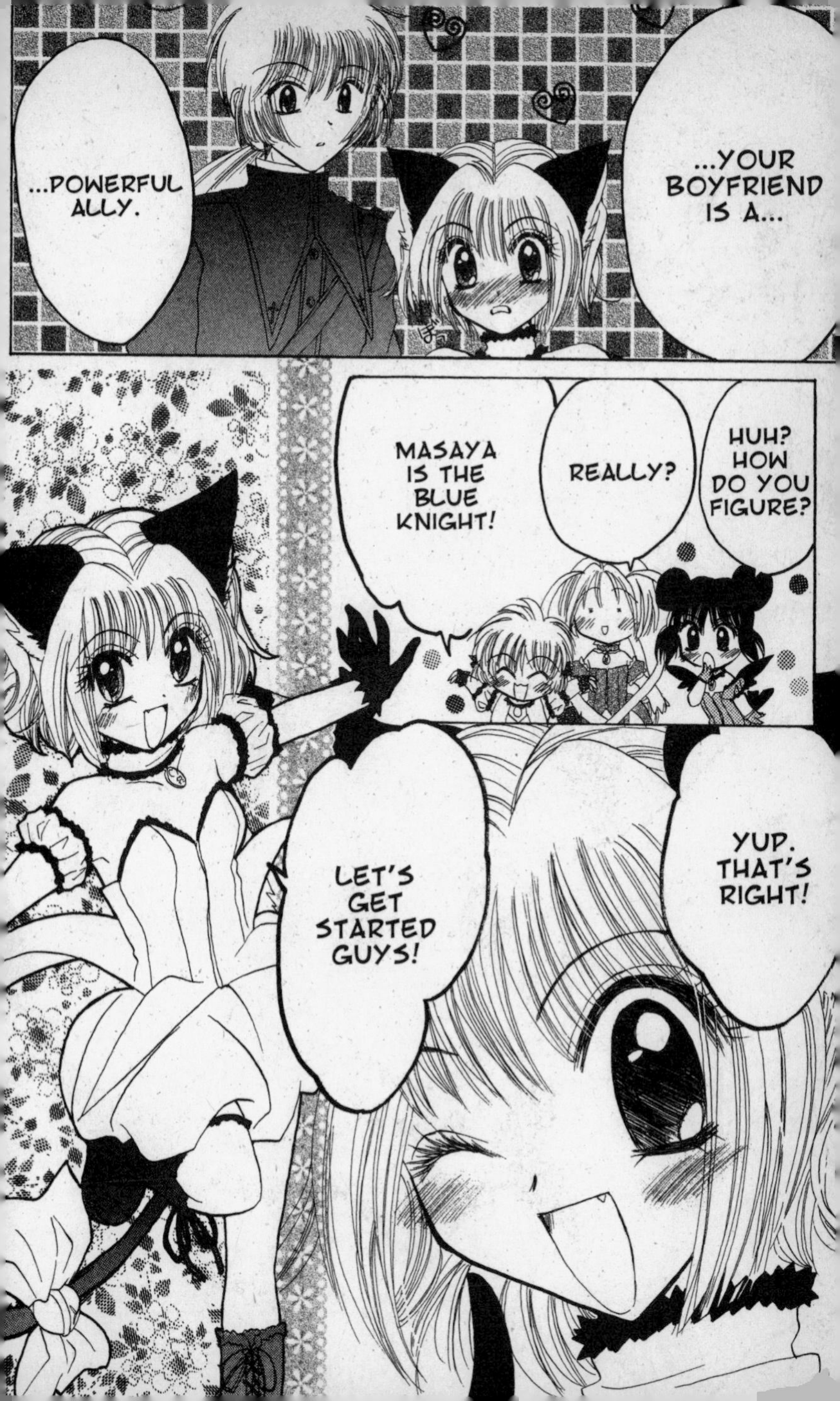
...YOUR BOYFRIEND IS A...
...POWERFUL ALLY.
HUH? HOW DO YOU FIGURE?
REALLY?
MASAYA IS THE BLUE KNIGHT!
YUP. THAT'S RIGHT!
LET'S GET STARTED GUYS!

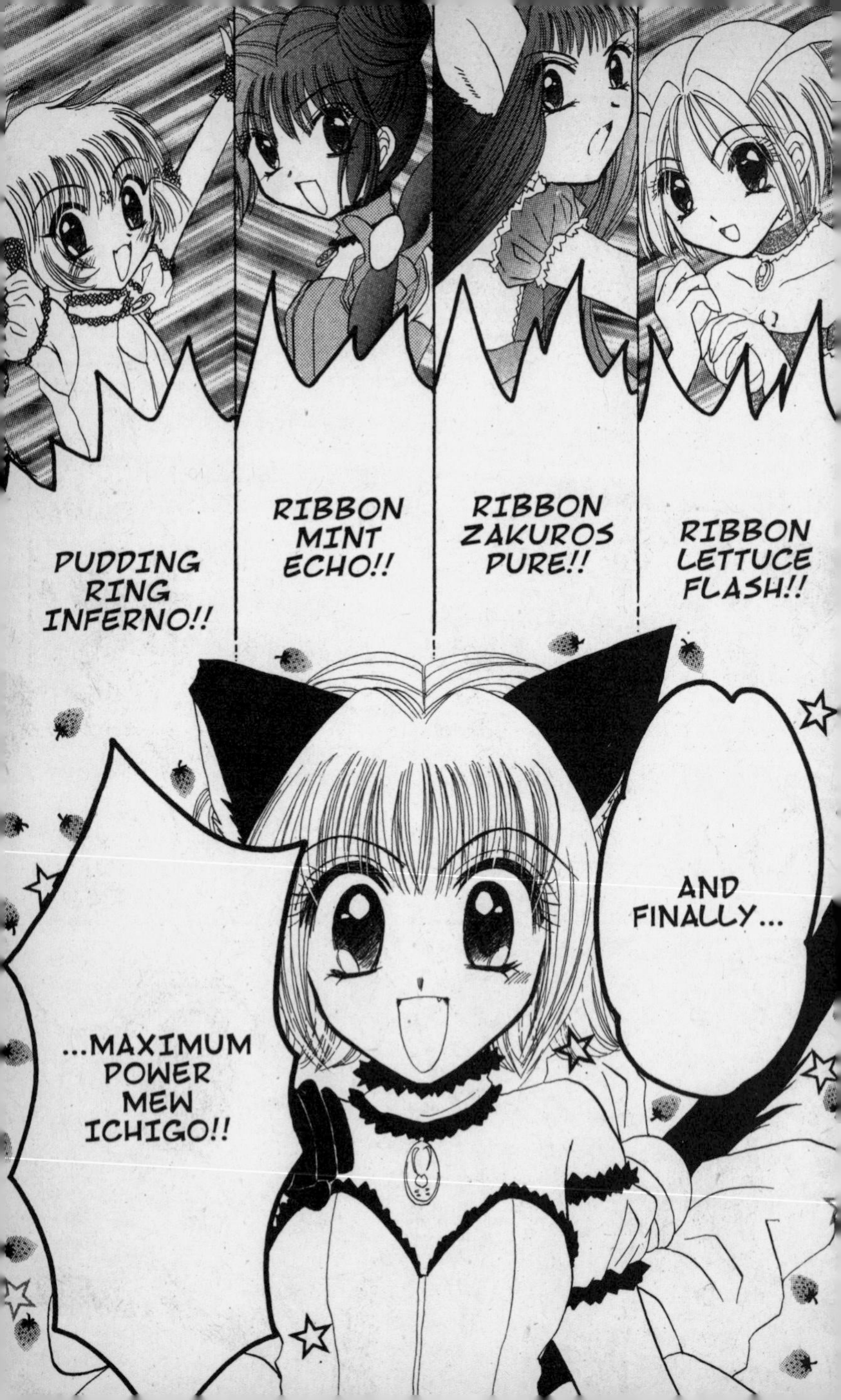

RIBBON LETTUCE FLASH!!
RIBBON ZAKUROS PURE!!
RIBBON MINT ECHO!!
PUDDING RING INFERNO!!
AND FINALLY...
...MAXIMUM POWER MEW ICHIGO!!

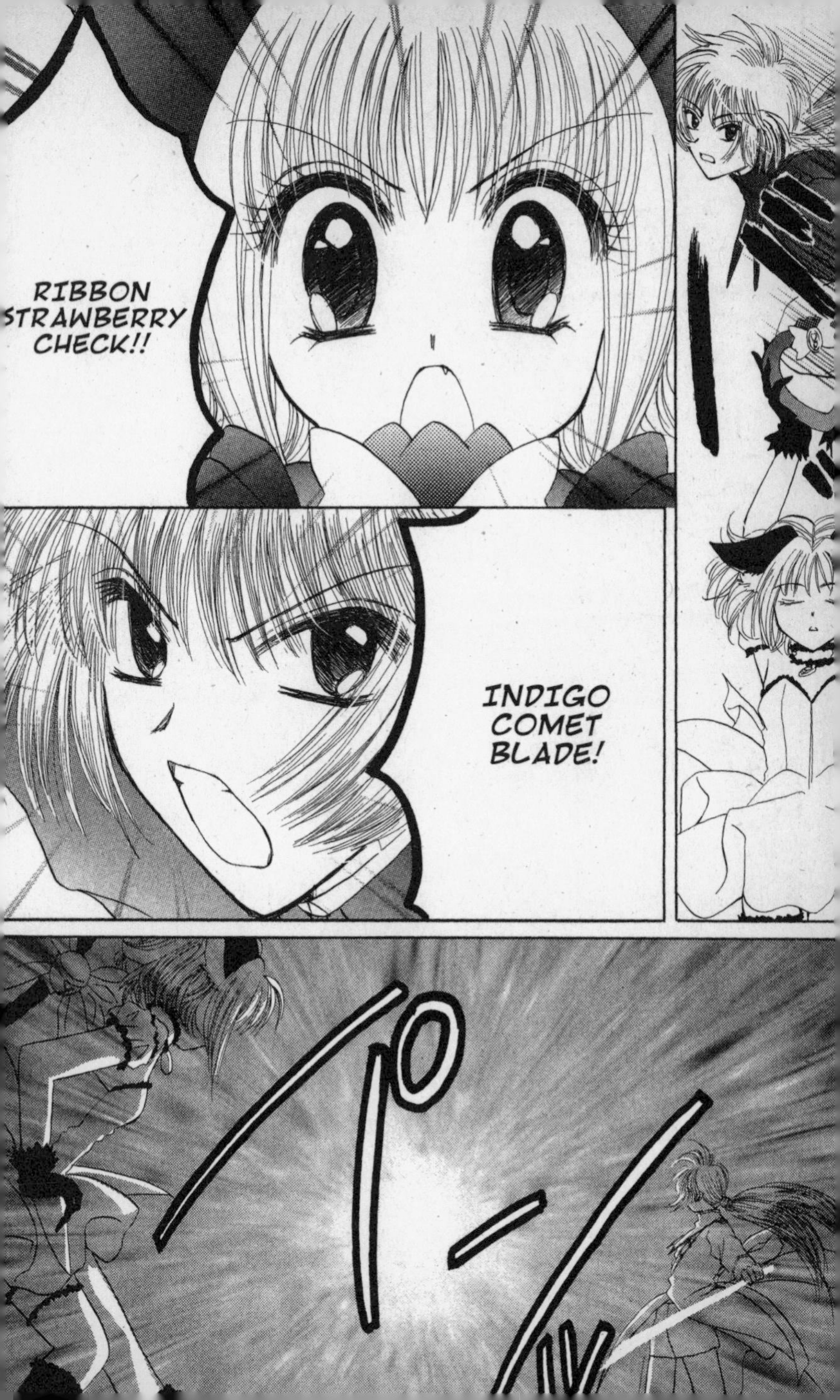
RIBBON STRAWBERRY CHECK!!
INDIGO COMET BLADE!

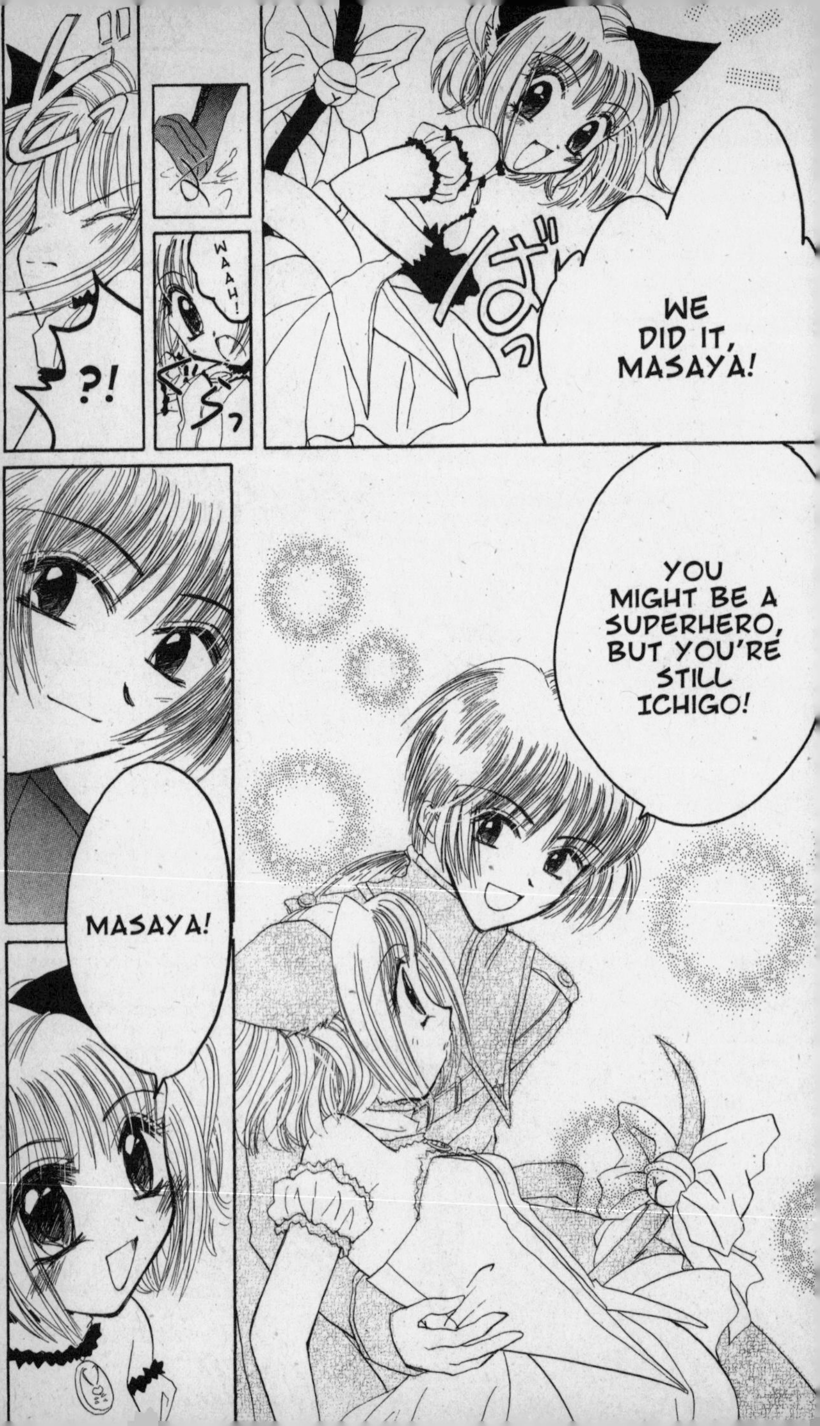
ばっ
WE DID IT, MASAYA!
WAAH!
?!
YOU MIGHT BE A SUPERHERO, BUT YOU'RE STILL ICHIGO!
MASAYA!

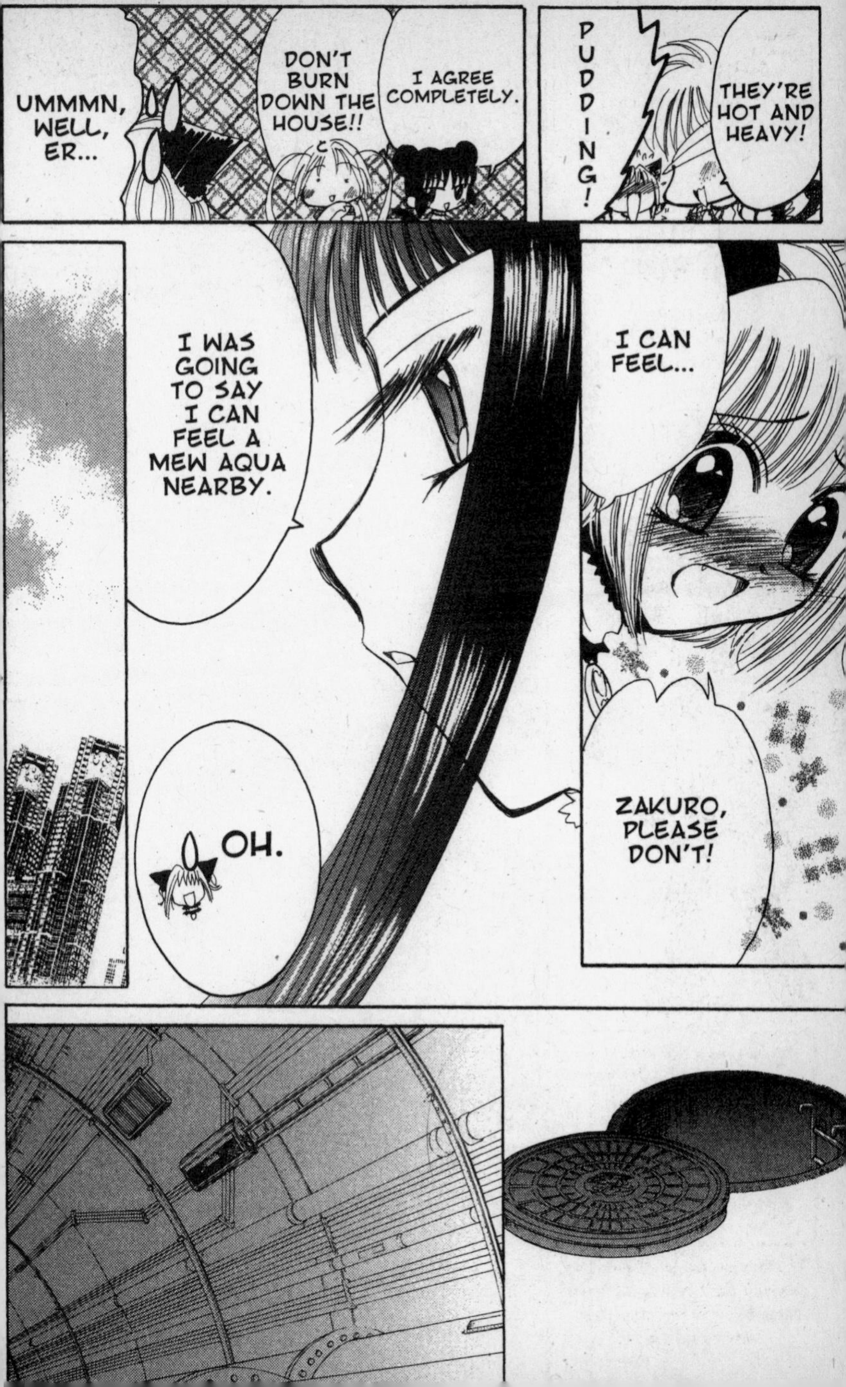
THEY'RE HOT AND HEAVY!
PUDDING!
I AGREE COMPLETELY.
DON'T BURN DOWN THE HOUSE!!
UMMMN, WELL, ER...
I CAN FEEL...
ZAKURO, PLEASE DON'T!
I WAS GOING TO SAY I CAN FEEL A MEW AQUA NEARBY.
OH.

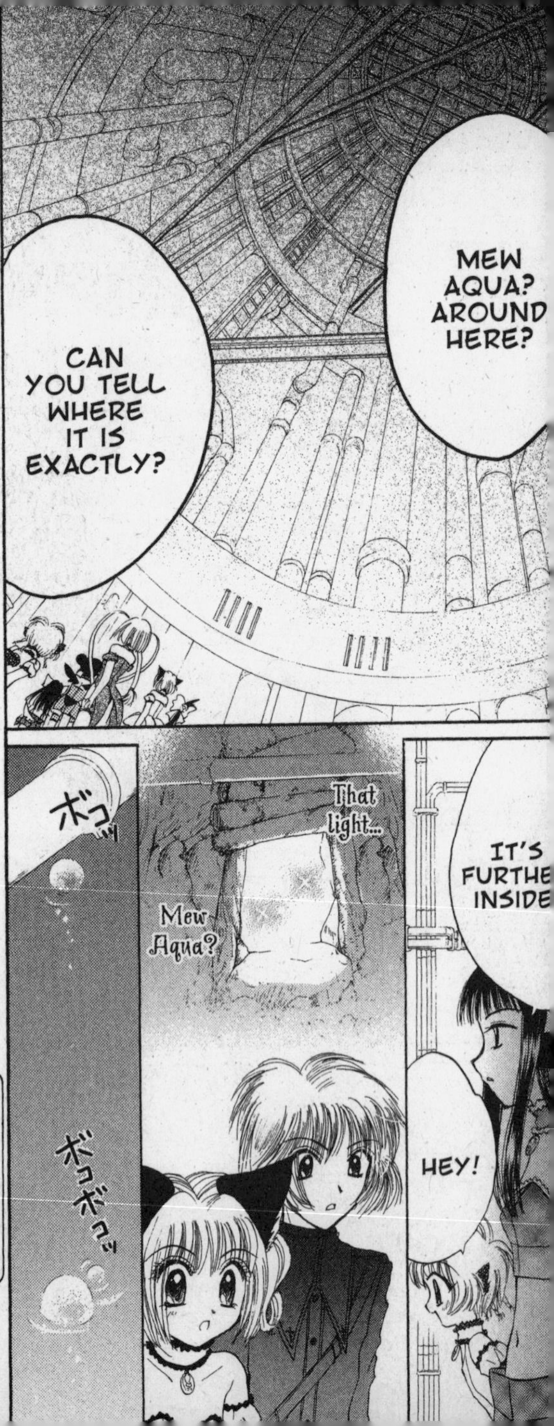
MEW AQUA? AROUND HERE?
CAN YOU TELL WHERE IT IS EXACTLY?
IT'S FURTHE INSIDE
HEY!
That light...
Mew Aqua?
ボコッ
ボコボコッ

Tokyo Mew Mew
Ichigo's Costume Designs Wanted!!

Cute Award

Emi Ibuya
Kanagawa Prefecture
11th Grade

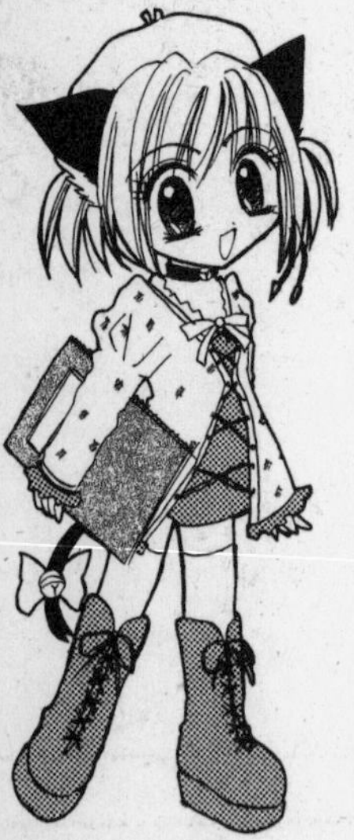

I can't remember some of the details of this design, so there will probably be a few minor differences. This is the cutest outfit possible for hanging out at the library! I'd love an overcoat like that for going out! It's a really cute design, perfect for a day of laid-back reading! ♥

Thanks so much for allowing me to present all six designs! I also want to thank everybody who entered the contest! ♥

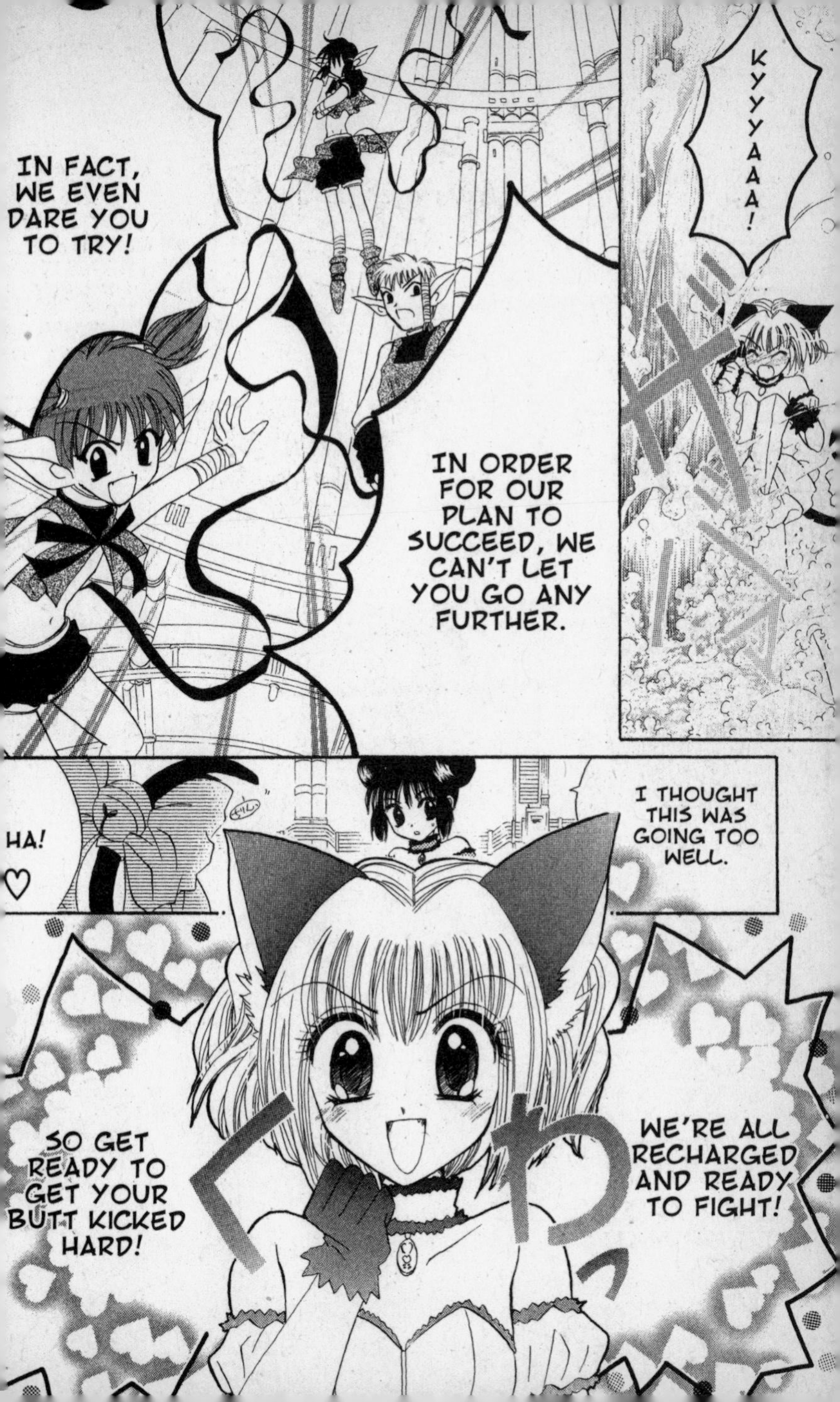
KYYYAAA!
IN ORDER FOR OUR PLAN TO SUCCEED, WE CAN'T LET YOU GO ANY FURTHER.
IN FACT, WE EVEN DARE YOU TO TRY!
I THOUGHT THIS WAS GOING TOO WELL.
HA! ♡
WE'RE ALL RECHARGED AND READY TO FIGHT!
SO GET READY TO GET YOUR BUTT KICKED HARD!

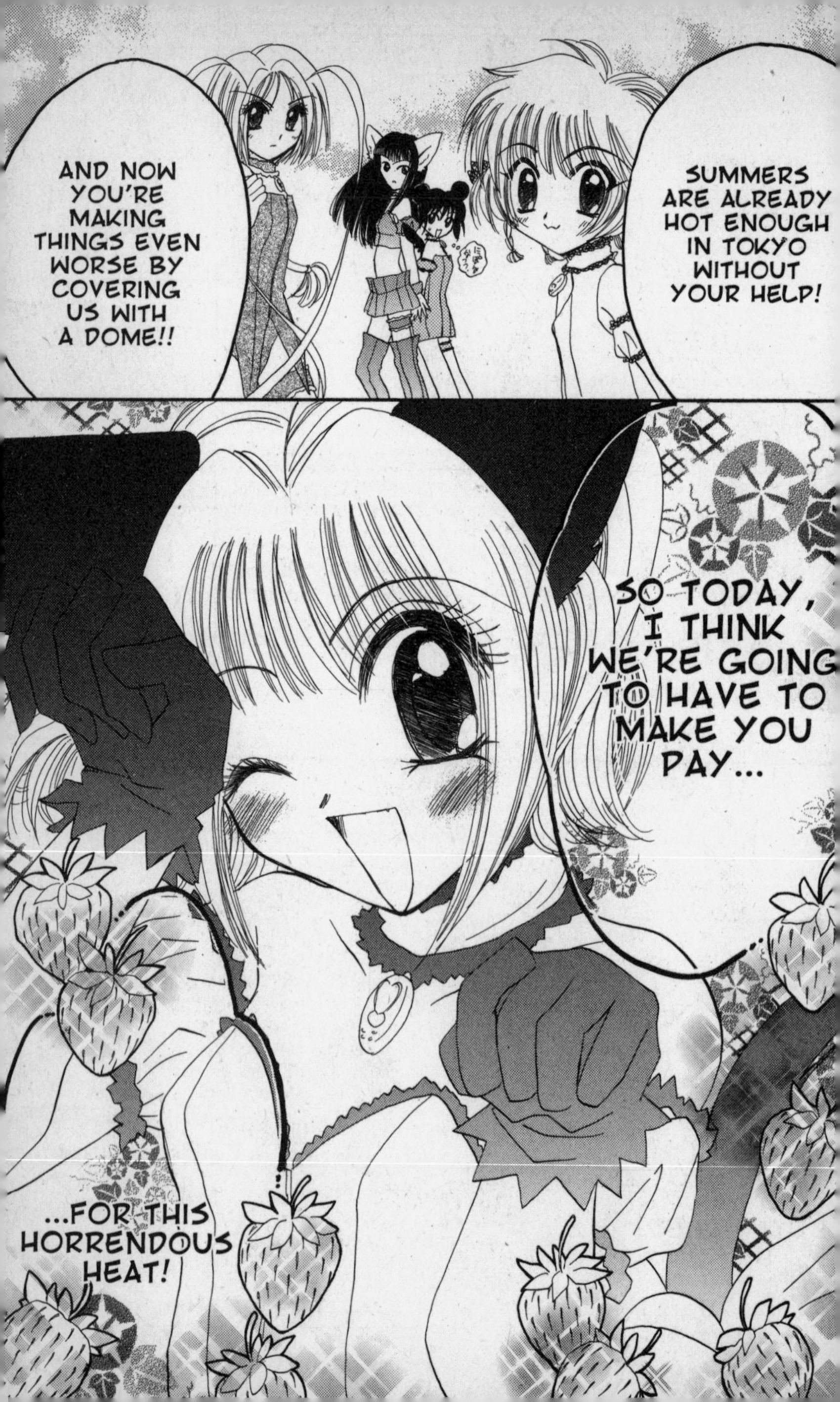
SUMMERS ARE ALREADY HOT ENOUGH IN TOKYO WITHOUT YOUR HELP!
AND NOW YOU'RE MAKING THINGS EVEN WORSE BY COVERING US WITH A DOME!!
SO TODAY, I THINK WE'RE GOING TO HAVE TO MAKE YOU PAY...
...FOR THIS HORRENDOUS HEAT!

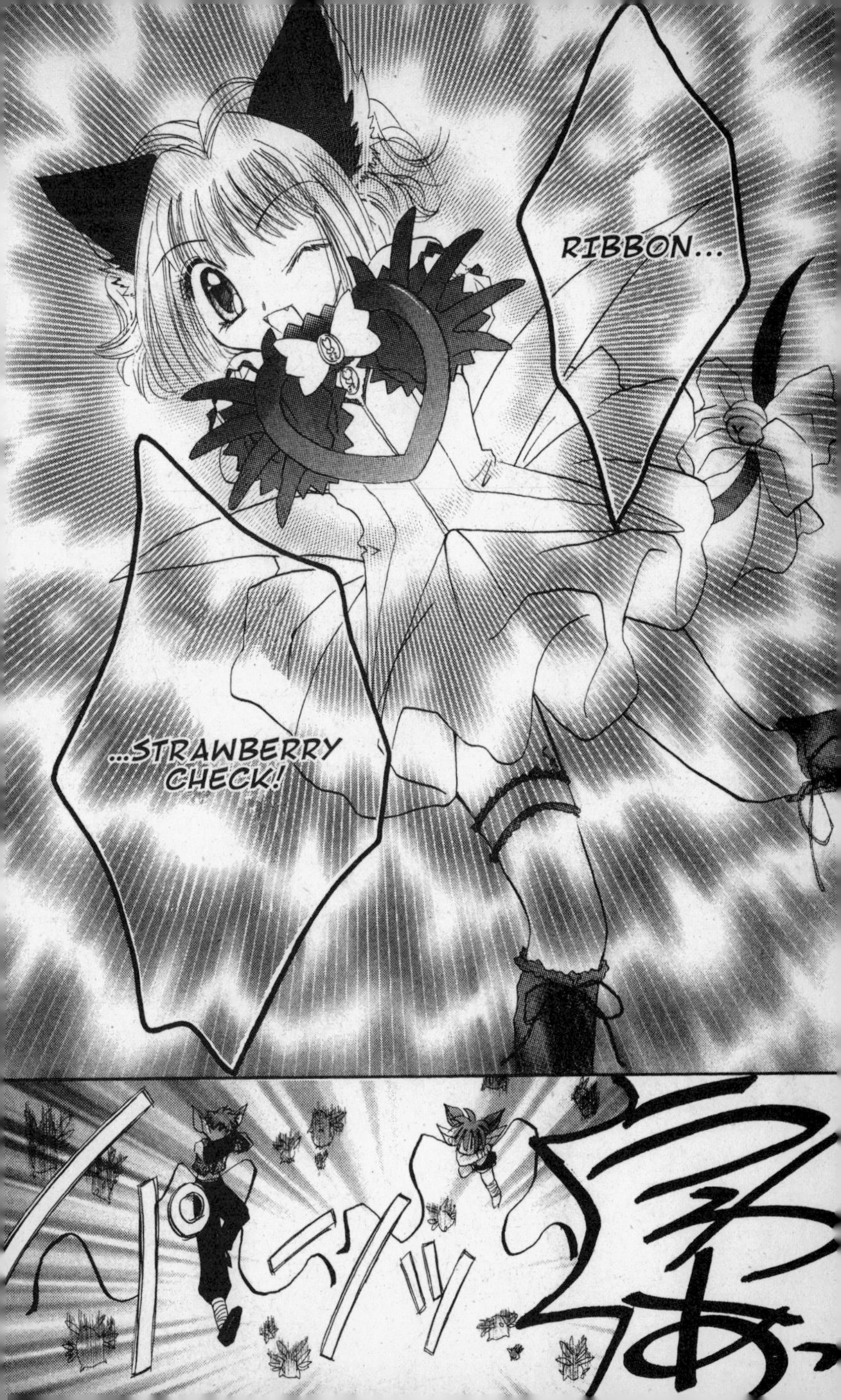
RIBBON...
...STRAWBERRY CHECK!
パシッ

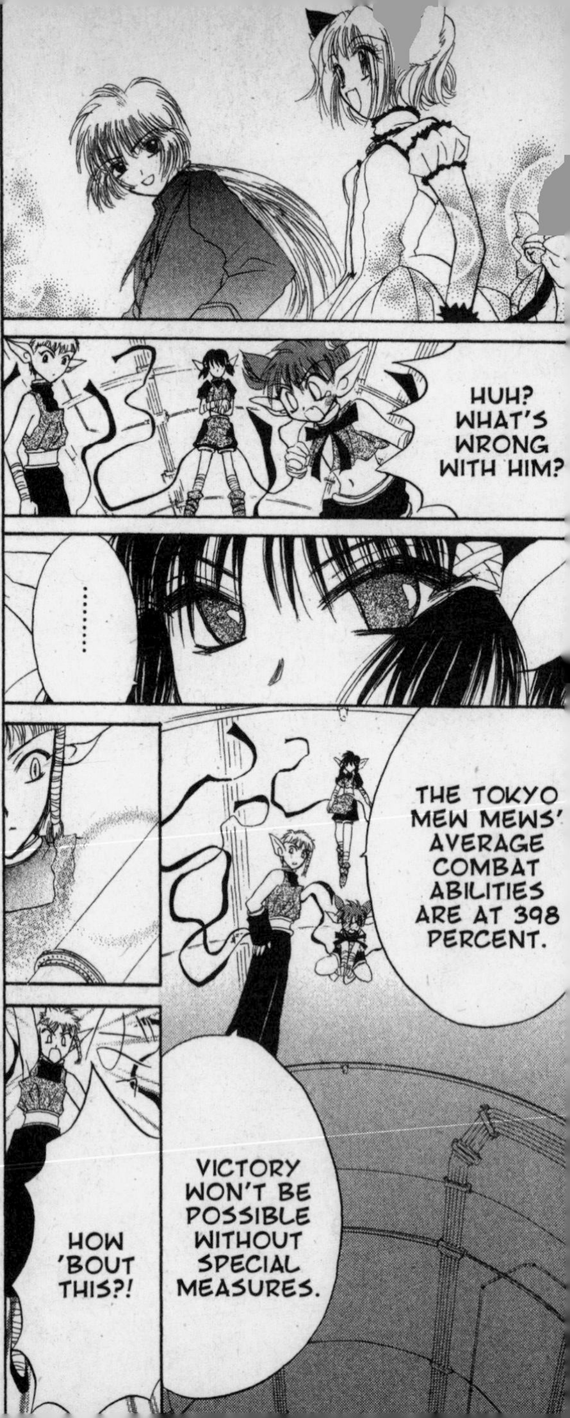
HUH? WHAT'S WRONG WITH HIM?
......
THE TOKYO MEW MEWS' AVERAGE COMBAT ABILITIES ARE AT 398 PERCENT.
VICTORY WON'T BE POSSIBLE WITHOUT SPECIAL MEASURES.
HOW 'BOUT THIS?!

SPECIAL THANKS!!

R.YOSHIDA

H.MATSUMOTO
M.OMORI

S.NAOHARA
K.HONDA
A.SUZUKI

A.OKAWA
S.NAKAZAWA

H.OIKAWA

T.INAWAKI

M.SEKIYA
S.SUDA

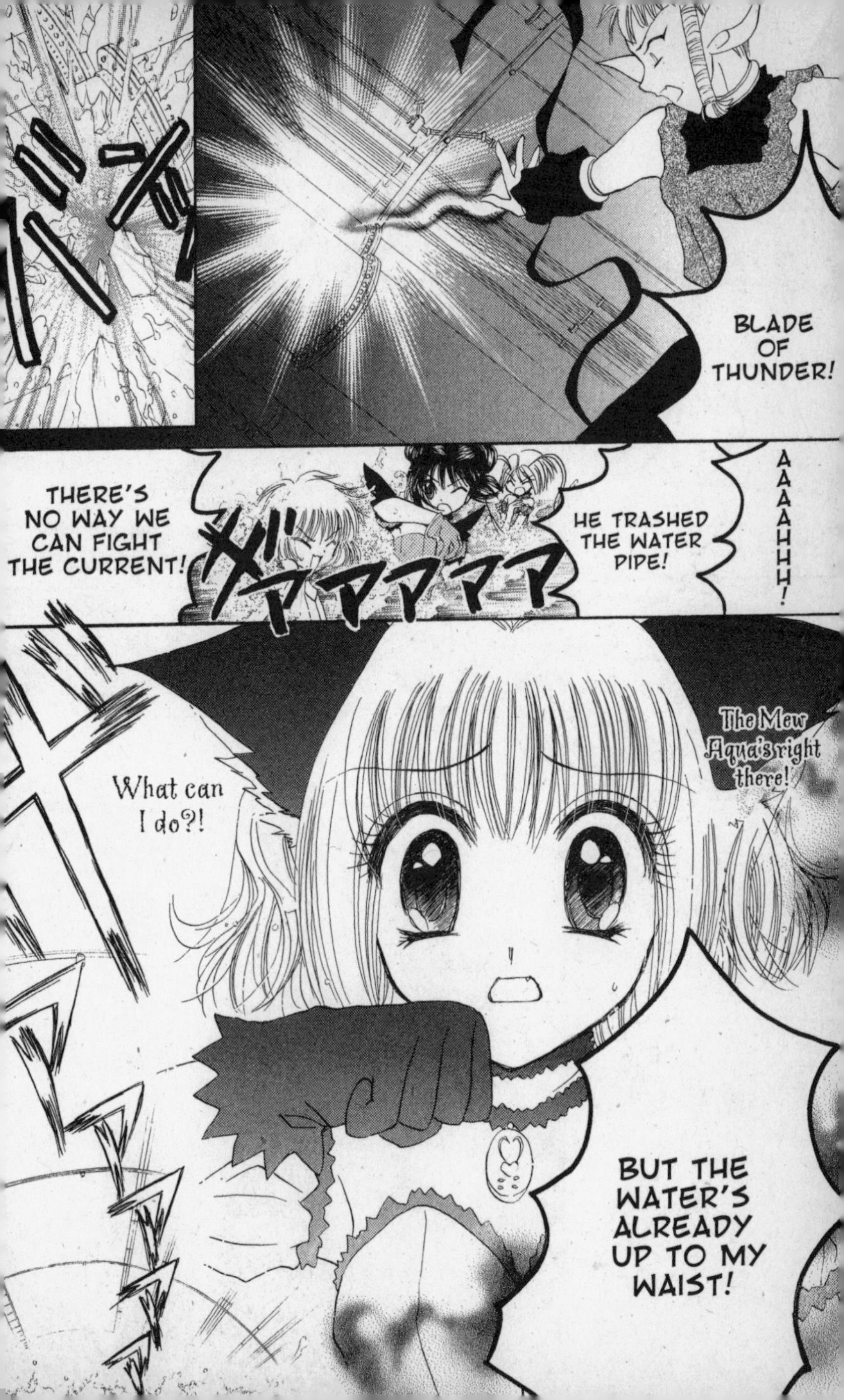
BLADE OF THUNDER!
AAAAAHHH!
HE TRASHED THE WATER PIPE!
THERE'S NO WAY WE CAN FIGHT THE CURRENT!
The Mew Aqua's right there!
What can I do?!
BUT THE WATER'S ALREADY UP TO MY WAIST!

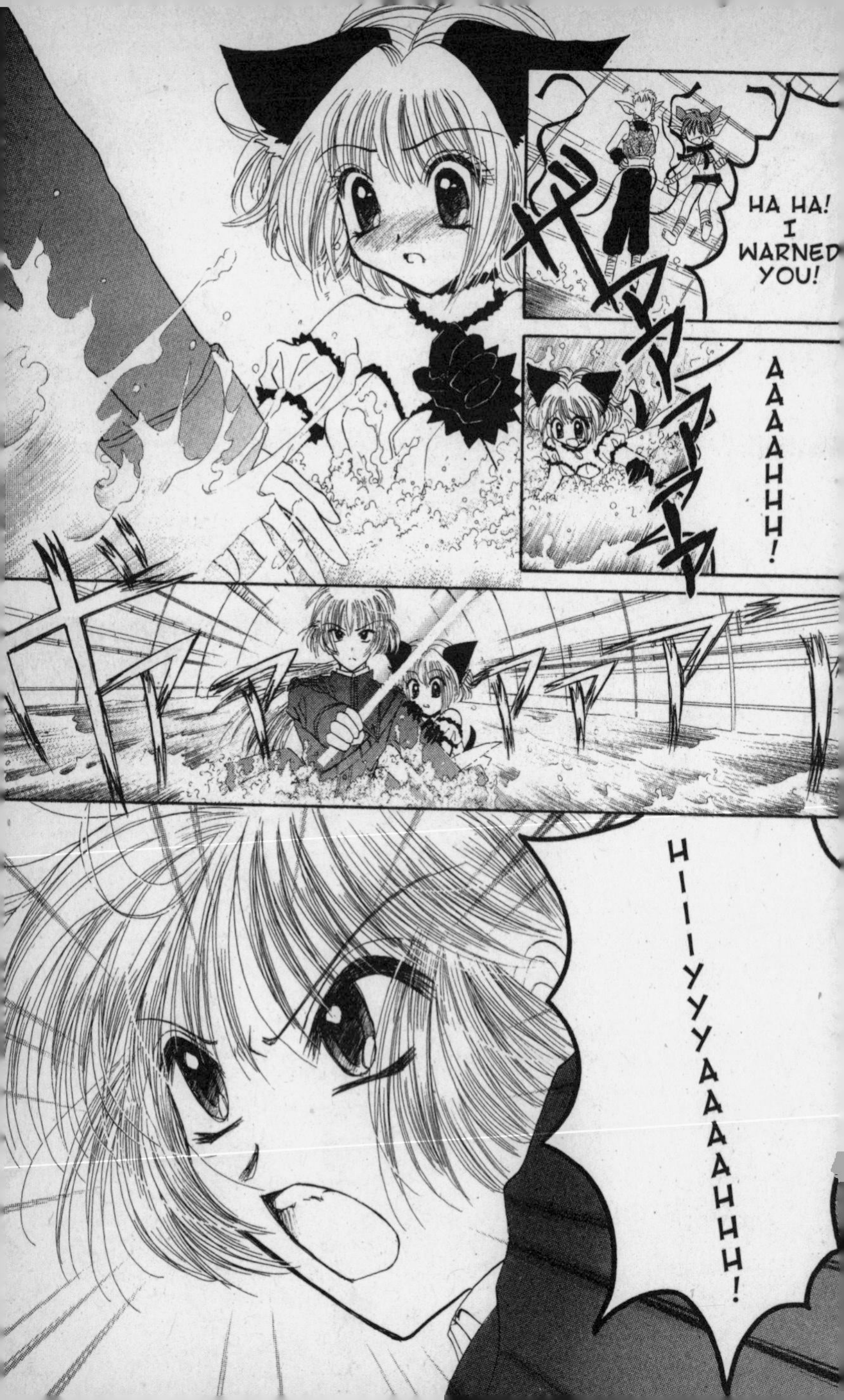
HA HA! I WARNED YOU!
AAAAHHH!
HIIIYYYAAAAHHH!

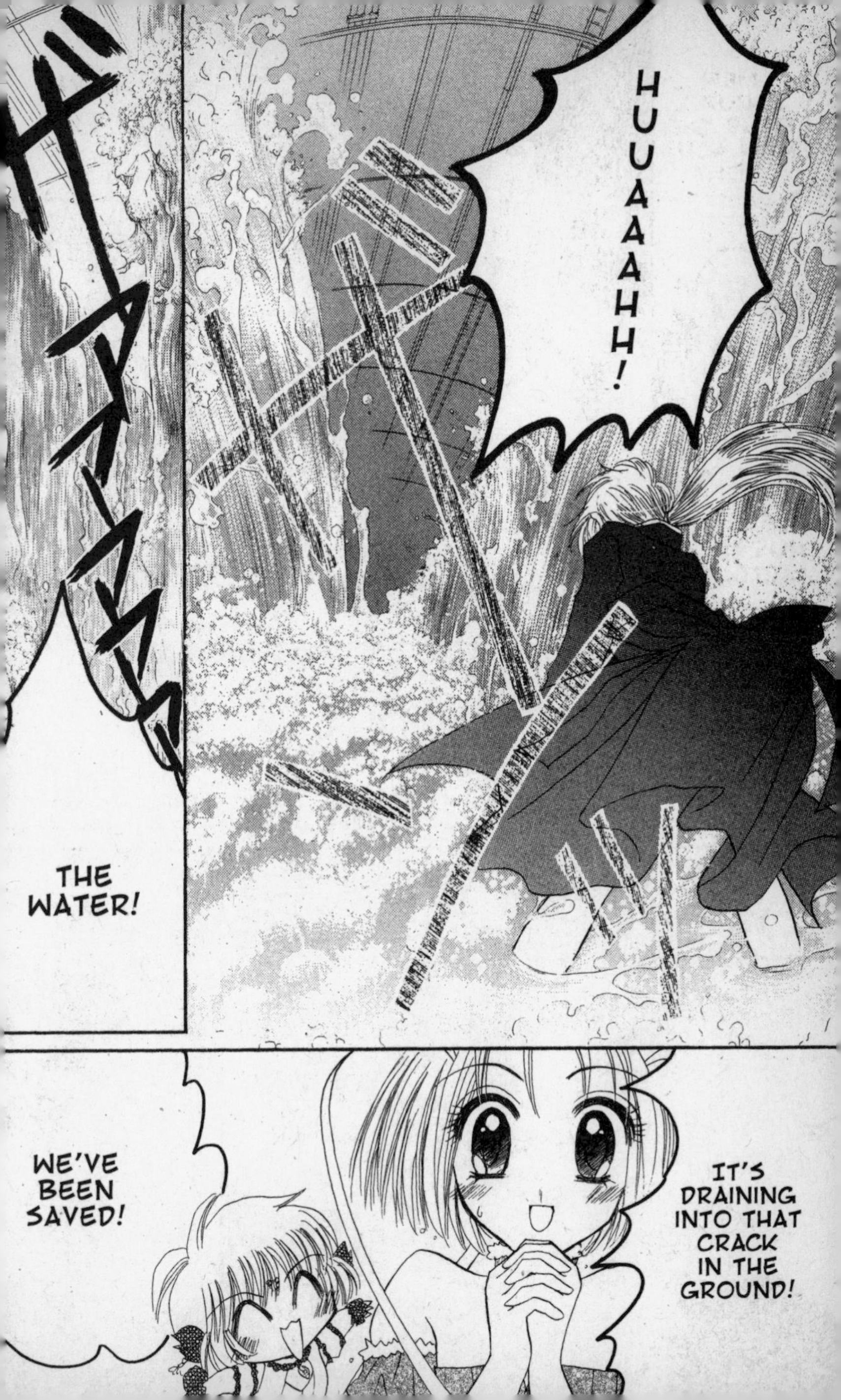
HUUAAAAHH!
THE WATER!
IT'S DRAINING INTO THAT CRACK IN THE GROUND!
WE'VE BEEN SAVED!

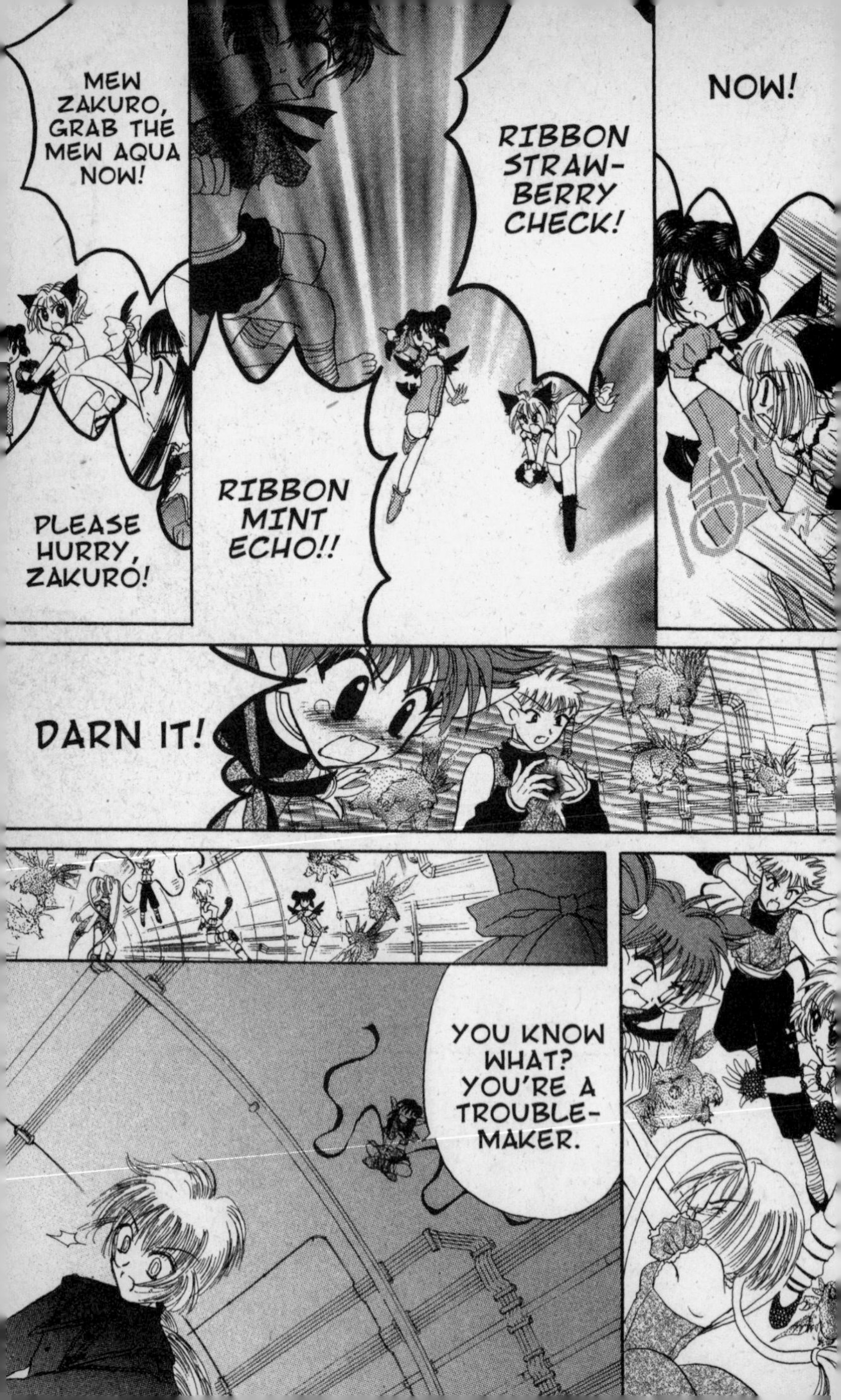
NOW!
RIBBON STRAW-BERRY CHECK!
RIBBON MINT ECHO!!
MEW ZAKURO, GRAB THE MEW AQUA NOW!
PLEASE HURRY, ZAKURO!
DARN IT!
YOU KNOW WHAT? YOU'RE A TROUBLE-MAKER.

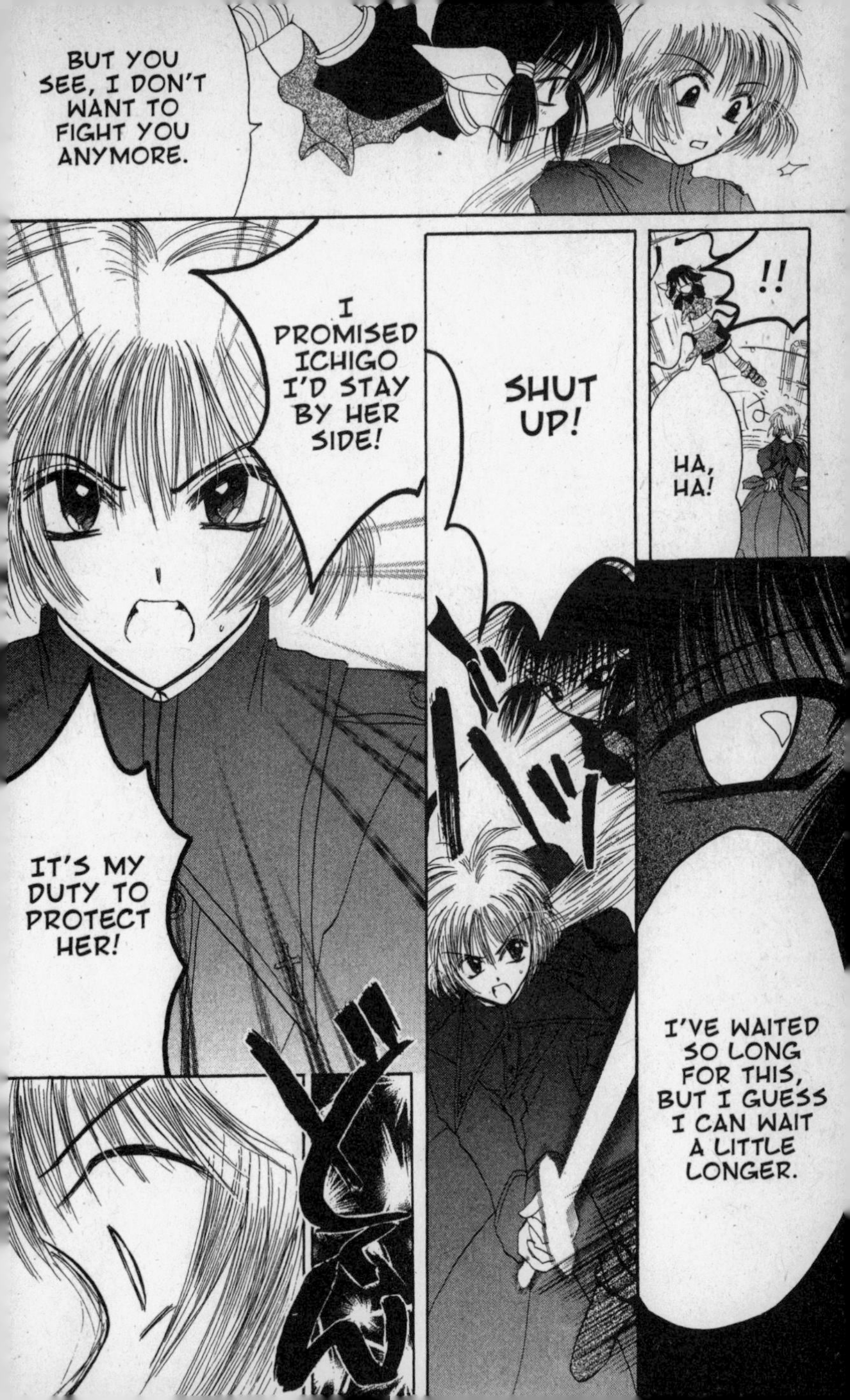
BUT YOU SEE, I DON'T WANT TO FIGHT YOU ANYMORE.
!!
HA, HA!
SHUT UP!
I PROMISED ICHIGO I'D STAY BY HER SIDE!
IT'S MY DUTY TO PROTECT HER!
I'VE WAITED SO LONG FOR THIS, BUT I GUESS I CAN WAIT A LITTLE LONGER.

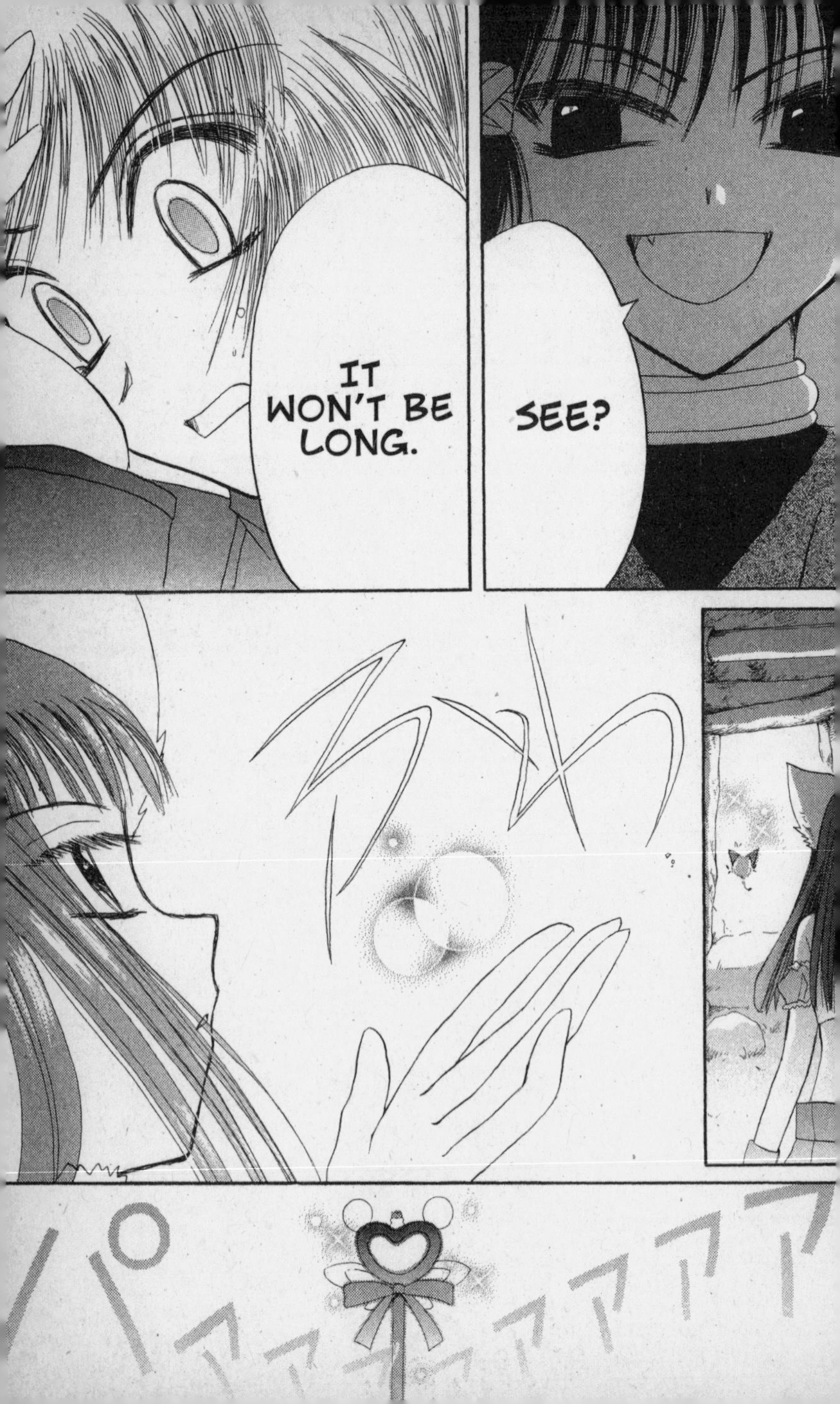
SEE?
IT WON'T BE LONG.

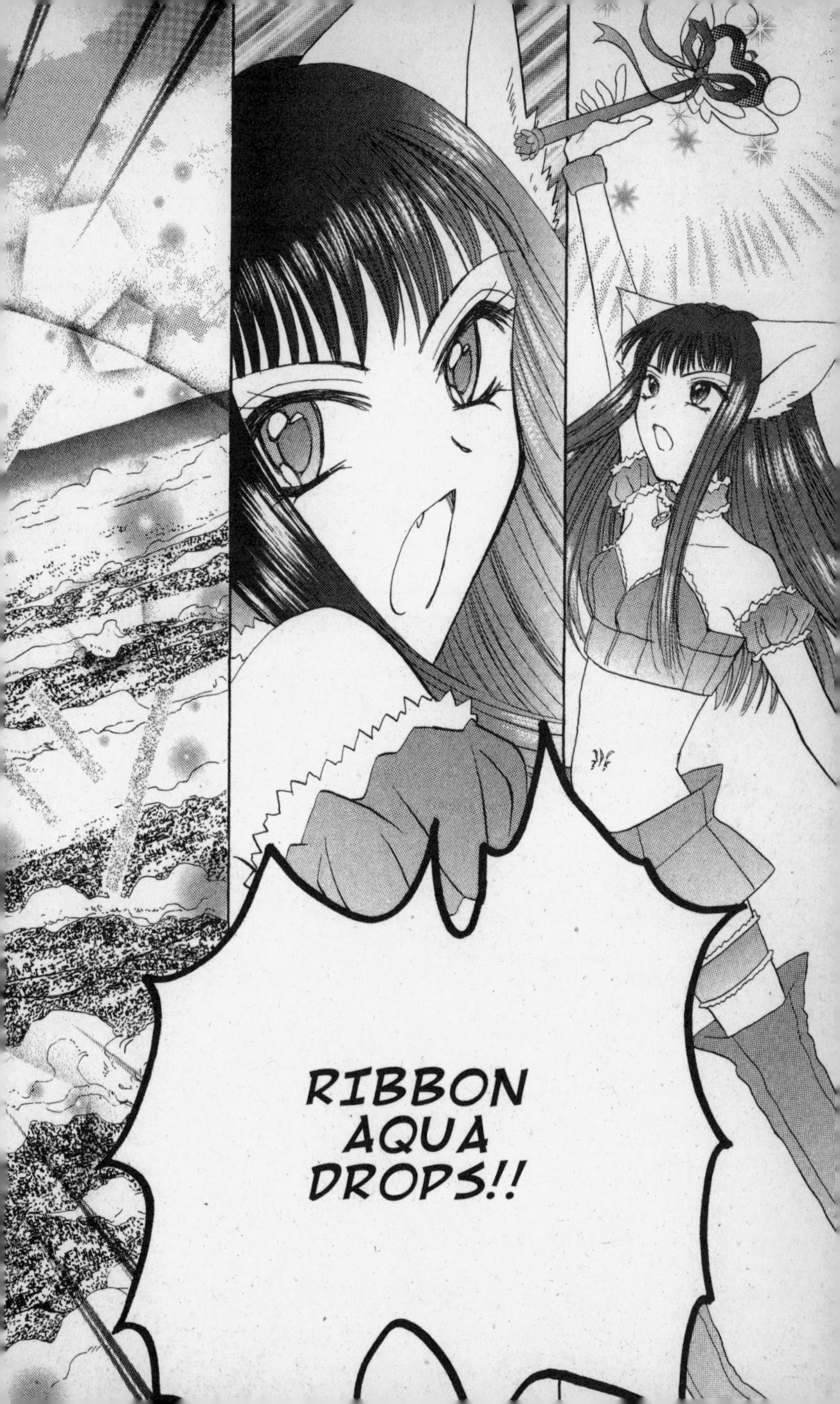
RIBBON AQUA DROPS!!

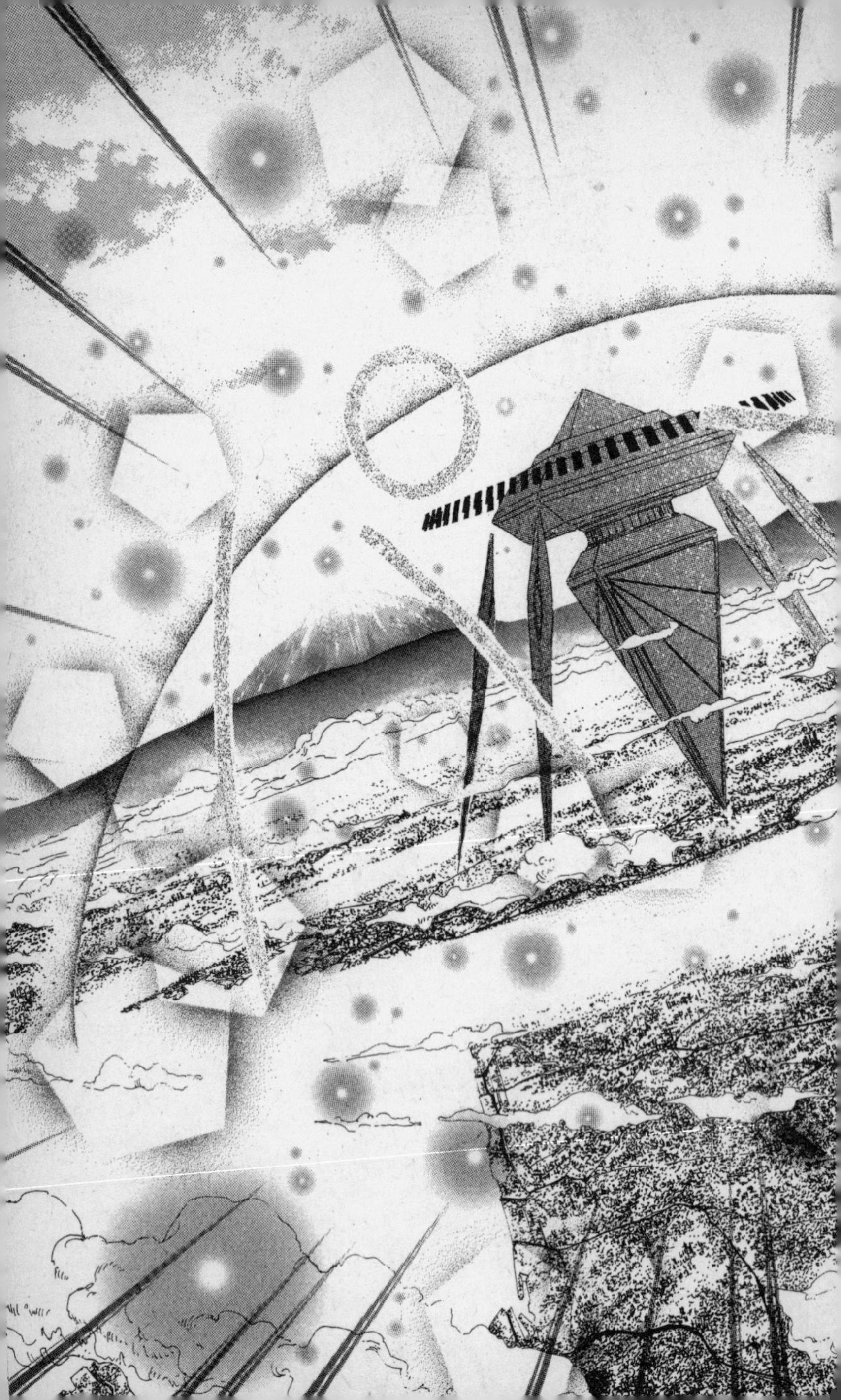

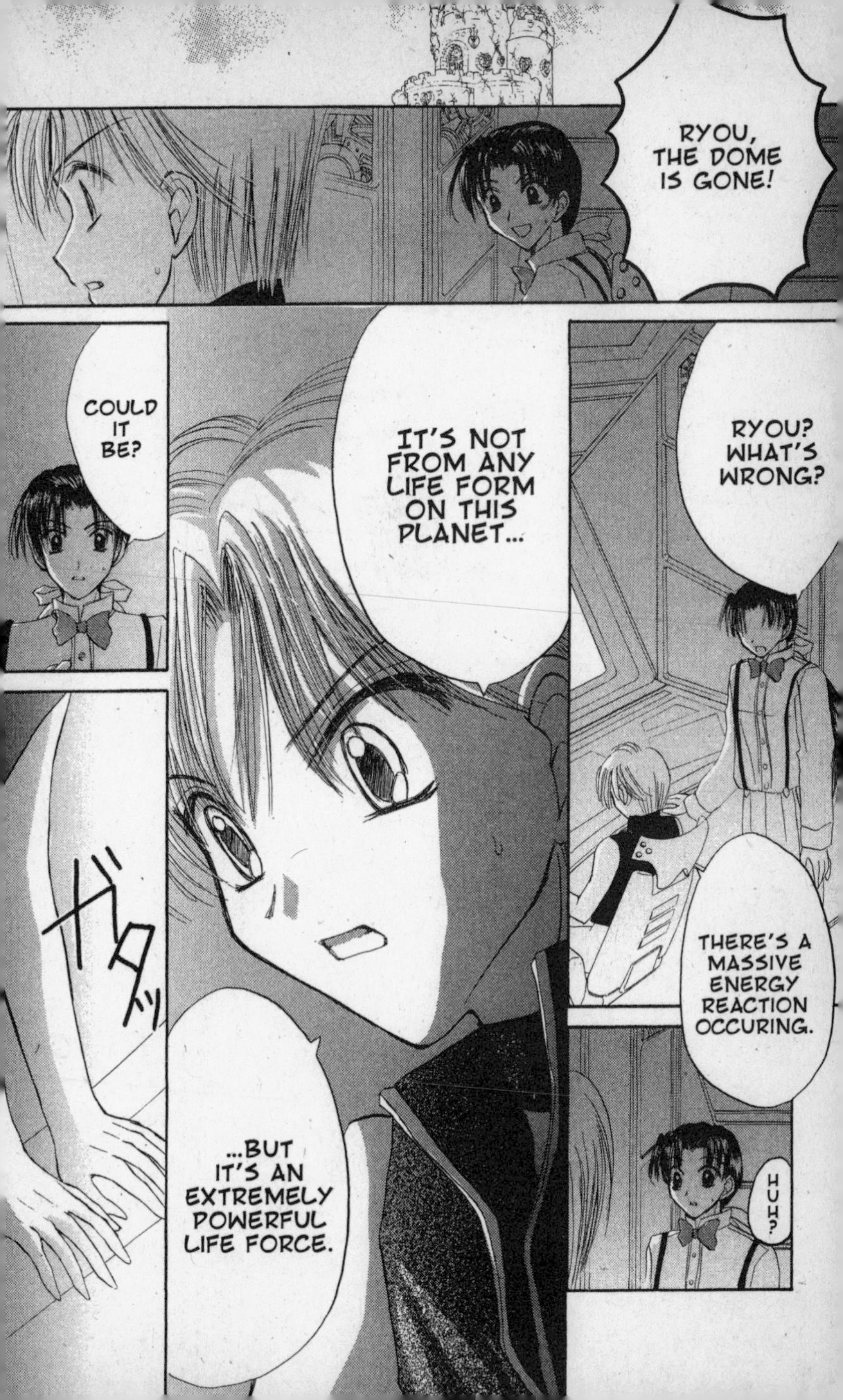
RYOU, THE DOME IS GONE!
RYOU? WHAT'S WRONG?
THERE'S A MASSIVE ENERGY REACTION OCCURING.
HUH?
IT'S NOT FROM ANY LIFE FORM ON THIS PLANET...
...BUT IT'S AN EXTREMELY POWERFUL LIFE FORCE.
COULD IT BE?
ガタッ

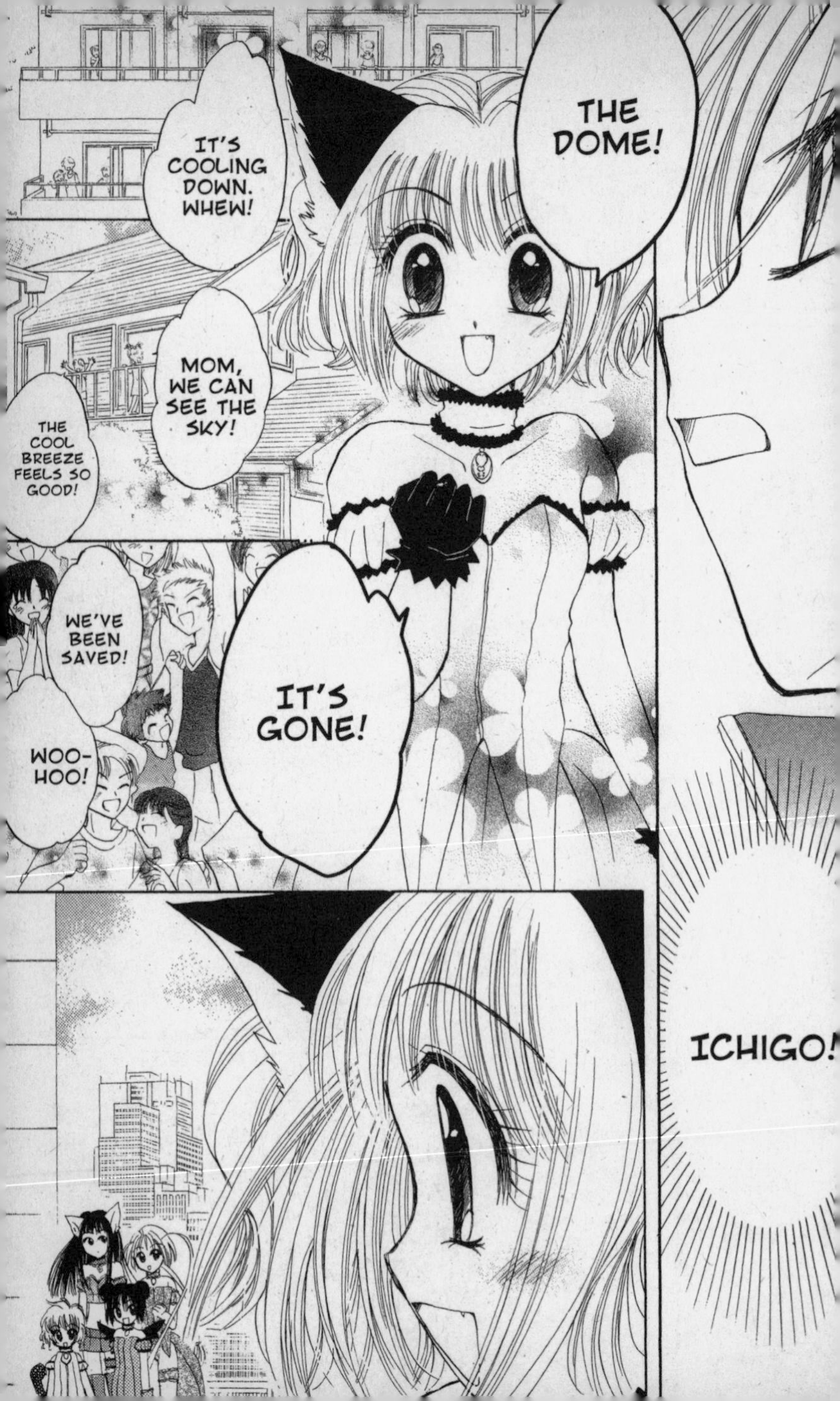
THE DOME!
IT'S COOLING DOWN. WHEW!
MOM, WE CAN SEE THE SKY!
THE COOL BREEZE FEELS SO GOOD!
IT'S GONE!
WE'VE BEEN SAVED!
WOO-HOO!
ICHIGO!

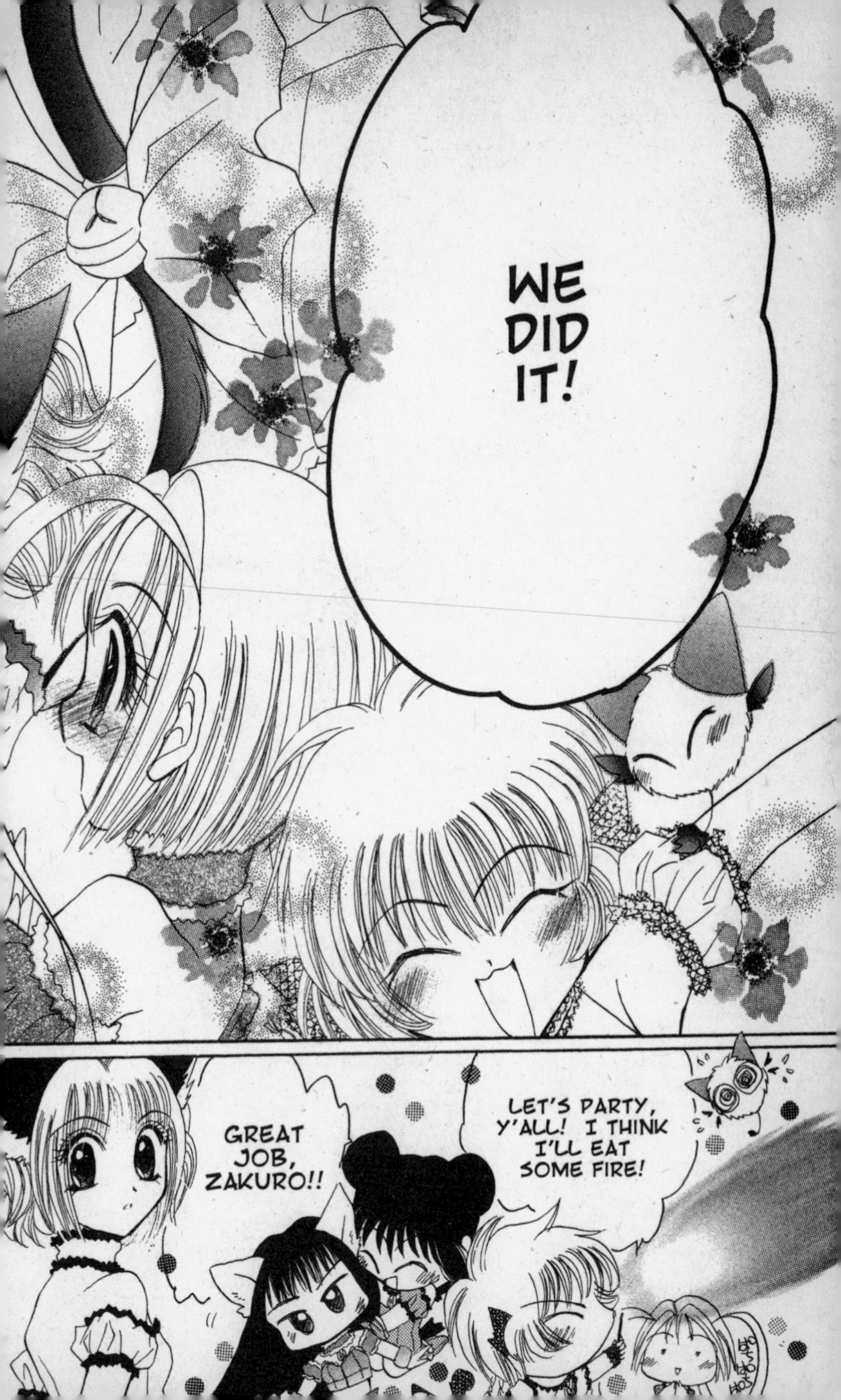
WE DID IT!
LET'S PARTY, Y'ALL! I THINK I'LL EAT SOME FIRE!
GREAT JOB, ZAKURO!!

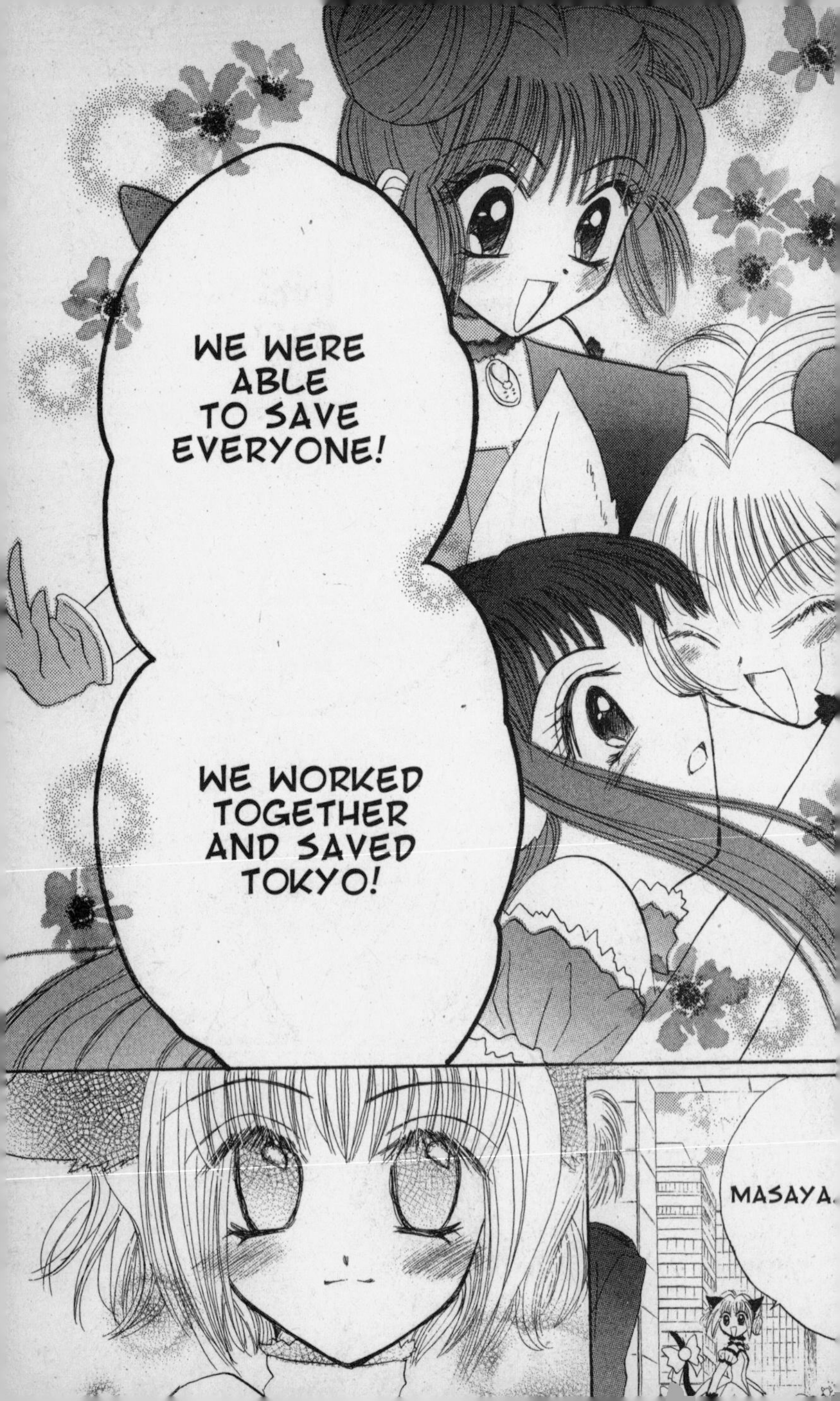
WE WERE ABLE TO SAVE EVERYONE!
WE WORKED TOGETHER AND SAVED TOKYO!
MASAYA.

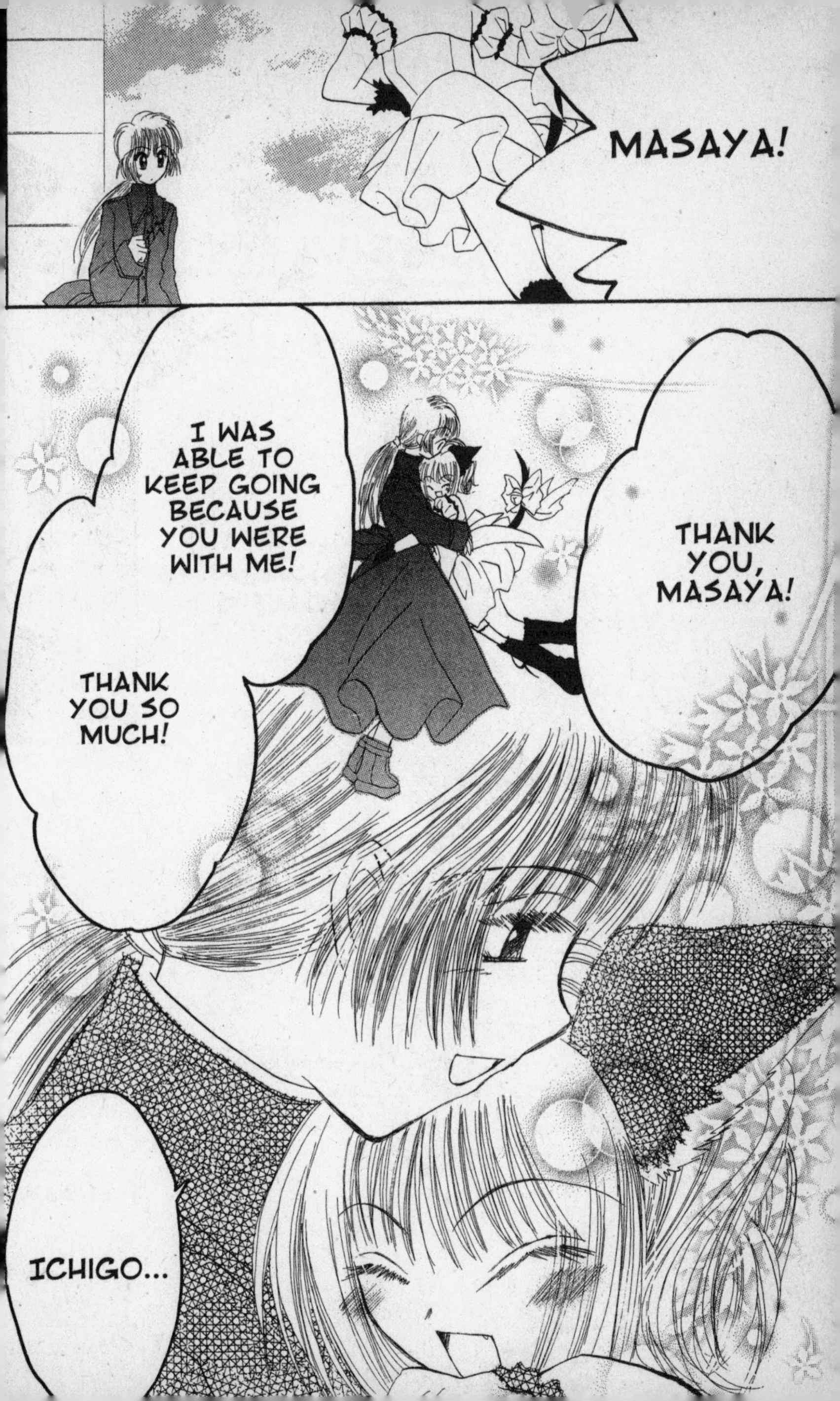
MASAYA!
THANK YOU, MASAYA!
I WAS ABLE TO KEEP GOING BECAUSE YOU WERE WITH ME!
THANK YOU SO MUCH!
ICHIGO...

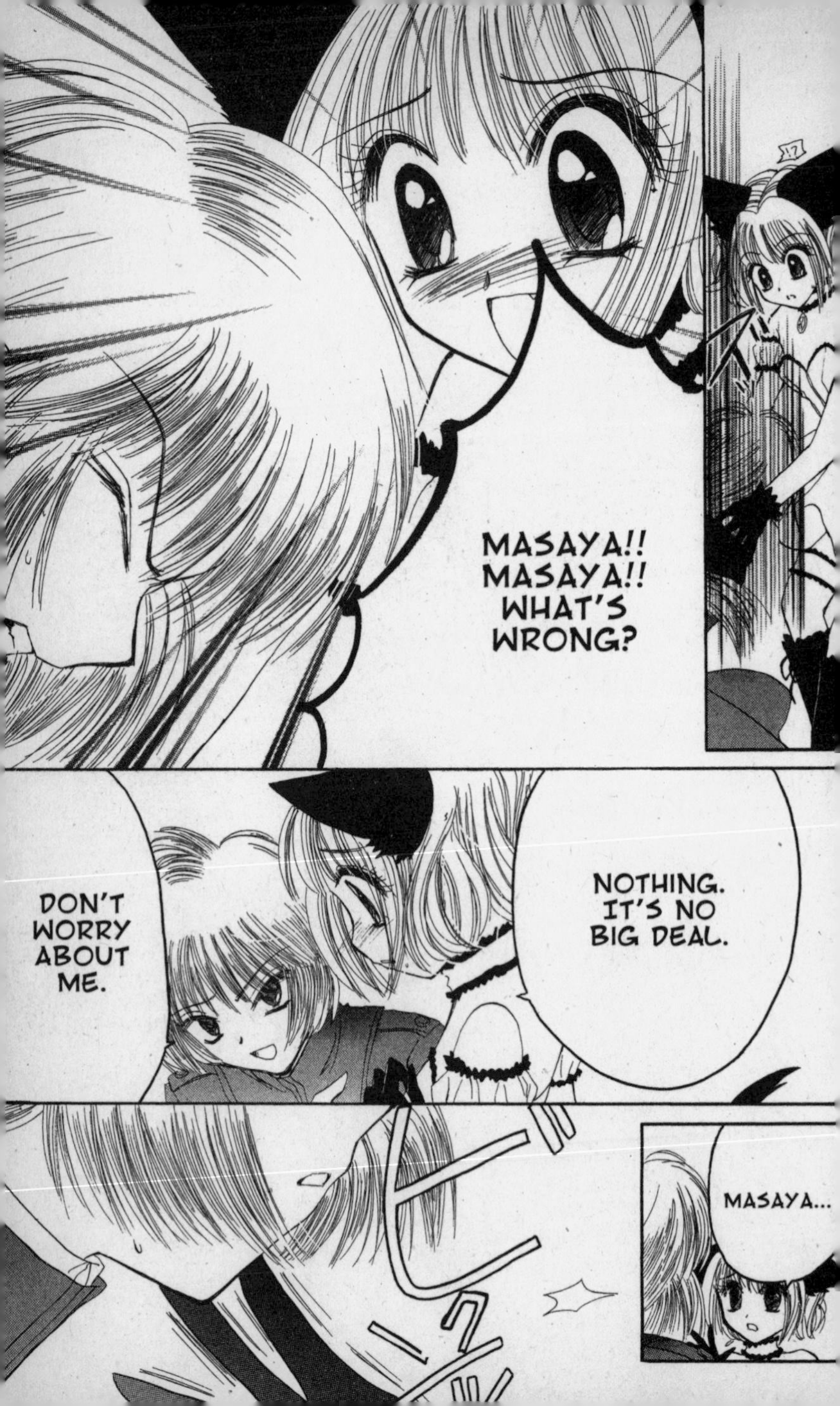
!?
MASAYA!! MASAYA!! WHAT'S WRONG?
NOTHING. IT'S NO BIG DEAL.
DON'T WORRY ABOUT ME.
MASAYA...

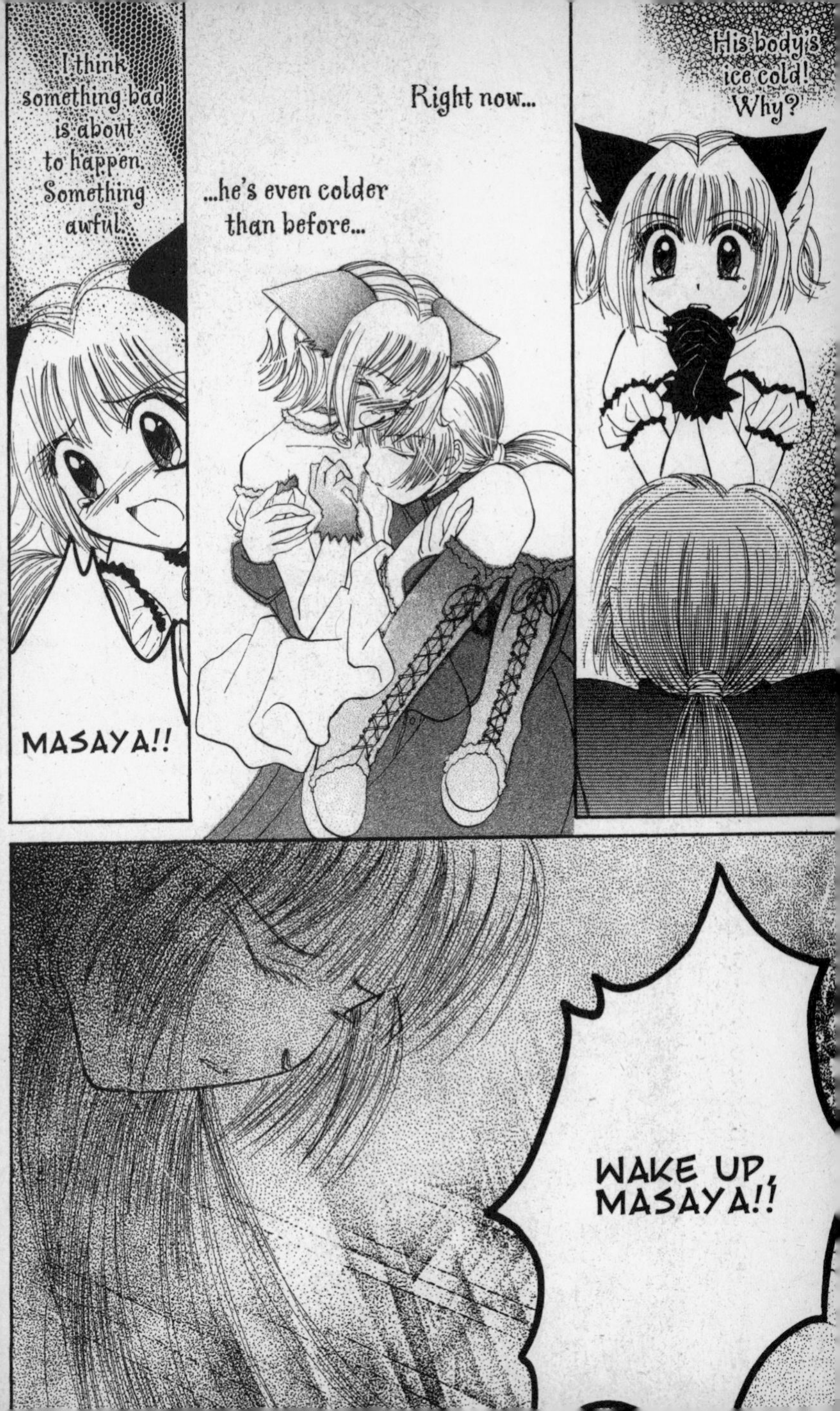
His body's ice cold! Why?
Right now...
...he's even colder than before...
I think something bad is about to happen. Something awful.
MASAYA!!
WAKE UP, MASAYA!!

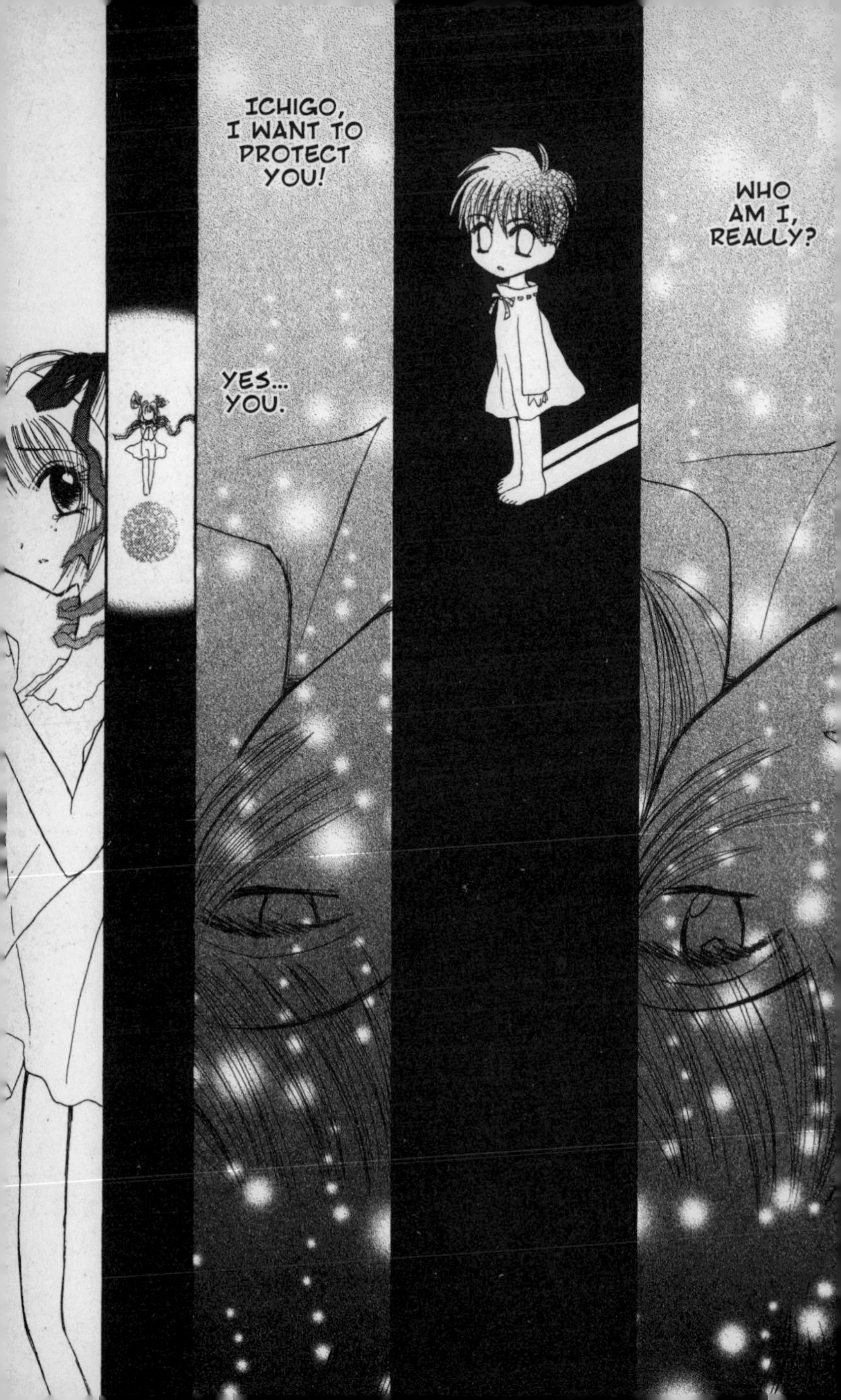
WHO AM I, REALLY?
ICHIGO, I WANT TO PROTECT YOU!
YES... YOU.

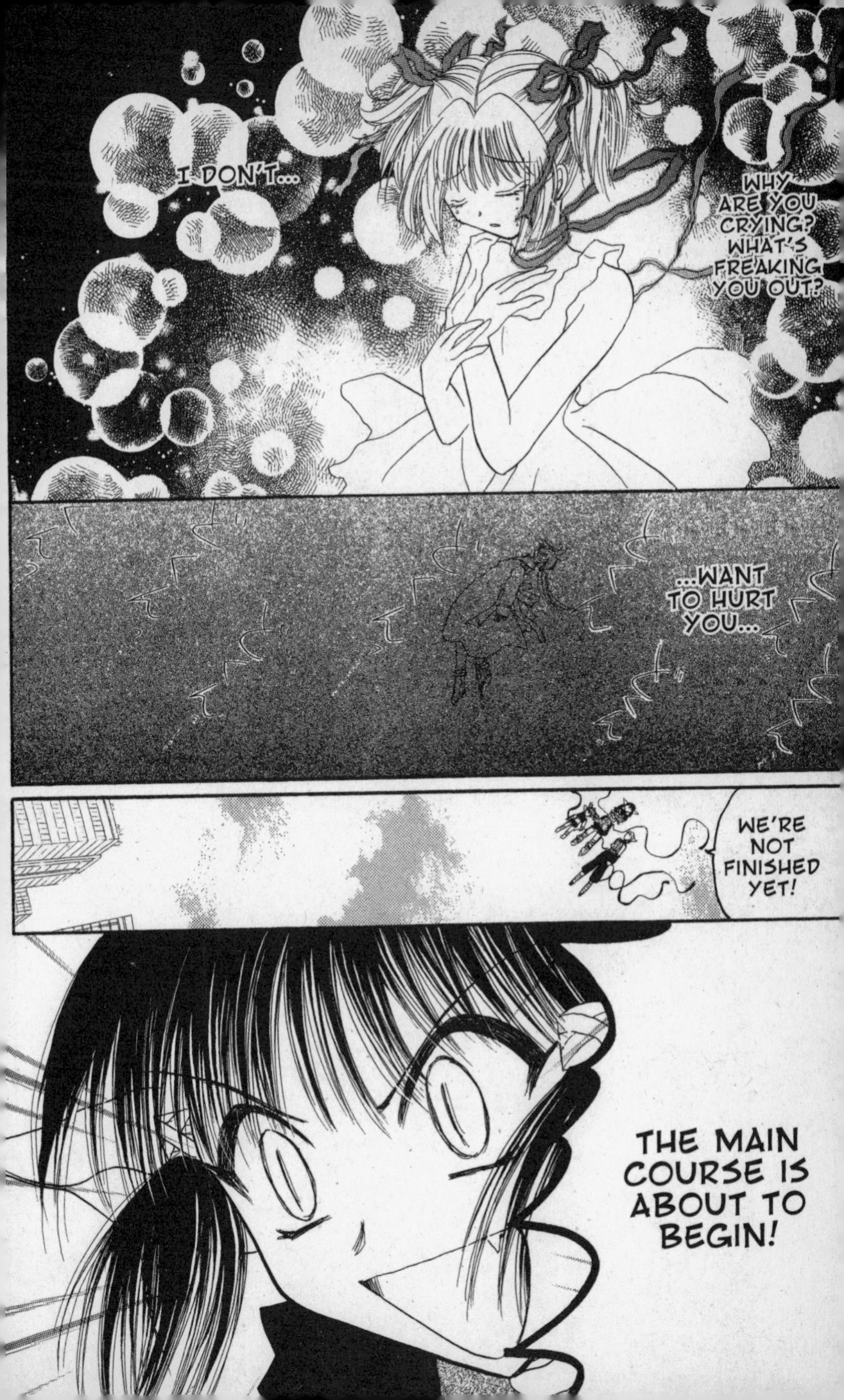
WHY ARE YOU CRYING? WHAT'S FREAKING YOU OUT?
I DON'T...
...WANT TO HURT YOU...
WE'RE NOT FINISHED YET!
THE MAIN COURSE IS ABOUT TO BEGIN!

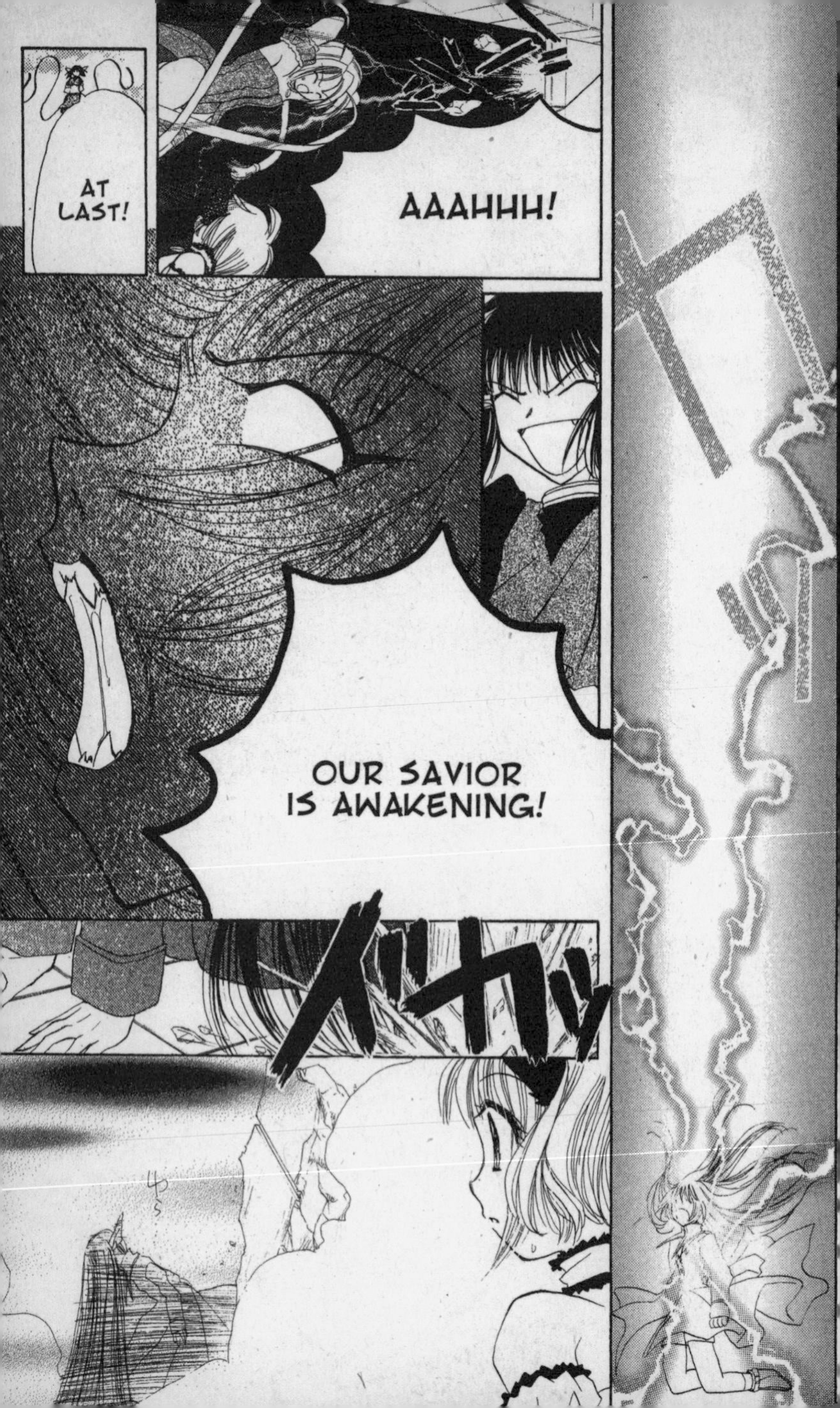
AAAHHH!
AT LAST!
OUR SAVIOR IS AWAKENING!

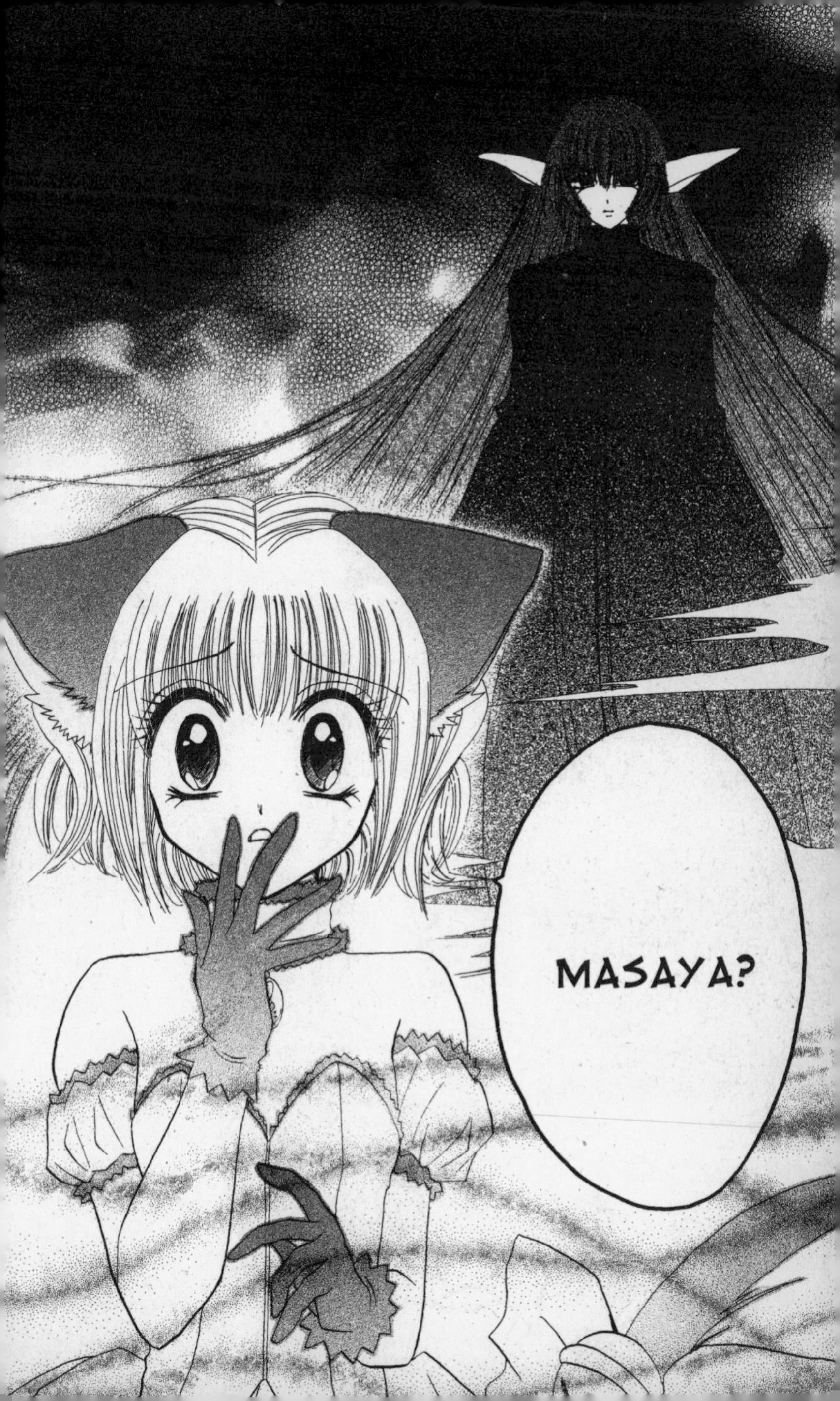
MASAYA?

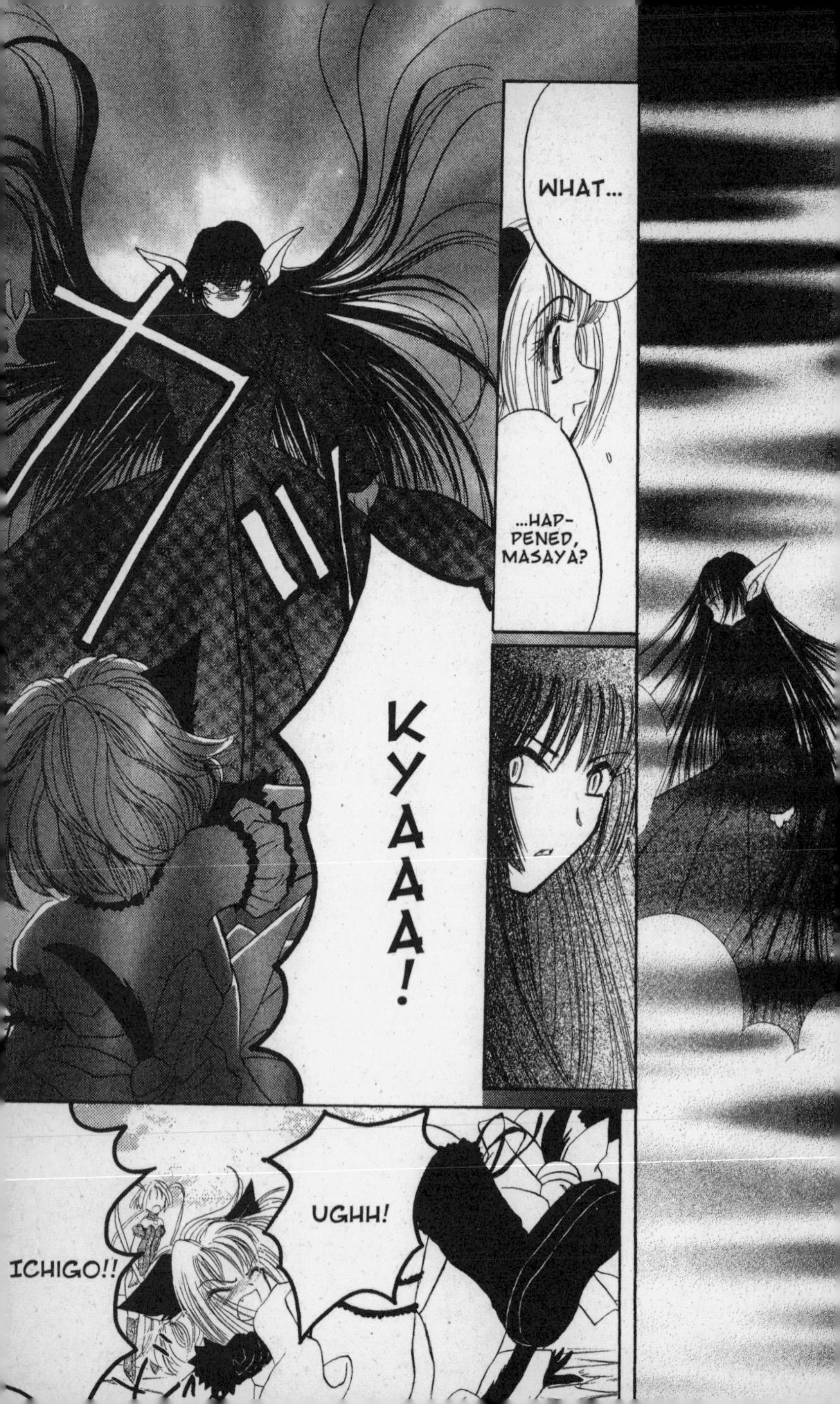
WHAT...
...HAP-PENED, MASAYA?
KYAAA!
UGHH!
ICHIGO!!

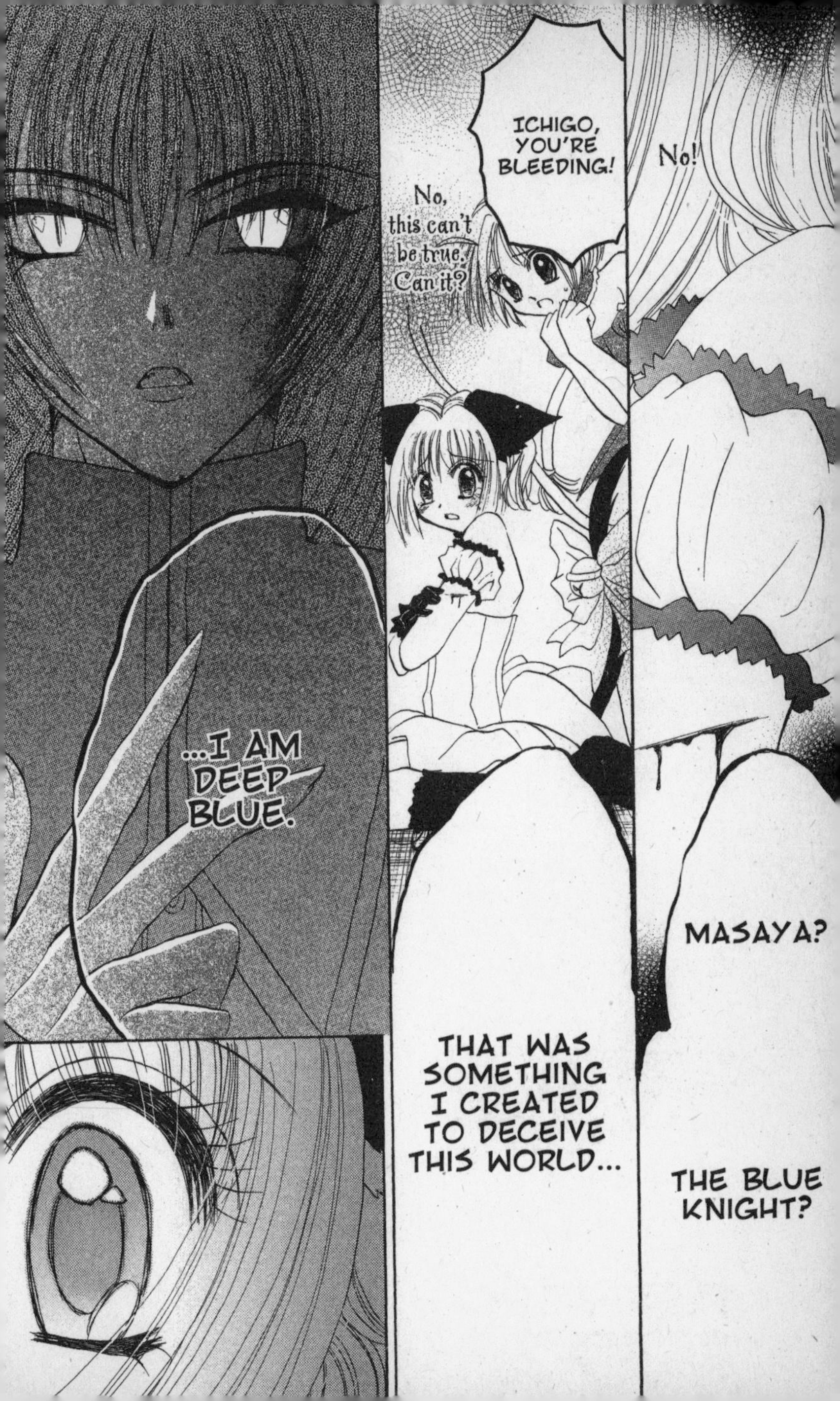
No!
MASAYA?
THE BLUE KNIGHT?
ICHIGO, YOU'RE BLEEDING!
No, this can't be true. Can it?
THAT WAS SOMETHING I CREATED TO DECEIVE THIS WORLD...
...I AM DEEP BLUE.

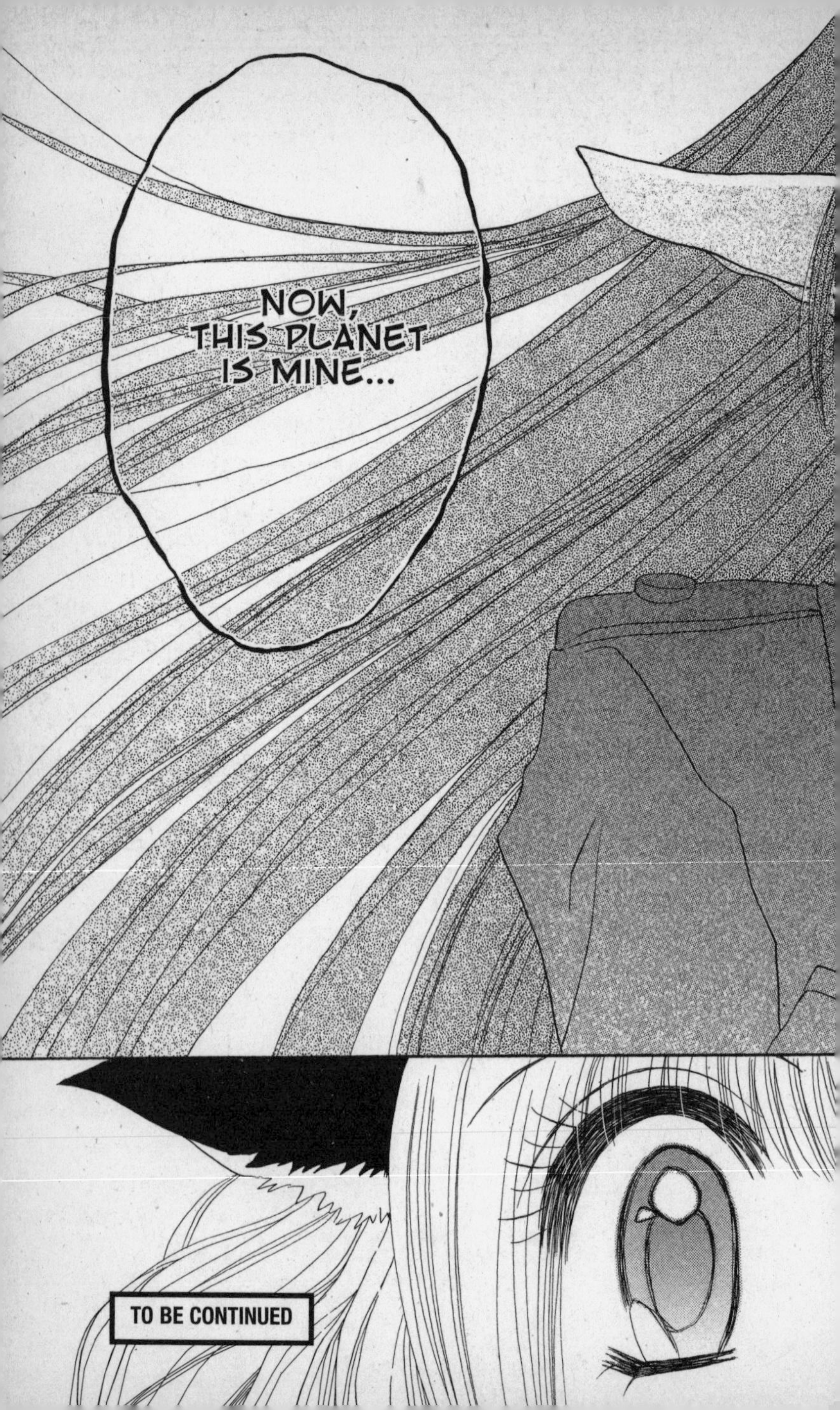
NOW, THIS PLANET IS MINE...
TO BE CONTINUED

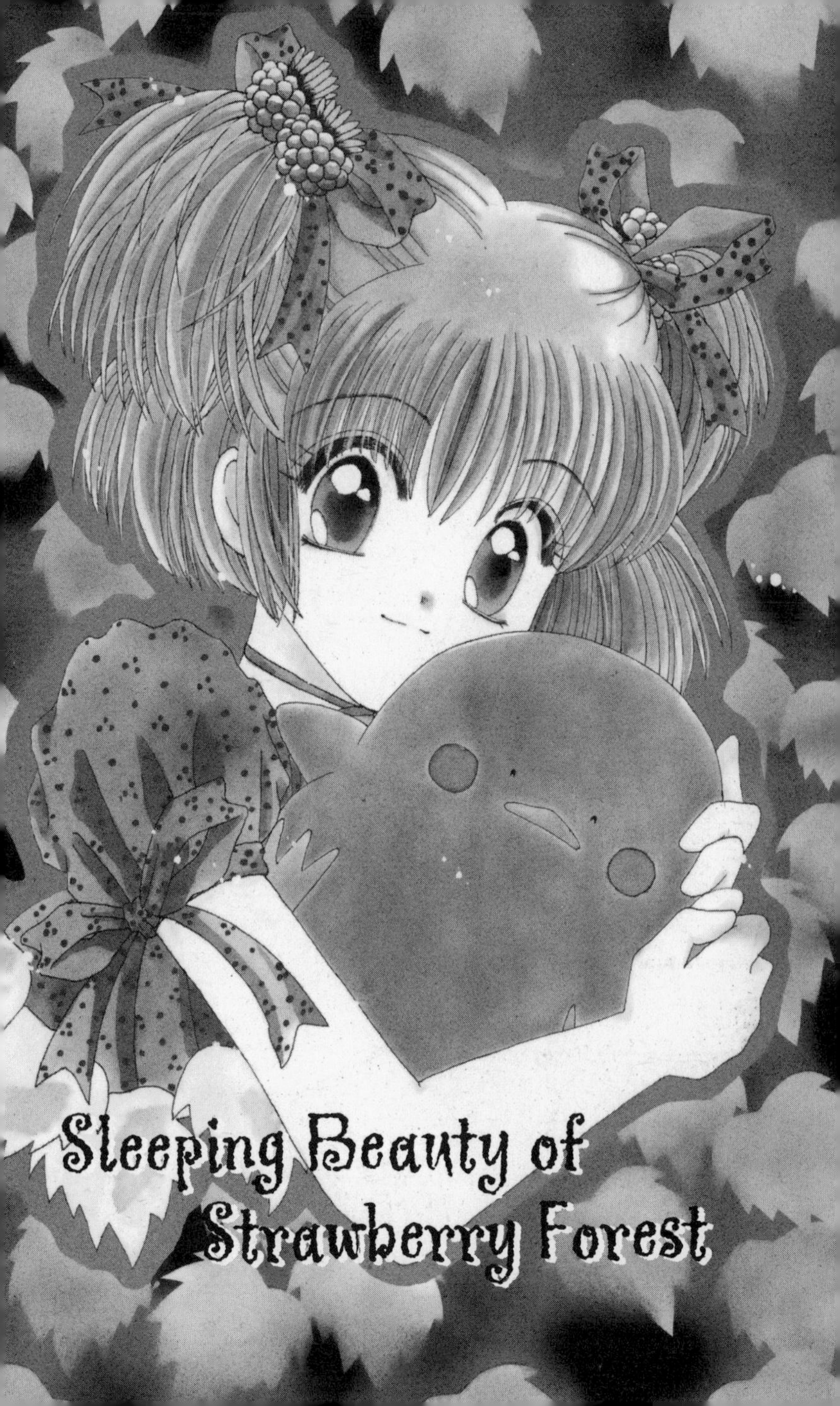
Sleeping Beauty of
Strawberry Forest

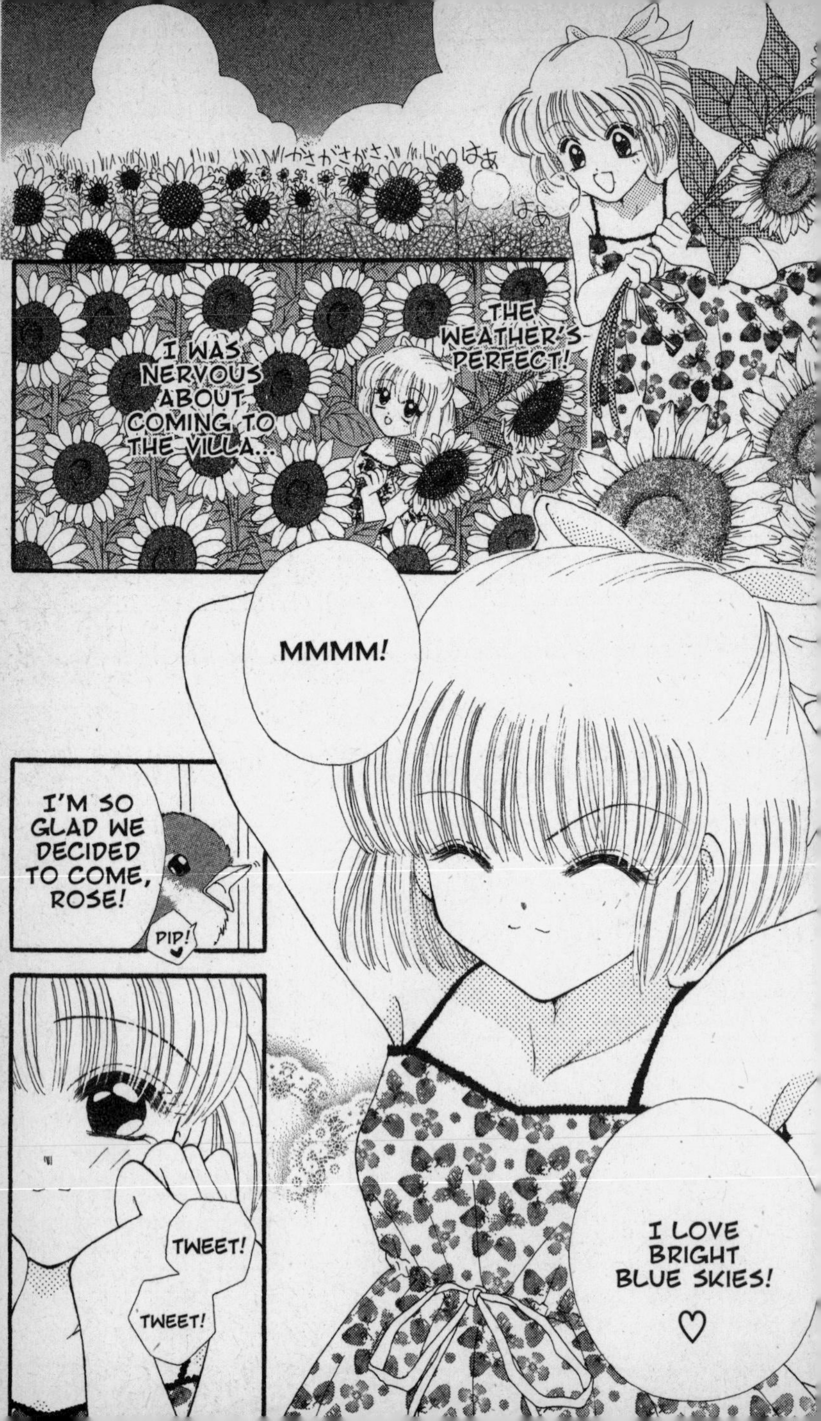

はあ
はあ
がさがさがさ
THE WEATHER'S PERFECT!
I WAS NERVOUS ABOUT COMING TO THE VILLA...
MMMM!
I LOVE BRIGHT BLUE SKIES! ♡
I'M SO GLAD WE DECIDED TO COME, ROSE!
PIP! ♥
TWEET!
TWEET!

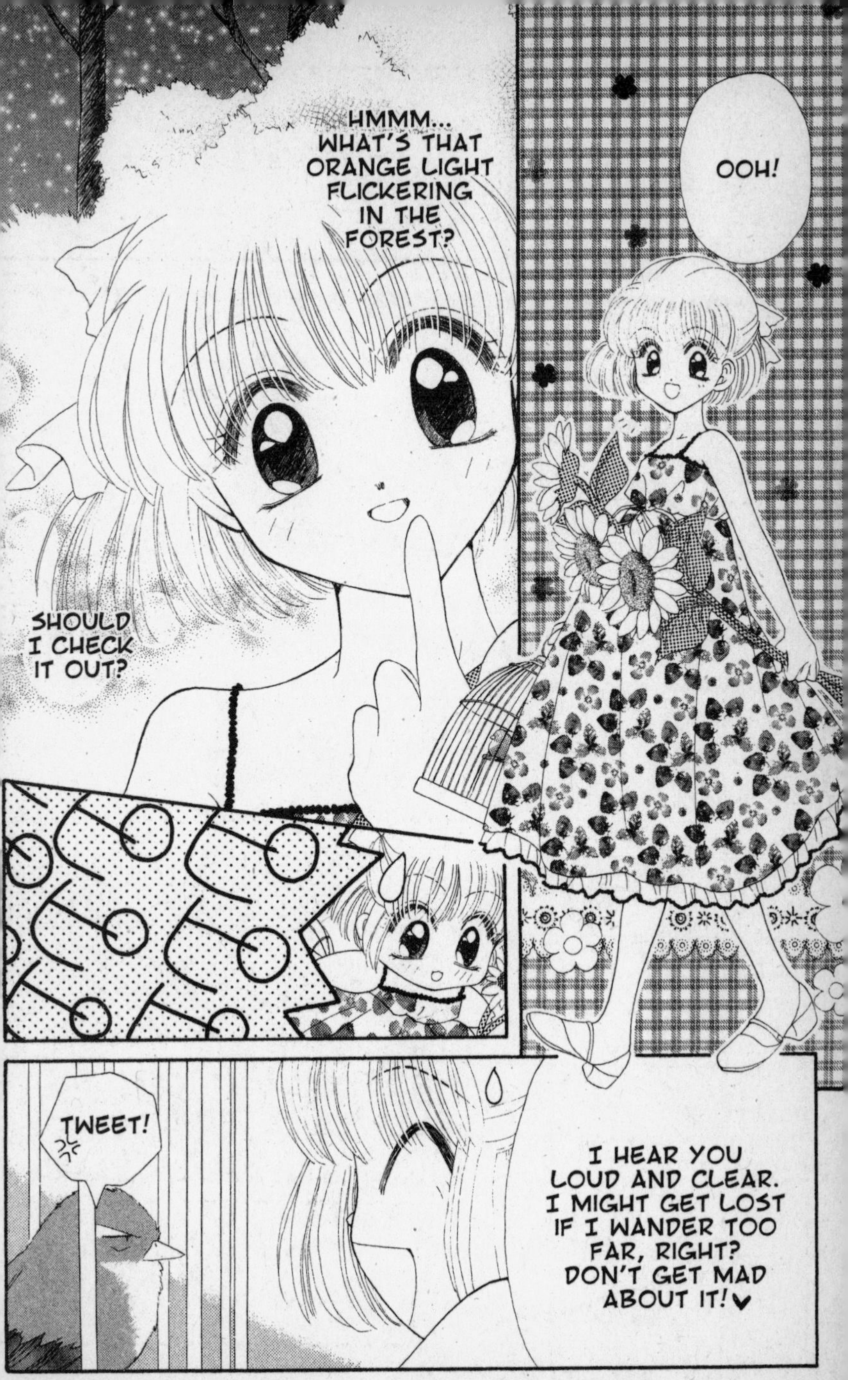
OOH!
HMMM... WHAT'S THAT ORANGE LIGHT FLICKERING IN THE FOREST?
SHOULD I CHECK IT OUT?
TWEET!
I HEAR YOU LOUD AND CLEAR. I MIGHT GET LOST IF I WANDER TOO FAR, RIGHT? DON'T GET MAD ABOUT IT! ♥

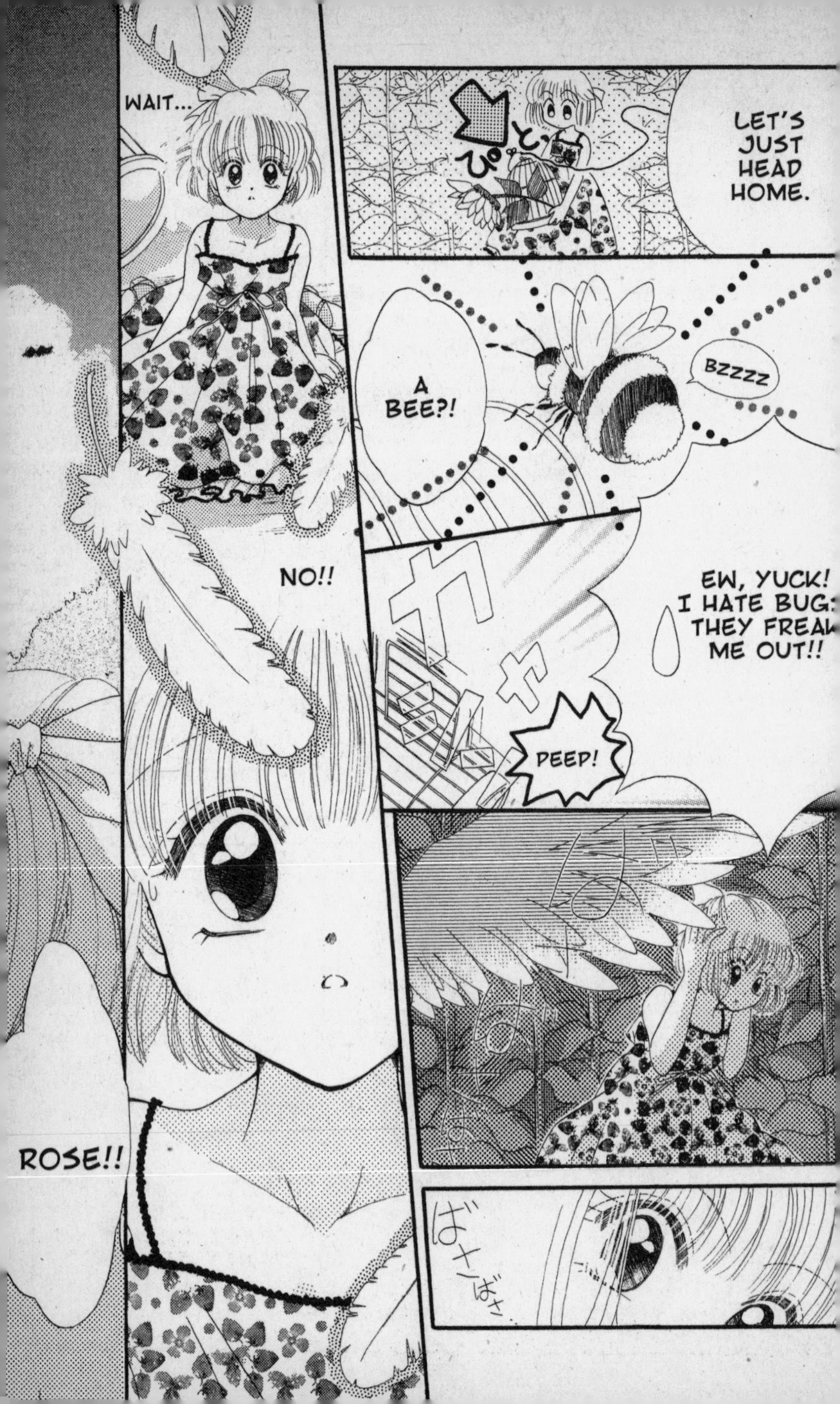

ぴと
LET'S JUST HEAD HOME.
BZZZZ
A BEE?!
EW, YUCK! I HATE BUG: THEY FREAK ME OUT!!
PEEP!
ばさばさ
WAIT...
NO!!
ROSE!!

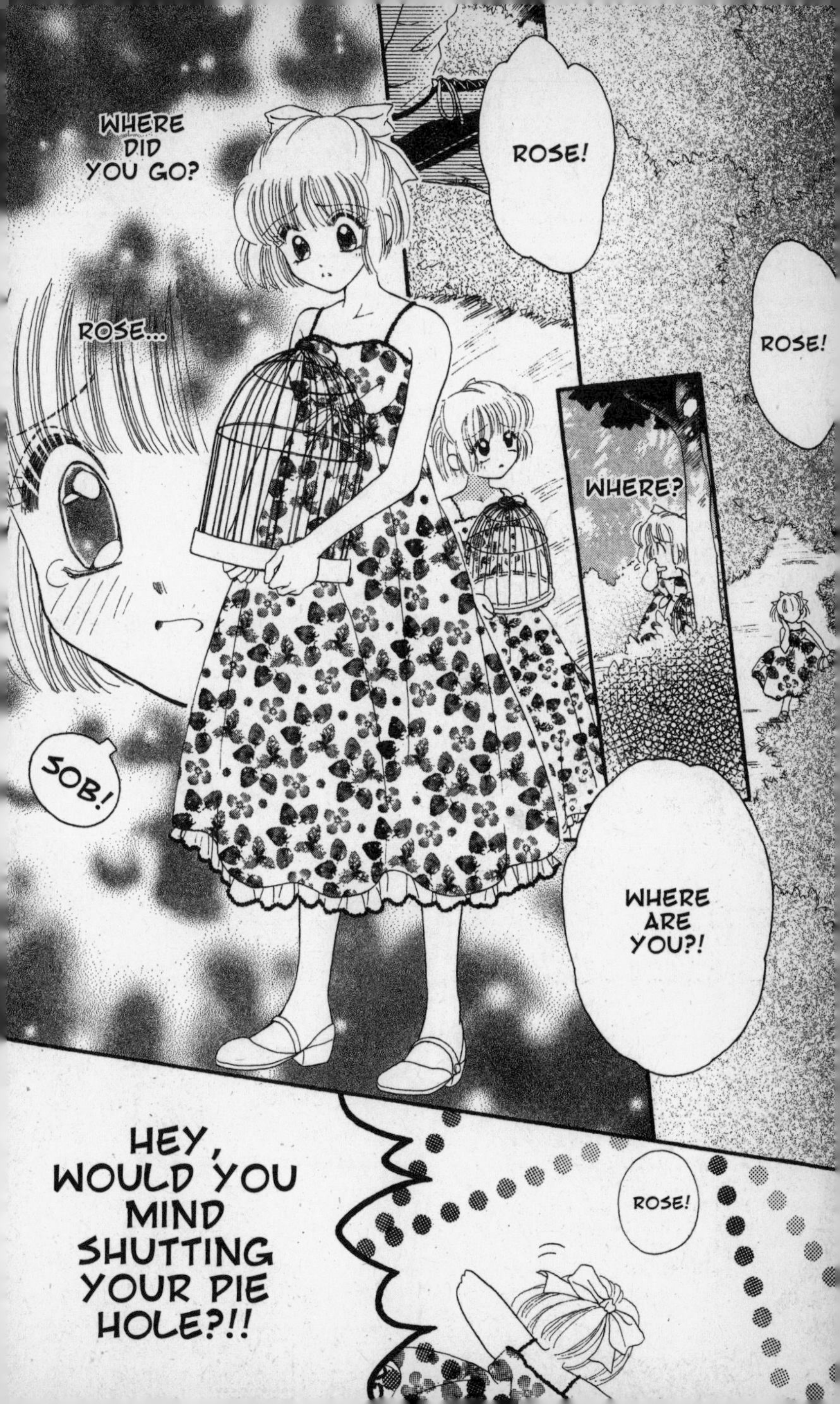
ROSE!
ROSE!
WHERE?
WHERE ARE YOU?!
WHERE DID YOU GO?
ROSE...
SOB!
ROSE!
HEY, WOULD YOU MIND SHUTTING YOUR PIE HOLE?!!

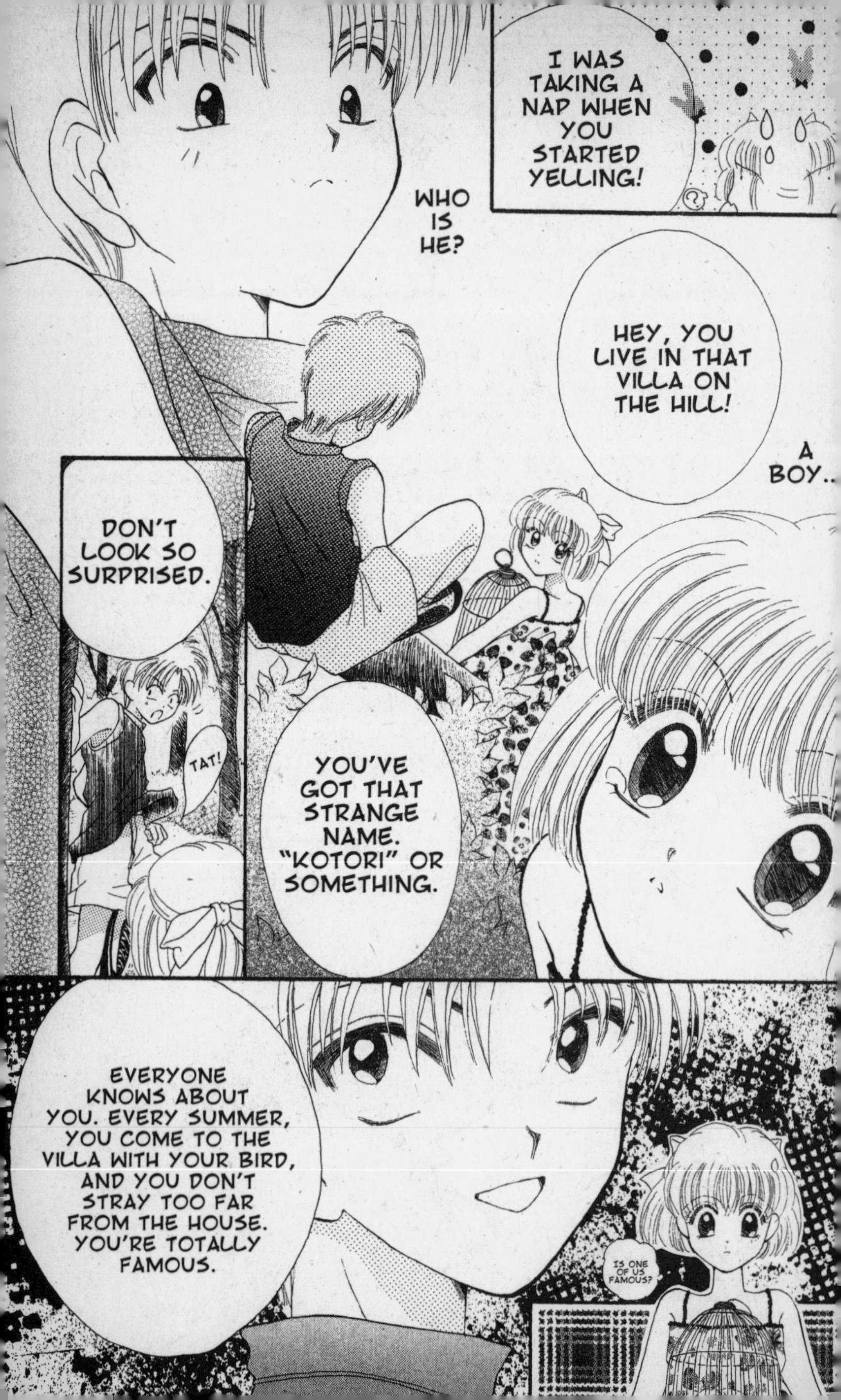

I WAS TAKING A NAP WHEN YOU STARTED YELLING!
WHO IS HE?
HEY, YOU LIVE IN THAT VILLA ON THE HILL!
A BOY...
YOU'VE GOT THAT STRANGE NAME. "KOTORI" OR SOMETHING.
DON'T LOOK SO SURPRISED.
TAT!
EVERYONE KNOWS ABOUT YOU. EVERY SUMMER, YOU COME TO THE VILLA WITH YOUR BIRD, AND YOU DON'T STRAY TOO FAR FROM THE HOUSE. YOU'RE TOTALLY FAMOUS.
IS ONE OF US FAMOUS?

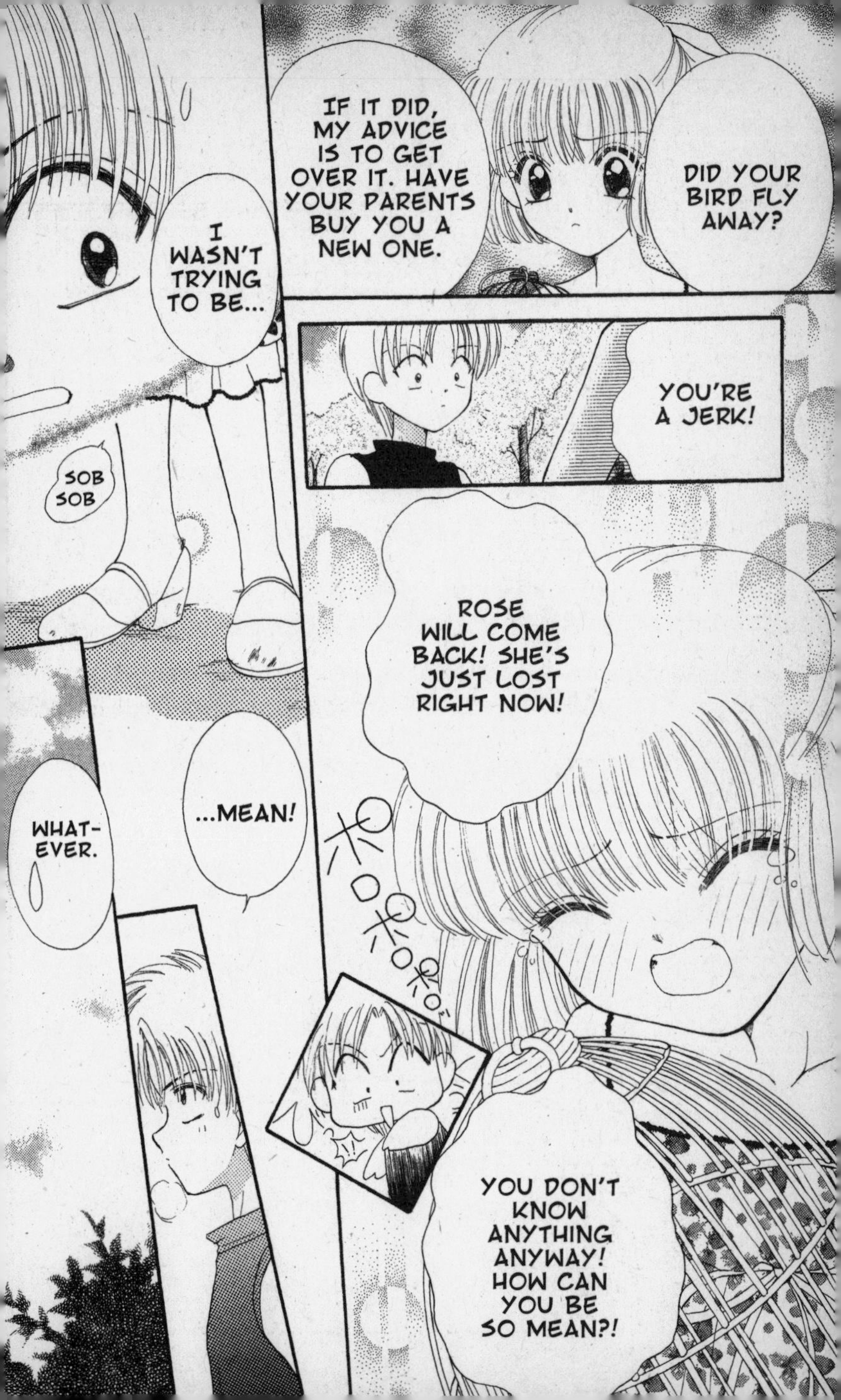
DID YOUR BIRD FLY AWAY?
IF IT DID, MY ADVICE IS TO GET OVER IT. HAVE YOUR PARENTS BUY YOU A NEW ONE.
YOU'RE A JERK!
ROSE WILL COME BACK! SHE'S JUST LOST RIGHT NOW!
YOU DON'T KNOW ANYTHING ANYWAY! HOW CAN YOU BE SO MEAN?!
I WASN'T TRYING TO BE...
SOB SOB
...MEAN!
WHAT-EVER.

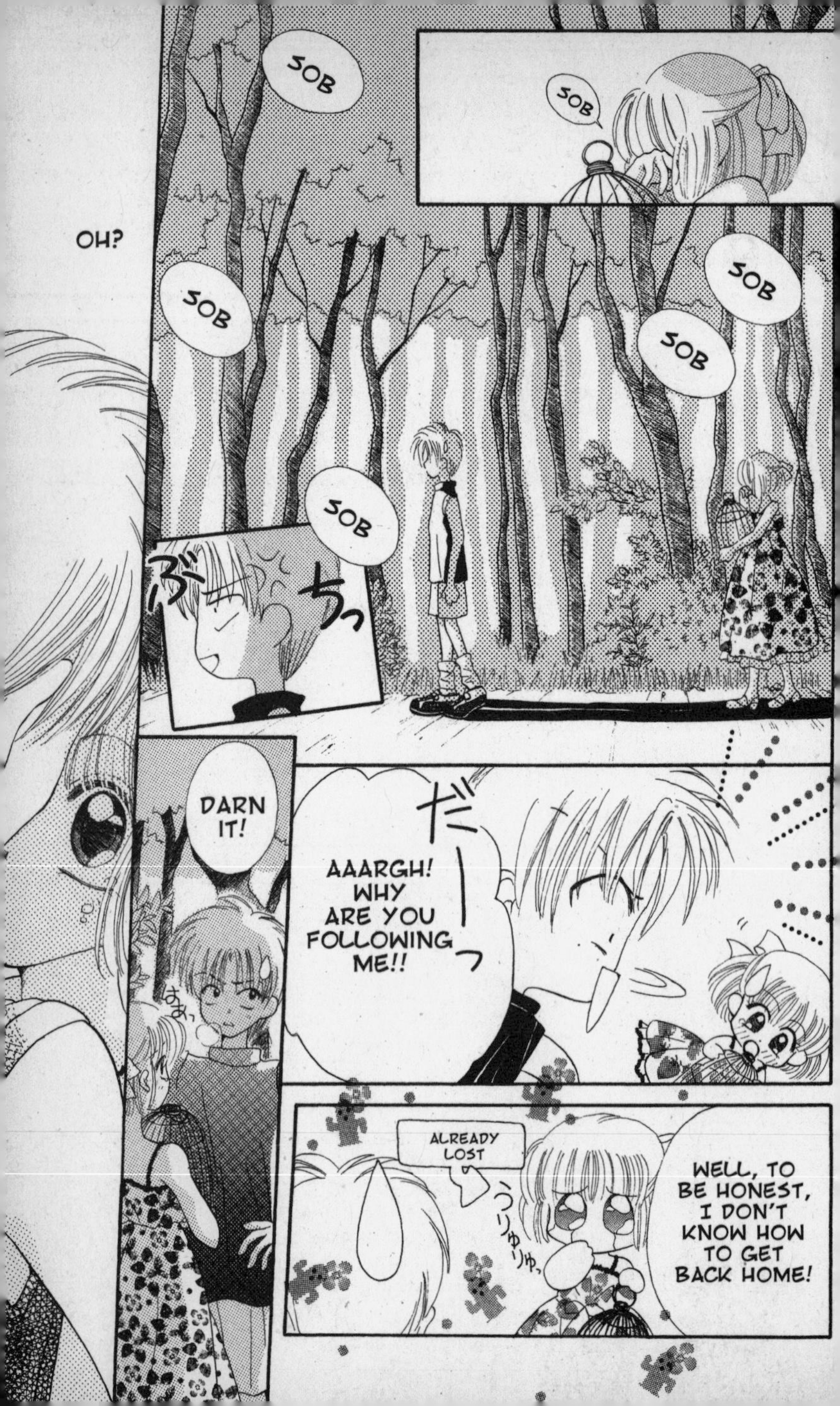
SOB
SOB
SOB
SOB
SOB
SOB
ぶ
ちっ
OH?
だーっ
AAARGH! WHY ARE YOU FOLLOWING ME!!
DARN IT!
WELL, TO BE HONEST, I DON'T KNOW HOW TO GET BACK HOME!
ALREADY LOST
うりゅりゅっ

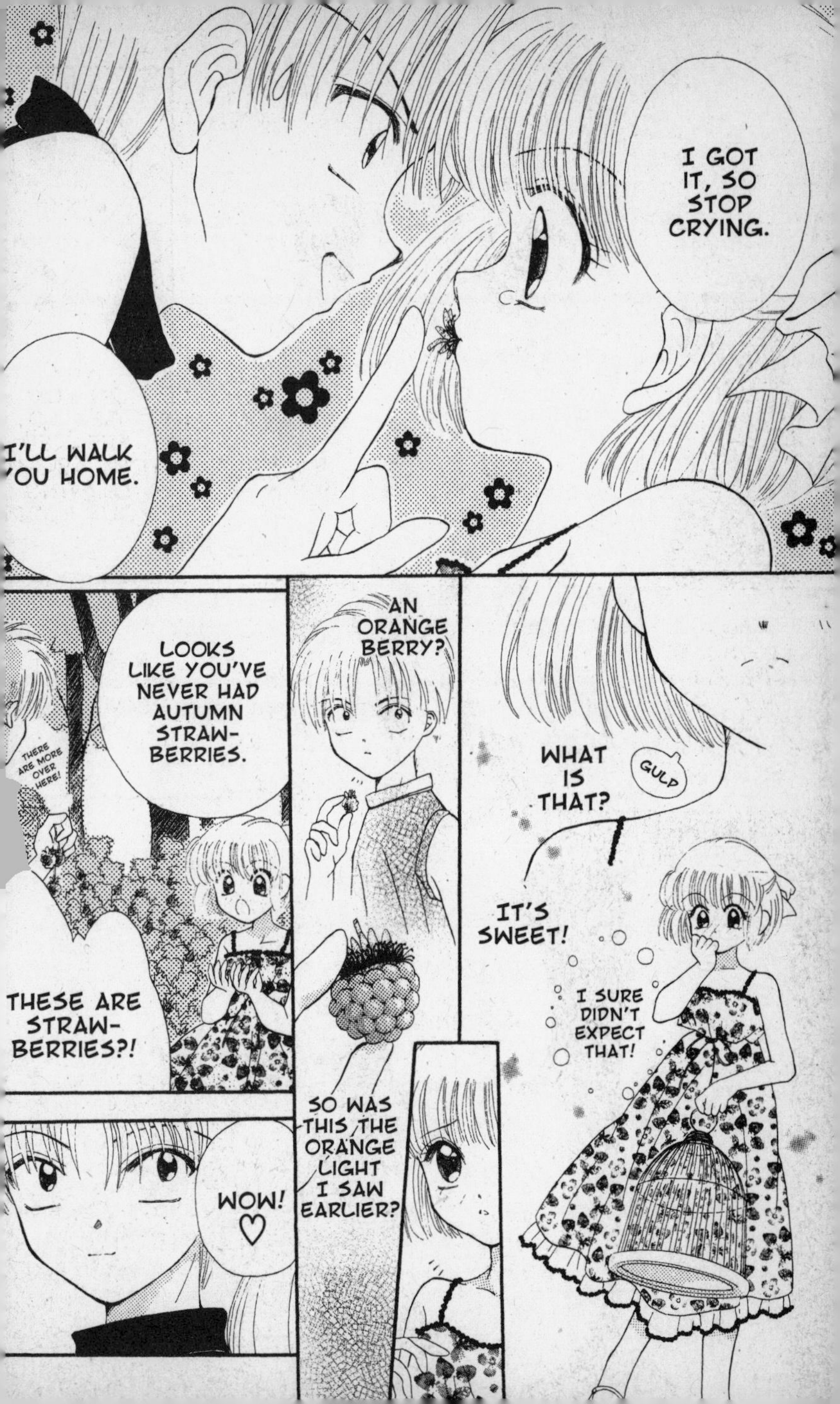
I GOT IT, SO STOP CRYING.
I'LL WALK 'OU HOME.
WHAT IS THAT?
GULP
IT'S SWEET!
I SURE DIDN'T EXPECT THAT!
AN ORANGE BERRY?
LOOKS LIKE YOU'VE NEVER HAD AUTUMN STRAW-BERRIES.
THERE ARE MORE OVER HERE!
THESE ARE STRAW-BERRIES?!
SO WAS THIS THE ORANGE LIGHT I SAW EARLIER?
WOW! ♡

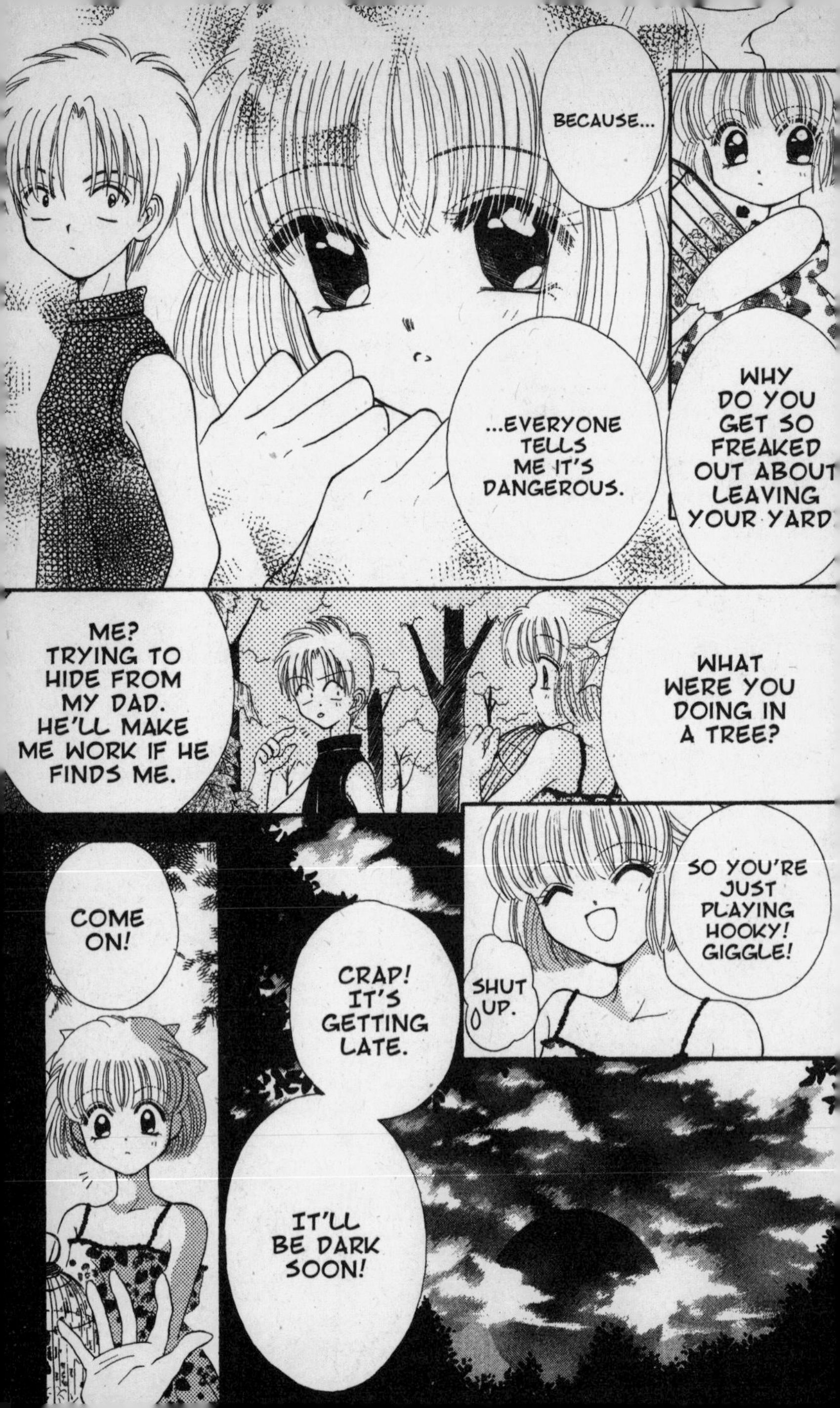
WHY DO YOU GET SO FREAKED OUT ABOUT LEAVING YOUR YARD
BECAUSE...
...EVERYONE TELLS ME IT'S DANGEROUS.
WHAT WERE YOU DOING IN A TREE?
ME? TRYING TO HIDE FROM MY DAD. HE'LL MAKE ME WORK IF HE FINDS ME.
SO YOU'RE JUST PLAYING HOOKY! GIGGLE!
SHUT UP.
CRAP! IT'S GETTING LATE.
IT'LL BE DARK SOON!
COME ON!

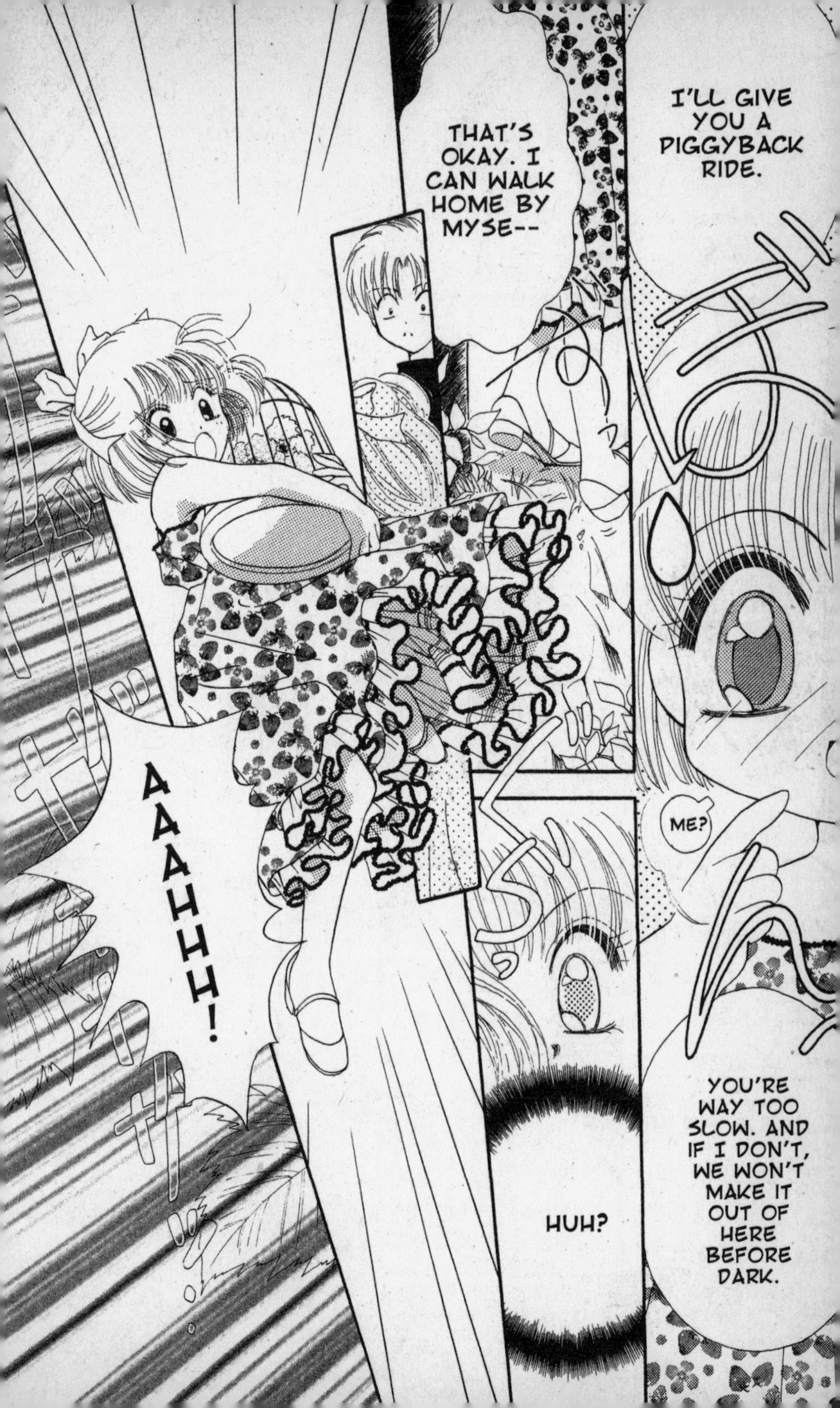
I'LL GIVE YOU A PIGGYBACK RIDE.
ME?
THAT'S OKAY. I CAN WALK HOME BY MYSE--
YOU'RE WAY TOO SLOW. AND IF I DON'T, WE WON'T MAKE IT OUT OF HERE BEFORE DARK.
HUH?
AAAHHH!

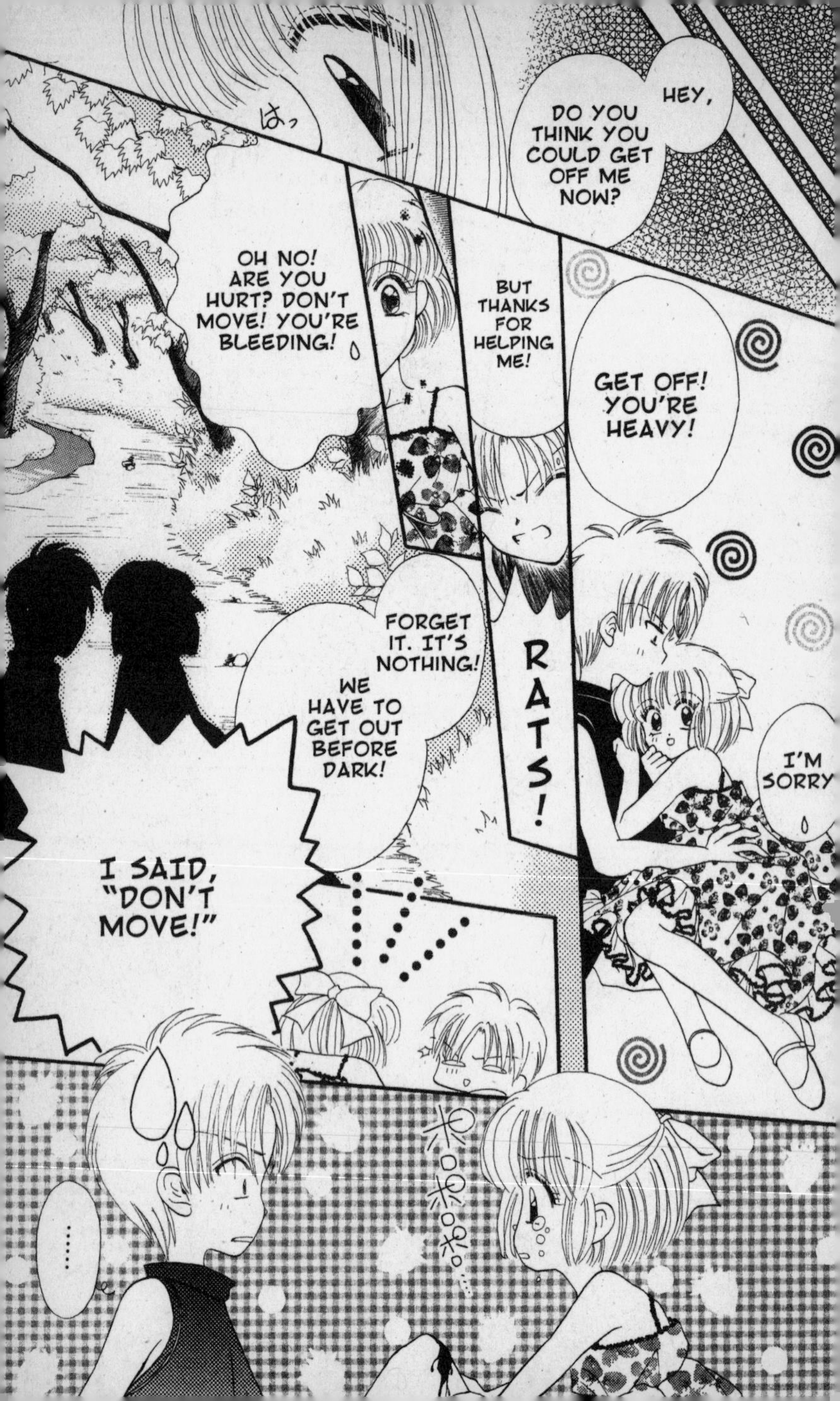
HEY, DO YOU THINK YOU COULD GET OFF ME NOW?
はっ
GET OFF! YOU'RE HEAVY!
I'M SORRY
BUT THANKS FOR HELPING ME!
RATS!
OH NO! ARE YOU HURT? DON'T MOVE! YOU'RE BLEEDING!
FORGET IT. IT'S NOTHING!
WE HAVE TO GET OUT BEFORE DARK!
I SAID, "DON'T MOVE!"
ポロポロ…
……

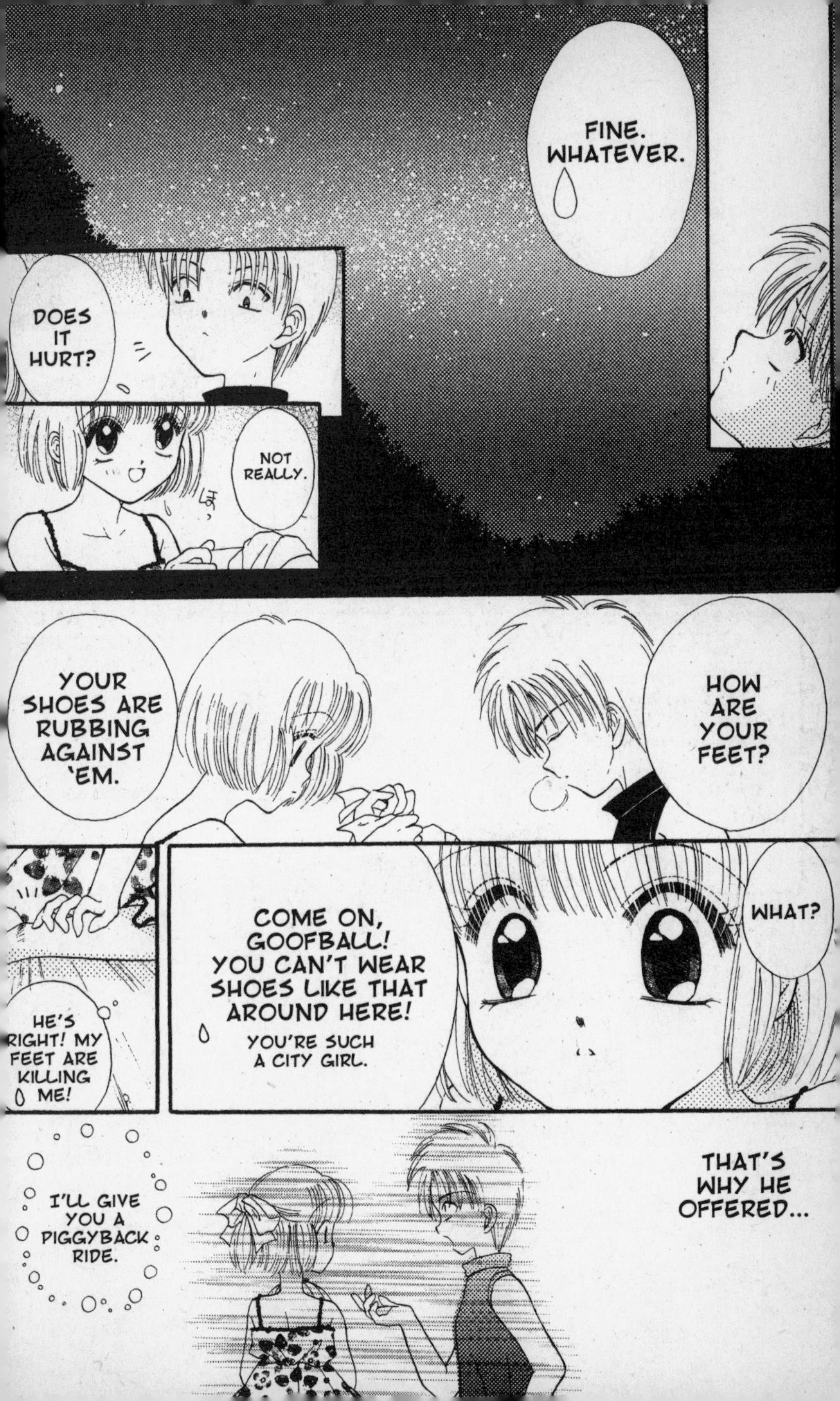
FINE. WHATEVER.
DOES IT HURT?
NOT REALLY.
HOW ARE YOUR FEET?
YOUR SHOES ARE RUBBING AGAINST 'EM.
WHAT?
COME ON, GOOFBALL! YOU CAN'T WEAR SHOES LIKE THAT AROUND HERE!
YOU'RE SUCH A CITY GIRL.
HE'S RIGHT! MY FEET ARE KILLING ME!
THAT'S WHY HE OFFERED...
I'LL GIVE YOU A PIGGYBACK RIDE.

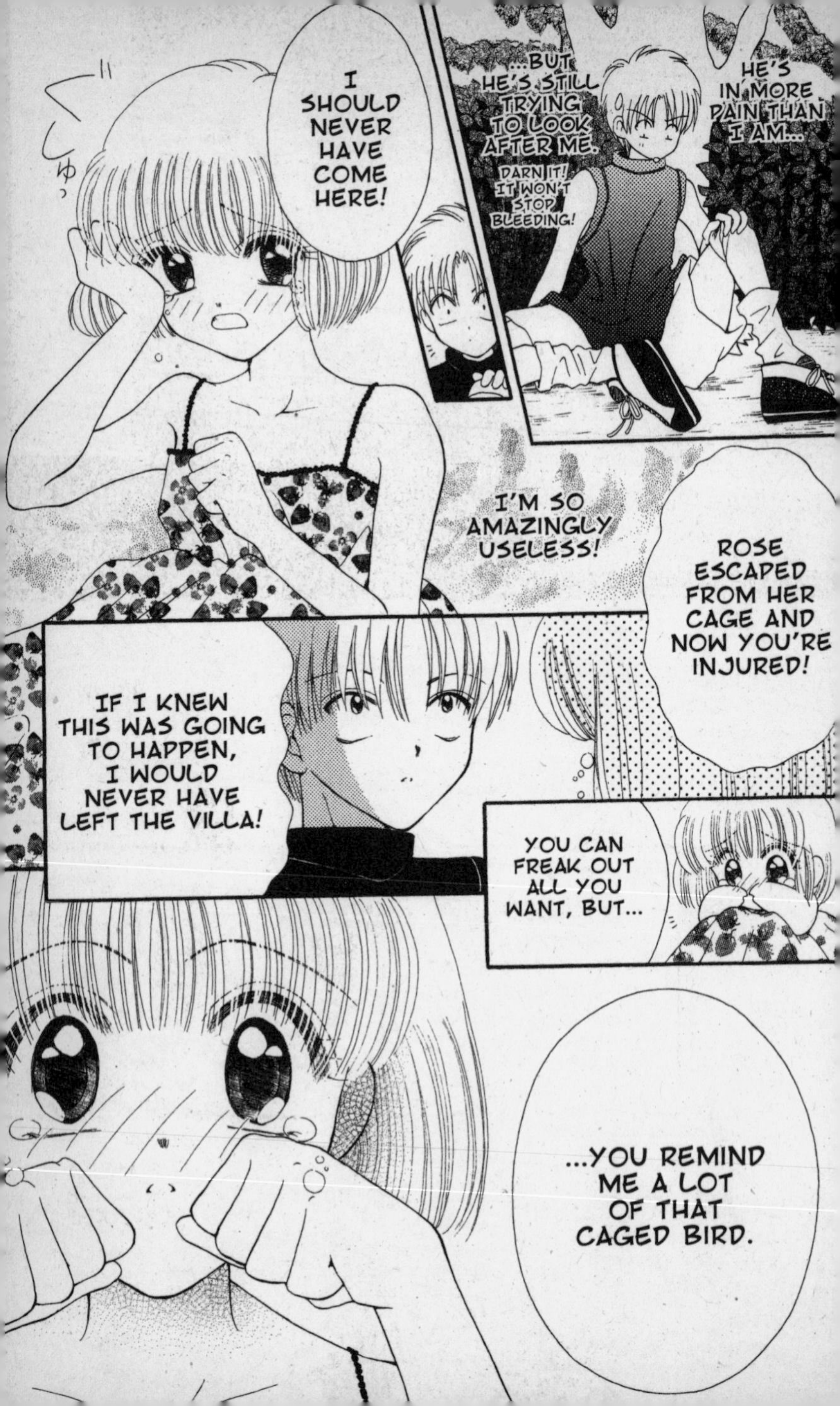
HE'S IN MORE PAIN THAN I AM...
...BUT HE'S STILL TRYING TO LOOK AFTER ME.
DARN IT! IT WON'T STOP BLEEDING!
I SHOULD NEVER HAVE COME HERE!
I'M SO AMAZINGLY USELESS!
ROSE ESCAPED FROM HER CAGE AND NOW YOU'RE INJURED!
IF I KNEW THIS WAS GOING TO HAPPEN, I WOULD NEVER HAVE LEFT THE VILLA!
YOU CAN FREAK OUT ALL YOU WANT, BUT...
...YOU REMIND ME A LOT OF THAT CAGED BIRD.

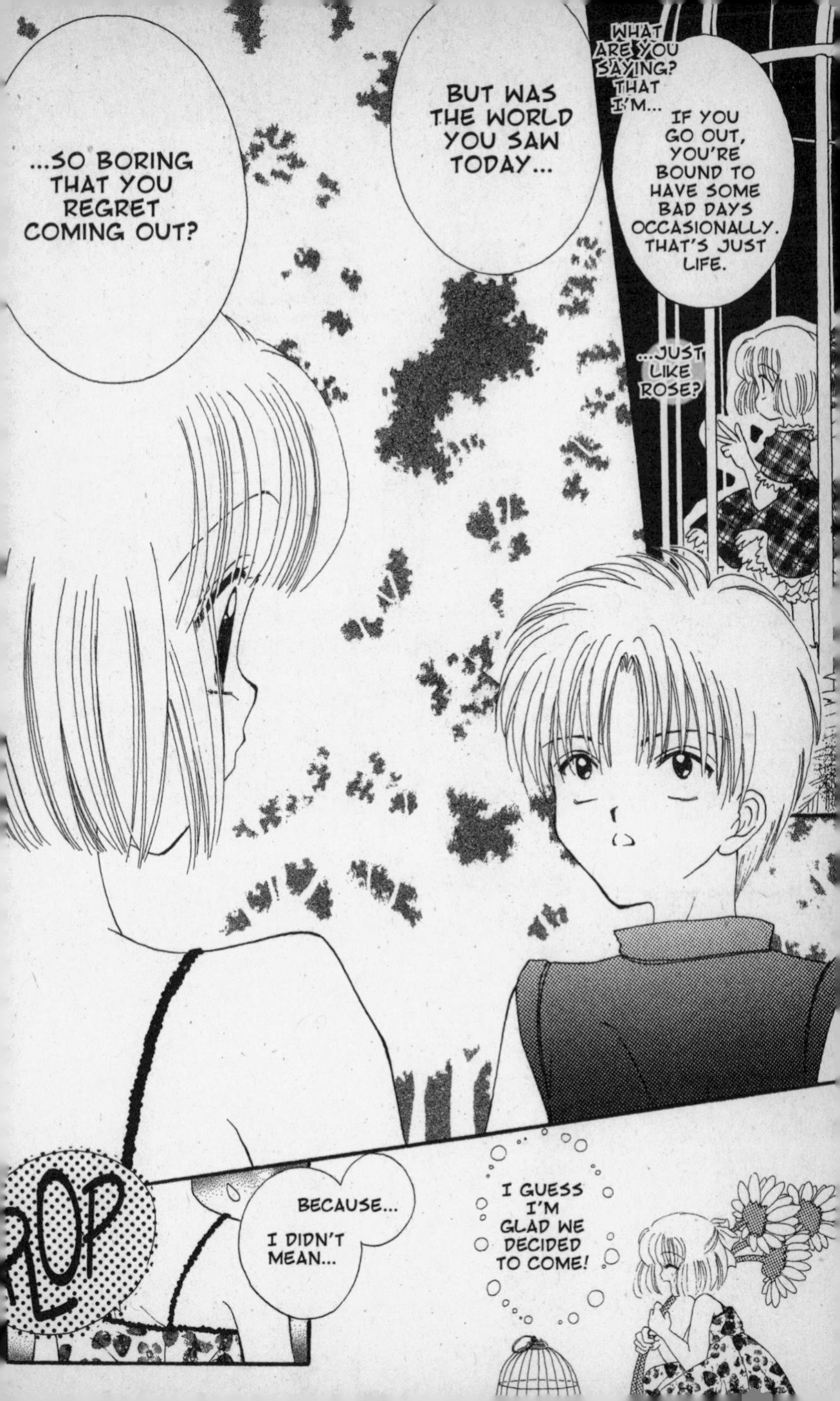
WHAT ARE YOU SAYING? THAT I'M...
...JUST LIKE ROSE?
IF YOU GO OUT, YOU'RE BOUND TO HAVE SOME BAD DAYS OCCASIONALLY. THAT'S JUST LIFE.
BUT WAS THE WORLD YOU SAW TODAY...
...SO BORING THAT YOU REGRET COMING OUT?
I GUESS I'M GLAD WE DECIDED TO COME!
BECAUSE...
I DIDN'T MEAN...

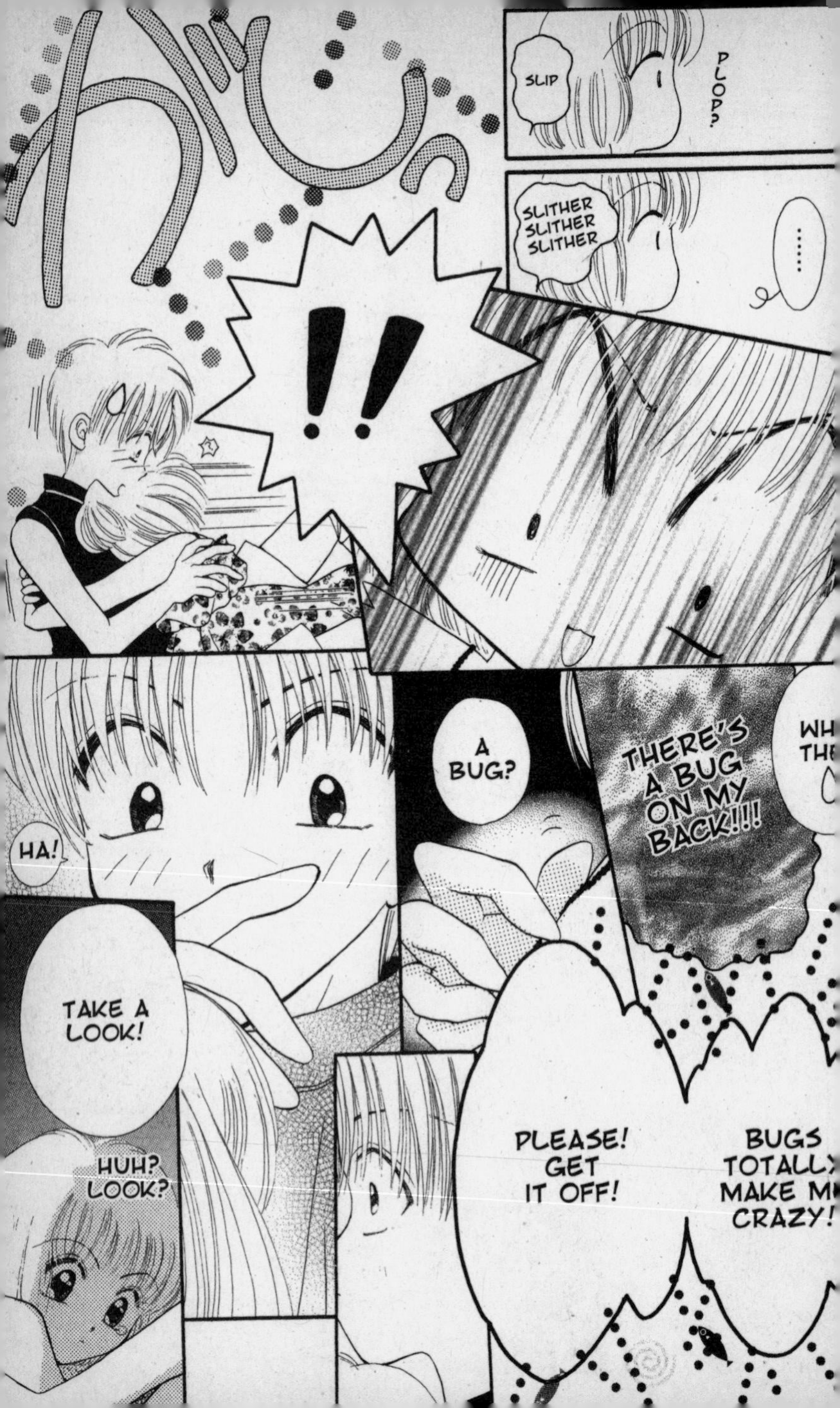
PLOP?
SLIP
......
SLITHER SLITHER SLITHER
!!
THERE'S A BUG ON MY BACK!!!
A BUG?
HA!
BUGS TOTALLY MAKE ME CRAZY!
PLEASE! GET IT OFF!
TAKE A LOOK!
HUH? LOOK?

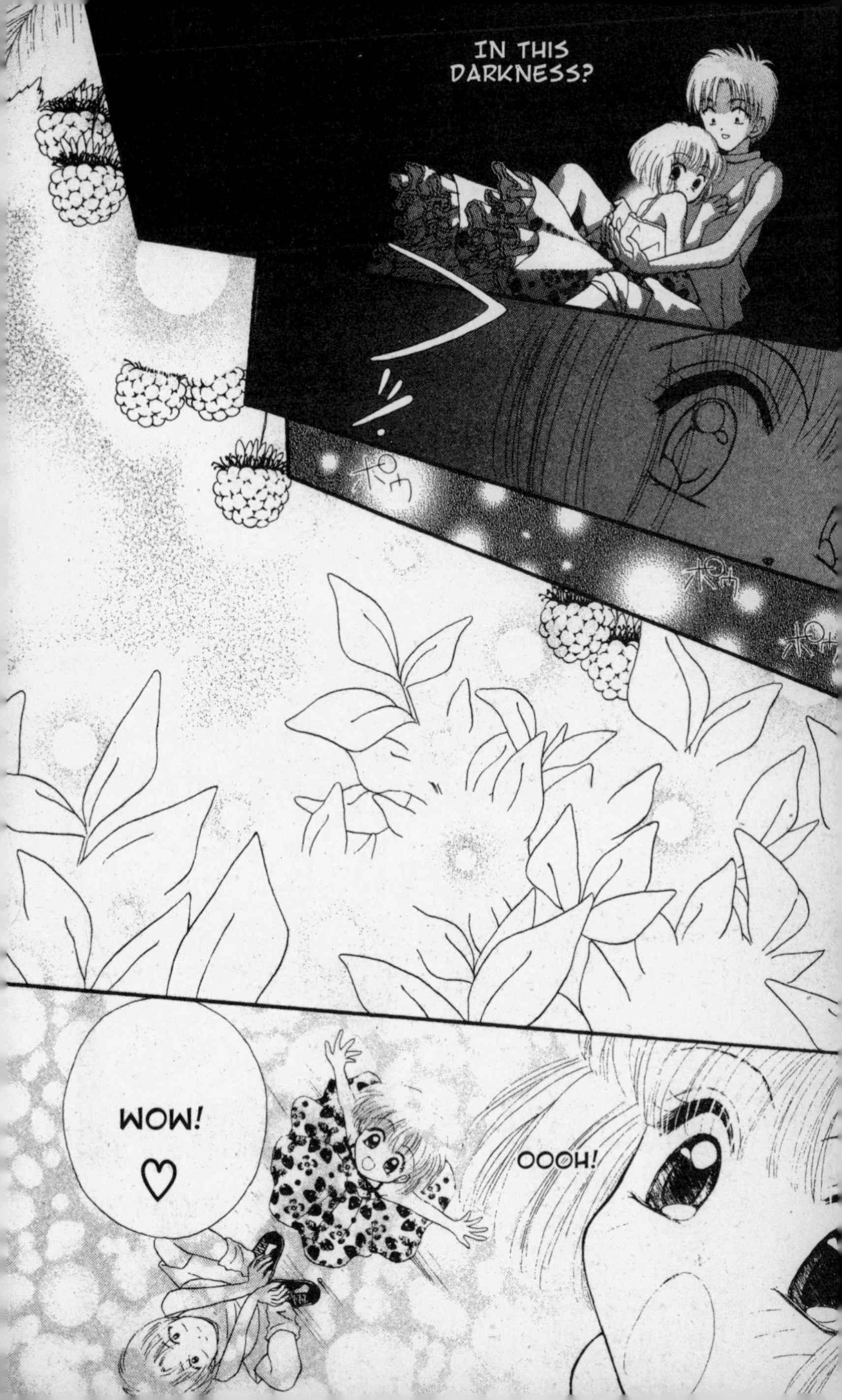
IN THIS DARKNESS?
OOOH!
WOW! ♡

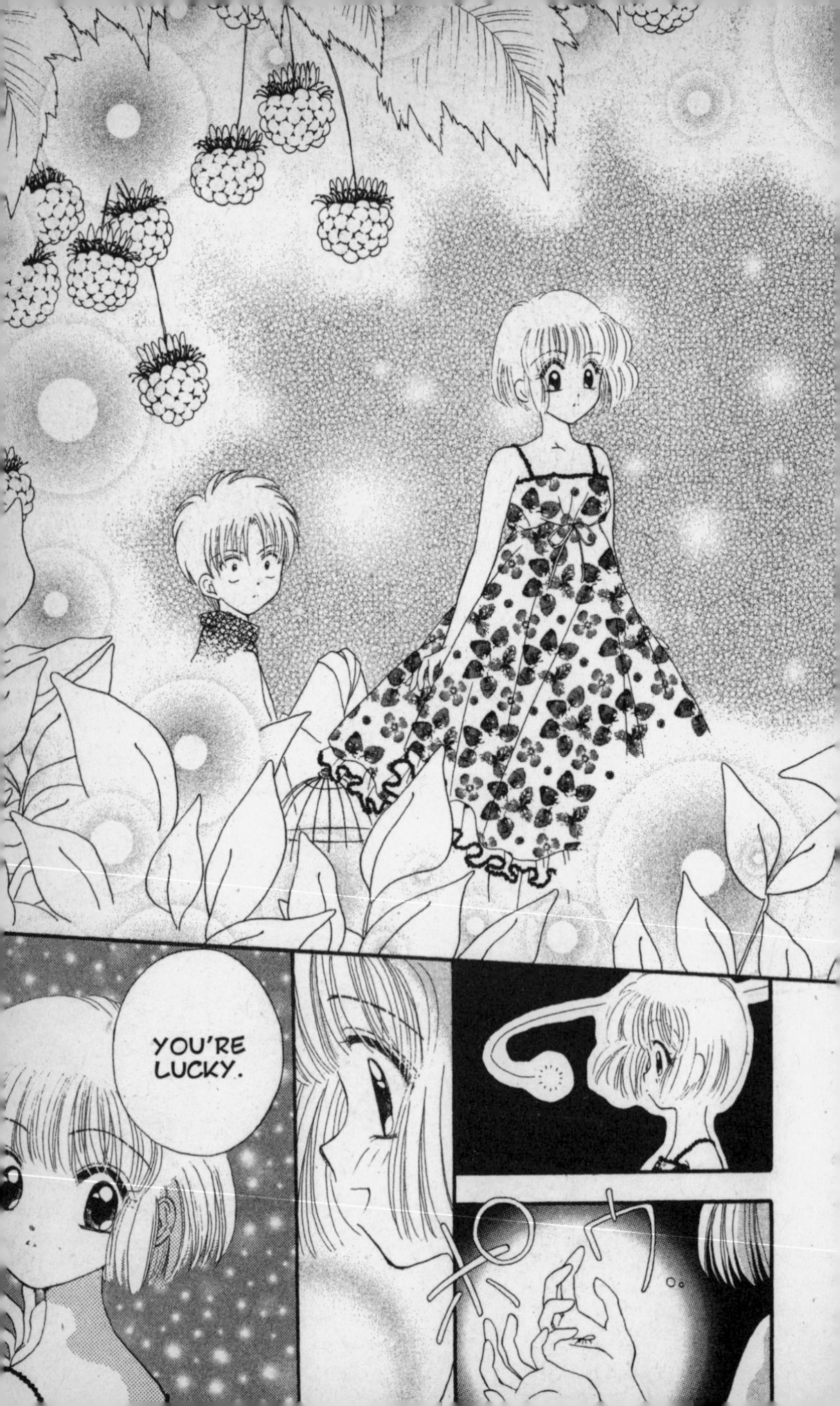
YOU'RE LUCKY.

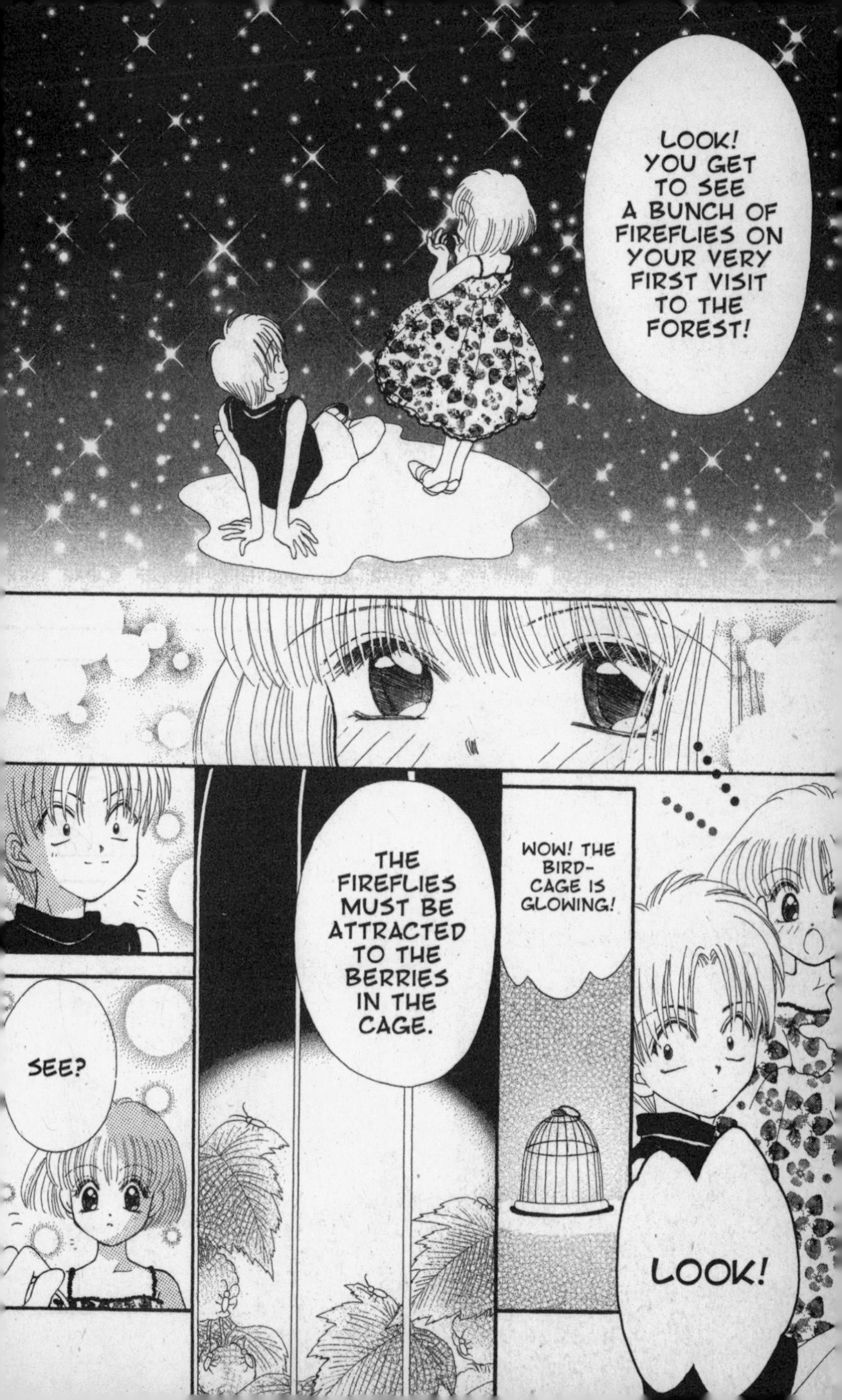

LOOK! YOU GET TO SEE A BUNCH OF FIREFLIES ON YOUR VERY FIRST VISIT TO THE FOREST!
LOOK!
WOW! THE BIRD-CAGE IS GLOWING!
THE FIREFLIES MUST BE ATTRACTED TO THE BERRIES IN THE CAGE.
SEE?

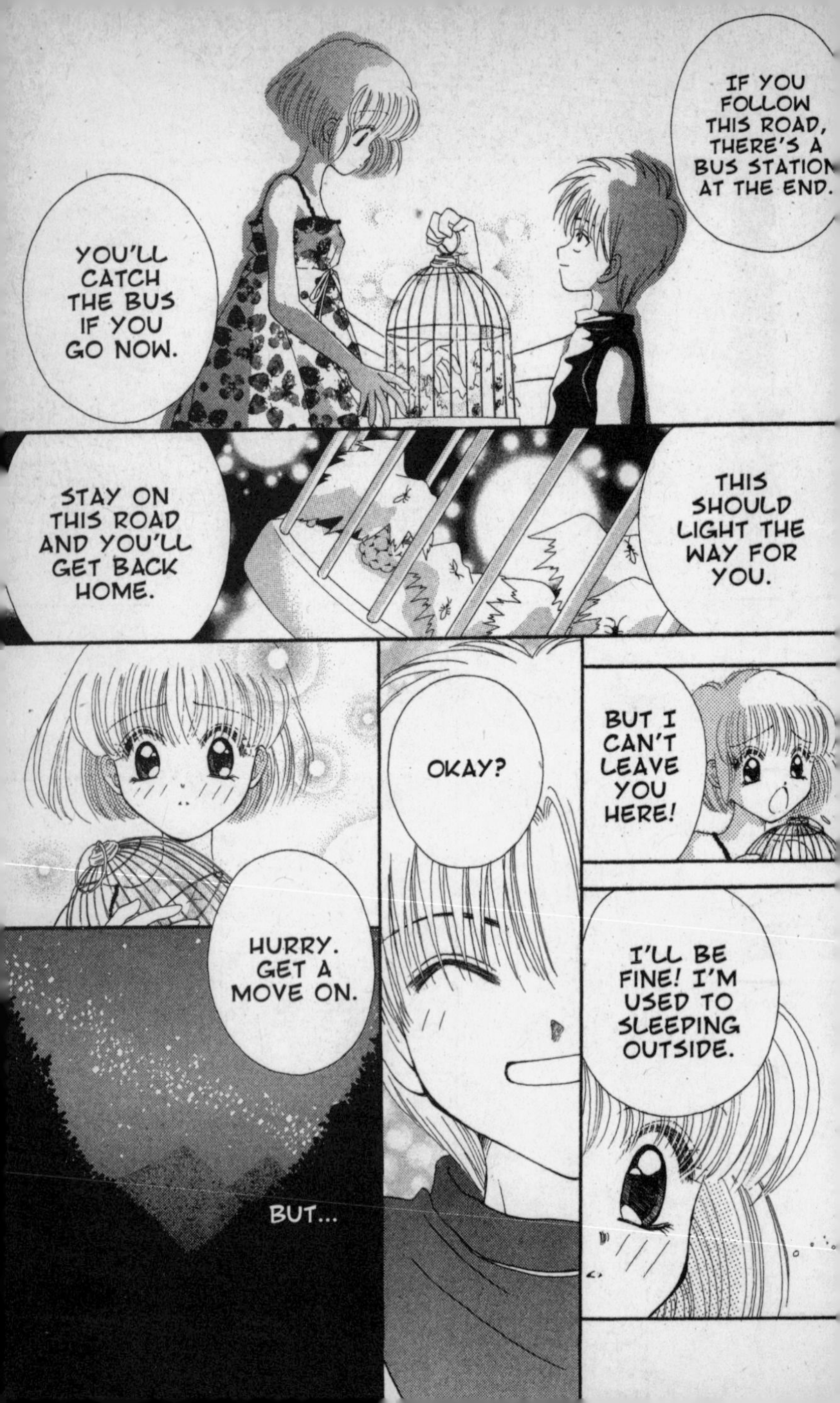
IF YOU FOLLOW THIS ROAD, THERE'S A BUS STATION AT THE END.
YOU'LL CATCH THE BUS IF YOU GO NOW.
THIS SHOULD LIGHT THE WAY FOR YOU.
STAY ON THIS ROAD AND YOU'LL GET BACK HOME.
BUT I CAN'T LEAVE YOU HERE!
I'LL BE FINE! I'M USED TO SLEEPING OUTSIDE.
OKAY?
HURRY. GET A MOVE ON.
BUT...

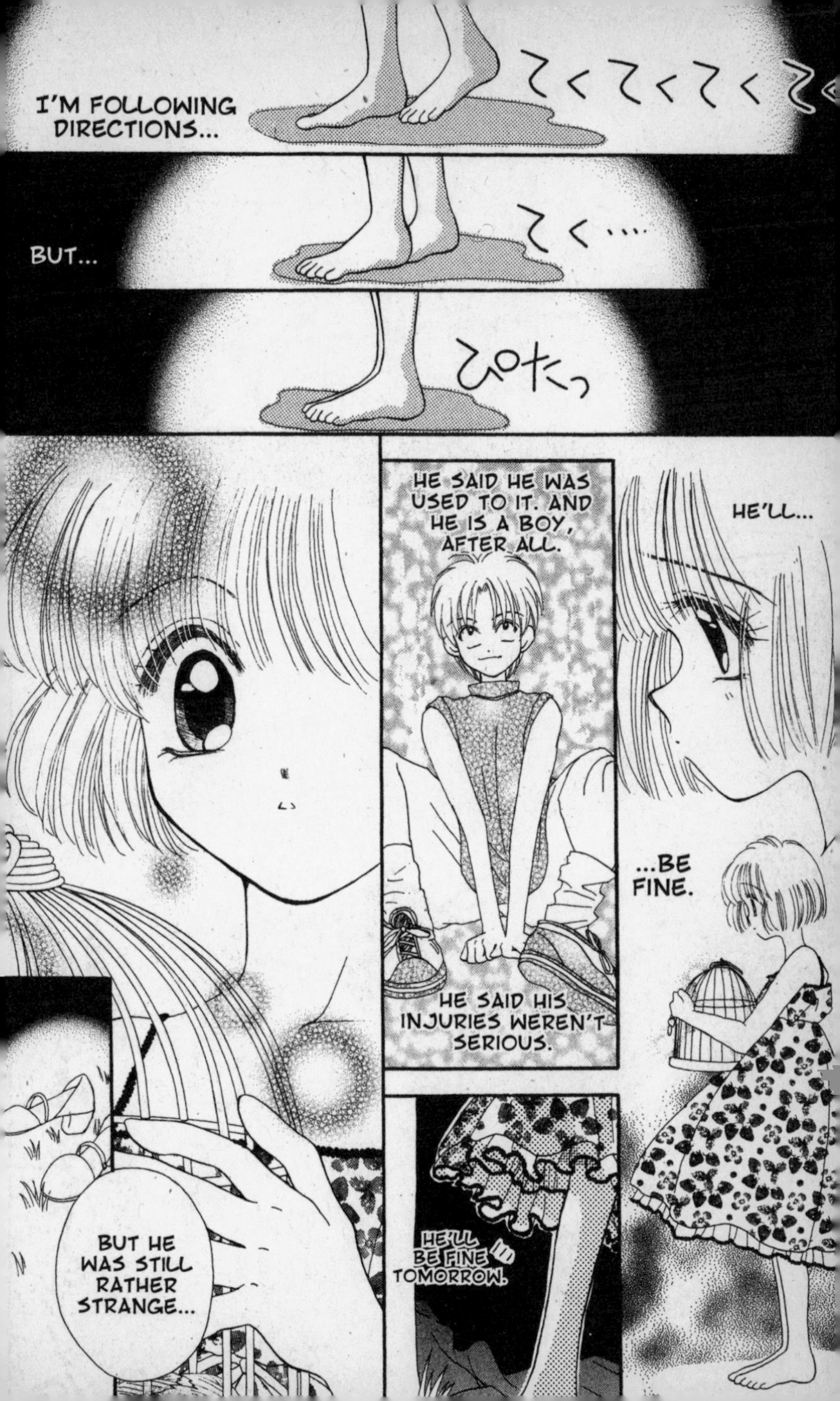

I'M FOLLOWING DIRECTIONS...
てくてくてくてく
BUT...
てく…
ぴたっ
HE'LL...
...BE FINE.
HE SAID HE WAS USED TO IT. AND HE IS A BOY, AFTER ALL.
HE SAID HIS INJURIES WEREN'T SERIOUS.
HE'LL BE FINE TOMORROW.
BUT HE WAS STILL RATHER STRANGE...

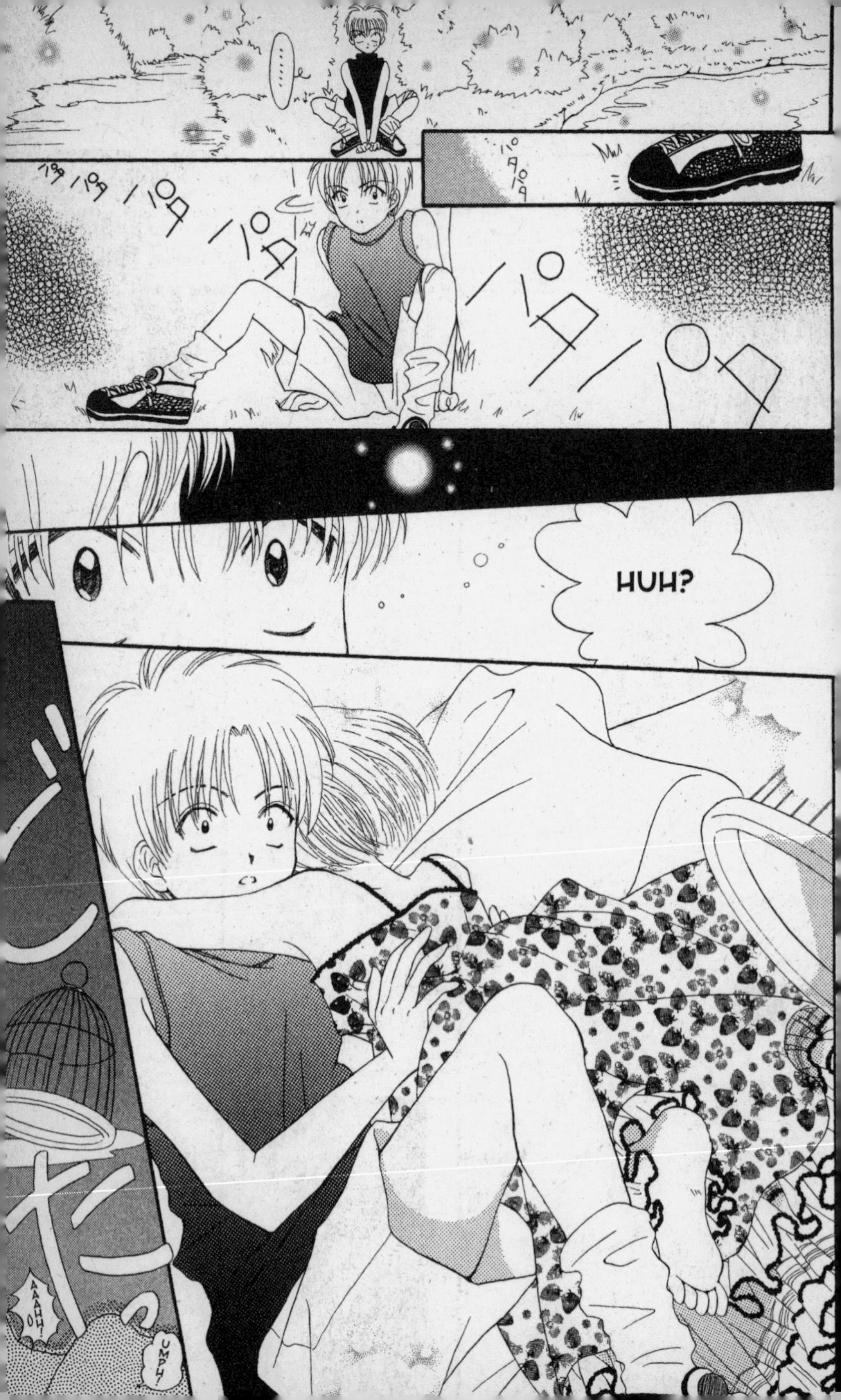
……
パタパタ
パタ パタ パタ パタ
パタ パタ
HUH?
UMPH!
AAAHH! O

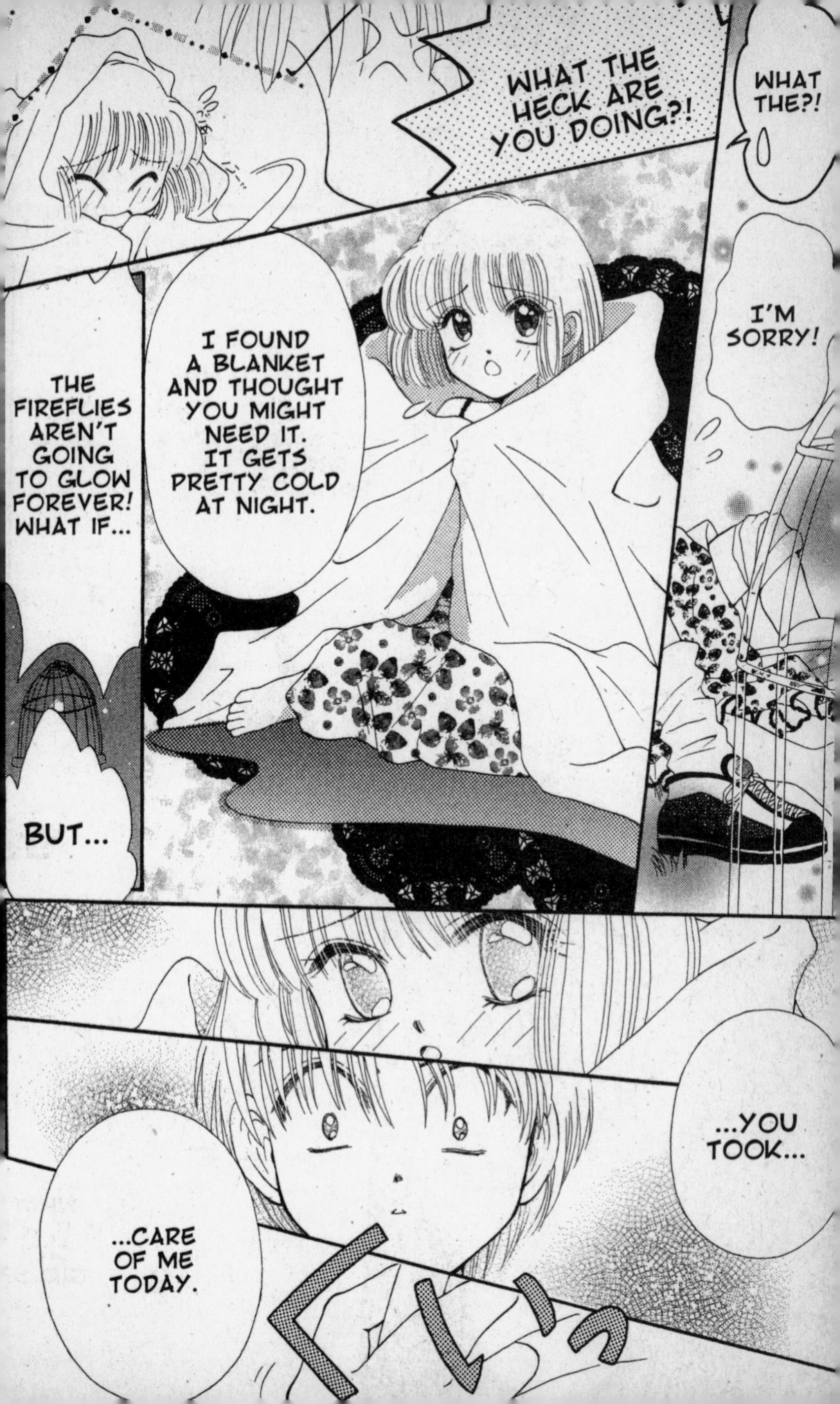
WHAT THE?!
WHAT THE HECK ARE YOU DOING?!
I'M SORRY!
I FOUND A BLANKET AND THOUGHT YOU MIGHT NEED IT. IT GETS PRETTY COLD AT NIGHT.
THE FIREFLIES AREN'T GOING TO GLOW FOREVER! WHAT IF...
BUT...
...YOU TOOK...
...CARE OF ME TODAY.

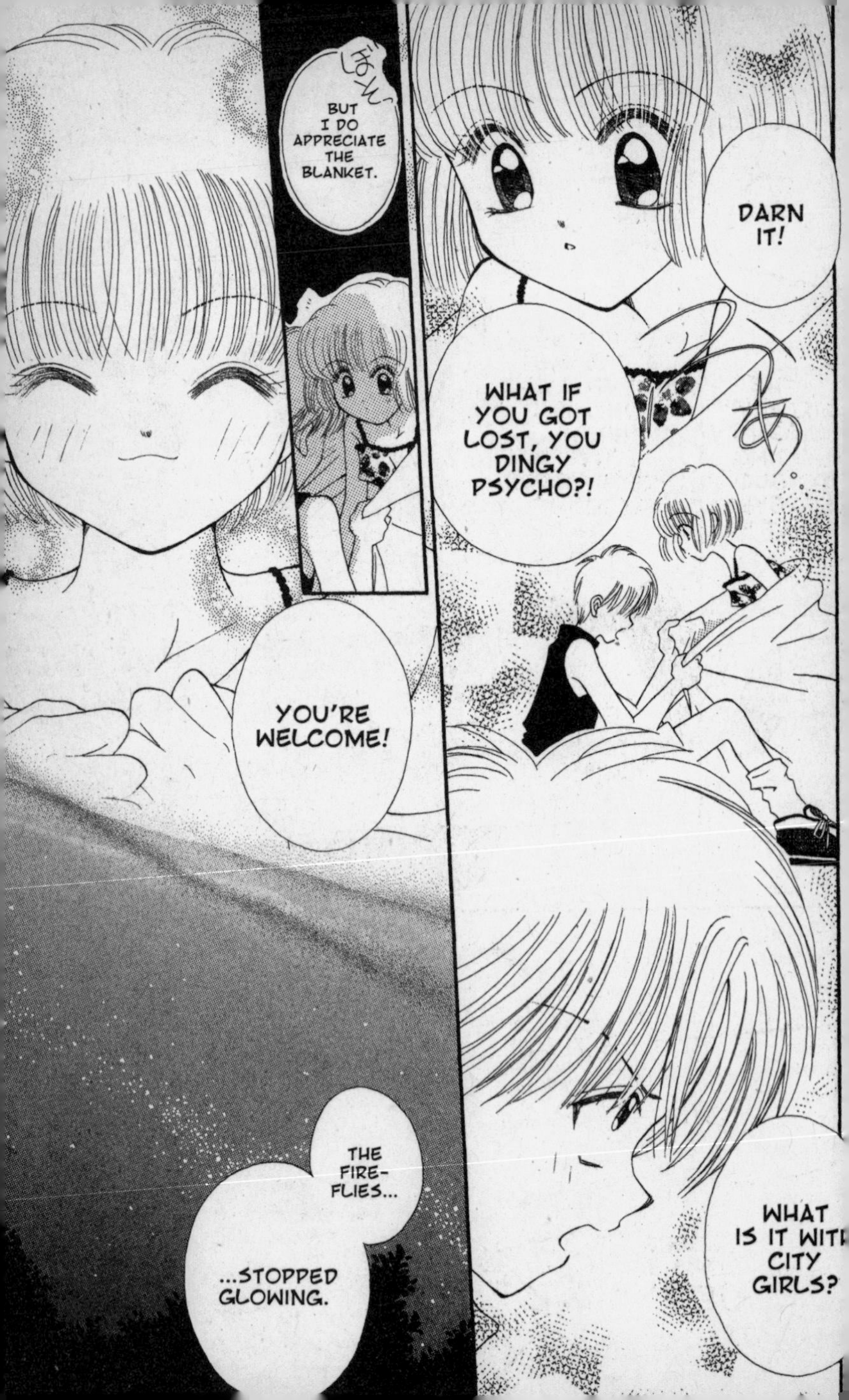
DARN IT!
WHAT IF YOU GOT LOST, YOU DINGY PSYCHO?!
WHAT IS IT WITH CITY GIRLS?
BUT I DO APPRECIATE THE BLANKET.
YOU'RE WELCOME!
THE FIRE-FLIES...
...STOPPED GLOWING.

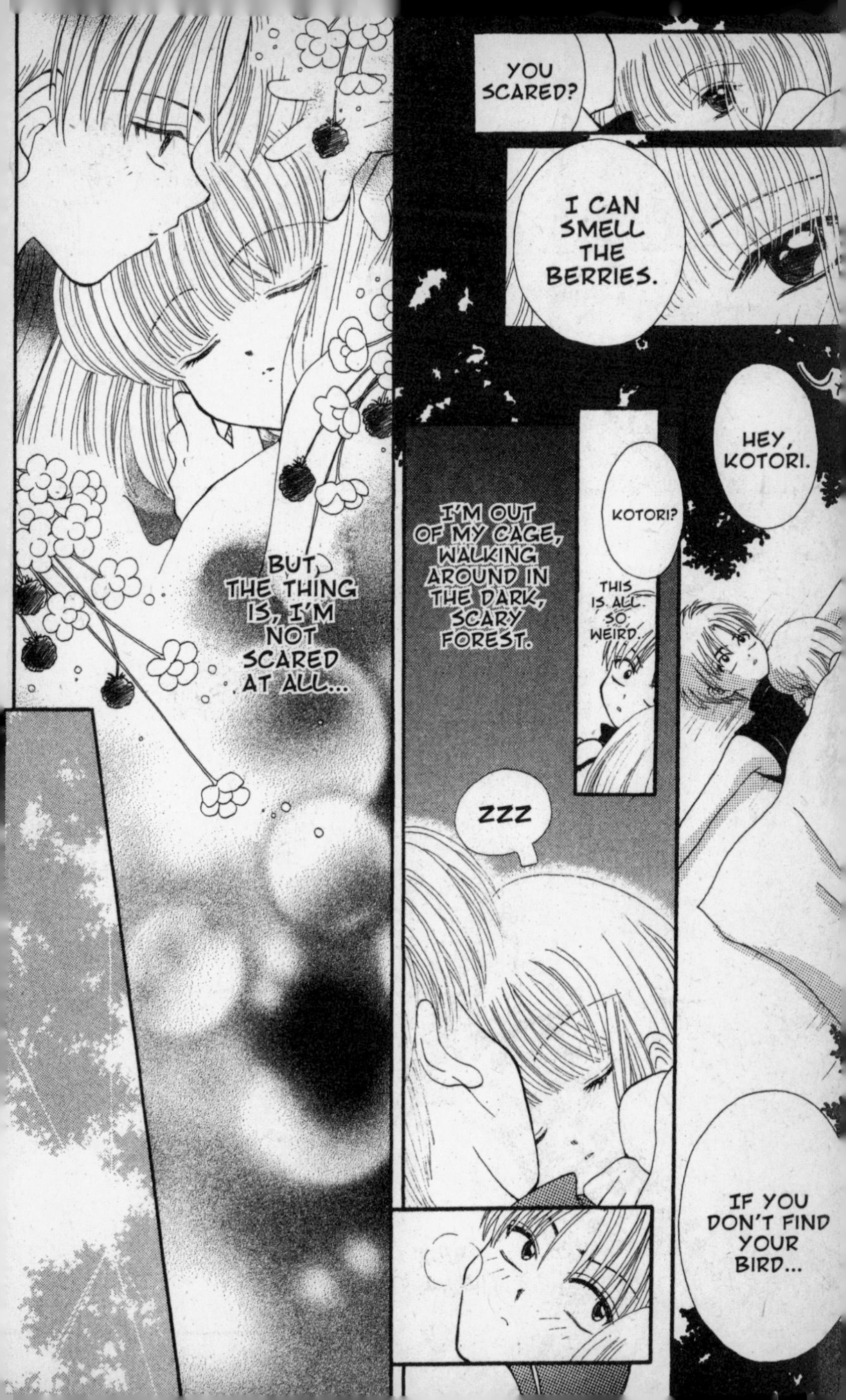
YOU SCARED?
I CAN SMELL THE BERRIES.
HEY, KOTORI.
KOTORI?
THIS IS ALL SO WEIRD.
I'M OUT OF MY CAGE, WALKING AROUND IN THE DARK, SCARY FOREST.
ZZZ
IF YOU DON'T FIND YOUR BIRD...
BUT THE THING IS, I'M NOT SCARED AT ALL...

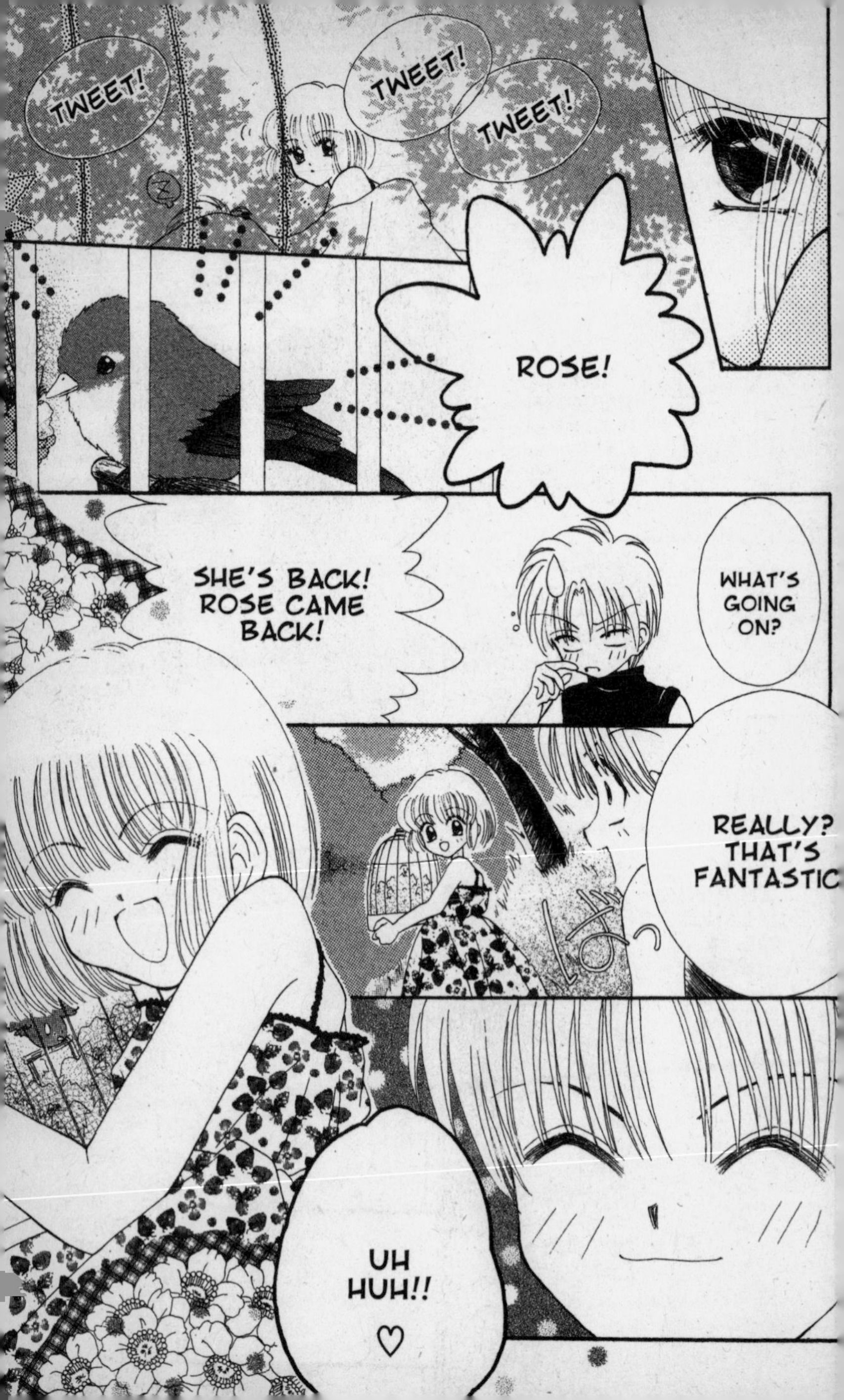
TWEET!
TWEET!
TWEET!
ROSE!
WHAT'S GOING ON?
SHE'S BACK! ROSE CAME BACK!
REALLY? THAT'S FANTASTIC
UH HUH!! ♡

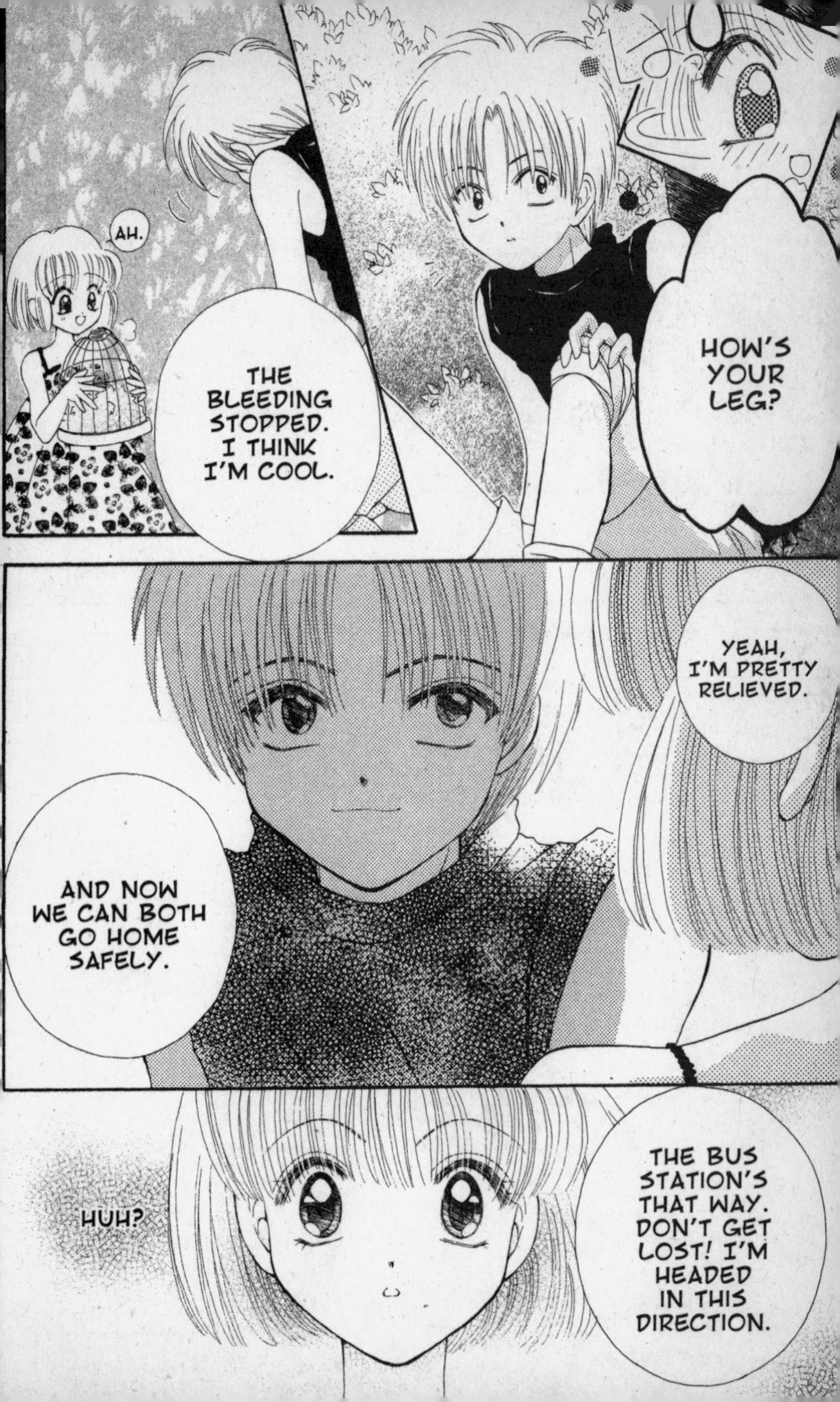
HOW'S YOUR LEG?
THE BLEEDING STOPPED. I THINK I'M COOL.
AH.
YEAH, I'M PRETTY RELIEVED.
AND NOW WE CAN BOTH GO HOME SAFELY.
THE BUS STATION'S THAT WAY. DON'T GET LOST! I'M HEADED IN THIS DIRECTION.
HUH?

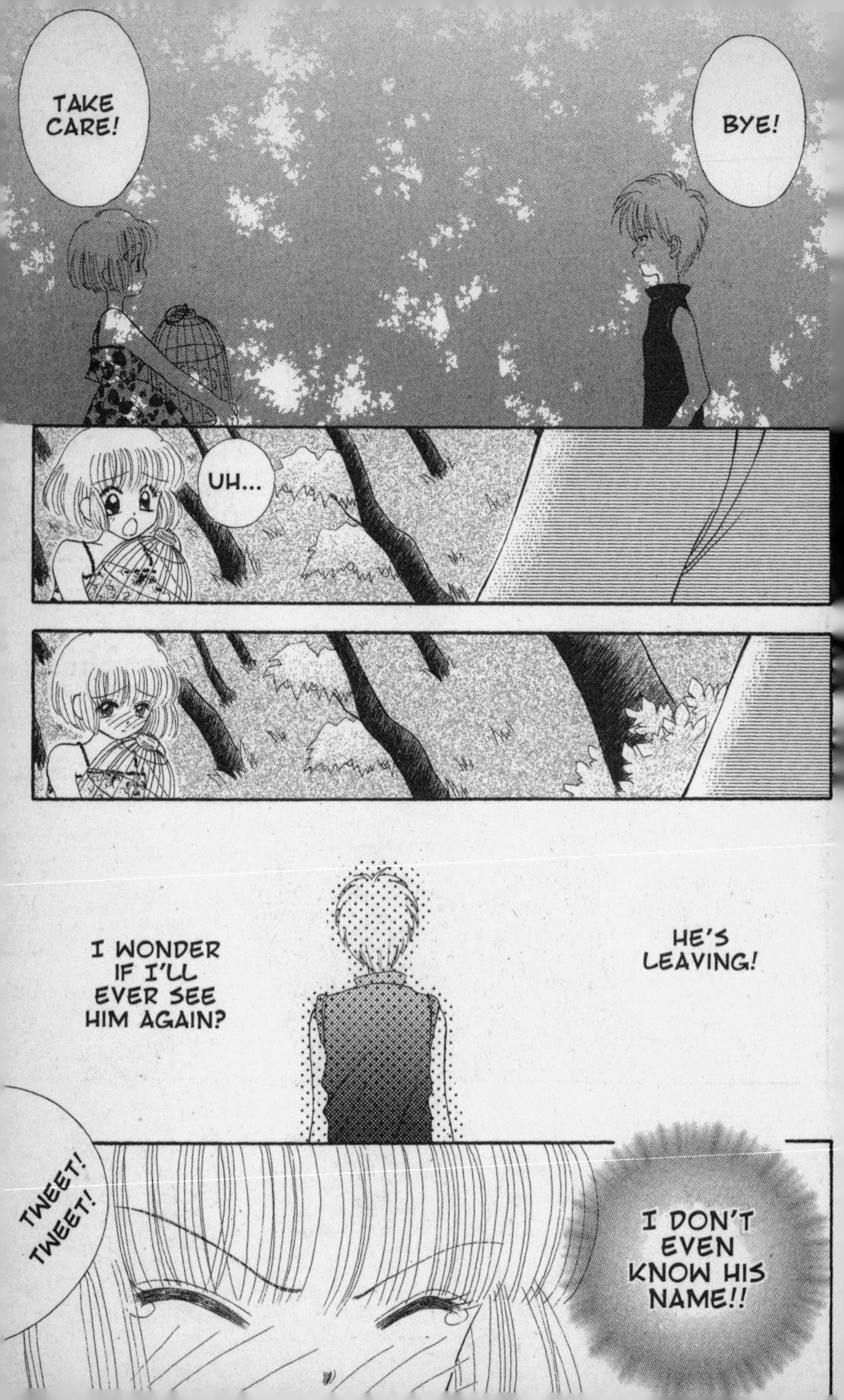
BYE!
TAKE CARE!
UH...
HE'S LEAVING!
I WONDER IF I'LL EVER SEE HIM AGAIN?
I DON'T EVEN KNOW HIS NAME!!
TWEET! TWEET!

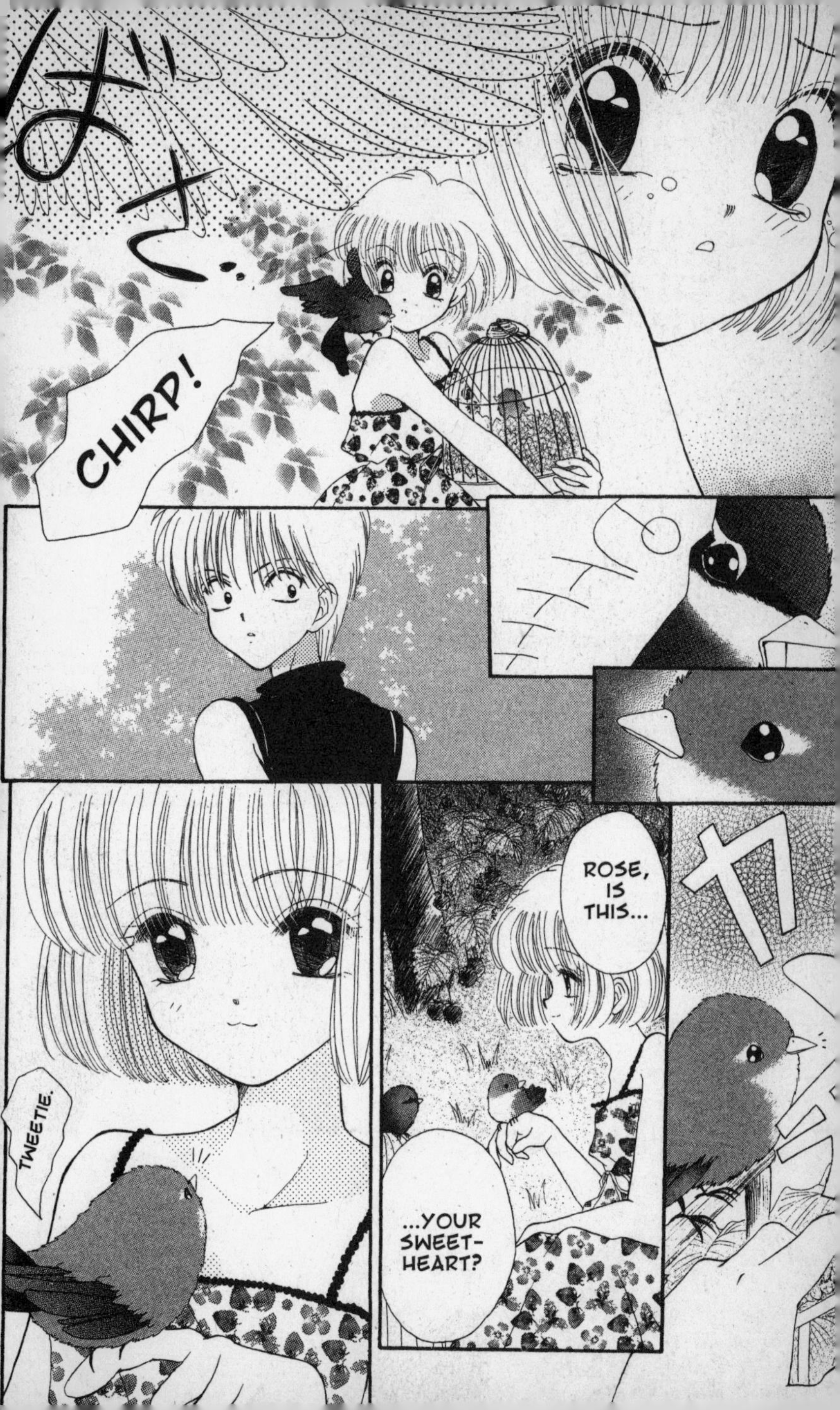
CHIRP!
ROSE, IS THIS...
...YOUR SWEET-HEART?
TWEETIE.

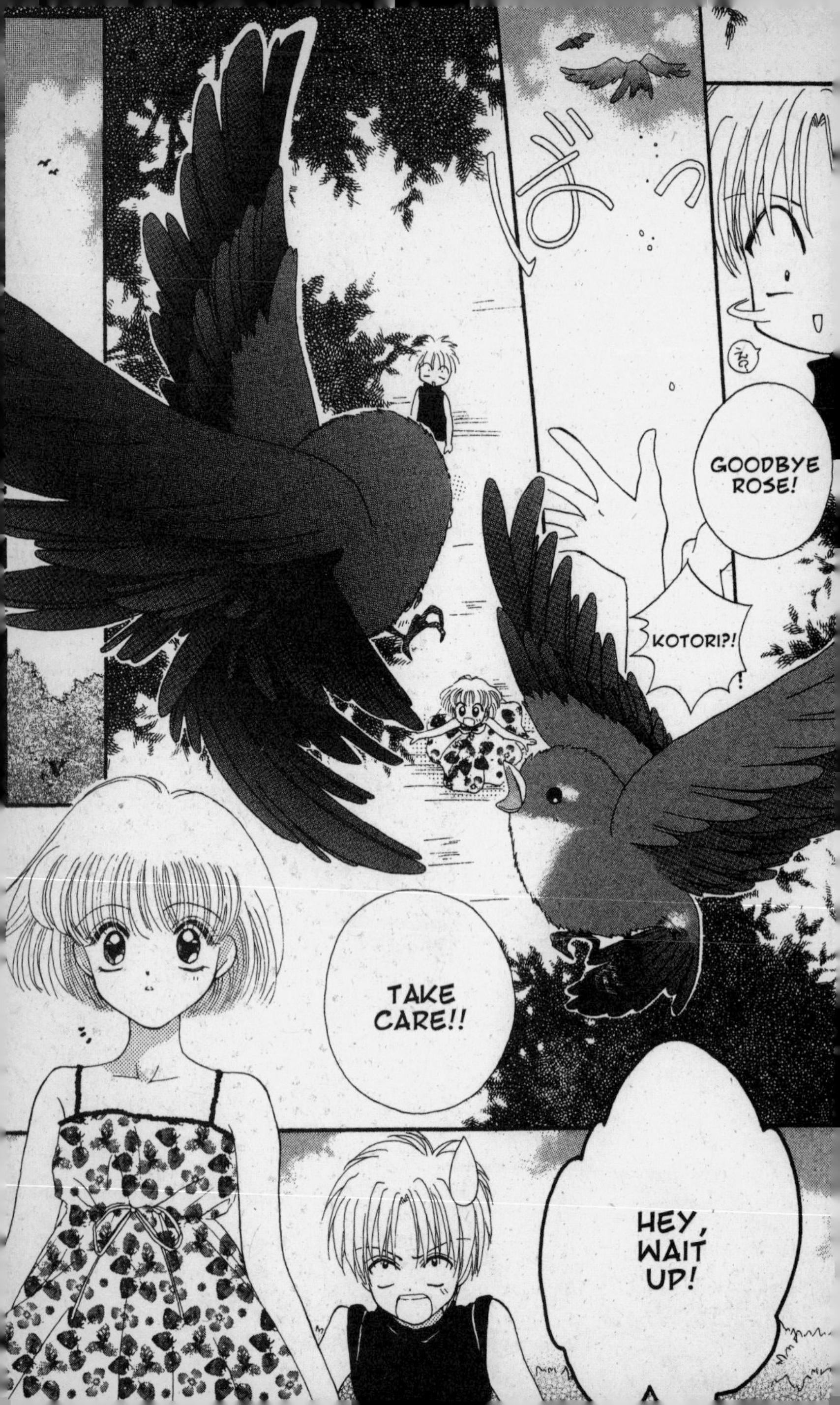
GOODBYE ROSE!
KOTORI?!
TAKE CARE!!
HEY, WAIT UP!

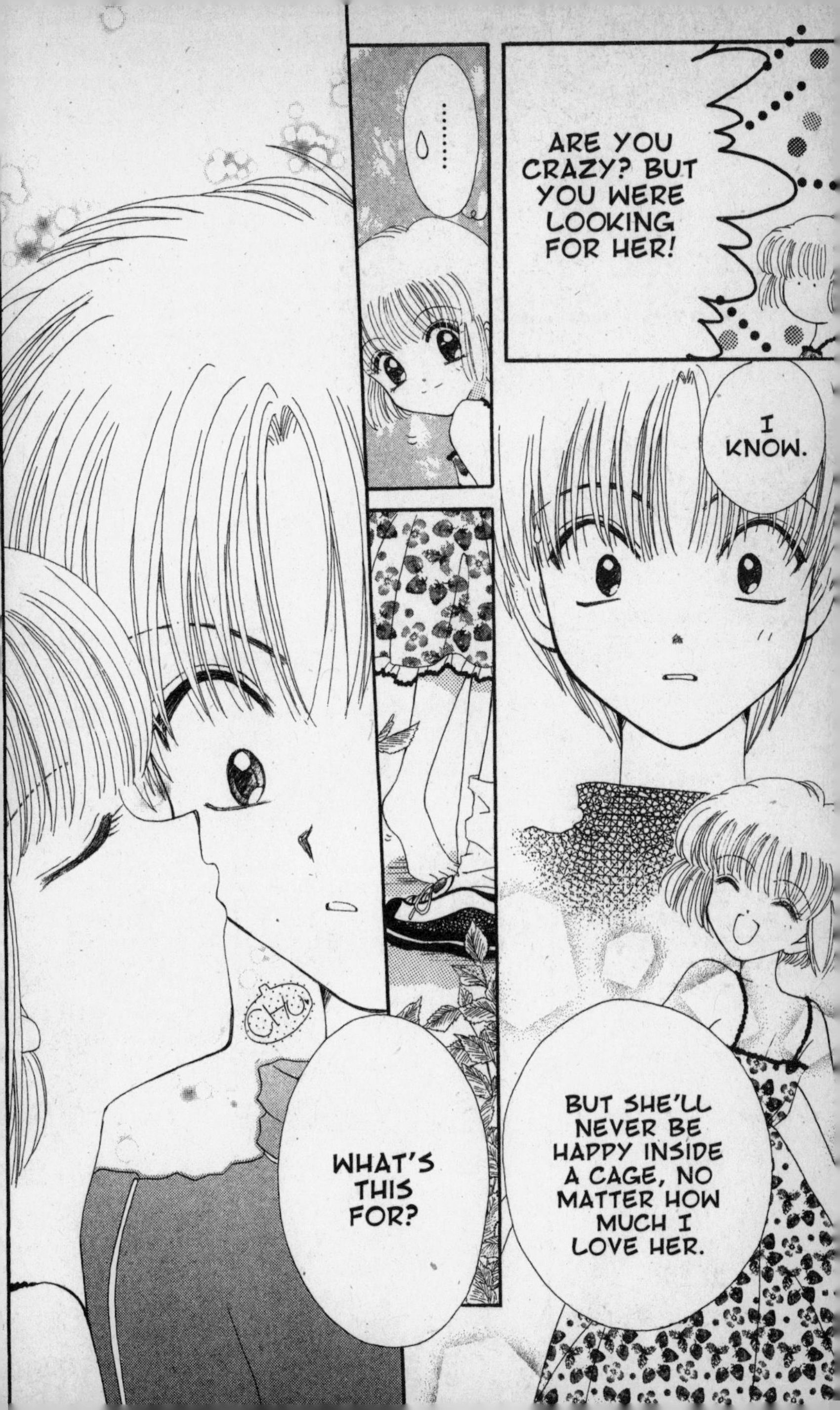
ARE YOU CRAZY? BUT YOU WERE LOOKING FOR HER!
......
I KNOW.
BUT SHE'LL NEVER BE HAPPY INSIDE A CAGE, NO MATTER HOW MUCH I LOVE HER.
CHU
WHAT'S THIS FOR?

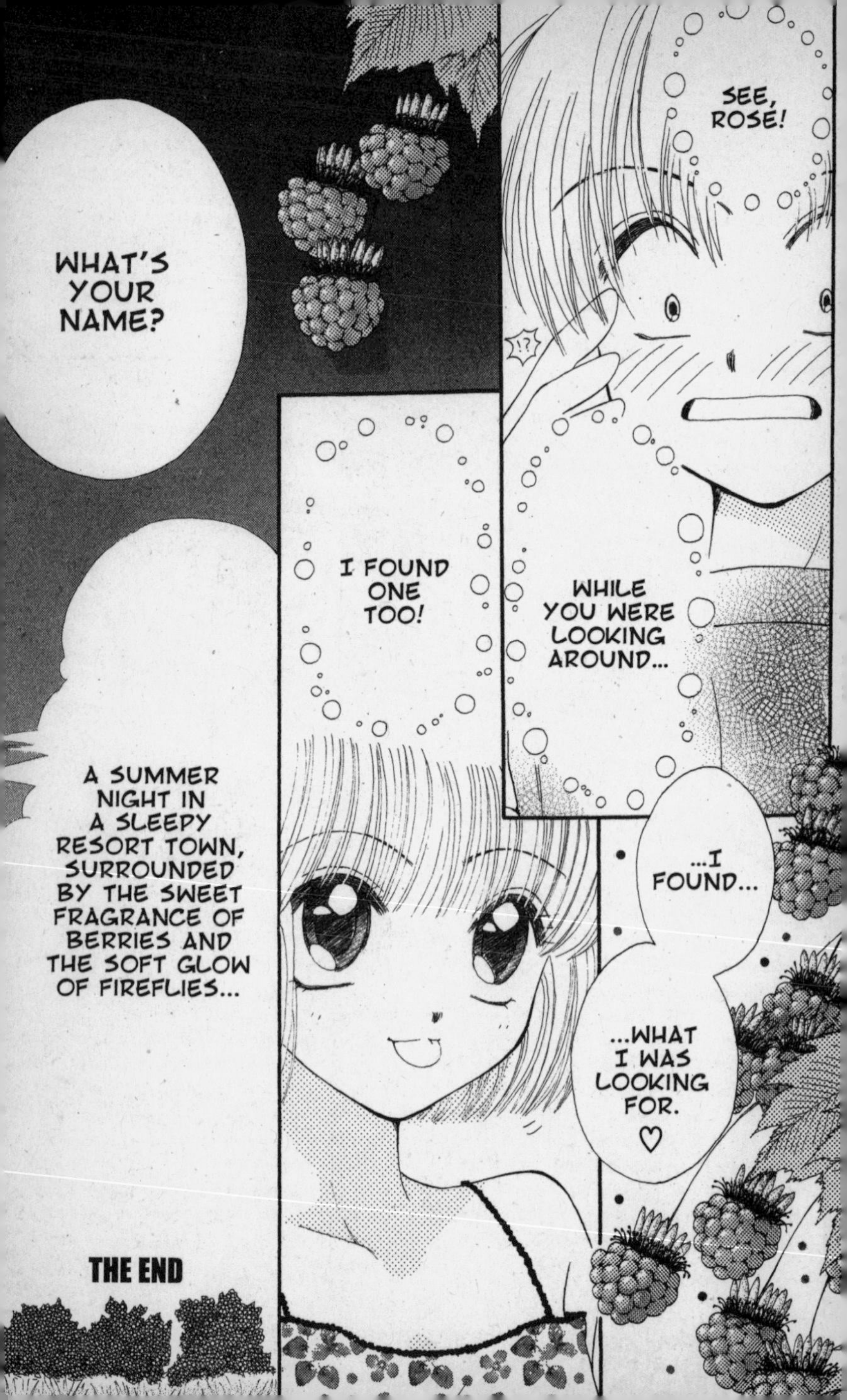
SEE, ROSÉ!
WHILE YOU WERE LOOKING AROUND...
I FOUND ONE TOO!
...I FOUND...
...WHAT I WAS LOOKING FOR. ♥
WHAT'S YOUR NAME?
A SUMMER NIGHT IN A SLEEPY RESORT TOWN, SURROUNDED BY THE SWEET FRAGRANCE OF BERRIES AND THE SOFT GLOW OF FIREFLIES...
THE END

Hi! It's me, Ikumi!

I'd like to thank my readers, both old and new alike! This is the sixth volume of Tokyo Mew Mew!

Wow! It's already the sixth volume! This year, we released four volumes! This is only possible because of all the support I get from my fans! Thank you very, very much!

This volume has tons of bonus material. Instead of side comics, I featured the designs from the "Tokyo Mew Mew Design Ichigo's Costume Contest"! There's a bonus comic that includes a page on my rough drafts, and an introduction to my new PS video game character, Ringo Akaii. Enjoy!

By the way, the illustration above is actually a cover of the script for the anime. The anime staff and voice actors make suggestions and requests, and I draw the cover accordingly whenever I can. The illustration for this cover was a request by Koichi Tochika, the voice actor for Ryou. He wanted the male characters dressed in drag for fun. The illustrations are based on my

impressions of many of the cast members (giggle). I usually don't request autographs from voice actors for my personal collection. After all, they're working while they're in the studio, so I feel bad about bothering them, although I've begged for a few autographs to give to my assistants. But for some odd reason, I really wanted them to sign this cover. I guess I'm taking full advantage of my position. Sorry! Don't you think it's fun, though? It's as if my characters, dressed in drag, autographed this cover! In all honesty, I guess I just wanted to brag about my little treasures (laugh). I told Mr. Tochika that I couldn't read his autograph, so he printed his name next to his signature (laugh). Thank you! Some of the other requests for illustrations have been Lettuce and Kish in love. Daisuke Sakaguchi, the voice actor for Kish, really likes Lettuce's character. There's also a request for an illustration of Mint eating lettuce, pomegranates (Zakuro means pomegranate in Japanese), strawberries (Ichigo means strawberry in Japanese) and pudding. Yumi Kakazu (voice actress for Mint)—I haven't gotten to your request yet! Please, be patient with me! Other requests include: Lettuce as a lettuce, Pudding as a pudding (Katsuyuki Konishi, who plays Shintaro Momomiya...how in the world should I draw that?) etc.

I hope I'll get opportunities to show you more of these illustrations!

Sleeping Beauty of Strawberry Forest

This was my very first project as a professional manga artist. A friend helped me with the screen tone, but I did everything else. At that time, I spent about a month on the rough draft, and another month working on the final draft. I remember being very meticulous with the artwork.

Actually, when this project was almost ready to be published, I thought I would have to do a lot of corrections and changes. All my painstaking efforts paid off though, because everything came out a lot better than I imagined. I don't know how to explain it, but it seems like this isn't my own work, although I know it is. Maybe it's because I took so long to complete it. I'm actually very fond of it. If you think I'm being stupid and a little full of myself, that's cool. It feels like this was done during a naive time in my life when I had a fresh attitude, though I'm not certainly not very naive anymore. I don't think I could draw something like this again. Again, you might think I'm weird, but I really love this work. It means a lot to me.

By the way, I drew this illustration earlier today. I don't think it's very different from the comic. Maybe I haven't grown as an artist. But that can't be, can it? I mean, come on, I've matured as an artist, right?

I wanted to let you know that the boy's name is Yota. I received a lot of letters from fans wanting to know his name. I'm glad I can finally answer that question!

Before Tokyo Mew Mew was serialized, Ryou's face looked a lot like Yota. I really like Yota's character. I'm also very fond of Kotori. She reminds me of a puppy. I really enjoyed drawing them. I want to draw another short manga like this soon.

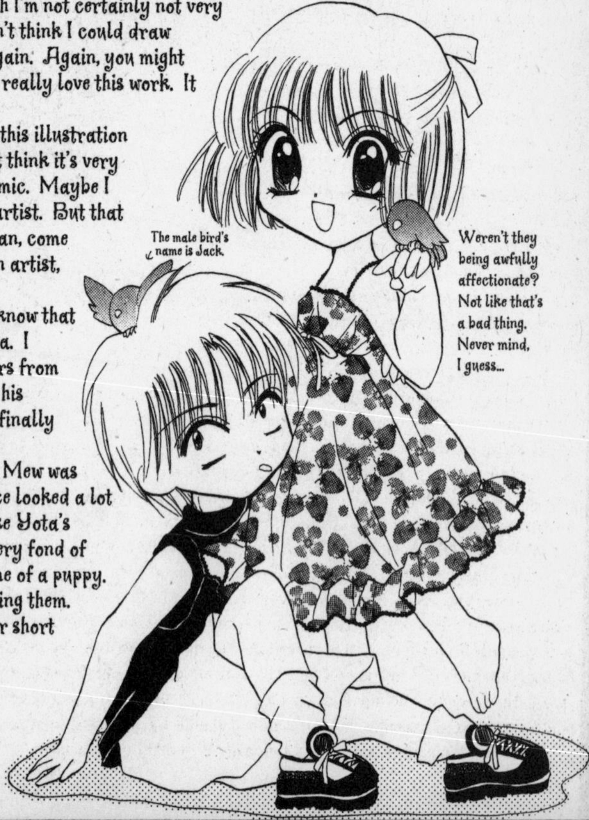
The male bird's name is Jack.
Weren't they being awfully affectionate? Not like that's a bad thing. Never mind, I guess...

We're proud to present Ikumi's ☆ "Rough Draft Pages!"

THESE ARE ROUGH DRAFTS THAT INCLUDE FRAMES, DRAWING AND LINES.

6
Today's the day...
...we're going to make you pay! ♡

17
RIBBON MINT ECHO!
RIBBON ZAKUROS PURE!
RIBBON LETTUCE FLASH!
PUDDING RING INFERNO!

These are the "Rough Draft Pages" for pgs. 100 and 101 of volume 6! It's one of my favorite scenes! The rough drafts aren't meant to be shown to the readers 'cause they can end up looking very sloppy! I try to make them as cute as possible (giggle)! I like to make them look like a picture book, although this can cause some wicked problems. After changing, editing and redrawing the storyboards several times, everything gets so messy. I hope I don't have to redraw too many times. Otherwise, they might publish an edition called "Mew Mew Rough Drafts." I seriously doubt it, but you never know. Ha ha ha!!

This scene reminds me of the last scene in this volume with Deep Blue (laugh)! I hope you have a better understanding about the creative process behind Tokyo Mew Mew. Did you enjoy it? I sure hope so!

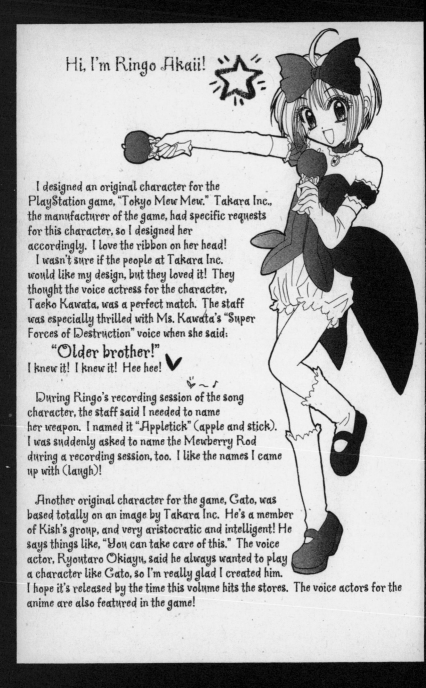

Hi, I'm Ringo Akaii!

I designed an original character for the PlayStation game, "Tokyo Mew Mew." Takara Inc., the manufacturer of the game, had specific requests for this character, so I designed her accordingly. I love the ribbon on her head!

I wasn't sure if the people at Takara Inc. would like my design, but they loved it! They thought the voice actress for the character, Taeko Kawata, was a perfect match. The staff was especially thrilled with Ms. Kawata's "Super Forces of Destruction" voice when she said:

"Older brother!" ♥
I knew it! I knew it! Hee hee!

During Ringo's recording session of the song character, the staff said I needed to name her weapon. I named it "Appletick" (apple and stick). I was suddenly asked to name the Mewberry Rod during a recording session, too. I like the names I came up with (laugh)!

Another original character for the game, Gato, was based totally on an image by Takara Inc. He's a member of Kish's group, and very aristocratic and intelligent! He says things like, "You can take care of this." The voice actor, Ryoutaro Okiayu, said he always wanted to play a character like Gato, so I'm really glad I created him. I hope it's released by the time this volume hits the stores. The voice actors for the anime are also featured in the game!

By the way, I totally wish this toy existed!

Ms. Kawata will be doing the voice.

When you shake the appletick, you'll hear, "My brother." How dreamy! Gentle whispers and scolding are both good (LOL)!

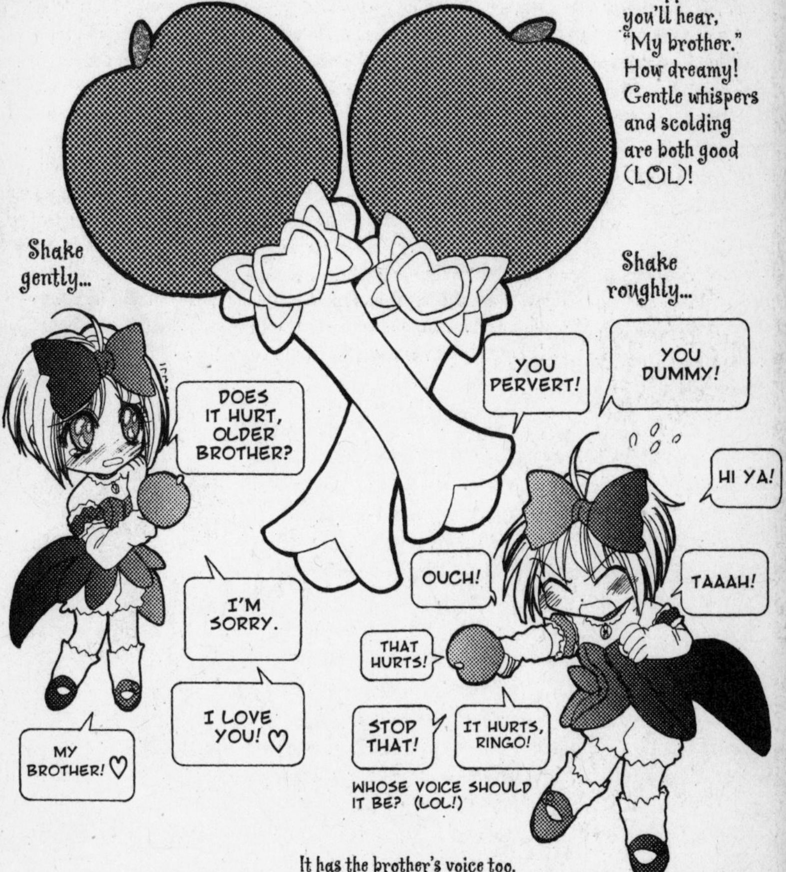

Shake roughly...
YOU DUMMY!
YOU PERVERT!
HI YA!
TAAAH!
OUCH!
THAT HURTS!
IT HURTS, RINGO!
STOP THAT!
WHOSE VOICE SHOULD IT BE? (LOL!)
Shake gently...
DOES IT HURT, OLDER BROTHER?
I'M SORRY.
I LOVE YOU! ♡
MY BROTHER! ♡

It has the brother's voice too.

Oh well! Hee hee hee!

Laugh! Laugh! Laugh!

I really adore Ringo. My fondness for her increases every time I draw her. I hope I can include her as a regular character one day. Pretty please? The people around me like her a lot. What do you think about her?

I'm feeling really good today. That's unusual, since I tend to stress out about negative things. It's not like there was anything special going on today to bring on my awesome mood. It's almost like a runner's high that you get during running or exercise, right after you overcome the fatigue (laugh). Maybe that's because I've been working non-stop without taking a day off. I'm writing this but I'm also working on an episode for the December volume. After I finish a heavy load of projects, I always feel a huge sense of accomplishment. But I still have a lot of work after I get finished with what I've started, so I have to keep going and going and going... If I keep feeling good, like I have a runner's high, I think I can do it, though I was feeling uber-overwhelmed just recently. During this project, we all had a great time at work. We were all laughing so much more than usual (giggle). It's so much better to have fun while working. Because of that, I guess, it's been difficult for me to get into a serious mood, so I wasn't able to draw dramatic, emotional scenes during those times. That was rough!! Oh well. Laughter is great for your health, so I think I'll keep laughing. Laughter helps work fly by!! ☆

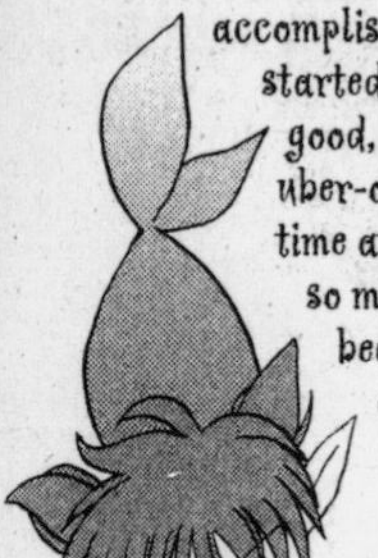

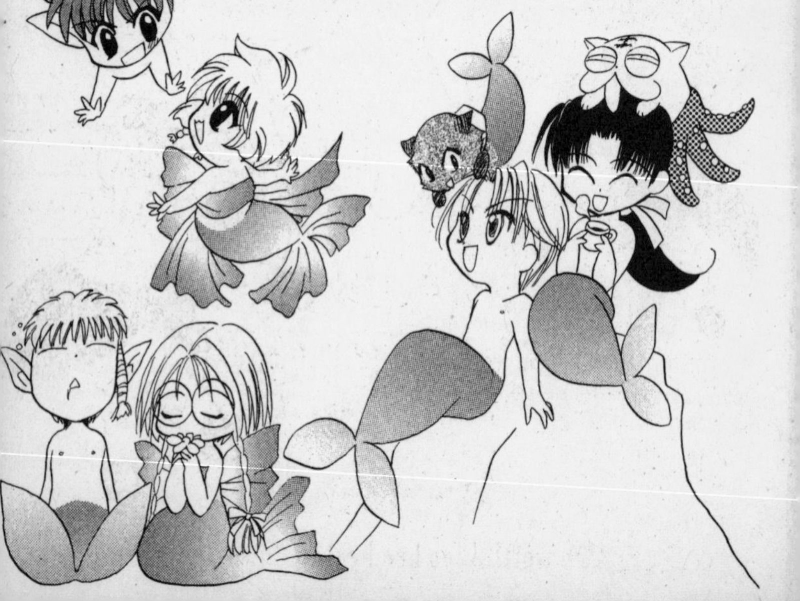

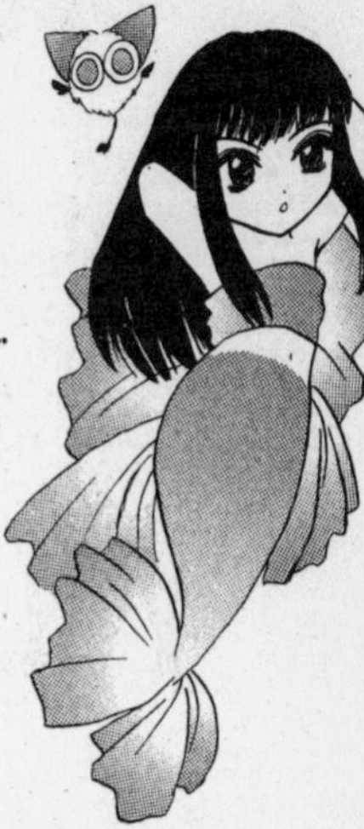

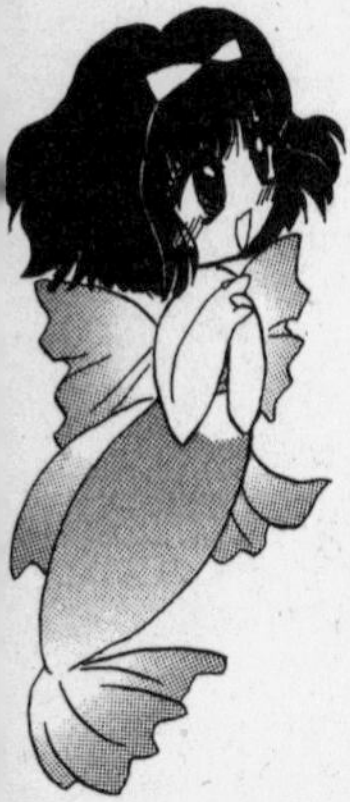

Finally...
To everyone who worked with me
to create this project...
To everyone who helped me in the past
with this project...
To everyone who has read this series...
And to everyone who has supported me...

I want to thank you so much!
I love you because you work so hard!
I'll do my very best too!

October 11, 2002
Mia Ikumi ☆

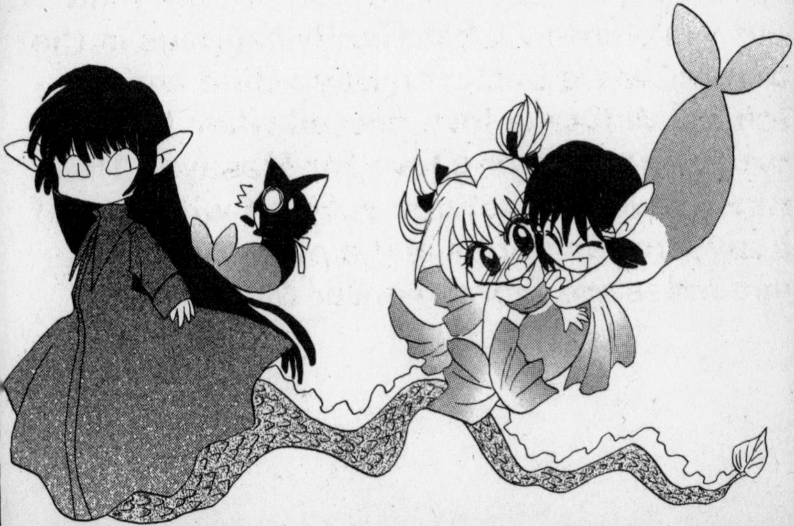

COMING SOON...

TOKYO MEW MEW

VOLUME SEVEN

Don't miss the last exciting volume of Tokyo Mew Mew as the fabulous crime-fighting felines are back once and for all to save Tokyo from utter destruciton. Find out in Volume 7 what finally happens in the brutal battle between Deep Blue and Ichigo! Will true love prevail when Ichigo proves her undying love for Masaya? This must-have last volume is filled with lots of bonus comic pages and a personal thank-you message from creator Mia Ikumi!

TOKYOPOP SHOP

SOKORA REFUGEES

Kana thought life couldn't get any worse—behind on her schoolwork and out of luck with boys, she is also the only one of her friends who hasn't "blossomed." When she falls through a magical portal in the girls' shower, she's transported to the enchanted world of Sokora—wearing nothing but a small robe! Now, on top of landing in this mysterious setting, she finds that her body is beginning to go through some tremendous changes.

Preview the manga at:
www.TOKYOPOP.com/sokora

T
TEEN
AGE 13+

SOKORA REFUGEES

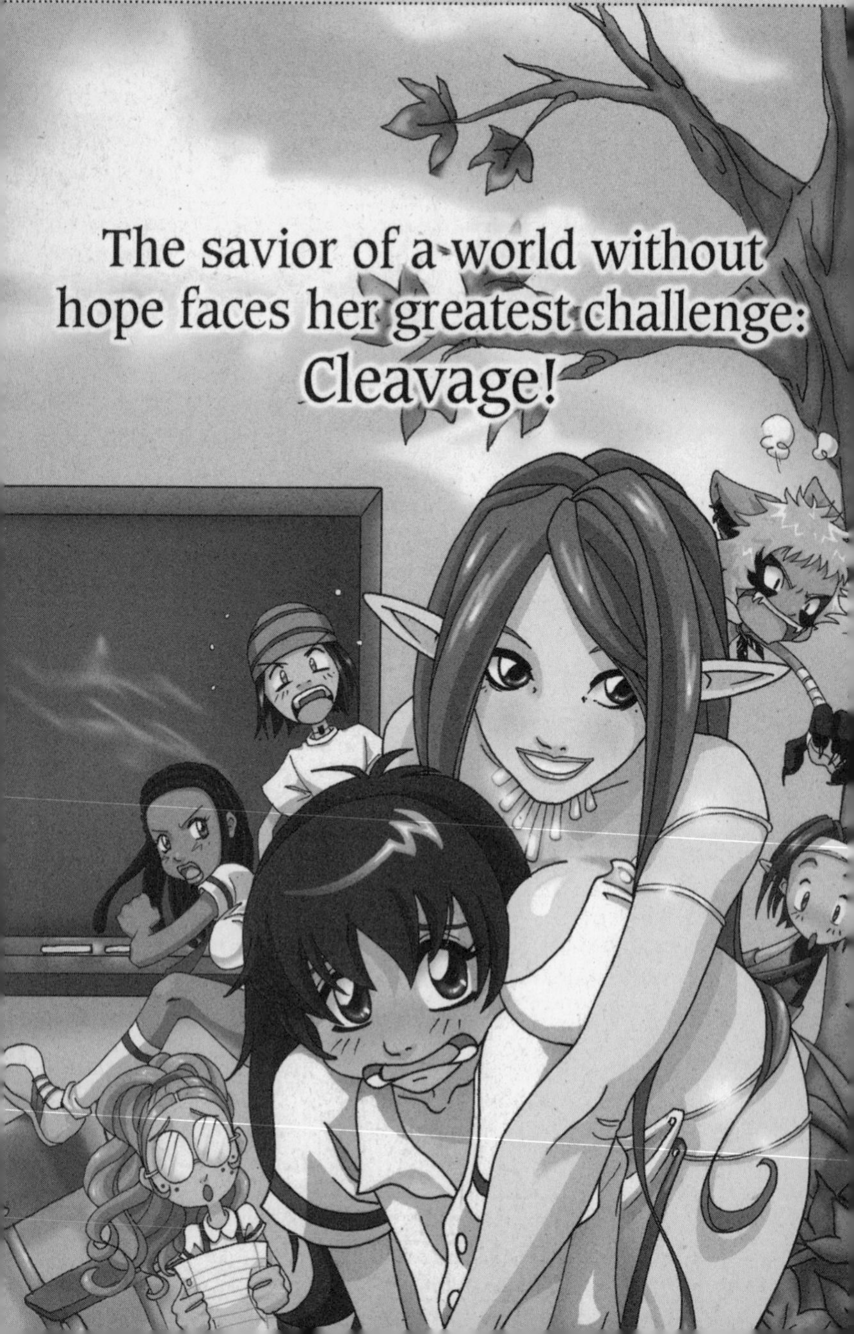
The savior of a world without hope faces her greatest challenge:
Cleavage!

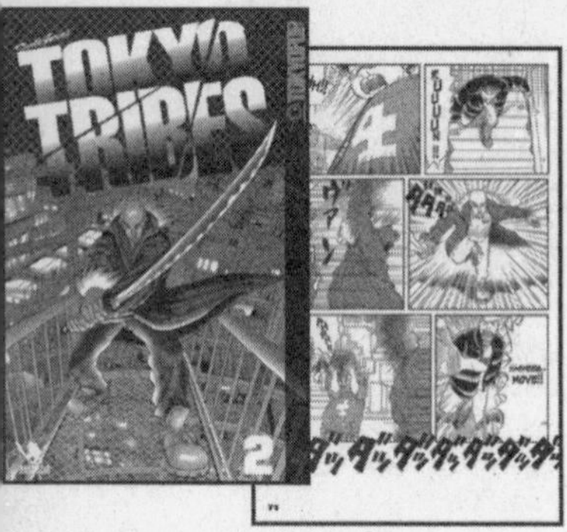
TOKYO TRIBES
2

BY SANTA INOUE

TOKYO TRIBES

Tokyo Tribes first hit Japanese audiences in the sleek pages of the ultra-hip skater fashion magazine *Boon.* Santa Inoue's hard-hitting tale of Tokyo street gangs battling it out in the concrete sprawl of Japan's capital raises the manga storytelling bar. Ornate with hip-hop trappings and packed with gangland grit, *Tokyo Tribes* paints a vivid, somewhat surreal vision of urban youth: rival gangs from various Tokyo barrios clash over turf, and when the heat between two of the tribes gets personal, a bitter rivalry explodes into all-out warfare.

~Luis Reyes, Editor

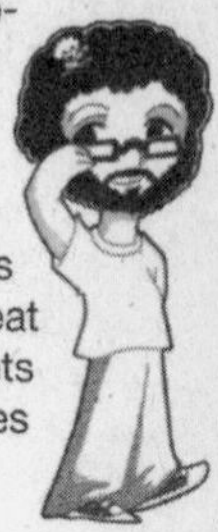

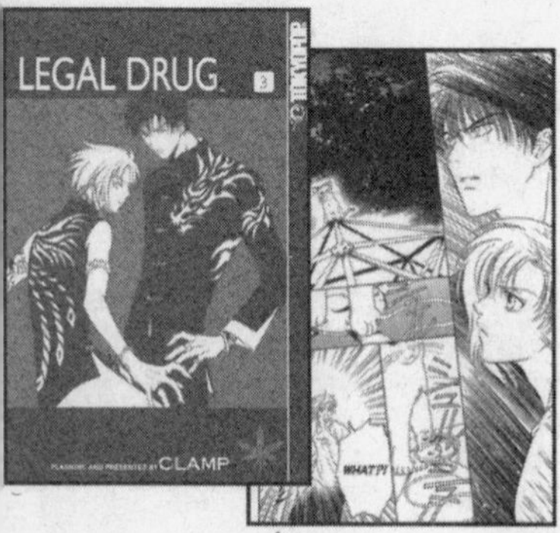
LEGAL DRUG
3
TOKYOPOP
CLAMP
WHAT?!

BY CLAMP

LEGAL DRUG

CLAMP is the four-woman studio famous for creating much of the world's most popular manga. For the past 15 years they have produced such hits as the adorable *Cardcaptor Sakura,* the dark and brooding *Tokyo Babylon,* and the sci-fi romantic comedy *Chobits.* In *Legal Drug,* we meet Kazahaya and Rikuou, two ordinary pharmacists who moonlight as amateur sleuths for a mysterious boss. *Legal Drug* is a perfect dose of mystery, psychic powers and the kind of homoerotic tension for which CLAMP is renowned.

~Lillian Diaz-Przybyl, Jr. Editor

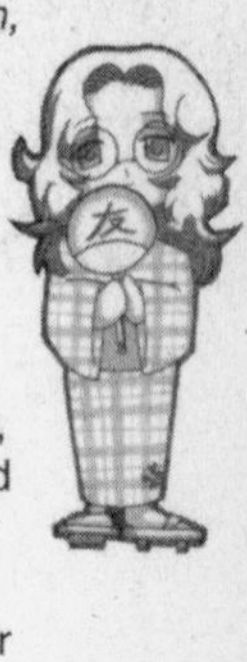

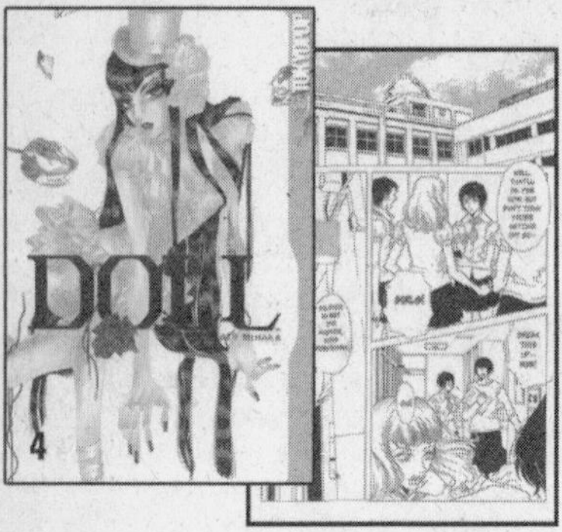
DOLL
4

BY MITSUKAZU MIHARA

DOLL

Mitsukazu Mihara's haunting *Doll* uses beautiful androids to examine what it means to be truly human. While the characters in *Doll* are draped in the chic Gothic-Lolita fashions that made Mihara-sensei famous, the themes explored are more universal—all emotions and walks of life have their day in *Doll*. *Doll* begins as a series of 'one-shot' stories and gradually dovetails into an epic of emotion and intrigue. It's like the *Twilight Zone* meets *Blade Runner!*

~Rob Tokar, Senior Editor

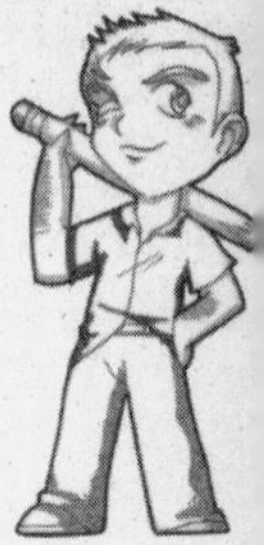

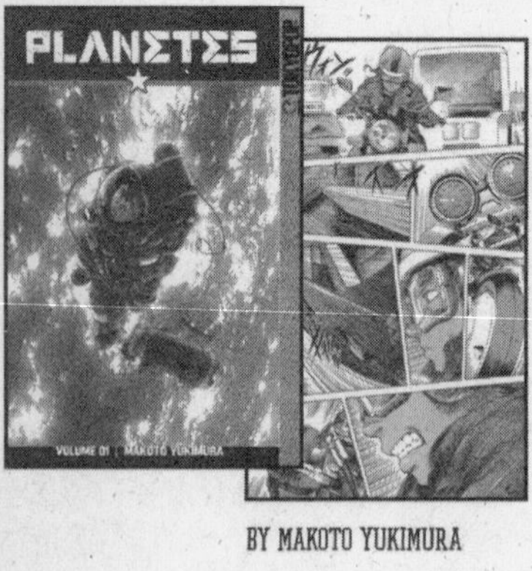
PLANETES
VOLUME 01 | MAKOTO YUKIMURA

BY MAKOTO YUKIMURA

PLANETES

Makoto Yukimura's profoundly moving and graphically arresting *Planetes* posits a near future where mankind's colonization of space has begun. Young Hachimaki yearns to join this exciting new frontier. Instead, he cleans the glut of orbital junk mankind's initial foray into space produced. He works with Fee, a nicotine-addict beauty with an abrasive edge, and Yuri, a veteran spaceman with a tragic past in search of inner peace. *Planetes* combines the scope of Jules Verne (*Around the World in Eighty Days*) and Robert Heinlein (*Starship Troopers*) with the philosophical wonder of *2001: A Space Odyssey.*

~Luis Reyes, Editor

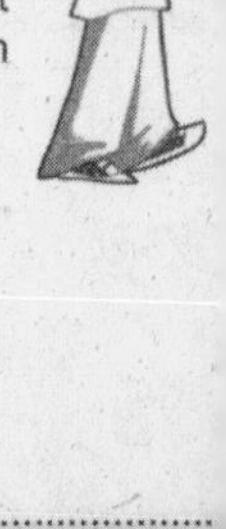

S0-BMV-587

STOP!

This is the back of the book.
You wouldn't want to spoil a great ending!

This book is printed "manga-style," in the authentic Japanese right-to-left format. Since none of the artwork has been flipped or altered, readers get to experience the story just as the creator intended. You've been asking for it, so TOKYOPOP® delivered: authentic, hot-off-the-press, and far more fun!

DIRECTIONS

If this is your first time reading manga-style, here's a quick guide to help you understand how it works.

It's easy... just start in the top right panel and follow the numbers. Have fun, and look for more 100% authentic manga from TOKYOPOP®!